the

Group Dynamics in Sport

Third Edition

Other Sport and Exercise Psychology Titles

at www.fitinfotech.com

Foundations of Exercise Psychology
Developmental Sport and Exercise Psychology: A Lifespan Perspective
Advances in Sport and Exercise Psychology Measurement
Psychology of Team Sports
Career Transitions in Sport: International Perspectives
Assessment in Sport Psychology
Exercising Your Way to Better Mental Health
Medical and Psychological Aspects of Sport and Exercise
Counseling College Student-Athletes: Issues and Interventions, 2nd Edition
Foundations of Exercise and Mental Health
The Practice of Sport Psychology
Sport Psychology: Linking Theory and Practice
Handbook of Research in Applied Sport and Exercise Psychology: International Perspectives
The Mental Game Plan: Getting Psyched for Sport
World Sport Psychology Sourcebook, 3rd Edition
Psychological Bases of Sport Injuries, 2nd Edition
Directory of Graduate Programs in Applied Sport Psychology, 7th Edition
Directory of Psychological Tests in the Sport and Exercise Sciences, 2nd Edition
Flow Scales Manual
Group Environment Questionnaire Test Manual
International Journal of Sport and Exercise Psychology

Group Dynamics in Sport

Third Edition

Albert V. Carron, Ph.D.
University of Western Ontario

Heather A. Hausenblas, Ph.D.
University of Florida

Mark A. Eys, Ph.D.
Laurentian University

Fitness Information Technology
A Division of the International Center for Performance Excellence
West Virginia University • 262 Coliseum, WVU-PE, PO Box 6116
Morgantown, WV 26506-6116

Library of Congress Card Catalog Number: 2005927268
ISBN: 1-885693-63-X

Production Editor: Corey Madsen
Copyeditor: Greg Leatherman
Cover Design: Scribe, Inc.
Proofreader/Indexer: Susan Case
Typesetter: Scribe, Inc.
Printed by Sheridan Books
Printed in the United States of America

10 9 8 7 6 5 4 3 2 1

Fitness Information Technology
A Division of the International Center for Performance Excellence
262 Coliseum, WVU-PE
PO Box 6116
Morgantown, WV 26506-6116
800.477.4348
304.293.6888 (phone)
304.293.6658 (fax)
Email: icpe@mail.wvu.edu
Website: www.fitinfotech.com

Contents

Detailed Contents

Foreword

Lawrence R. Brawley, PhD
Canada Research Chair:
Physical Activity for Health Promotion
and Disease Prevention
University of Saskatchewan

Group Dynamics in Sport is now in its third edition. Like its predecessors from 1988 and 1998, the content reflects the latest thinking and literature on the topic and provides us with the new directions in the field. Clearly, it will remain the most influential book on this subject in the field of sport psychology. The book is an exceptionally well-written resource about sport group dynamics that is both readable and user-friendly.

I wrote the foreword for the 1998 edition and my reaction to the new 2005 version remains very positive. Once again, I urge everyone in sport psychology to use this text not only because this is the most comprehensive reference on the topic, but also because it is insightful. While there are a number of researchers who have made selected contributions to the group dynamics literature in sport, it would be fair to say that none of us have examined and commented on it in a way that gives meaning to 40 years of research. However, this book serves to gel and give order to this diverse literature. Few individuals have made such influential contributions that can affect the direction of an entire field, but this contribution is significant because it has this impact.

In this edition, Bert Carron partners with two former PhD students who are accomplished individuals in their own right. Dr. Heather Hausenblas and Dr. Mark Eys were award-winning young investigators in their period of training with Dr. Carron. In the present volume, they bring new developments in the field to the book. They offer information on the relationship between the group and individual level constructs such as role clarity and ambiguity, on the shared beliefs of group members, and on the meta-analyses of group effects. Also, the authors give us organizational frameworks to follow in considering the basic and applied research presented. They continue to strive to offer implications for the effectiveness of sport groups in the realm of practice. As with previous editions, the authors capture our attention with quotes from people in sport who have experienced the powerful impact of the group, and they provide us with visual aids that facilitate teaching and learning.

Given the prevalence of group influences on sport endeavors within North America and across the world in youth sport, school sports, recreation and leisure programs, and elite and professional sport, there can be little doubt that sport groups are important. Given the community and national level efforts of physical activity organizations to engage people in activity, there can be little doubt that sport group dynamics is important. If the goals of kinesiologists, exercise scientists and physical educators are to train students to meet the needs of the public by promoting physical activity and sport, *this book should be a compulsory reference for their training*. If the goal of sport psychology organizations, which advocate professional certification and training, is to give the consumer the most knowledgeable and competent professionals and certified consultants, the information in *this book should be a compulsory reference for their training.*

Edited multi-chapter volumes in sport psychology texts frequently offer single chapters on the topic of group dynamics. By definition, these chapters, however well written, always underrepresent the magnitude of information available. I know, as I have authored some of this work. If undergraduate and graduate students, researchers, and consultants only rely on these books to help with their education about groups, they will be deficient in their fundamental understanding of the topic. Some readers may feel that I am referring only to individuals who wish to become experts in sport group dynamics. Those who take this perspective are naïve about the powerful social forces that impact our society. They are in the greatest need of this book. Those who are wise enough to obtain this reference to guide their thinking, teaching, and consulting will have insight into how groups can be used as agents of change to motivate and alter the behavior of participants. I believe this book will be an indispensable resource for those wise people.

Concerning forewords, most readers expect a positive endorsement of the book, and doubly so when the contributor is a colleague of the authors, as I am of Drs. Carron, Hausenblas, and Eys. However, *I believe that books that make a strong contribution to an entire field need strong endorsement.*

In my opinion, there is no other group of authors that could offer this work to the field of sport psychology, and this field would be less without their effort on this volume. I have used the 1998 version in much of my previous work and will make the same future use of the 2005 edition. To do less would undermine the quality of my work, a risk I am unprepared to take as I continue to conduct research on the influence of groups.

Saskatoon, Saskatchewan
April, 2005

Preface

Here we are with a third edition! Who would have thought it in 1988, when the first edition appeared? Having said that, however, if there was enough content pertaining to group dynamics in sport to justify a first edition 17 years ago, and then enough new content to justify a second edition 10 years later in 1998, this third edition is certainly necessary and timely. Over the past seven years, there has been a burgeoning research interest in group dynamics in sport. As was the case with the second edition, our general purpose in producing this third edition was to review what is currently understood about group dynamics in sport teams.

What do we know about group dynamics in sport? Well, it isn't rocket science—but not for the reasons that you might think. For most of us, understanding groups is far more important than understanding rocket science. In the first chapter of the book, we pointed out that Roy Baumeister and Mark Leary (1995) argued that the need to belong—the desire for interpersonal attachments—is a fundamental human motivation. Quite simply, we have a basic need to be with people. Consequently, not surprisingly, each of us has membership in a large number and variety of sport teams and physical activity groups (as well as other groups, of course) in our lifetime. Not all of these groups work well some of the time or all of the time. Understanding is the first step in change. If we better understand our environment, we are in a better position to operate in it and change it if need be.

Another way group dynamics in sport differs from rocket science is its pervasiveness. Look around. Daily, the popular media are full of references to the dynamics of sport teams. In fact, throughout our book, we have illustrated all of the theoretical constructs discussed by using quotations from the popular sport media—newspapers and magazines.

How does this third edition of *Group Dynamics in Sport* differ from the second edition? The fundamental difference is in the nature and amount of new content. Considerable amount of research has recently been conducted on such phenomena as the home advantage, role relationships in sport teams, the correlates of team cohesion generally, the relationship of team cohesion to team performance specifically, collective efficacy, and team building in sport. Thus, the chapters that focus on these phenomena are considerably different in content and organization from their 1998 counterpart. Finally, other chapters in this third edition, although they might appear at first glance to be similar to those in the 1998 version, have profited considerably from new research and new insights.

In all ventures of this type, we as authors owe a debt of gratitude to a number of people. That can only be done individually, so we'd like to change the format to do so.

Bert: For 25 years I have had Larry Brawley and Neil Widmeyer as professional colleagues and personal friends. From a professional perspective (and as I have indicated in other instances), they have contributed immeasurably to the breadth and depth of my understanding in the area of group dynamics. Most of what I communicate about group dynamics is influenced by our conversations, research, and writing. On the personal level, it is difficult for me to imagine anyone being blessed with better friends.

Over my professional lifetime, I have had the good fortune to be exposed to outstanding colleagues and graduate students (many of whom are now colleagues). It has been suggested that scientists stand on the shoulders of the people who have gone before them. That's true. But we also get a lift onto those shoulders from our colleagues. I'd like to acknowledge my debt and say thanks.

Heather: Many people have played a significant role in the writing of this book—without their assistance its completion would certainly have not been possible. First, I would like to acknowledge my former advisor, Bert Carron. His leadership, guidance, mentoring, and professional approach were, and continue to be, inspiring. I am truly indebted. Second, my past and present colleagues and graduate students have often lightened my labors and enriched my scholarship. But most importantly, I thank them for their gift of friendship. Third, although the role played by my parents was somewhat indirect, their love, patience, and support were of utmost importance and always appreciated. Finally, I thank my husband, Todd, and our two precious children, Tommy and Scotty, for their unconditional love. They are my sunshine, and I am humbled to call them my own.

Mark: My experiences in life and in academia have been made extremely enjoyable and enlightening through my involvement in and exposure to a number of different groups. First, I am extremely honored to have been included with Bert and Heather as a contributor to the third edition of this book. Second, I would not be investigating issues in group dynamics without the initial encouragement and continued guidance of Bert, Neil Widmeyer, Larry Brawley, Steven Bray, and numerous other colleagues and friends. Finally, a special acknowledgement to my two most important groups who continue to support me: my parents, Shirley and Adrian, and my wonderful wife, Stephanie, and daughter, Abigail. It is to the above groups that I am truly thankful.

The Team: It is our hope that the 21 chapters in our book will serve to introduce readers to the complexity and simplicity, as well as the practical and theoretical significance, of group dynamics in sport teams. Interest in understanding the dynamics of sport and physical activity groups has grown considerably in the past 25 years. It is our hope that our book will stimulate even more interest in the future.

Albert V. Carron
Heather A. Hausenblas
Mark A. Eys
April, 2005

SECTION 1

INTRODUCTION

Being part of a team is not something your grandparents can buy for you. No one can give this to you as a gift. You have to earn it yourselves. (Blais, 1995, p. 102)

Chapter One

THE NATURE OF GROUPS

> *If you've ever wondered why the most talented teams don't always win . . . here's the reason. Chemistry is what's up. Team's nuclei. Their bonding and combustion. Stable elements and volatile ones. The critical nature of the mix and what Connecticut coach Jim Calhoun calls "the vapor that just sort of hangs over a team." (Wolff, 1995, p. 34)*

Membership and involvement in groups is a pervasive characteristic of our society. We enter life as a member of society's strongest and most significant group—the family. As we grow and develop, we become members of and are influenced by other important groups in social and work settings. We attend school in groups, worship in groups, socialize in groups, and carry out business in groups. Also, play, exercise, and sport are group activities. Even so-called individual sports like wrestling, badminton, and tennis are group activities since at least two people—(the minimum number of people necessary to constitute a group) are required for competition. In group settings, we influence the behaviors, cognitions, and attitudes of other people and, in turn, are influenced ourselves.

The groups to which we belong also have a powerful, significant impact on our lives (see Box 1.1). In the quote used to introduce the first section, the coach of a women's high school basketball team pointed out at the first practice that becoming a team requires effort and sacrifice (cited in Blais, 1995). Effort and sacrifice pay more dividends, however, if the right chemistry develops among team members, as the quote that led off this chapter highlights.

Although membership in groups is not always associated with the positive outcomes described by Blais, our involvement in groups seems inevitable. Roy Baumeister and Mark Leary (1995), drawing on research evidence from a wide cross section of areas in psychology, stated that the need to belong, the desire for interpersonal attachments, is a fundamental human motivation

A number of conditions must be present before a state, need, or condition is truly fundamental. The desire for interpersonal attachments satisfies all of these. It

a) is present across a wide variety of situations,
b) has an important influence on thought and emotion,
c) leads to health or adjustment problems if it is not satisfied,
d) stimulates behavior designed to satisfy it,
e) is present in all people,

Box 1.1

Teamwork is Considered Important for Individual and Team Success in Sport

Bill Bradley, formerly of the New York Knicks of the National Basketball Association: "I have always believed that there was a larger purpose to basketball than individual achievements. Excellence has been defined for me in terms of the team's success. In high school, it was whether our team from a very small school in a small town could defeat the bigger, city teams. In college, it was whether a team of students who played basketball to their collective potential could compete with the best in the country. In the pros, it was whether a team without a dominant star could be the best in the world. And, in the U.S. Senate, a moment of insight came when I realized that the passage of legislation, like teamwork, required getting people with different backgrounds, different interests, and different personal agendas to agree on a shared goal, and to work toward it" (Bradley, 1976, p. iii).

On Red Auerbach, General Manager of the Boston Celtics of the National Basketball Association: "The success of the Celtics is based on a philosophy wholly opposed to individualism. The basic Auerbach commandment is that to win, the individual must fit in; he must subordinate his desires and skills to those of the team. He must, to use an Auerbach watchword, 'sacrifice himself,' in his life and on the court, to the working of the team" (Greenfield, 1976, p. 205).

On Greeces unexpected success in the 2004 Union of European Football Associations (UEFA) championship: "For a tournament in which the big names have so often failed to deliver what they promised, it was fitting that UEFA EURO™ was ultimately won by rank outsiders. Greece's incredible achievement was a triumph of teamwork and camaraderie, and after another never-say-die performance in the final no one can begrudge them their finest hour" (Szreter, 2004).

---

f) is not a product of some other motive (such as the need for safety), and

g) has an influence on a large number of behaviors (Baumeister & Leary, 1995).

Because the need to belong is a fundamental motivation, it cannot be satisfied through mere social contact with strangers or individuals we dislike. Neither can it be satisfied through pleasant social interactions with strangers. Baumeister and Leary emphasized that "first, people need frequent personal contacts or interactions with the other person [and] second, people need to perceive that there is an interpersonal bond or relationship marked by stability, affective concern, and continuation into the foreseeable future" (p. 500).

Sport is one of the primary aspects of society that satisfies our need to belong. What do we know about the group in sport? Possibly not as much as we know about the family, army unit, or work group, but that picture is changing. Our general purpose in writing this book was to review the body of research literature about group dynamics in sport groups, but before we present that discussion, it is useful to outline the thoughts of various theoreticians about the nature of groups.

The Reality of Groups

The object of psychology as a science is to describe, explain, predict, and control behavior. But, a group is an abstraction, or theoretical construct; only its individual members are real. The presence of a theoretical construct cannot be directly observed; it can only be inferred from behavior. Therefore, it is not surprising that social scientists have historically had difficulty agreeing on the real nature of groups. Conversely, the behavior of individuals, either alone or in collective situations, can be described, explained, predicted, and/or controlled. As a consequence, Fred Allport (1924), a prominent psychologist in the 1920s, argued that groups are not real, and that any scientist who wished to understand human behavior should focus on the individual, not the group. Allport stated,

> *The only psychological elements discoverable are in the behavior and consciousness of the specific persons involved. All theories that partake of the group fallacy have the unfortunate consequence of diverting attention from the true locus of cause and effect, namely the behavioral mechanisms of the individual . . . if we take care of the individuals, psychologically speaking, the groups will be found to take care of themselves. (p. 9)*

This issue may seem to be simply philosophical to the coach or athlete who could argue, "Of course, we have a team. We meet and practice, travel together, compete against other teams, have a history, and so on." And, they would be correct. But the issue raised by Allport is not whether an organization exists, whether it is successful, or whether it is recognized as a distinct entity. When he questioned the reality of groups, Allport questioned whether groups were anything more than the sum of the individual members.

Consider the hypothetical case of two mixed doubles tennis teams in competition. Allport might have argued that if the two males were identical in their ability, experience, and so on, and the two females were also identical in every way, then the two mixed doubles teams would be identical, including their behavior and performance. In short, Allport proposed that a group is simply a sum of its parts. If the parts are identical, the groups will be identical. And, as an extension of this fact, if we wish to describe, explain, predict, or control the behavior and performance of the doubles tennis teams, we must describe, explain, predict, and control the behavior and performance of the individual members. Inherent in this viewpoint is the assumption that there is no special chemistry that sets off one group or team from another.

In the decades following the publication of Allport's book, psychologists, sociologists, and anthropologists debated the reality of groups. Currently, there is almost universal agreement that groups are "real," that they differ from the simple sum of member attributes, and that group behavior and performance cannot be understood by simply examining individual behavior and performance. To illustrate, it might be useful to look at one case supporting the conclusion that groups are real.

Theodore Mills (1984), a sociologist, pointed out that group goals are quite distinct from the goals established by individuals for themselves. He used the game of chess to illustrate his point. In chess, the goal of each of the two individual participants is to win;

this personal goal is identical for both contestants. But, the goal of the dyad (the two contestants when they are considered together as a group) can't be "to win." There is no opponent for the unit represented by the two chess players. So, can we assume that this unit, the two chess players as a group, has no goal? Mills argued, "On the contrary, there is an idea in the minds of the two parties which refers to a desirable state of the dyad: it is to have a high-quality contest which each party wants to win, wherein play is imaginative, in which superior play does win. The group goal, as distinct from personal goals, then, is to have a good contest" (Mills, 1984, p. 94).

The point made by Mills has often been echoed by coaches and athletes. For example, in the 1987 Canada Cup Series, Canada and the USSR played four superb games. The first ended in a tie. The next two were tied in regulation time and extended to sudden-death overtime. One of these overtime games was won by the USSR, the second by Canada. In the final game, Canada scored a goal within the final two minutes of the third period to win 6-5. Prior to the last game, Mike Keenan, the coach of the Canadian team commented,

> *There's a synergism involved in this and it has taken the game to greater levels than ever before. The chemistry in both teams and what it has brought out in each other is incredible. Both have been challenged to the ultimate and it has brought out the very best in both. To play at this level, the best players in the world have played as well as they've ever played. They're enjoying it. You can see it in their faces. (quoted in Kernaghan, 1987, p. C1)*

Ken Dryden, a former goaltender for the Montreal Canadiens, provides another example of the synergism between two competitors. In his autobiography, Dryden stated,

> *A good opponent [is] a rare and treasured thing for any team or player . . . By forcing you to be as good as you can be, such an opponent stretches the boundaries of your emotional and playing experience . . . It is why good players and good teams, good enough to stand alone, stand straighter and more vividly with a good opponent. (Dryden, 1983, p. 127)*

Mills, Keenan, and Dryden were essentially discussing the same thing. There's no doubt that the two opponents in any competition have the identical goal of winning, but they also share a common goal of playing a satisfying game. The fact that they share a common goal is evidence of the reality of groups. In summarizing his discussion, Mills pointed out,

> *Two points need emphasis. First, the group goal is not the simple sum of personal goals, nor can it be directly inferred from them. It refers to a desirable state for the group, not simply a desirable state for individuals . . . the second point is that the mental construct of the group goal resides not in some mystical collective mind, but in the minds of group members . . . It may be shared by most or all group members, but since many other ideas are shared, that is not its distinction. What sets the concept of group goal apart is that in content and substance it refers to the group as a unit—specifically to a desirable state of that unit. (p. 95)*

Groups are real. They have goals, aspirations, character, and a personality different from the simple sum of the goals, aspirations, character, and personality possessed by individual group members. Further, individual behavior is different within group situations. The influence of the group can lead to increased conformity, deviance, tenacity, or many other behaviors individuals might not exhibit alone. Similarly, individual performance is different within group situations. Frequently, individual athletes who cannot or do not stand out by themselves are outstanding in a group setting.

The Utility of Groups

Given that scientists have had doubts about the reality of groups, it probably shouldn't be surprising that both lay people and social scientists have had misgivings about whether groups are positive or negative, good or bad, useful or detrimental. Box 1.2 contains some of the old adages and popular bromides that have been passed on to succeeding generations (also see Illustration 1.1). It should be apparent why these old adages are confusing to a layperson. That is, our old adages offer more contradictions than solutions (Steiner, 1972).

The contradictions are understandable if we consider the disagreements among scientists. In 1978, Christian Buys, a social scientist, wrote what he described as a partly tongue-in-cheek, partly serious article entitled "Humans Would Do Better without Groups" (Buys, 1978a, 1978b). In this article, Buys presented a rather large list of negative, destructive consequences associated with group involvement. His fundamental point was that these negative consequences clearly show that otherwise rational, logical individuals often behave quite the opposite when they are within group situations.

One negative consequence of group involvement is *social loafing:* the reduction in individual effort that occurs when people are involved with group activities. The reasons for this phenomenon seem to be that individuals a) save their best effort for those instances where they perform alone (and are evaluated personally), b) are motivated to get by with as little effort as possible and the group provides them with a good opportunity to coast, c) reduce their personal efforts in order to reduce the likelihood that other group members will take advantage of their efforts, or d) assume that other group members are better qualified and, therefore, reduce effort accordingly.

Box 1.2	
Popular sayings about the utility of groups for task productivity have been contradictory	
The Group as a Benefit	**The Group as a Liability**
Two heads are better than one.	Too many cooks spoil the broth.
The more the merrier.	Three is a crowd.
Many hands make the work lighter.	If you want things well done, do them yourself.
There is unity in numbers.	A camel is a horse developed by a committee.

Illustration 1.1. The more the merrier?

A second, negative aspect of groups is the tendency *toward self-deception*. There is a tendency for ingroup members to overvalue ingroup members, processes, and products and to undervalue those from the outgroup. This process of self-deception begins almost as soon as groups form. We categorize ourselves socially, which produces perceptions of "we" versus "they," and this social categorization is an important element of group formation. With intragroup cooperation, intergroup competition, and increasing group cohesiveness, an evaluation bias becomes established and there is an increase in outgroup rejection.

Conformity is a third, negative aspect of groups. In order for any group to be effective and operate in a coherent, unified fashion, its membership must ascribe to common standards and hold similar perceptions of what is acceptable and unacceptable. When individuals accept without question a group's decision to engage in destructive or anti-social behavior, it provides an excellent example of the negative potential group conformity.

A fourth, negative correlate of group involvement is *groupthink*. The choice of the term, groupthink, was influenced by George Orwell's book, *1984*. According to Irving Janis (1972), groupthink is a mode of thinking engaged in by members of highly cohesive groups that are strongly motivated to maintain unanimity. A catalyst for Janis' work was an interest in exploring the bases for some well-known, disastrous group endeavors, such as the Bay of Pigs invasion, the inadequate defense of Pearl Harbor prior to World War II, and the escalation of the Vietnam War. Janis proposed that bad decisions can be made by groups if members develop a closeness, an *esprit de corps*, and critical thinking is suspended or rendered ineffective. A set of unconscious, shared illusions emerge that are accepted by all group members without serious dissent. Chapter 18 contains a more comprehensive discussion of groupthink; also, a number of examples of groupthink are provided in Box 18.2.

A fifth negative aspect of group involvement is *deindividuation*: the loss of personal identity, self-awareness, and inner restraints resulting from the individual's submersion in the group. When Festinger, Pepitone, and Newcomb (1952) first introduced the term, they characterized deindividuation as follows: "individuals are not seen or paid attention to as individuals. The members do not feel that they stand out as individuals. Others are not singling a person out for attention nor is the person singling out others" (p. 282). The individual loses his/her sense of personal identity and becomes an indistinguishable part of the group. As a result of deindividuation, individuals in groups may behave in ways that are atypical of them when they are alone.

A good example of deindividuation in action comes from the 1972 USSR-Canada hockey series. In Moscow, during the closely contested final game, a tying goal was scored by a Canadian player midway through the third player. However, the goal judge was slow in flashing the red light. Jack Ludwig (1972) described what happened next:

> *The goal judge seemed to be clearing it with Brezhnez. And in the stands, [Team Canada manager] Alan Eagleson, seeing that the light hadn't gone on, thought it had been disallowed and blew up, and was launching himself toward the scorer's bench when two policemen grabbed him. He hollered and Pete Maholovich, not having much to do while the hassling was going on, happened to be counting the house. Who should he see but old agent, Alan Eagelson, dangling from the cops' arms like a New Year's baby from a stork's bill! . . . Big Pete, 6'8" in his naked steel skates, charged the boards, vaulted up, and over, his shoulder pads four cops wide, his stick ready, offering to trade peace for Eagleson! In two seconds, twenty other Team Canada players were out there . . . Eagleson [who was] reclaimed . . . who cried out against injustice, was the great hero, though Eagleson, to free himself from the encumbrance of unnecessary adulation, looked back at the cops and the enemy and flashed first a one-finger salute, and, perhaps thinking himself stingy, unselfishly gave the cops his whole arm. (pp. 175-176)*

The actions of Eagleson and Team Canada when the goal judge failed to signal the goal were consistent with what would be expected of individuals in a state of deindividuation. A loss of self-regulation occurred.

Inevitably, Buys' thoughts produced a number of responses in which his conclusion was criticized and alternate perspectives offered (Anderson, 1978; Green & Mack, 1978; Kravitz, Cohen, Martin, Sweeney, McCarty, Elliott, & Goldstein, 1978; Shaffer, 1978). Essentially, four major points were made in these rebuttals. One was that it isn't groups that are responsible for these negative behaviors, it is individuals. Consequently, if the behavior of individuals could be improved, groups would not be a problem. A second was that some of the phenomena listed by Buys are characteristic of the collective behavior of individuals in crowds, not groups. A third was that many of the consequences listed by Buys can be negative or positive depending on the context. A social movement would be negative, for example, if it contributed to fascism and led to the elimination of civil liberties; it would be positive, on the other hand, if it contributed to the enhancement of human dignity. And, finally, it was pointed out that Buys ignored many of the positive functions served by groups: the pursuit of civil liberties by action groups, the charitable work done by humanitarian groups, the effectiveness of the family unit in raising children, and so on.

The debate set off by Buys' article is informative. The rebuttals leave no doubt concerning the question of whether groups can or should be eliminated from society—a view echoed by Buys himself. As he pointed out, "Clearly, many forms of groups are beneficial, if not essential to humans. Indeed, it seems nonsensical to search for alternatives to human groups" (Buys, 1978b, p. 568). Groups are a necessary, integral, generally beneficial part of society.

Definition Issues in the Study of Groups

In the previous two sections, it was pointed out that there has been some debate about both the reality of groups and their utility. Consequently, it probably does not come as a surprise to hear that there also has been considerable divergence in how a group should be defined. Definition clarity is essential for effective communication; it insures that people are discussing the same phenomenon. Thus, for example, we might state that sport is a useful vehicle to teach children "aggression." Different sets of readers might define aggression quite differently and take a different meaning from that statement. For one set, aggression and motivation might be synonymous; for another aggression and violence might be synonymous. The nature, antecedents, and consequences of those contrasting synonyms are dramatically different. So, it should be obvious that for the sake of definition clarity, it is important to insure that there is consistency in our understanding of what we mean by the term group.

What a Group is Not

Joseph McGrath (1984) pointed out that "groups are not just any aggregate of two or more people" (p. 6). He defined a groups as "social aggregates that involve mutual awareness and potential mutual interaction" (McGrath, 1984, p. 7), and then pointed out what types of social aggregations lack these criteria (and, therefore, cannot be considered a group). According to McGrath, these include

- *Artificial aggregates* such as a *statistical group* formed on the basis of a common property such as age, sex, social class (e.g., Danish cross country skiers),
- *Unorganized aggregates* such as a) an *audience* that is attending to a common set of stimuli (e.g., people watching a tennis match), b) a *crowd* that is in physical proximity attending to a common set of stimuli (e.g., Indianapolis 500 attendees), or c) a *public* that has and is attending to a common set of issues, has indirect interaction on these issues but may not be in physical proximity (e.g., the International Olympic Committee),
- *Units with patterned relationships* such as a) a *culture* where the members share common customs, language, etc. (e.g., Canadians), b) a *subculture* where members share common customs, language, etc. that are in contrast in specific ways to that of the surrounding culture (e.g., French Canadians), or c) a *kinship group* where members are related by birth or marriage,
- *Structured social units* such as a) a *society* where members share a geographical region, political system, and relationships characterized by interdependence, or b) a *community* which is a subdivision of a society, and
- *Deliberately designed social units* such as a) an *organization* where a large aggregate of people is recruited for specific roles (e.g., United Way), or b) a *suborganization,* which is a portion of a large organization (e.g., the University fund-raisers for the United Way),
- *Less deliberately designed social units* such as an *association* which are formed for specific purposes and where interaction among members is present (e.g., Rugby's Five Nations Championships among France, England, Wales, Scotland, and Ireland).

McGrath pointed out that groups may develop within these settings; the potential is present. But, he emphasized that the above list of aggregates does not inherently satisfy the criteria that help to constitute a group.

Even a very superficial examination of the above list of aggregates would highlight the fact that none of these are characteristic of sport teams. Cricket teams, volleyball teams, rugby teams, wrestling teams, and so on would fall under the category of deliberately designed social units (i.e., in the case of organized sport teams competing in a league) or the category of less deliberately designed social units (i.e., in the case of sport teams not competing in formal competitions but nonetheless satisfying the criteria for a group outlined below).

What a Group Is

Every group is like all other groups, like some other groups, and like no other group. A therapy group, a social group, and a sport group are similar in some ways, but they are significantly different in numerous aspects. Consequently, theoreticians studying different types of groups have focused on different aspects. That is, the definitions for a group fall into a number of categories or types, each of which highlights an important aspect of the nature of groups.

One general category of definitions emphasizes that groups are characterized by a *common fate* for their members. Individuals may contribute to the team outcome but in basketball, cricket, netball, and field hockey, the group wins or loses. The following definition serves as an example of the common fate definition of a group:

> *A set of individuals who share a common fate, that is, who are interdependent in the sense that an event which affects one member is likely to affect all. (Fiedler, 1967, p. 6)*

A second category of definitions highlights the fact that membership in groups—in contrast to being present in a crowd of people—is associated with *mutual benefit* for the individuals. It was pointed out above that we have a fundamental need to form interpersonal attachments. It is enjoyable and rewarding to be a member of a badminton team; those rewards and benefits are not present when the individual is a member of a crowd awaiting the arrival of a bus. An example of a definition that emphasizes the mutual benefit aspects of a group is

> *A collection of individuals whose existence as a collection is rewarding to the individuals. (Bass, 1960, p. 39)*

Because all groups are characterized by a stable pattern of relationships among members, one of the two most common approaches has been to define a group through its *social structure*. Thus, for example, status differences, roles, and group norms are not relevant (or present) in a collection of individuals meeting for a class for the first time; they are relevant (and present) in a synchronized swimming team. The following definitions highlight elements of social structure:

> *Its members share norms about something . . . [including] norms concerning the roles of the group members . . . These distinctive features—shared*

*norms and interlocking roles—presuppose a more than transitory relation-
ship of interaction and communication. (Newcomb, 1951, p. 3)*

*A group is a social unit which consists of a number of individuals who
stand in (more or less) definite status and role relationships to one another
and which possess a set of values or norms of its own regulating the behavior of individual members, at least in matters of consequence to the group.
(Sherif & Sherif, 1956, p. 144)*

Another very common approach to the definition of a group highlights important
group processes such as interaction and communication among members. Since interaction and communication can occur among strangers in a movie lineup, for example, definitions focusing on group processes characteristically elaborate upon the quality of the
relationship among the individuals. Some examples are

- *Two or more persons who are interacting with one another in such a manner
  that each person influences and is influenced by each other person; (Shaw,
  1981, p. 8)*
- *For a collection of individuals to be considered a group there must be some
  interaction; (Hare, 1976, p. 4)*
- *The face-to-face interaction of two or more persons in such a way that members are able to recall the characteristic of the other members accurately . . .
  Some additional characteristics of small groups that provide further definition of the concept and serve to distinguish the small group [include] . . . frequent interaction . . . the development of a group personality . . . the
  establishment of group norms . . . coping behavior . . . role differentiation . . .
  interdependent goals . . . The final unique characteristic of small groups is
  something called the assembly effect bonus. This refers to extra productivity
  that is caused specifically by the nature of groups; (Burgoon, Heston, &
  McCroskey, 1974, pp. 2-5)*
- *A group is an aggregation of two or more people who are to some degree in
  dynamic interrelation with one another; (McGrath, 1984, p. 8) and*
- *We mean by a group a number of persons who communicate with one
  another, often over a span of time, and who are few enough so that each person is able to communicate with all others, not at second hand, through other
  people, but face-to-face. (Homans, 1950, p. 1)*

One difficulty with definitions that are based on common fate, mutual benefit, social
structure, and group processes is that all of these characteristics could be present without
guaranteeing the existence of a group. For example, two strangers might independently
sneak into a gymnasium to shoot baskets on a Sunday morning. If the custodian discovers
them, they would suffer a common fate: eviction. The presence of a second person could
be beneficial from the perspective of having company, retrieving a stray ball, sharing the
blame for sneaking in, and so on. It would also be possible for interaction and communication to occur and norms (e.g., retrieve the other person's ball if it rolls close) and role
relationships (e.g., teacher and pupil) to develop. But, the two individuals would not be a
group if they didn't consider themselves to be a group. Therefore, some authors have proposed that a fundamental characteristic of a group is *self-categorization*. Examples of definitions which highlight the self-categorization aspect of groups are

- *Two or more individuals [who] . . . perceive themselves to be members of the same social category; (Turner, 1982, p. 15) and*
- *A group exists when two or more people define themselves as members of it and when its existence is recognized by at least one other. (Brown, 1988, pp. 2-3)*

All of these characteristics have relevance for the definition of a sport team or group.

A Sport Team Defined

Drawing on each of the above characteristics, a sport team can be defined as a collection of two or more individuals who possess a common identity, have common goals and objectives, share a common fate, exhibit structured patterns of interaction and modes of communication, hold common perceptions about group structure, are personally and instrumentally interdependent, reciprocate interpersonal attraction, and consider themselves to be a group.

A basketball team, whether it in an organized league or competing in 3-on-3 competitions, serves to highlight the components of the definition of a group. There are, of course, at least two people involved. The common identity exists when individual team members, opponents, and non-team members all view the group as a unit distinguishable from other units. In sport, a common identity can result from the team's name if the team is competing in an organized league. Even in informal competitions, however, self-categorization produces a sense of common identity in athletes competing against an opponent.

The very specific objective of every sport competition—winning—serves to ensure that there is at least one shared common purpose in a sport team. Also, the common fate that is universal among sport teams is winning or losing.

Numerous examples are available for the structured patterns of interaction that exist within a sport team. The most obvious example is the offensive and defensive alignments that the team adopts. Any newcomer to a team requires some time to become completely familiar with the specific system. Another example is the distinctions made implicitly or explicitly between rookies and veterans early in training camp. The locker room assignments, uniform distinctions, and hazing practices are a manifestation of structured patterns of interaction.

The language of basketball generally—(screen, back door, two-man) and the specific manner in which it is selectively used on particular teams provides one example of a structured mode of communication. The specific terminology conveying particular offensive and defensive assignments is another. Although members of a team can readily translate these apparently meaningless symbols into something meaningful, a non-team member or uninitiated observer cannot.

The structure of any group consists of roles, norms, positions, and status. As soon as individuals begin to interact and communicate, status differences evolve, positions are assumed, and role expectations and norms begin to form. On a basketball team, positions are established almost immediately. Status differences evolve because of differences in ability or knowledge, and roles (e.g., rebounder, shooter, captain) and norms (e.g., we all rebound and play tough defense) develop from individual interactions and communications.

Personal and task interdependence are inherent within the nature of the sport itself; the rules of sport dictate the size, general structure, and organization of the sport team. Therefore, an individual cannot play basketball alone; a specific number of players are permitted on the field at any given time; there are general rules on how they must be aligned; interaction with opponents must conform to certain standards, and so on. In essence, each team member is dependent on his or her teammates if competition is going to occur.

Interpersonal attraction generally evolves from sport team participation— although there are documented exceptions, friendships are usually present to some degree on most teams.

The final criterion—self-categorization—is generally the first one present when a team forms. Even in a 2-on-2-basketball game played on the playground with strangers, the distinction of "we" versus "they" evolves as soon as the teams are formed.

Group Dynamics Defined

This book includes the term group dynamics. Inclusion of that term was quite deliberate, so it may be useful to outline what it is intended to mean. Kurt Lewin (1943, 1948, 1951), the generally acknowledged catalyst for the study of group issues, is credited with introducing the term to represent two aspects: the study of groups and the energy, vitality, and activity characteristic of all groups. As a field of inquiry, group dynamics is thought to be "dedicated to advancing knowledge about the nature of groups, the laws of their development, and their interrelations with individuals, other groups, and larger institutions" (Cartwright & Zander, 1968, p. 7). Our book deals with this aspect of group dynamics: we have attempted to summarize the body of research that has focused on the nature of sport teams and their development, and their interrelationships with individuals and larger institutions.

Also, however, sport teams are characterized by energy, vitality, and growth and development; they are dynamic, not static. That dynamism is manifested in the developing nature of the structure of sport teams, their cohesiveness, and their collective efficacy, for example. It is also manifested in interaction and communication among team members, group decision-making, and team achievements. Our book also focuses on the nature, antecedents, and consequences of the dynamic group processes characteristic of sport teams.

Conceptual Frameworks for Groups

A conceptual framework or model is a simplified representation of reality. Conceptual frameworks representing sport teams offer some disadvantages and advantages (Carron, 1984b). One disadvantage that might be obvious is that any conceptual framework, because it is a simplified representation, can never adequately portray the total phenomena. The developers of a conceptual framework are like the fabled three blindmen who were placed at different parts of an elephant and asked to provide a description. Each was a good scientist and provided a completely reliable and objective description of the elephant. But, none of the individual descriptions was adequate as a portrayal of the total elephant. In the same vein, a conceptual framework, no matter how comprehensive, cannot provide a valid portrayal of a theoretical construct.

A second disadvantage is that human behavior is dynamic while conceptual frameworks tend to present a static picture; they are a photograph rather than a video representation. A photograph freezes its objects in a particular time and place. Thus, for example, a portrait of a sport team taken today might include smiling, contented athletes. Another portrait taken tomorrow could present a different picture.

A third, somewhat related disadvantage is that conceptual frameworks generally represent simple linear causal relationships. Thus, in the conceptual framework used to organize the material for our book, group structure, one aspect of which is role acceptance, for example, is portrayed as leading to group cohesion, which, in turn is portrayed as leading to group processes (an aspect of which is communication). However, there is a reciprocal relationship among all three: between communication and role acceptance, cohesion and role acceptance, and cohesion and communication. A linear causal framework does not reflect these dynamic relationships.

Despite these shortcomings, there are advantages to the use of a conceptual framework. One major advantage is that complex topics can be simplified and more readily explained and understood. If the group is so abstract that early psychologists even questioned its existence, how can any sense be made out of it without a simplified representation?

A second advantage is that assumptions can be more readily drawn about how the individual components of the complex phenomena are related. In the case of the sport team, a conceptual framework might permit us to make assumptions about the interrelationship of role clarity, role acceptance, team cohesion, and team performance.

Finally, a conceptual framework can help clarify what is known and unknown about a phenomenon, and, consequently, provide some direction for further research. Again, if we take a sport team as an example, a conceptual framework might serve to highlight the fact that we know very little about the relationship of density and group size to athlete satisfaction in sport. A conceptual framework could serve as a catalyst for research to examine this issue.

What follows are some useful conceptual frameworks which help to highlight the complexity of groups generally and sport teams specifically.

A Conceptual Framework for Group Effectiveness

All groups strive to be effective, but, effectiveness takes on different meanings for different groups. A police force might judge itself effective if the community has a low crime rate, while an effective sorority could be one that maintains its annual membership, and an effective investment club is likely to be one that makes money for its members.

What makes a sport team effective? Is it finishing first in the standings or is it simply having more wins than losses? In both of these instances, effectiveness is equated to performance outcome. Since a sport team competes with other teams, its performance outcome is dependent upon not only its own performance but also upon the performance of its opponents. Thus to judge a team's effectiveness by its performance outcome is somewhat misleading and, at times, unfair. A better indicator of team effectiveness is team performance. Team performance refers to how well the team carries out (executes) its tasks. Some examples of team performance include minimizing the number of turnovers in basketball, maximizing the number of shots on net in hockey or team handball, and increasing the percentage of successful passes in soccer or football.

Ivan Steiner (1972) advanced a simple and popular conceptual framework of group effectiveness. A schematic representation of this conceptual framework is presented in Figure 1.1. As Steiner pointed out, actual productivity is the performance that is attained, whereas potential productivity is the performance that might be obtained, based upon the relevant resources in the group. The group's resources include the knowledge, ability, and skills of the individual players, their respective level of training, the adequacy of their equipment, and so on. The actual steps, actions, or behaviors taken individually or collectively by group members to carry out the group task represent the group processes. When individuals work in groups, communication, coordination, and interaction are necessary. These can be relatively ineffective and losses in efficiency can occur. Steiner proposed that the two major sources of losses that occur in any group are the result of faulty coordination and reduced motivation.

Steiner's conceptual framework can be illustrated with a hypothetical example of a tug-of-war team. In the case of a two-person team, each individual might be able to pull 100 kg. Thus, the potential productivity of the group based on the group's resources is 200 kg. However, the group would likely pull less than this (possibly 180 kg.), because of the inability of the two people to coordinate their efforts and/or because each person might expect the other to carry the main load. Therefore, the group would have experienced a process loss of 20 kg.

As a group increases in size, its potential productivity increases. A volleyball team that keeps 30 members throughout the season has a greater likelihood of having the necessary resources to handle almost every situation. There will always be enough players for scrimmages, replacements will be available in case of injuries, specialized lineups can be used against certain teams, and so on. But, with an increase in resources, there will also be an increase in the number of problems associated with effectively and efficiently managing the group. With 30 players, it is more difficult for the coach to run an effective practice in which all of the players are active. Frequent personal communication with each individual player is difficult. If lineups are rotated, the players will not be as familiar with each other. Also, and more importantly perhaps, social loafing can increase; with increased numbers in the group, individual team members may suffer a loss in motivation and personal accountability.

The application of Steiner's conceptual framework to the effectiveness of sport teams in general is illustrated in Figure 1.2. In this example, Team A will be more effective than Team B if

a) it possesses greater relevant resources and experences fewer process losses,

or

b) it has greater relevant resources and experiences approximately equal process losses,

or

c) it has approximately equal relevant resources and experiences fewer process losses.

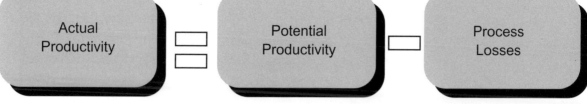

Figure 1.1. Steiner's (1972) conceptual framework of group effectiveness

In professional sport, where the desire for league parity has led to efforts to equalize team resources (e.g., the weakest team drafts first), potential productivity is crucial. In amateur sport, where coaches have limited control over their resources (they generally coach the talent available and have very little opportunity to supplement or change their roster during a season), the reduction in process losses is crucial. How can process losses be reduced? How can group effectiveness be increased?

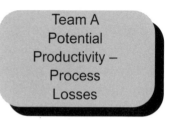

Research in psychology, sociology, anthropology, and business has been concerned with these questions since their origin as sciences. Fortunately, information is available to provide the coach with some guidelines and insights.

A General Conceptual Framework for the Nature of Groups

VERSUS

Joseph McGrath (1984) has provided a useful conceptual framework for the study of groups. This is illustrated in Figure 1.3. According to McGrath, the soul or essence of a group is group interaction processes: team members interacting with one another. Members of a netball team, for example, practice together regularly, interact for social and for task purposes, and come to decisions that have both personal and collective implications. In short, members are constantly interacting together in some way that is meaningful to them.

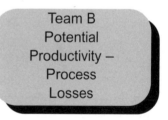

Figure 1.2. The application of Steiner's conceptual framework of group effectiveness to the analysis of sport teams

McGrath also pointed out that five general categories of factors influence group interaction processes. One of these is the *properties of the group members*. Thus, for example, members of the netball team could differ in ability, age, personality, height, weight, religion, and a host of other biological, social, and psychological attributes. These attributes have the potential to influence the interactions that occur among team members.

McGrath also identified group structure as another potentially important set of properties influencing group interaction processes. The properties of the group members (their ability and age for example) have an influence on the development of status differences, role responsibilities, player positions, and so on. In turn, group structure influences and is influenced by group interaction processes. An older, more skillful netball player, for

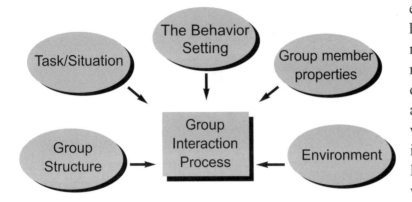

Figure 1.3. A conceptual framework for the study of groups (McGrath, 1984)

example, is likely to have higher team status than the majority of other team members. As a consequence, in any team interactions, her opinions would likely have more impact on the collective. Further, the manner in which teammates respond to high and low status colleagues is qualitatively and quantitatively different.

Properties of the *environment* also influence interactions within groups. Members of a netball team could be training together in the off-season. A crowded, noisy weight room would be less conducive to task (e.g., weight training techniques) or social (e.g., family concerns) interactions than a spacious, quiet weight room. The physical, socio-cultural, and technological properties of different environments influence group interaction processes.

Finally the nature of the *task/situation* also influences group interaction processes. The members of a netball team could be together to train, to compete against another team, to attend a banquet, or to participate in the wedding of a teammate. The fundamental nature of these tasks/situations differs and, consequently, the nature of the group interaction processes would vary accordingly.

A Conceptual Framework for Sport Teams

The conceptual framework for a sport team that was used as the organizational framework for this book is presented in Figure 1.4. This is a linear conceptual framework consisting of inputs, throughputs, and outputs. The outputs, the major consequences in effective sport groups, are individual products such as individual performance and adherence, and group products such as team outcome and group stability. The throughputs are the group's structure, processes, and cohesiveness. Finally, the inputs are the attributes of individual group members, and the nature of the group's environment.

There are 21 chapters in this book, presented in seven sections entitled Introduction, Group Environment, Member Attributes, Group Structure, Group Cohesion, Group Processes, and Building the Group. The first section, which contains two chapters, serves to introduce the concept of a group and outline how groups develop. The next five sections deal with the major factors influencing group formation and group functioning. The final section, which contains one chapter, provides an introduction to the types of interventions used to develop more effective teams. An analogy that helps to outline specifically how each of the last six sections (and the final 19 chapters) are related to one another is the purchase and operation of a bicycle.

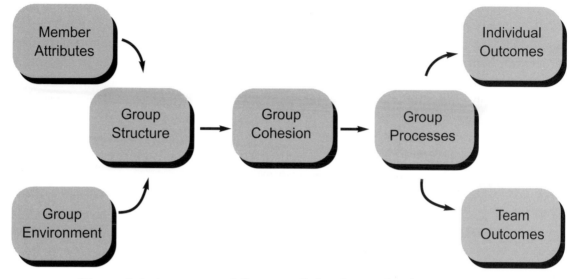

Figure 1.4. A conceptual framework for the study of sport teams

Group effectiveness is influenced by environmental factors. Similarly, the relative effectiveness of 3-speed, 10-speed, and/or mountain bikes also depends on environmental factors such as the terrain on which they will be used. A 10-speed is impractical to deliver newspapers; a mountain bike is ineffective for the Tour de France. In the three chapters in the second section, factors associated with the group's environment are introduced.

A group's resources are its individual members. The attributes of those members directly influence the group's effectiveness. A bike is also composed of component parts that represent its "resources." It should be obvious that the resources used to construct different bikes vary in number, function, and quality. For example, there are over a thousand components for some bikes, the components for a standard bike differ from those for a mountain bike, and it's possible to spend either a minimal or a large amount of money for the same component. Not surprisingly, the quality of a bike is strongly influenced by the quality of its component parts. This same truism also applies to teams—the quality of a team is strongly influenced by its component resources. In the four chapters of the third section, factors associated with member attributes and group effectiveness are discussed.

In every bike, the various parts are put into position according to their functions and roles—the component parts make up the bike's structure and foundation. Groups also have a formal structure that develops when their members assume positions and take on different functions and roles. The six chapters in the fourth section are concerned with the development of group structure.

When the bike is put together, each part is tightened into place. Also, care is taken to insure that the wheels don't rub on the frame, that the gears work smoothly, that oil is applied where necessary. In short, the bike is drawn together into a tight integrated unit. This process is analogous to the development of group cohesiveness. Cohesiveness is the bond that accounts for the fact that many athletes with differing needs, personalities, motives, and goals can be formed together into one strong effective group. In the two chapters in the fifth section, the issues associated with group cohesiveness are discussed.

The construction of the bike is not an end in itself. It is put together for some purpose, such as competing, socializing, working, or recreating. During the periods in which it is used, the bike's effectiveness is influenced by many different interdependent (related) processes. Some of these, for example, involve regular maintenance such as putting oil on the chain and air in the tires, insuring that the gears operate in a smooth coordinated fashion, and so on. These functions are associated with the process of operating the bike. A group also forms for some purpose such as competing, socializing, working, or recreating. During the period in which it is engaged in its activities, various processes also influence its effectiveness. The four chapters in the sixth section focus on group processes.

Finally, bikes do not always work as well as they should. Consequently, they need a tune up. Similarly, groups sometimes suffer from problems of poor leadership, member conflict, poor cohesiveness, and so on. When this is the case, the group requires a tune up as well. In group dynamics, this tune up is referred to as team building. The last chapter outlines protocols used for team building in sport teams.

Chapter Two

GROUP DEVELOPMENT

> "We'll get better, but we ain't going to make it a total turnaround," the 37-year-old [Scottie] Pippen says. "It's impossible because of the makeup of our team. It's always new personnel; it's always, now we've got to see how this guy plays and how we're going to fit him in. You can't keep doing that." He blames the team's woes on owner Paul Allen and president Bob Whitsitt, arguing that they have assembled the deepest roster in the league with little regard for team chemistry. (Thomsen, 2002, p. 152)

If you consider the situations in which you are able to participate as a member of a sport group, it is quickly apparent that there are a large number and variety: competitive sports, intramural sports, physical education classes. In each instance, the collection of individuals may differ in many important aspects —in terms of the number of members, the extent to which there is social interaction, the level of intimacy, the degree to which there is an interest in the success of the group, the amount of mutual help and assistance provided, and the extent or frequency that the participants refer to the whole as "we" and to other social bodies as "they." In short, the collections of individuals present in these various sport settings may differ markedly in the degree to which they constitute a "group." So, given the number, variety, and dissimilarities among groups, how is it possible to study groups in a general sense? How is it possible to generalize across groups?

Kluckhohn and Murray (1949) observed that each individual is like all other people, like some other people, and like no other person. Cissna (1984) pointed out that the same is undoubtedly true for groups:

> *Every group is like all groups in some respects, like some—or perhaps even most—groups in some respects, and like no groups in other respects. Groups do change and develop in common similar ways; some things about some groups, perhaps all groups, do not change; and all groups are also unique in changing and in staying the same. (p. 25)*

In short, the study of groups is difficult but not impossible because, despite their differences, there are also some strong similarities present across even the most widely differing groups. Among these similarities are the general way in which groups develop, in the structure that is characteristic of all groups, and in the types of interactions that occur within and between groups.

The Nature of Group Development

Group development has been defined as "the degree of maturity and cohesion that a group achieves over time as members interact, learn about one another, and structure relationships and roles within the group" (Mennecke, Hoffer, & Wynne, 1992, p. 526). Numerous theories have been proposed in an attempt to define how groups develop over time. In 2004, a summary of the past 50 years of literature pertaining to group development (Arrow, Poole, Henry, Wheelan, & Moreland, 2004) highlighted five general categories that encompass these various theories.

The Sequential Stage (Linear) Perspective

In the sequential stage perspective of group development, it is assumed that the group progressively moves through different stages of change. Critical issues arise in each successive stage and when they are successfully dealt with the group moves on. Arrow and colleagues (2004) noted that one of the most cited examples of this type of model was advanced by Bruce Tuckman (1965).

Tuckman initially reviewed 50 studies in a search for common interpretations on how groups develop. On the basis of his analysis, he proposed that all groups go through four stages as they develop and then prepare for and carry out the group's task. These were referred to as *forming, storming, norming,* and *performing.* Subsequently, Tuckman and Jensen (1977) modified this original proposal and added a fifth stage that they referred to as *adjourning.* The Tuckman and Jensen perspective on group development is presented in Table 2.1 (see Illustration 2.1).

Table 2.1
Stages of group development (Adapted from Tuckman & Jensen, 1977)

Stage	Interpersonal Characteristics	Task Characteristics
Forming	Individuals become familiar with each other and bonds develop within the group.	Members determine what the group task is and what methods are suitable to carry it out.
Storming	Tension develops and conflict occurs among group members and with the leader.	Resistance arises to group methods and the group task.
Norming	Cohesiveness and group harmony develop and group roles are established.	Task cooperation among members is prevalent.
Performing	Relationships are stabilized.	The group's orientation is on productivity and performance.
Adjourning	Member contact decreases and emotional dependency among individual members is reduced.	The task of the group is completed and the duties of members are finished.

Illustration 2.1. The orientation phase of group development.

In the first stage, *forming*, the group members become familiar with each other and begin to identify the group's task. A fraternity group that makes the decision to enter a team in an intramural basketball league would go through this stage—even though all of the individuals belong to the same fraternity and know each other well. It would still be necessary for them to become familiar with each other's skills and abilities and to determine what offensive and defensive systems the team should use. The forming stage is essentially an orientation phase and issues of inclusion and dependency are a major focus (Arrow et al., 2004).

In the second phase, tension and conflict arise in the group as interpersonal disagreements occur, resistance to the group's leader develops, and members begin to question the group's approach to the task or the task itself. Generally, these issues have to do with power and authority (Arrow et al., 2004). In the case of the fraternity team, *storming* might be reflected in disagreements about how the offense or defense should be run, who should make the decisions on substitutions, who should do most of the shooting, and so on. During the storming stage, various group members attempt to resist the group's influence and impose their preferences on the group.

Following the storming that occurs in stage two, the group begins to draw together again in a stage referred to as *norming*. Group roles and group norms are established in terms of both social relationships and task productivity. A dominant person, an outstanding player, or even a senior member of the fraternity might become assertive within the team and be acknowledged as the leader. Other group roles are also assigned or assumed: team peacemaker, comedian, social director, playmaker, and shooter, for example. Essentially, the norming stage is characterized by cooperation, cohesiveness, and consensus on the group's goals and objectives.

In the fourth stage, *performing*, interpersonal relations are stabilized and the group's energy is directed toward successful execution of the group's task. The fraternity team's leader, peacemaker, playmaker, and shooter now know and accept their roles. In the performing stage, the team becomes completely focused on achieving team success.

When the group's task has been completed, there is a termination of duties, a reduction in dependency on the group, and possibly the breakup of the group. This is referred to as the *adjourning* phase. Adjourning would occur in the fraternity team—at least in terms of playing basketball—when the basketball season was over. The roles that the various fraternity members had filled on the team such as leader, comedian, and so on would disappear with the breakup of the team. When the team members went back to just being members of the fraternity, the roles and responsibilities developed in this other context would prevail.

Three important points should be highlighted about the Tuckman and Jensen schema. First, the five stages are sequential. That is, when one stage is successfully completed, the group passes on to the next. Second, the duration of time spent at any one stage is variable for different groups. One group might spend a considerable amount of time in the forming stage but pass quickly through the storming stage. In fact, Hill and Gruner (1973) noted that a group that is essentially re-forming may completely skip aspects of a stage that it has already gone through. Thus, for example, a college basketball team that is returning for another season with a majority of veterans might not have to go through some of the orientation procedures of a completely new team. However, it's possible that this group might have a storming stage that is prolonged. A final point is that all effective groups must go through the various stages. If a group hopes to be productive, it must form, storm, norm, perform, and ultimately, when production is completed, adjourn.

Another model of group development proposed by Garland, Kolodny, and Jones (1965) is typical of the sequential stage perspective. The Garland et al. model includes five stages that are referred to as pre-affiliation, power and control, intimacy, differentiation, and termination-separation. In the *pre-affiliation* stage, individuals explore the possibility of joining together in a group. At this point, some potential group members might decide not to become involved. In the *power and control* stage, the individuals who have formed the group define, formalize, and test intra-group relationships. Also, subgroups may form. In the *intimacy* stage, interpersonal relationships become intensified and cooperation and sharing are strong. The *differentiation* stage is characterized by high cohesion and strong acceptance of the individuality of other group members. Finally, the *termination-separation* stage is associated with social interactions and communication centers around maintaining the group. The group reminisces and evaluates past group activities.

An example of the above model is illustrated in a study by Jaroslav Cikler (1967). He charted the actual group development and eventual breakup of fourteen 11-year-old boys who met to play soccer. The overriding consideration that drew the 14 boys together initially was their interest in soccer. This interest became the catalyst for their formation into a group. It also became the factor that drew the boys into a cohesive group. In the early stages, the structure within the group was very basic. Two captains who were elected by the total group formed teams. The role of team captain tended to be rotated among four different individuals while the composition of the two teams tended to vary from one day to the next. Also, all of the boys retained some input into the composition of the two teams. Conflicts and disagreements were minimal. In short, the total group developed some structure (e.g., dominant individuals, captains) but the two teams that were formed to compete were spontaneous and unstructured.

Over time, the overall group became much more structured. Practices were often held instead of games in order to improve the quality of play of all group members. Eventually, elections were no longer held—captains who selected the two teams simply assumed the leadership role. Ultimately, the number of individuals in this role was reduced from four to two and the composition of the two teams became stabilized. The number of disagreements increased and began to dominate the play.

After approximately a year and a half, the group began to disintegrate. Interest in soccer began to fade and members of the group began to develop interests outside the group. Possibly it was due to the fact that the original group of 14 was now, for all intent and purposes, two groups of 7. Possibly it was due to the increased emphasis on playing well (e.g., practices and training sessions). Or possibly it was due to the conflicts and disagreements that arose during games. It's even possible that other factors such as increasing age, changing interests, and added responsibilities outside of the group were the main "causes" and the factors observed by Cikler were "effects." Whatever the origin, the group began to break up and after approximately two years it was extinct.

The Repeating Cycles (Pendulum) Perspective

The majority of linear models are based on the underlying assumption that groups possess an inherent static development that is unresponsive to the demands of the environment (Gersick, 1988). In contrast, the repeating cycles perspective of group development (Worchel, 1994) represents a less deterministic view of group development by emphasizing the shifts that occur in interpersonal relationships during the growth and development of the group. It is assumed that a group does not move progressively through various stages in a linear fashion from the instant it forms. In short, cycles of development repeat and resolution to certain issues are considered temporary (Arrow et al., 2004).

Arrow and colleagues provided an example illustrating the repeating cycles perspective. It was proposed that group development is a repeating cycle of five stages. The first stage, *discontent*, occurs when group members feel alienated from the group and do not consider it as part of their identity. Initially, these feelings would exist for individuals trying out for a new sport team. They would likely not be included in conversations among the veteran players and, because they have not yet been selected, probably do not consider themselves part of the group.

The second stage, *group identification*, is reflective of increased commitment to the group and the identification of individuals who are members and non-members. The movement from the first stage to the second stage is typically founded on some event that begins to unite the group. The posting of those members who have made the team is a precipitating event that immediately identifies who are members and who are not.

The third stage is marked by increased activity and energy within the group as it strives toward a goal (i.e., *group productivity* stage). Once the team begins practices and games, the focus for individual members turns to production and finding a way to contribute to the team. To allow for this in sport, it's quite common for coaches to book an exhibition schedule to get his or her team ready for the upcoming competitive season. However, as the group begins to attain its goals during this period of the schedule, it starts to enter the *individuation* stage whereby members look for and demand recognition for their own contributions. For example, the very early part of a season could be thought of as a honeymoon where the individual members are just happy to be part of the group. However, once the honeymoon is over, there are desired (e.g., starter) and undesired (e.g., bench player) roles to fulfill and athletes want meaningful roles to play on a team. These roles could be fully spelled out as the exhibition season continues and athletes may or may not consider these roles as reflective of their abilities.

As this process of individuation continues, the group enters a final stage of *decay,* in the sense that the group puts less energy into achieving its goals and individual members become less interested in retaining their membership (i.e., the group returns to the discontent stage and potentially cycles through the process again). To continue the example, it's possible towards the end of the exhibition portion of the schedule that athletes become weary of constant practices and the prospect of playing meaningless games. For intercollegiate athletes, concerns about school may take precedence over athletics. Regardless, one's interest in his or her membership in the group may begin to decline. However, the beginning of the regular competitive season will likely renew the group's energies and the cycle will repeat itself . . . perhaps to be renewed once again if the team makes the playoffs.

Another example of a pendulum model of group development is one developed by William Schutz (1966). The main elements in Schutz's theory—the need for inclusion, the need for control, and the need for affection—are discussed in more detail in Chapter 8 (see Table 8.1). Schutz proposed that all groups from dyads to the largest groups must sequentially and successfully handle problems in the areas of inclusion, control, and affection. Essentially, different interpersonal problems are predominant in different phases of the group's development. He also emphasized that "these are not distinct phases . . . these problem areas are emphasized at certain points in a group's growth. All three problem areas are always present but not always of equal salience" (p. 171).

Schutz's model is similar to a linear perspective. However, it is considered to be a pendulum model because it contains the assumption that the three problem areas reappear during the life of the group. Thus, when a group has gone through the sequence of inclusion to control to affection, it begins another cycle.

Generally, problems of *inclusion* predominate during the initial phases of group development. These problems center around how much communication, interaction, and involvement different individuals want with each other and with the group. Obviously, if the majority of individuals want little or no interaction, communication, or involvement, the chances that they will form and develop into a strong group are minimal. On the other hand, if the majority of members want and express a great deal of inclusion behavior, the group has a solid foundation from which to proceed.

Issues related to control characterize the second problem area. Group members must resolve who will make the decisions, how the group will be led, and where the primary power and influence will lie. The control phase in Schutz's model of group development is similar to the storming stage in the Tuckman and Jensen model.

Finally, as the group develops, interpersonal concerns in the area of *affection* arise. Concerns center around how friendly, intimate, or affectionate group members want to be with each other.

Schutz proposed that when a group breaks up (disintegrates), it does so in a reverse sequence: affection to control to inclusion. That is, affection is the last to develop in the group; it is the first to go. After the decline in affection, issues relating to control, power, and influence begin to decline in importance. Eventually, group members simply don't care "who's in charge." Finally, contact, communication, and involvement decline to the point where the members no longer meet as a group.

A common link between the various repeating cycle models reflects what most athletes come to understand after being a member of a few sport teams. That is, there are ups and downs in the development of the group. More specifically, after group members become oriented to one another, group existence is marked by instances of conflict and differentiation followed by resolution and cohesion that could be followed by additional conflict and differentiation, and so on. Table 2.2 presents examples of two such case histories.

The first example comes from the book, *A Season on the Brink,* by John Feinstein (1987). During the 1985-86 college basketball season, Feinstein was given complete access to coach Bobby Knight and the Indiana Hoosiers. He attended practices, team meetings, and games, traveled with the team and recorded what he saw and heard. That season might be considered successful by most sport team's standards, but in 1986-87, the year after Feinstein was with them, the Indiana Hoosiers won the NCAA National Championship. The bulk of Feinstein's book deals with 1985-86 but in an epilogue he does present an overview of the championship year. The quotes in Table 2.2 overlap both seasons.

The second example comes from the book *Face-off at the Summit* by Ken Dryden and Mark Mulvoy (1973). It is the result of a diary maintained by Dryden during the 1972 Canada-Russia hockey series and which was subsequently developed into a book in collaboration with Mulvoy. The year 1972 marked the first opportunity for professional hockey players from North America to compete against European amateurs. From the mid-1950s, the Russians had enjoyed a clear superiority over Canadian amateur hockey teams in international exhibitions, in the Olympics, and in World Cup championships. Canadian sport fans felt that the Russian's success was achieved against inferior opposition. Thus, in 1972 when an All-Star team of professionals was selected from the National Hockey League, popular consensus was that "Canada's best" would soundly beat the Russians 8-0 in the eight-game series. Many Canadians considered the outcome of the first four games (which were played in Canada) a national disaster. The Russians led the series with two wins, one loss, and a tie. Team Canada eventually won the series with four wins, three losses, and one tie. The winning goal was scored in the eighth and deciding game with only 34 seconds left to play.

As Table 2.2 illustrates, cohesion is assumed to be relatively high when a group first comes together. This is a period of *orientation* and general feelings of team unity arise from the common expectations, experiences, anxieties, and aspirations that all the prospective team members share. In the Team Canada and Indiana Hoosier examples, the feelings of unity might have been a result of the sacrifices that all athletes made during the summer (e.g., training). Or, it may have been the result of the common goals and aspirations that the athletes had for the upcoming competition/season. The essential point is that when the team first gets together, there is a relatively high feeling of unity.

Following the orientation period, the pendulum swings and there is *differentiation and conflict*. Differentiation refers to the fact that the group physically and psychologically subdivides into smaller units and conflicts arise as athletes compete for a limited number of positions on the team. In many sports, breaking the total group into smaller units for practice is a natural consequence of the way the sport is organized; offense versus defense, forwards versus defense, setters versus spikers, and so on. The Team Canada quotation in Table 2.2 serves to highlight the potential conflicts that can arise as a result of the competition for a starting position on the team; the Indiana Hoosier quotation highlights the drudgery, monotony, and feelings of boredom that arise when a team is confronted with

Table 2.2
An example of a pendulum model of group development in a basketball setting (the Indiana Hoosiers as described by John Feinstein, 1987) and a hockey setting (Team Canada as described by Ken Dryden & Mark Mulvoy, 1973)

Team Canada	Indiana Hoosiers
Stage 1. Orientation: Cohesion and feelings of unity are high, the athletes share many common feelings, anxieties, and aspirations	
Practices Start: "One surprise aspect of the first week was the absolute lack of temper flare-ups—like high sticks— between people who go out of there way to knock each other down during the regular season" (p. 27).	*Practices Start:* "In college basketball, no date means more than October 15. On that day, basketball teams all around the country begin formal preparation for the upcoming season" (p. 27).
Stage 2. Differentiation and Conflict: The group physically or psychologically subdivides into smaller units; conflicts often arise as athletes compete for positions on the team	
Pre-series Practices Continue: "All of us desperately want to play on Saturday night because it is Game 1 of a historic event. It will mean so much to be one of the best seventeen and two—that is seventeen skaters and two goaltenders" (p. 32).	*Pre-season Practices Continue:* "November is the toughest for any college basketball team. The excitement of starting practice . . . has worn off and practice has become drudgery . . . There is just day after day of practices— the same faces, the same coaches, the same drills, the same teammates" (p. 59).
Stage 3. Resolution and Cohesion: Cohesion increases as group members share common concerns and feelings as they prepare to face a common threat	
The First Game: "After we finished our work, Sinden names the lineup for the opening game. Red Berenson, one of the centers, told Sinden and Ferguson to get lost for a couple of minutes . . . 'Look,' Red said to us. 'We have thirty-five outstanding hockey players here right now but only nineteen will be dressing tomorrow night. It's no disgrace not to be playing . . . this is a team of thirty-five men. Let's keep it that way'" (pp. 41-42).	*The First Game:* "The tension in the locker room was genuine. All the reminders about Miami, all the memories of last season, not to mention the memories of forty-eight practices that had led to this afternoon combined to create a sense of dread" (p. 96).

Table 2.2 (continued)

Stage 4. Differentiation and conflict:
Team unity is weakened as different individuals are rewarded
or punished, setting them off from the group

During the Series: "I practiced this morning with the Black Aces and tonight I'll be in the stands with them. The Black Aces of a hockey team are the spares . . . As expected, the Black Aces were flat at practice. Disappointed, down, depressed, none of us is used to watching a game from the stands" (pp. 60-61).

During the Season: "The locker room would not have been much quieter if Kent State had won the game . . . Mentally, Knight had decided he needed Hillman and Smith in place of Robinson and Brooks. They were deep in the doghouse . . . After [the team] showered, he blistered them one more time. Only three players had pleased him" (p. 102).

Stage 5. Termination:
If the season has been successful, feelings of cohesion are high.
If the season has been unsuccessful, feelings of cohesion are low

Termination: "I just looked around the room; everyone's uniform was soaked with sweat. I felt really proud . . . for all of us. I didn't know more than a handful of them six weeks ago, but now I felt that I knew everyone of them in a way you rarely know anyone. We had gone from the heights to the depths—and now we were back on top again" (p. 178).

Termination: "They jumped on each other, pummeled each other and cried . . . Finally, they went back to the locker room. When it was quiet Knight spoke briefly. 'What you did,' he told them, 'was refuse to lose. You've been that kind of team all year'" (p. 348).

constant early season practices and no games. Both examples help to illustrate the decline in cohesion and team unity that follows the orientation period.

Inevitably, the group draws together again as the pendulum swings forward in the opposite direction. This is what is referred to as *resolution*. In sport groups, resolution usually occurs when the team is about to meet an opponent. Competition within the group decreases and consensus is reached on general team goals and objectives. In the Team Canada quotation, a respected team member has reminded the total group about the importance of group solidarity. In the Indiana Hoosier example, the shared aspirations for upcoming season and the memory of a failure in the previous season both contribute to team unity in terms of a common shared anxiety: the fear of not doing well.

As the season progresses, the sequence described above is repeated. Differentiation and conflict are followed by resolution and cohesion, which are followed by differentiation and conflict, which are followed by resolution and cohesion. The group continues to grow and develop over the course of the season but there are pendulum-like shifts until the team dissolves.

When the team is successful, the final pendulum swing is toward high cohesiveness. In fact, in a meta-analysis examining the relationship between cohesion and sport performance, Carron, Colman, Wheeler, and Stevens (2002) reported that success is a strong predictor of subsequent cohesiveness. When teams win, feelings of cohesiveness are extremely high, and when they lose, they're low. The Team Canada quotation in Table 2.2 best serves to illustrate this; feelings of closeness accompany team success.

Additional Models of Group Development

In their review of group development models, Arrow and colleagues (2004) noted that there are additional theories that differ slightly from the linear and pendulum models. These fall under three general categories. The first category, *adaptive response models*, emphasizes that patterns of development are idiosyncratic (i.e., unique) for all groups based the demands and obstacles they must overcome. Essentially, this category rejects the notion that all groups move through similar sequential stages.

The second category, termed *robust equilibrium models*, highlights the fact that group development is marked by early activity and change followed by a relatively stable period. As Arrow and colleagues noted, it is presumed that "once a group has emerged from its early period and finished settling, the structure of interest will stay relatively constant" (p. 85). This model does have application to the development of structure in sport teams. For example, the early stages of a sport team's development require the delineation of roles, selection of leaders (i.e., captains), among other structural concerns. Generally, there are only slight modifications to the overall structure of teams after this process is complete.

A final category of group development models, a variation of the above, is termed *punctuated equilibrium models*. In this category, group development is viewed as consisting of stable periods of time punctuated with instances of sudden instability where the group is reorganized. This reorganization could be the result of the reassignment of roles or a turnover in group membership.

Turnover in Group Membership

Typically, in all organizations including sport, an issue that has attracted more attention than group development has been member turnover. It could be argued that even the addition of one new member results in the formation of a "new group." That is, any membership change alters the team's dynamics—a fact alluded to in the quote by Scottie Pippen of the NBA Portland Trailblazers that introduced this chapter.

The result of adding new members isn't always as disruptive as was apparently the case for Pippen's Portland Trailblazers. Nonetheless, although interscholastic, intercollegiate, professional, and amateur sport teams continue to function year after year, there is a regular turnover in a team's composition as a result of graduation, resignation, retirement, promotion, transfer, and dismissal. Even in championship professional sport teams, there is a regular turnover in personnel. For example, Grant Fuhr, a former goaltender for the Edmonton Oilers, winners of the Stanley Cup in four of the five years between 1984 and 1988, observed that "every year, there's a turnover—three or four guys every year, it seems like . . . That's life in the NHL" (quoted in Wiley, 1988, p. 68). Fuhr's impressions of the Oilers seem still to be applicable to the NHL.

In studies of organizational effectiveness in non-sport settings, it has repeatedly been shown that the replacement process is time consuming. The recruitment, training, and assimilation of new personnel are also expensive. Satisfaction and effective communication among group members is adversely affected. Established routines are disrupted. Also, group productivity and group effectiveness generally suffer (e.g., Caplow, 1964; Evan, 1963; Gaertner & Nollen, 1992; Irvine & Evans, 1995; Shelley, 1964).

A number of researchers have examined the implications of personnel changes in a sport organization in terms of (1) team performance, (2) the consequences for the organization if the turnover occurs in management (coaches, general managers) or among the athletes, and (3) the consequences for the organization if the turnover occurs in specific playing positions, e.g., goaltenders versus forwards in hockey, infielders versus outfielders in baseball, quarterbacks versus defensive backs in football.

The Replacement of Management

In amateur sport, when things do not go well, the coach usually makes changes in the athletes on the roster. However, in college and professional sport, when things do not go well, a regular and frequent occurrence is the replacement of coaches and managers. Box 2.1 illustrates two reasons why management turnover may occur. While some might argue that this is not unreasonable—that effective coaches should be retained and ineffective coaches should be released/fired—former college basketball coach Fran Fraschilla provides another perspective:

> *The line [determining] how a coach is perceived is so thin and so fluid . . . I always go back to what [Houston Rockets coach] Jeff Van Gundy told me a long time ago: "Biggest game of the year. You're down one. You get a good shot. The ball is in the air. It hangs there. Good coach or bad coach? Good coach or bad coach? Good coach or bad coach?" (cited in Wertheim, 2004, p. 57-58).*

There is research evidence that shows that firing the coach is not necessarily the best solution. A considerable body of research shows that there is a negative relationship between the replacement of a coach or manager and team effectiveness. Teams that change their coaches and managers a great deal are less successful than teams that don't (see Table 2.3). The only exception appears to be in professional hockey.

Care must be taken in the interpretation of the general findings in Table 2.3, however. There is no doubt that managerial turnover is associated with a lack of team effectiveness. But, correlational data do not provide any real insight into causation. When a seat belt sign comes on in an airplane, the ride generally gets rougher. But would it be reasonable to ask the pilot not to turn the sign on in order to insure a smooth flight? Certainly not, because the turbulence is associated with the seat belt sign, not caused by it.

Research has also shown that the negative relationship between manager/coach turnover and team success documented in Table 2.3 is influenced by a number of moderator variables including (a) the coaching ability of the successor, (b) the timing of the

Box 2.1
Managerial turnover in sport teams

Factor	Quotation
Losing as the Basis for Managerial Turnover	The Canadiens, after missing the playoffs last spring for the first time in a quarter of a century, were outscored 22-4 in losing their first five games this season, and the only appropriate accompaniment for the grim events at hockey's shrine was a dirge. Or a laugh track. But in a giddy, logic-defying and wildly successful makeover that began with the Oct.17 firing of general manager Serge Savard and coach Jacques Demers, the Canadiens, under Tremblay and new G.M. Rejean Houle, have rekindled the passion that makes hockey in Montreal distinct. The Canadiens had grown musty after their 1993 Stanley Cup victory, and following their abysmal start this year there was an outcry for team president Ronald Corey to bring in outsiders with fresh ideas, to air out the franchise before the move to the new Forum in March. (Farber, 1995, p. 26)
Player Dissatisfaction as the Basis for Managerial Turnover	When Missouri basketball coach Norm Stewart, 64, retired last week after 32 years of guiding the Tigers, he left behind an impressive record: 731 victories (seventh-highest all time), eight conference championships, and 16 NCAA tournament appearances. Yet while Stewart is revered in his home state, storm clouds had been gathering around Stormin' Norman since midway through last season, when reports of conflicts between him and his players surfaced. Although Stewart insisted that the retirement was his decision, many close to the team believe Stewart left under pressure from athletic director Mike Alden and several players, who reportedly threatened to transfer if Stewart returned. (Mravic & O'Brien, 1999, p.31)

succession (e.g., midseason versus end-of-season turnover), (c) the choice of inside (those hired from inside the team) versus outside successors (those hired from outside the team), and (d) the length of the replacement (short-term versus long-term succession).

Insofar as the *coaching ability of the successor* is concerned, Pfeffer and Davis-Blake (1986) examined the coaching ability of successors in the National Basketball Association for the 1977 through 1981 seasons. They found that coaches with (a) better prior win-loss records, (b) with previous professional coaching experience, or (c) who had improved the performance of other teams were associated with better performance after succession. The authors suggested that this finding illustrates the need for organizations to select new coaches with the best performance records.

Insofar as the timing of succession is concerned, Allen and his colleagues (1979) found that professional baseball teams experiencing a succession during the season performed worse over the year than teams with a succession between seasons. They also found that inside succession was slightly less disruptive than outside succession. Grusky

Table 2.3

The relationship between managerial turnover and team effectiveness

Sport	Period	Results	Reference
Professional Baseball	1920-1941 1951-1958	Higher managerial turnover was associated with lower team effectiveness. (r = -.43)	Grusky (1963)
Professional Baseball	1949-1968	Higher managerial turnover was associated with lower team effectiveness. (r = -.54)	Loy (1970)
Professional Baseball	1951-1960	Higher managerial turnover was associated with poorer win-loss, league standing, and games behind first place. No differences between internal vs. external changes.	Theberge & Loy (1976)
Professional Baseball		1920-1923 Teams replacing managers during season performed worse than teams replacing managers between seasons.	Allen, Panian, & Lotz (1979)
Professional Baseball	1951-1990	Managerial replacement was followed by improvement in team performance.	Fabianic (1984,1994)
College Basketball	1930-1970	Higher coaching turnover was associated with lower team effectiveness. (r = -.24)	Eitzen & Yetman (1972)
College Basketball	1930-1970	Higher coaching turnover was associated with lower team effectiveness. (r = -.24)	Eitzen & Yetman (1972)
Professional Basketball	1977-81	The poorer the team's record in the previous season, the greater the chances of a coaching change. (r = -.31)	Pfeffer & Davis-Blake (1986)
Professional Ice Hockey	1950-1966	Coaching change was unrelated to team success	McPherson (1976a)
Professional Ice Hockey	1938-1988	Coaching change was associated with improved team performance in the short term but not after a long term.	McTeer, White, & Persad, (1995)
Professional Football	1960-1988	Coaching change was associated with improved team performance in the short term but not after a long term.	McTeer, White, & Persad (1995)

(1964) pointed out that because inside successors are more familiar with the players, the management, and the owners, there should be less disruption to the team. Also, the successor should be better able to anticipate and avoid the difficulties of the previous manger/coach.

Insofar as the length of the replacement, McTeer, White, and Persad (1995) examined the short- and long-term effects of manager/coach turnover in professional baseball, basketball, football, and hockey. They found short-term performance improvements for all four sports during the remainder of the season following manager/coach turnover. The performance improvements, however, were not long term. That is, beyond the season during which the succession took place, coach/manager replacement had little effect on performance. Thus, replacement of coaches/managers, while associated with improved performance during the latter half of the replacement season, failed to improve performance in the following season.

Gamson and Scotch (1964) pointed out that the relationship between manager turnover and team success can be interpreted from three perspectives. In the *common sense* perspective, it is assumed that a new manager is a catalyst for improved team performance. That is, it is assumed that the coach/manager has a meaningful impact on performance, and that a change in leadership provides fresh new ideas, new perspectives, and a rejuvenated atmosphere to the sport organization, resulting in improved team performance. Thus, managers are fired because their teams performed poorly and it is expected that performance will improve under new management.

Second, the *ritual scapegoating* perspective assumes that the actual effect of the manager on team performance is minimal. Thus, managers of faltering teams are made ritual scapegoats. A central part of this perspective is that the ritual surrounding the managerial change is important in that it reduces anxiety, but the change itself is relatively unimportant to the subsequent performance of the team. Thus, the manager is the seat belt sign in the airplane of sport. The interpretation is that some other factor or factors are the cause of the turbulence, but the manager, like the seat belt sign, is eliminated.

A third explanation is the *vicious-circle* perspective that states that manager turnover disrupts performance. This perspective suggests that following poor team performance, managerial turnover occurs. Managerial succession results in disruption of the established patterns of action and relationships on the team and this, in turn, leads to further decline in performance. This explanation views team performance and succession as being a reciprocal relationship.

Gamson and Scotch tested these perspectives but could not find clear support for any of them. Notwithstanding the difficulty of determining what's cause and what's effect, it is reasonable to assume that some permanence in coaching is best. If a coach is going to have any effect, that effect is more likely to be felt over the long term rather than a short term. Interestingly, Eitzen and Yetman (1972) found that there is an inverted-U relationship between coaching stability and team success:

> *Coaches who left after eight or nine years tended to leave as winners in comparison with their early years. Coaches whose tenure lasted ten, eleven, or twelve years were split evenly into those whose records were improving and those whose records were deteriorating. For those coaches whose longevity at one post exceeded twelve years . . . every year but one showed a disproportionate number of coaches ending their career at a school with last-half records poorer than their first. (p. 115)*

When coaches stay at one institution for a long period of time, they have an opportunity to build a program and their record improves. Subsequently, their record tends to level off and, eventually, it declines. This decline may be due to complacency, decreasing motivation, or some other factors. Whatever its causes, there is an optimal tenure for coaches (Donnelly, 1975).

The Replacement of Team Members

A quote presented earlier from Grant Fuhr, a former goaltender of the Edmonton Oilers, testified to the annual replacement of team members in professional hockey. Fuhr felt that three or four players per year were replaced on the Oilers, a figure slightly under the 5.88 average in the league as a whole (McPherson, 1976a). Turnover or member replacement is a consistent fact of life in all sport. The turnover may be due to injuries, trades, the draft, or retirements and it affects some teams in some sports more than others. Player turnover is also an attempt to rebuild unsuccessful teams. The biggest trade in baseball in 37 years occurred when the unsuccessful San Diego Padres made a 12-player trade with the Houston Astros in December, 1994 (Verducci, 1996). Although the fundamental purpose of member turnover in sport teams is to enhance team success, as Box 2.2 illustrates, team success doesn't always follow player turnover.

Although player turnover may be frequent in professional sports, the rate varies across sports. For example, Schwartz (1973, reported in Loy, McPherson, & Kenyon, 1978) examined the rate of turnover in professional baseball, basketball, and football between 1960 and 1969. Turnover was defined as the ratio of players used by a team in a season who were not present in the previous season divided by the total number of players used by a team. He found that baseball had the highest ratio (.403) followed by basketball (.367), and football (.334).

Schwartz suggested that the internal dynamics of the three professional sports might account for differential personnel succession rates. For example, he proposed that teamwork,

Box 2.2	
Player turnover in sport teams	
Factor	**Quotation**
Player Turnover	The Gretzky years? All the Los Angeles Kings got out of them were increased ticket prices (choicest seats rose from $17.50 to $90), a much needed revenue stream from expansion fees (thanks to Gretzky, a regional sport became national in the 1990s as teams were added in San Jose, Tampa Bay, Miami, and Anaheim) and despite all that, bankruptcy. It was not that much of a success story when you think about it. A good idea going in—star-driven Los Angeles trades for the greatest star in hockey—but not so brilliant coming out. After seven and a half seasons together the Kings were again well under .500, attendance was in decline, and Wayne Gretzky, hockey's most important resource, was distracted, miserable, and 35 years old. And in all that time the Kings didn't win a Stanley Cup. That's the main thing that didn't happen. (Hoffer, 1996, p. 22)

interaction, and performance of mutually interdependent tasks seem more characteristic of football than basketball, and in turn, more characteristic of basketball than baseball (an assumption that might be challenged). Since effective teamwork requires that players on a given team interact as a cohesive unit over a significant period of time, turnover rates should vary as a function of the number of dependent and coordinate tasks required of positional occupants in a specific sport.

Not only does the rate of turnover vary across sports, it varies within a sport as well. Barry McPherson (1976a) examined player turnover rates for specific positions within professional hockey teams from 1950 to 1966. He found that the turnover rate per year for goaltenders was the lowest (2.50), followed by defenseman (4.72), forwards (7.53), and centers (8.25). McPherson suggested that the higher turnover rates for centers were due to their clearly defined roles (e.g., leader in goals and assists), which are easily evaluated. Thus, a center must produce or he will be replaced. As well, due to the centrality of the position, centers receive a high level of prestige and, therefore, many young athletes aspire to the role. This high level of aspiration results in a large labor supply, leaving management with a sizable pool of talent from which to initiate a turnover.

What are the implications of player turnover to team effectiveness? As Table 2.4 shows, teams that have the highest rate of turnover on their rosters are the least successful. As was the case with manager turnover, the only exception to the generalization about athlete turnover and team effectiveness is professional hockey (McPherson, 1976a).

Five points should be emphasized about these findings. The first, which was mentioned above, is that the data on player turnover and team effectiveness are correlational. Thus,

Table 2.4
The relationship between professional athlete turnover and team effectiveness

Sport	Period	Results	Reference
Baseball	1960-1969	Higher athlete turnover was associated with lower team effectiveness. ($r = -.51$)	Schwartz (1973)
Baseball	1951-1960	Higher athlete turnover was associated with poorer win-loss, league standing, and games behind first place.	Theberge & Loy (1976)
Basketball	1960-1969	Higher athlete turnover was associated with lower team effectiveness. ($r = -.47$)	Schwartz (1973)
Basketball	1977-1981	Number of new players was associated with fewer games won. ($r = -.59$)	Pfeffer & Davis-Blake (1986)
Ice Hockey	1950-1966	Athlete turnover was unrelated to team success.	McPherson (1976a)
Football	1960-1969	Higher athlete turnover was associated with poorer team success.	Schwartz (1973)

they are subject to the same limitations and reservations raised about the managerial data on turnover. It is not possible with correlational data to conclude that one factor caused another.

The second point is that too little turnover in a playing roster can also be a problem for team effectiveness. For example, baseball manager Billy Martin (Martin & Pepe, 1987) suggested that without turnover, motivation can diminish and complacency can develop on a team (see Box 2.3).

A third, related point is that there is an optimal time for player turnover; if player turnover is either too fast or too slow, a team's effectiveness suffers. This point is well illustrated in a study by Loy, Theberge, Kjeldsen, and Donnelly (1975). They examined the relationship between player turnover in professional baseball and the number of games behind first place. The operational definition for player turnover was the duration of time to *half-life*—the duration of time required for the team to be reduced (through player changes) to one half of its original complement. Thus, a team roster might contain 40 athletes in 1988. Through trades, retirements, injuries, and other factors, only 20 of those original 40 members might still be present on the roster in 1990. In this case, the duration to half-life would be two years. Loy and his colleagues found that there is an inverted-U relationship between the duration of time to half life and team success.

The fourth point is that turnover in some positions is undoubtedly less disruptive than turnover in other positions. If an individual has a peripheral role on the team, his/her departure has less effect than the departure of an individual who occupies a more critical, central position. Theberge and Loy's (1976) study with professional baseball supported this proposition, although McPherson's (1976a) study with professional hockey did not.

A final point that should be raised is that the studies with sport teams that have examined the member turnover and team effectiveness issue have focused on one measure of effectiveness—win-loss record. There are a number of other indices of effectiveness which might be influenced by turnover including team morale, job satisfaction, costs associated

Box 2.3 *Implications of a lack of player turnover in sport*	
Factor	**Quotation**
A viewpoint on potential problems associated with team stability.	Long-term contracts are often harmful. I'm not saying it's true with all players, but it is with many of them. They lose incentive, their motivation, if they have a long-term contract. Subconsciously, they just don't seem to try as hard. If a guy is a fringe player and it's time to sign him to a new contract, I'd like to see baseball just let him go. Bring in somebody else, somebody who won't cost as much money and who is hungrier, who is not set in his ways with all those bad habits. I'm not talking about a Don Mattingly or a Dave Winfield or a Ricky Henderson. Keep them. But get rid of the fringe players, just keep turning them over. That will stop all that nonsense of threatening the manager and the owner. (Martin & Pepe, 1987, p. 148)

with moving, training and accommodating new personnel, and the number of spectators in attendance (McPherson, 1976b).

The latter measure, the number of spectators in attendance, may seem like a strange barometer of organizational effectiveness. However, in professional sport, spectator attendance is possibly the ultimate criterion of effectiveness. And, player turnover adversely influences spectator attendance. A case study that clearly illustrates this point is the Canadian Football League in the 1980s. In 1987, the league was in danger of folding. One of the primary reasons cited for the declining attendance was excessive player turnover. As Reilly (1987) noted,

> *You can't tell the players without a scorecard—except of course in the CFL, where you can't tell the players even with a scorecard. Because teams are desperate to win . . . turnover is outrageous . . . "The people who make money out of the CFL are the airlines" says John Hudson, a vice-President of Labatt's. "They run a shuttle business like you cannot believe. (pp. 40-43)*

Whether turnover causes organizational ineffectiveness or whether turnover occurs because the organization is ineffective is not clear. What is clear is that there are no major benefits associated with large turnovers but there are numerous potential problems.

SECTION 2

GROUP ENVIRONMENT

Renovating and purchasing land for brand new sports arenas is becoming as common as SportsCenter reruns on ESPN . . . Justifying the expense is only one of the problems that people have to consider when deciding whether or not to build a new stadium. Another is looks and fan appeal. The arenas of old cater to the fan by providing concession stands on all concourses and parking relatively close to entrances. Newer arenas have become more extravagant with waiters to bring people their food, areas for expensive skyboxes for the V.I.Ps., and reserved parking spaces and red carpet for superstars . . . Ticket prices are soaring and the love for the game seems to be fading with every new skybox that is built and every marketing scheme that is utilized to attract money and superstars to the event. The ultimate essence of the game is lost and the true fans are left to watch the game at home. And it all starts with the stadium. In the future, newer, bigger, and fancier will determine what kinds of fans attend games. (Shakula, 2001)

Chapter Three

GROUP SIZE

> Every year he would recruit some ninety freshmen, even though he knew that he would ultimately find places for no more than sixteen or seventeen. He signed up the extras, he told his associates, "so that Woody and Bear and Ara can't get their hands on them." (Mitchener, 1976, p. 177)

Researchers have had a long-standing interest in questions related to the effect of group size. Approximately 100 years ago, what is generally considered to be the first social psychology (and sport psychology) laboratory experiment was undertaken and issues associated with group size were part of the focus. Norman Triplett (1897) was interested in determining why cyclists rode faster when they raced in groups or pairs versus when they rode alone. Cycling times under three conditions were compared: a) unpaced where the cyclists raced alone against time, b) paced where the cyclist raced alone against time but in conjunction with a pacer (a tandem bicycle containing 3 to 4 confederates), and c) paced competition where the cyclist raced against a competitor with both cyclists being paced. He found that the paced competition and paced conditions were 39.55 sec/mile and 34.4 sec/mile respectively faster than the unpaced condition. In other words, working in group situations proved beneficial to the cyclists. Triplett then devised a laboratory study to examine this effect further. In that study, children told to wind string on a fishing reel as rapidly as possible, wound faster when working with other children than when working alone.

The issue of group size has remained one of the most frequently examined topics in social and industrial psychology. The quote by James Mitchener that introduces this chapter clearly highlights one of the implications associated with increases in group size. Increasing the number of freshmen recruited and retained on the roster of a team does increase the probability that the necessary resources for team effectiveness will be available (and, at the same time, will not be available to a competitor). However, in the situation outlined by Mitchener, not all of the recruited freshman retained on the team roster would have the opportunity to eventually compete. For many sport teams, an excessive roster can lead to a large number of problems such as player dissatisfaction, crowding, and lack of both adequate instruction and feedback from the coach. Thus, one pertinent question concerning group size is "What is the optimal number of extra competitors to retain for a group?"

Optimal Group Size

Work and Social Groups

Questions regarding optimal group size had their origin in problem solving groups and work crews. Is one individual as effective as two? Are two people as effective as three? The poem by Jack Prebitsky (1983) which is presented in Box 3.1 endorses a "more the merrier" perspective. But, there are different views on what is optimal. Hare (1981), based on a review of the research conducted between 1898 and 1974, concluded that five is the optimal number for social groups, work groups, and families because

- With an odd number of individuals, a strict deadlock is not possible;
- If a split occurs and subgroups form, individuals in the minority subgroup are not socially isolated (i.e., as would be the case if the original group was comprised of only three members); and
- A group of five is large enough for the members to shift roles easily and withdraw from awkward positions without necessarily having an issue resolved.

Other authors, however, have preferred to make reference to a *critical group size* under the assumption that optimal group size will vary with the situation. This was the viewpoint adopted by Ivan Steiner (1972), who observed that

> *The number of members constituting a critical size undoubtedly depends upon the nature of the task and the resources of the participants. The size beyond which productivity begins to decline clearly reflects the demands of the task, and three-person groups with insufficient resources may welcome a new member whereas those with adequate resources may not . . . However, there is reason to believe that certain group sizes may be critical in a fairly wide variety of situations. (p. 98)*

Thelen (1949) advocated that groups should adopt the principle of *least group size*: the group should be just large enough to include sufficient members with the social and task skills necessary to carry out its activities. Bray, Kerr, and Atkin (1978) advanced a similar perspective: the principle of *functional group size* should be the most important consideration insofar as group size is concerned. The number of people necessary to carry out the group's activities represents the functional group size for any activity. As the number of group members increases beyond this functional complement, the number of individuals not participating also increases.

Sport Teams

In sport situations, the principles of least group size and functional group size would provide support for the suggestion that, all things being equal, a sufficient number of individuals should be retained in order to practice efficiently and effectively. What this means is that the necessary resources should be available to scrimmage in team sports and compete in individual sports. Consequently, a basketball team might retain 10 to 12 members; a volleyball team might retain 12 to 14 members, and a wrestling team, 20 to 24 members (approximately 2 individuals per weight class). This would insure that there would not be a large number of individuals inactive at any given time. Opportunities for personal instruction, reinforcement, and reward would also be available. Also, the amount of individual participation and high feelings of personal responsibility, commitment, and accountability to the group would be present.

It is important to keep in mind that the application of the principles of functional group size and least group size are not a fixed standard. They can vary from group to group and sport to sport. For example, there is evidence that very large groups usually subdivide into smaller subgroups (e.g., Baker, 1981). Sometimes this might even occur because of the organizational structure adopted. American football provides a good example. Traditionally, large rosters are maintained in this sport and the total roster is generally subdivided into smaller units, each of which has its own coach. A total squad of 80 people might be subdivided into an offensive unit, a defensive unit, and, in some cases, a special unit associated with the kicking game. These units represent subgroups within the total team roster. Each of these subgroups can have all of the characteristics of an independent group—leadership, roles, structure, and so on. Thus, a football team of 80 may not differ substantially (insofar as functional size and "extra" group members is concerned) from a basketball team of 12 to 15 people.

The application of the principles of least group size and functional group size can also vary from one team to another within the same sport. American football again provides a good example. On one team of 80 athletes, the coaches might decide to use some of their best athletes on both offense and defense. On another team of 80 athletes, the coaches might decide to have their personnel specialize on either offense or defense. From a social and a task point of view, there is considerable difference between the teams in these two contexts. In the case of the team with the roster of 80 and no subgroups, the principles of least group size and functional group size might lead the coaches to conclude that they had at least 15 players too many on the roster. These 15 would be non-participants who could become dissatisfied and detract from group morale. Therefore, the coaches might consider it best to release the non-participants. On the other hand, an entirely different conclusion might be reached in the case of the team with the roster of 80 subdivided into two units of

---

Box 3.1
A "more the merrier" perspective from the bird kingdom

The Prelutsky (1983) proposition.

Whatever one toucan can do
Is sooner done by toucans two
And three toucans (it's very true)
Can do much more than two can do.
And toucans numbering two plus two can
Manage more than all the zoo can.
In short, there is no toucan who can
Do what four or three or two can.

A qualifying perspective: The Carron, Widmeyer, & Brawley (1996) corollary.

Are there any exceptions you might ask?
Our answer is it depends upon the task.
Two toucans adding food to a common pot
Will produce what a single toucan cannot
But one toucan sufficient for a complex job
Will be badly hampered by a milling mob

40 each. As a result of the specialization between offense and defense, the coaches might conclude that there were no unnecessary "extras."

Questions about critical group size have not been perceived to be an important issue in sport teams. Little empirical work has been carried out, and as a result, discussions on group size have drawn on the theoretical perspectives developed in psychology and sociology. One possible reason for the lack of research might be that the practical applications seem limited because the rules of sport explicitly limit team size.

Another possible reason might be that group size can be operationally defined in different ways in different sports. Neil Widmeyer (1971) originally made this point when he stated that there are three possible indices of group size in sport. One is the *action unit*: the number of people on the playing surface at one time. Using this index, for example, a basketball team includes five members in the action unit; a volleyball team, six.

Another index of group size in sport is the *dress roster:* the number of individuals in uniform during competition. League rules and budget considerations usually influence this number. The dress roster for competition might be ten to twelve athletes for a basketball team, twenty to twenty-six athletes for an ice hockey team.

A third possible index is the *team roster:* the total number of athletes retained on the team. Many athletes practice with a team during a season but never have the opportunity to compete against another team. One basketball team might have 20 athletes on its team roster while another might have only 15. Considered from the perspective of the action unit, the dress roster, and the team roster, a basketball team is composed of 5, 10 to 12, and 15 to 20 athletes, respectively. Obviously, if a researcher or coach was interested in determining how team size influences other variables such as adherence, absenteeism, satisfaction, or cohesion, the measure used to represent "team size" could affect the answer obtained.

Carron, Widmeyer, and Brawley (1989) did attempt to determine what constitutes an ideal roster size in sport. They asked athletes from basketball, volleyball, soccer, and hockey what they felt would be "ideal," "too large," and "too small" for their sport team. As the results in Table 3.1 show, the athletes' perceptions of an ideal roster size were generally less than the roster size traditionally adopted by coaches (with basketball being the exception). In addition, a roster size that was approximately 25% greater than the perceived ideal was considered to be too large; one that was 25% smaller than the ideal was considered too small.

The athletes were also asked to list as many potential advantages and disadvantages as possible for sport teams that are too small and too large. There were three major findings. First, the athletes listed more task-related advantages and disadvantages for being on either small or large teams than social-related advantages and disadvantages. A task-related advantage of a small roster is that "there are more opportunities to participate;" a disadvantage is that "the team does not have enough depth." A task-related advantage of a large roster is that "there are opportunities to rest"; a disadvantage is that "the team's organization suffers."

A second finding was that the advantages and disadvantages listed were overwhelmingly (by 3 to 1 ratio) game or competition related rather than practice related. Opportunities to compete are the main interest of athletes. Any factors that detract from

Table 3.1

Perceptions of group size in sport teams (from Carron, Widmeyer, & Brawley, 1989).

Sport	Action Unit	Ideal Size	Too Large		Too Small	
			Size	Percent	Size	Percent
Basketball	5	11.9	15.1	127.0	8.7	74.0
Volleyball	6	9.8	12.6	125.6	7.4	75.1
Soccer	11	16.3	19.7	121.6	12.7	78.4
Hockey	6	16.1	20.5	131.5	12.9	80.1

the possibility of competing are considered to be a disadvantage; any factors that contribute to the possibility of competing are considered to be an advantage.

The third result was that the athletes generated a substantially greater number of disadvantages associated with rosters that are either too large or too small than advantages. As far as athletes are concerned, there are a few perceived advantages in being a member of a team that is too large or too small; however, there are numerous disadvantages.

The Group Task and Group Size

Approximately 25 years ago, Ivan Steiner (1972) reviewed the research that had been conducted on group size and concluded that it was in a "chaotic state of affairs" (p. xiii). In an attempt to provide a frame of reference and interject some order into that chaos, Steiner concluded that much of the confusion could be eliminated if the nature of the group's task was taken into consideration (see Box 3.1 again). Consequently, he developed a task typology to differentiate among groups.

The Basis for a Task Typology

The typology of tasks developed by Steiner is based on three main questions. The first concerns whether the task is divisible (i.e., it can be broken down in subunits) or unitary (i.e., no subunits are present). A sprint relay team performs a divisible task. There is a leadoff runner, a fourth or anchor runner, and the second and third runners. On the other hand, a rowing team carries out a unitary task; all the rowers perform the same task at the same time.

The second question concerns whether the group product is measured by qualitative or quantitative standards. Figure skating and gymnastics are sports in which quality is the most important criterion for judging performance effectiveness. On the other hand, weight lifting and track and field are sports in which performance effectiveness is assessed through quantitative standards. How much? How fast? How high?

The third question concerns how the individual inputs are combined to yield the group's product. Six ways are possible—each of which corresponds to a specific task-type identified by Steiner in his taxonomy of tasks. On some tasks, a larger group size is better; on others, one good individual is more effective than a group. Steiner's taxonomy of tasks went a long way toward shedding light on the question of when and why groups are more or less effective than one individual operating independently.

Steiner's Task Typology

The types of tasks in which increases in group size may not lead to an increase in group effectiveness were referred to by Steiner as eureka disjunctive, unitary conjunctive, and noneureka disjunctive. *Eureka disjunctive* tasks are those in which only one solution to the problem is taken from all the possibilities raised by group members. The solution to the problem is usually yes/no or either/or. In this type of task, increases in group size may not necessarily lead to an increase in group effectiveness. A group of statisticians calculating the batting averages of individual baseball players is one example of an eureka disjunctive task. All statisticians may start to calculate the average of any single player. But, when one statistician has the solution, the group's task is completed because that individual's solution is readily assumed to be the group's solution.

Because, in eureka disjunctive tasks, the most successful member's score is adopted by the group, one intelligent, competent member is at least as effective as a group. In fact, one person may even be more effective than a group. A single person can work more quickly and with less interference because there is no need to communicate strategies and discuss progress. Also, if the group possesses only mediocre statisticians and no calculators, its solution might not be correct. So even if the individual and the group arrived at the same solution, the individual would be more efficient in terms of time spent.

Unitary conjunctive tasks are those in which all members of the group must complete the task or contribute to the group's product in order for the group to finish. Also, no matching of individuals to roles is possible. Consequently, the group is only as strong as its weakest member. For example, in mountain climbing, every member of the team must successfully complete the climb. A poor climber with inadequate technique or poor conditioning holds the group back.

Tasks in which a variety of approaches to the problem and/or solutions are possible are called *noneureka disjunctive.* A panel of experts struck to determine who is the best player in the World Cup Soccer Championship would be one example. Also, the question of which athletes should be chosen for a nation's representative cricket team is another example. In noneureka disjunctive tasks, increases in group size lead to increases in resources and, therefore, produce a broader perspective. Thus, a larger group should be more effective than a smaller group or single individual. However, a selection panel may not be as effective as one highly competent person because one person working alone doesn't need to convince, justify, explain, or achieve consensus. So, using a group rather than one competent individual might be a disadvantage.

The types of tasks in which increases in group size should lead to an increase in group effectiveness were referred to by Steiner as additive tasks, compensatory tasks, and disjunctive divisible tasks. An *additive* task is one in which the group output is determined by summing individual outputs. The total number of problems solved by a group in a finite period of time will always be greater than the number solved by one individual. Increases in group size will lead to increases in team effectiveness when team scores in individual sports are required. For example, at wrestling, gymnastics, and track and field meets, a specific number of points is given for each individual performance. These points are then summed to determine a team total. A team with the maximum number of competitors allowed within the rules generally should be superior to a team with an incomplete roster. As another example, a single rower should not be able to cover the same distance in the same time as a pair of rowers or a crew of eight. Increases in the number of crewmembers in a boat should result in improvements in speed.

Compensatory tasks are those in which the group product is obtained from the average of the individual member inputs. This is what occurs when gymnastics events, aerobic competitions, and figure skating competitions are judged. The scores of the various judges are pooled and an average value is obtained—sometimes after eliminating the highest and lowest values. In this type of task, one highly competent individual may be more accurate than the group but, generally, a group score is more reliable and, therefore, a group typically outperforms a substantial number of it members.

Divisible conjunctive tasks are those in which there is a division of labor and individuals are matched to the tasks which best match their skills. Specialization is required and individuals must carry out specific group roles. Most sport teams fall under this category. Athletes are designated as setters or spikers in volleyball, pitchers or catchers in baseball. In the case of divisible conjunctive tasks, a larger group is much more effective providing that (a) the individuals can be matched to the appropriate tasks and (b) the group is not too large.

Group Size and Productivity and Performance

Steiner's Framework

The relationship of group size to performance can best be understood within the framework outlined by Steiner (1972), illustrated in Figure 3.1. Steiner proposed that as the number of members in a group increases, the potential for that group to be more productive also increases. The reason for this is quite simple—there are more resources available to draw upon. But, this occurs at a decelerating rate. That is, when the number of group members increases, the resources that are available also increases, but only to a point. Eventually, as group size continues to increase, the resources available to the group plateau. This reflects the facts that at some point all of the expertise necessary for a group to complete

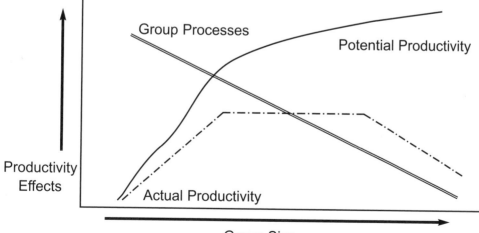

Figure 3.1. Steiner's (1972) model for the effect of increases in group size

its mission is available. Continually adding new members beyond this point doesn't produce additional payoffs in increased group productivity.

An ice hockey coach, for example, might normally keep 18 players on the team's roster—three regular forward lines, three regular defense pairs, two goal tenders, and one role player. However, the coach might conclude that this contingent of players has failed to provide the team with sufficient flexibility to make adjustments for special situations. Consequently, he or she might add additional players—a penalty-killing unit, offensive specialists, an extra goaltender, and so on. At some point all of the players that could possibly be used would be on the team roster. There would be no purpose in continually adding more players (resources) because a plateau had been reached.

As the group size increases, it also becomes more difficult for the coach to coordinate practices, to use all the players in games, to provide everyone with instruction in practices, and to communicate effectively with the total roster. It would also become more difficult for each player to interact with every other player. As a result, with increases in resources there is also a decrease in process efficiency—where process efficiency reflects the effective coordination of resources.

Not surprisingly, increased size influences the absolute output of the group and the relative output of each individual group member. Figure 3.1 also illustrates this effect. Steiner proposed that as group size continues to increase, the absolute productivity of the group increases initially and then shows a decrease. What Steiner highlighted is that eventually, the group becomes so large it cannot effectively carry out its task. The relative productivity of each individual member also declines systematically with increases in group size. An example that illustrates this relationship is a volleyball team. If twelve players are kept on the roster, the team is able to scrimmage effectively, run specialized drills for setters and spikers, and so on. Thus, a team of twelve is better off than if only six players are retained on the roster. In a twelve-person roster, however, each individual player has less opportunity to spike, set, or work with the coach than in a six-person roster. Thus, the relative productivity of each individual decreases.

The Ringelmann Effect

One of the earliest studies on the effect of group size on group productivity was a classic unpublished study on individual and group performance in a rope-pulling task conducted by Ringelmann over 100 years ago (cited in Kravitz & Martin, 1986). Male volunteers were asked to pull on a rope as hard as they could, in tug-of-war fashion (additive task), in groups of varying size. The rope was connected to a strain gauge that measured the group's total effort. Ringelmann's results are summarized in Table 3.2.

Using individual productivity as a baseline, Ringelmann computed group efficiency. Assuming that one person worked at 100% efficiency, then the individuals in the 2-person groups worked at only 93% of their potential, the individuals in the 3-person groups at only 85% of their potential, the individuals in 4-person groups at only 77% of their potential, and the individuals in the 8-person groups at only 49% of their potential. The results showed that as group size increased, the group's performance was increasingly inferior to what might be predicted from the simple addition of individual performance.

Table 3.2

A summary of Ringelmann's research on the effect of group size on group productivity (Adapted from Kravitz & Martin, 1986, and Steiner, 1972)

No. of Individuals	No. of Coordination Links	Relative Performance per Person	Group Productivity	Process Losses
1	0	1.00	---	---
2	1	0.93	1.86	0.14
3	3	0.85	2.55	0.45
4	6	0.77	3.08	0.92
5	10	0.70	3.50	1.50
6	15	0.63	3.78	2.22
7	21	0.56	3.92	3.08
8	28	0.49	3.92	4.08

Why did individual performance decrease as the number of people in the group increased? Steiner (1972) proposed two possible causes for the decrease in relative individual productivity with increasing group size: a) reduced individual motivation (it is more difficult to motivate individuals when personal accountability is reduced), and b) coordination losses (it is more difficult to coordinate the efforts of larger groups of people). Steiner favored the latter explanation, concluding that individuals may fail to synchronize their efforts in a maximally efficient manner, thus producing less productivity, but not necessarily effort.

Steiner's preference for coordination as the explanation does make sense. A problem that arises with increasing group size is that it becomes increasingly difficult for each individual to interact with every other individual, either in a task or social context. If one person is operating alone, there is no interaction, no need to work in a coordinated fashion, no need to be concerned with the feelings of someone else. In short, there are no coordination links—where a coordination link represents the interaction between two people. As the group increases in size, the number of coordination links increases dramatically. The number of possible two-person links in groups of varying size can be determined with the following formula:

$$\text{No. of Coordination Links} = \frac{N^2 - N}{2}$$

In a two-person group, there is one link; in three-person groups, there are 3 links; and in eight-person groups, there are 28 coordination links. Thus, in comparison to a two-person group, an eight-person group has four times the resources to draw upon but 28 times as many links to coordinate.

In an attempt to determine whether Ringelmann's results could be reproduced and to determine whether motivation or coordination was the primary cause of reduced individual effectiveness in larger groups, Allan Ingham, George Levinger, James Graves, and Vaughn Peckham replicated the Ringelmann study in 1974. In two different studies, individuals were tested alone and in groups of 2, 3, 4, 5, and 6 people.

In the first study, Ingham and his colleagues found results similar to those reported by Ringelmann for groups up to the size of three people (see Table 2.3). That is, if a single individual can be considered to be working at 100%, the individuals in two-person groups worked at 91%; the individuals in three-person groups, at 82%. However, contrary to Ringelmann findings, progressive increases in group size did not lead to corresponding progressive decreases in individual efficiency. Rather, there was a general leveling off from three-person groups onward so that individuals in groups of six pulled at an average of 78% of their potential.

The purpose of the Ingham et al. second study was to determine whether the losses resulting from increased group size were primarily due to poor coordination or reduced motivation. Again, individuals were tested alone and in groups of 2, 3, 4, 5, and 6 people. However, in actuality, pseudo-groups were employed. That is, in every instance, only one individual was actually tested. In the conditions where 2, 3, 4, 5, and 6 people were involved, the balance of the group was made up of confederates (accomplices) of the experiment. The only real participant was placed in the front of the line and the confederates assumed positions behind. The confederates made all the appropriate sounds of effort but, in reality, the real participant pulled alone. Any decrease in performance could then be attributed to a loss in motivation rather than a loss in coordination (because only one person was actually pulling the rope).

As Table 3.3 shows, the results of Study 2 were almost identical to those found in Study 1. That is, there was a decline in relative individual productivity in groups up to the size of three people and then a plateau occurred. More importantly, these results showed that coordination was not the most important factor in the process losses. The decline in relative individual performance was primarily the result of a loss in motivation. Presumably, with groups of increasing size, there is a decreasing sense of personal accountability and, therefore, a decrease in motivation.

Social Loafing in Work and Social Groups

Bibb Latané and his colleagues referred to the reduction in individual effort when people work in groups as social loafing (Harkins, Latané, & Williams, 1980; Latané, 1981; Latané, Williams, & Harkins, 1979; Williams, Harkins, & Latané, 1981). Latané and his colleagues (1979) suggested that social loafing is a type of social disease, having "negative consequences for individuals, social institutions, and societies" (p. 831). As they also pointed out, the phenomenon of social loafing seems to contradict many popular

Table 3.3

Relationship between group size and rope-pulling performance (Percentage of potential productivity for groups differing in size)

| | Group Size | | | | | |
	1	2	3	4	5	6
Ringelmann	100	93	85	77		
Ingham et al. (1974, Study 1)	100	91	82	78	78	78
Ingham et al. (1974, Study 2)	100	90	85	86	84	85

stereotypes. One of those popular stereotypes is, of course, that many hands make the work lighter. Another stereotype that is held in sport is that a sense of solidarity and commitment to the team leads athletes to put in a special effort in order to not let teammates down.

Social loafing also contradicts social psychological theory. It has been repeatedly documented that when others are present—either as spectators or as co-actors—individual performance in simple, well-learned tasks will improve (Zajonc, 1965). Thus, the presence of co-actors should be expected to enhance, not diminish individual performance.

Because social loafing does appear to contradict previous research and common assumptions, it also raises a number of questions. First, how generalized is the phenomenon? Social loafing was demonstrated by Ingham and his colleagues with rope pulling. Does it occur in other tasks and/or under other conditions? Second, is social loafing a problem in real teams competing in actual sport situations? Third, what are the factors that contribute to social loafing? Can social loafing be reduced?

Since 1974, nearly 80 studies have been conducted on social loafing; individual effort while alone has been compared with individual effort in a collective situation. Collective efforts occur when individuals working in the real or imagined presence of others combine their inputs to produce a single group product.

Given the presence of a large amount of research on social loafing, Karau and Williams (1993) used meta analysis (i.e., the results from individual studies are combined statistically to determine an overall size of effect) to integrate the findings. Karau and Williams concluded that social loafing occurs across "a wide variety of tasks, including physical tasks (e.g., shouting, rope-pulling, and swimming), cognitive tasks (e.g., generating ideas), evaluative tasks (e.g., quality ratings of poems, editorials, and clinical therapists), and perceptual tasks (e.g., maze performance and vigilance tasks on a computer screen)" (p. 682).

Also, social loafing is not a characteristic of one type of population. Karau and Williams found that social loafing is evident in males and females and in different cultures—although the effect is smaller for women and for individuals from Eastern cultures. These provocative findings suggest that women and individuals in Eastern cultures are less likely to engage in social loafing because they have more group-oriented priorities than do men and individuals in Western cultures.

The findings from the Karau and Williams meta-analysis also illustrated that there are a number of conditions under which the tendency to engage in social loafing is increased. These include situations where

- The individual's output cannot be evaluated independently,
- The task is perceived to be low in meaningfulness,
- The individual's personal involvement in the task is low,
- A comparison against group standards is not available or possible,
- Other individuals contributing to the collective effort are strangers,
- The individual's co-workers are expected to perform well, and
- The individual perceives that his/her contribution to the collective outcome is redundant.

Social Loafing in Sport Groups

Working with strangers on a lab task undoubtedly influences the coordination among individuals as well as motivation to carryout the task. Thus, at first glance, it seems possible that social loafing might not occur in sport teams. The strong commitment that individuals have made to their team, the experiences and sacrifices that they have shared, and the significant, important goals that they hold in common might help to keep motivation at a high level. Allan Ingham and his colleagues (1974) raised this point in the discussion of their results with the tug-of-war task:

> Since the groups used in our experiments were quasi-groups, coordination problems would probably be greater than in established groups who are used to working together. One might ask whether the discrepancy between actual and potential productivity would be reduced if our subjects had been team members on the same rowing crews. (p. 383)

In an effort to test this possibility, Ingham et al. examined the performance times of rowing crews from Olympic Games held in the period 1952 to 1964. They found that the coxed fours were only 13% faster than the coxed pairs and that the eights were only 23% faster than the pairs. Although, there are differences in boat size, water displacement, and so on, it can be assumed that some social loafing did occur in the rowing crews.

In a field experiment, Sharon Huddleston, Susan Doody, and Karen Ruder (1985) also found evidence of social loafing in a sprint relay. After female athletes were timed running a 55-yard sprint alone, they were formed into a 4-person team for a shuttle relay. One half of the groups were provided with information about the phenomenon of social loafing under the assumption that this insight might help to alleviate the problem. It had no effect. Performance times over the 55-yard distance were faster when the athletes ran alone than when they ran in teams.

Mark Anshel (1995) also found evidence of social loafing in elite female rowers who performed a simulated rowing task under alone and group conditions for durations of one-stroke, 1.5 minutes, and 10 minutes. Performance was measured as distance covered. Loafing was not manifested when individuals performed under the one-stroke and 1.5 minute group conditions. However, social loafing did occur under the relatively prolonged (10 min.) condition. This illustrates that social loafing can occur in tasks that are meaningful or important, have intrinsic interest, and involve competition (Hardy & Latané, 1988).

Since social loafing is a common occurrence when individuals work collectively and without accountability, many hands do not always result in light work (as the popular stereotype suggests). Given the negative consequences for individuals and social institutions, it is importance to know how to reduce social loafing. Based on the findings in their meta-analysis, Karau and Williams (1993) suggested several ways in which social loafing might be reduced or overcome in natural settings:

- Provide individuals with specific feedback about personal performance or the group's performance,
- Monitor individual performance or make individual performance identifiable,

- Assign individuals to meaningful tasks,
- Make each person's task unique so that all individuals feel more responsibility for their work,
- Enhance the cohesiveness of the group, and
- Make each individual feel that his/her contributions to the task are important.

Group Size and Psychosocial Outcomes

Cohesion

Sport Teams. The size of a group is related to its cohesiveness. In work and social groups, increasing group size is negatively related to group cohesiveness. Sticking together as a total entity, developing strong social relationships, and/or maintaining group consensus on goals and objectives increases in difficulty with increasing group size.

Widmeyer, Brawley, and Carron (1990) examined the relationship of team roster size to cohesion in two studies. In Study One, the number of members on a basketball team was manipulated. Individuals in a 3-on-3 recreational basketball league were initially matched on ability and then formed into teams consisting of 3, 6, or 9 members. After a week of practice, the teams played 2 games a week for 8 weeks. The results revealed that task cohesion was greatest in the 3-person teams and lowest in the 9-person teams. On the other hand, the 6-person groups had the highest social cohesion and also were the most successful (see Figure 3.2).

Apparently, in the smallest teams it was easiest to develop consensus and commitment around common group goals and objectives (i.e., task cohesion). But, with no substitutes available, there was not enough opportunity to develop social cohesiveness or to compete successfully against the 6-person groups. The largest groups, on the other hand, had too many resources and this hindered the development of task cohesion, social cohesion, and the ability to compete effectively. The curve for performance success in Figure 3.2 is very similar to the hypothesized curve for productivity proposed by Steiner and illustrated in Figure 3.1.

In their second study, Widmeyer and his colleagues examined the relationship between the size of the action unit (i.e., the number of group members actually competing at any given time) and group cohesion. College students participated in volleyball tournaments in which three different sized action units were

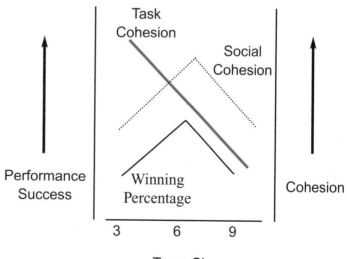

Figure 3.2. Performance success from groups of varying sizes competing in a 3-on-3 basketball league (Adapted from Widmeyer, Brawley, & Carron, 1988)

used: 3 vs. 3, 6 vs. 6, and 12 vs. 12. The level of group cohesion was greatest in the smallest unit and least in the largest.

Individual Affect

Affect, a term used to represent emotions such as satisfaction and dissatisfaction, pride and shame, enjoyment and lack of enjoyment, is influenced by group size. This has been observed in a wide variety of different groups with widely varying purposes (e.g., sport teams, work units, army platoons). For example, in their study with recreational volleyball teams, Widmeyer et al. (1990, Study 2) found that individual enjoyment decreased as the number of individuals in the action unit increased. Further, in an industrial setting, it was found that coal miners became highly dissatisfied with their work when the number of individuals in a work crew was increased from 3 to 40 to 50 (Trist & Bamforth, 1951). Also, business students working on an idea-generating task were more satisfied and effective in groups of 3 than 9 (Valacich, Dennis, & Nunamaker, 1992). Finally, in research carried out in the American army, satisfaction was higher when soldiers were sent to the front lines as replacements in mutually chosen groups of four buddies rather than alone (Chesler, Van Steenberg, & Brueckel, 1955). On the basis of a review of previous research, Neil Widmeyer (1971) concluded that increases in group size have a major effect on individual satisfaction and group morale (see Table 3.4).

Individual Cognitions and Behavior

Table 3.4 also highlights a number of cognitions and behaviors influenced by increases in group size. One of those is *reduced individual participation and feelings of responsibility*.

Table 3.4
The effect of increases in group size on group member satisfaction
(Adapted from Widmeyer, 1971)

Factor	Effect of an Increase in Group Size	Effect on Member Satisfaction and Group Morale
Member Participation	Decreases	Decreases
Feelings of Responsibility	Decreases	Decreases
Participation in the Group	Decreases	Decreases
Density and Crowding	Increases	Decreases
Feelings of Personal Threat and Inhibition	Increases	Decreases
Communication	Decreases	Decreases
Attention, Instructions, and Reinforcement	Decreases	Decreases
Leadership Opportunities	Decreases	Decreases
Opportunities to Meet Other People	Increases	Increases

On a volleyball team with six members, the participation of the individual athletes at practices and games would be 100 percent. As the size of the roster increases, the absolute participation and feeling of responsibility for the team's welfare would decrease in each athlete. Initially, increases in size might be viewed favorably since each individual would have some opportunity for a rest and the burden placed on any one person would be reduced. But, with further increases in group size and the resultant decrease in individual participation and responsibility, satisfaction and group morale would decrease.

Another factor influencing the amount of satisfaction individuals experience is their level of involvement or participation within the group. In their 1963 review of the group size literature, Thomas and Fink noted that with increasing numbers, each individual in a group has less opportunity to assume a leadership role, interact and communicate with all others, and/or contribute in a meaningful way to the group product. Individual members are also more likely to consider the group poorly organized. As a consequence, satisfaction is diminished.

Crowding and Density

Widmeyer et al. (1990, Study 2) attempted to identify the factors most highly associated with individual enjoyment in action units of 3, 6, and 12 volleyball players. The individuals evaluated the degree to which they perceived they 1) had obtained exercise and experience fatigue, 2) were crowded, 3) were conspicuous, 4) had influence and responsibility, and 5) were on a team that possessed organization and used strategy during competitions. The results showed that all five factors contributed to enjoyment for the action units of 3, 6, and 12 people. In the action units of 3 and 6, the degree to which each individual felt that he or she obtained exercise and experienced fatigue were the most important for enjoyment. In action units of 12, however, the factors that were most important for enjoyment were the degree to which the individual perceived he or she had had influence and responsibility and had not been crowded. Those individuals who least enjoyed the experience of participating were those who felt that they had little responsibility or influence and were crowded while participating.

Illustration 3.1 portrays an exaggerated instance of crowding. In this type of context feelings of anxiety and inhibition can occur. Consider a badminton team that adds six additional members to its roster. The amount of space available for workouts/practices is reduced. Consequently, it becomes difficult for the individual to relax and focus solely on the activity. Individuals are constantly aware of the presence of others and the possibility of contact or collision.

Despite, the above, it is safe to say that we know very little about the effect of team roster size on perceptions of crowding/density. In order to better understand the nature of this relationship in sport and physical activity, it is necessary to separate the three dimensions of crowding and density: a) the group's size as represented by the number of individuals present (social density), b) the amount of space afforded each member (spatial density), and c) the interpersonal distance present between members (proximity) (Knowles, 1983; Paulus, Annis, Seta, Schkad, & Matthews, 1976). A large soccer team of 40 members might not seem crowded if practices are held on a field large enough to insure that spatial density and proximity are not a hindrance to participation. By contrast, a

Illustration 3.1. Increases in group size may provide the coach with more resources, but a large roster can lead to increased crowding and density.

smaller team of 20 members might feel very crowded if its practices are held on a field where team members cannot move freely without the risk of contact.

Paulus and his colleagues (1976, Study 1) examined the three crowding/density variables (proximity, group size, and room size) in a controlled laboratory setting. The task required each person to trace a multiple maze. Proximity was varied by manipulating the distance between the individuals (they were placed either 6 inches or 18 inches apart), group size by having individuals work in groups of four or eight, and room size by using two test rooms with one being approximately twice as large as the other. Paulus and his colleagues found that individuals in the large group made more errors on the maze than those in the small group. Neither room size nor proximity had an effect on performance.

Communication

Another factor influenced by the size of the group is the level of communication present (see Table 3.4 again). On the basis of extensive research with three organizations, Indik (1965) concluded that an organization's size directly influences the amount of communication among its members. He suggested that the larger the organization, the greater the likelihood that communication among members will be inadequate to carry out the organization's goals and objectives. He also proposed that this reduced communication, in turn, leads to lower interpersonal attraction.

With increases in group size, it is also more difficult to give each group member personal attention and involve them in the social activities of the group. Also, opportunities for personal instruction are reduced, as anyone who has been in large physical education classes can testify. Instruction becomes more group-oriented. Not surprisingly, the amount of reinforcement and rewards provided to each individual also decreases. Each of these contributes to reduced individual satisfaction and lower group morale.

Positive Benefits of Increased Group Size

One of the few positive psychosocial outcomes of an increase in group size is that there is an increase in opportunities available to meet other people who are perceived to be interesting and attractive. In a pairs team in figure skating, for example, there is only one other person available in the "group" for friendship and communication. If the two individuals don't like each other, the group offers little in the way of social satisfaction. Conversely, when a group increases in size, the number of potential friends who are available also increases.

Group Size and Leadership

Group size has four principal implications for leadership. First, with an increasing number of group members, the opportunity for any one individual to participate in the leadership of the group diminishes. Second, more demands are placed on the formal leader. Third, the formal leader has less opportunity to interact and communicate with individual members. Finally, as groups increase in size, there is an increasing tendency for group leaders to become more authoritarian and adopt a more centralized leadership style (Hare, 1981; Stogdill, 1974; Widmeyer, 1971). As an example, the coach of a soccer team with 25 members on its roster is more likely to be autocratic and authoritarian than the coach of a soccer team with 12 members. Individual input into decision making is not only more difficult to coordinate in larger groups, it is less efficient to solicit it. The group can experience "paralysis of analysis" if an overly democratic approach is used.

There are differences in the subjective impression of the effectiveness of leaders in groups of varying sizes. For example, Perry and Bauman (1973) and McDaniel and Feldhusen (1971) have observed that teacher evaluations systematically decrease as class size increases. There is also some evidence, however, that the relationship between instructor evaluation and class size is not simply linear in nature. Centra and Creech (1976), in a study of 4,760 class sections, found that the mean ratings assigned to instructors decreased for class sections having from 70 to 150 students. On the other hand, Pohlmann (1975), in a study with 1,247 class sections, reported that higher instructor ratings were obtained in smaller classes (less than 80 students) and larger classes (120 students or more) than in moderate size classes (80 to 120 students).

Chapter Four

GROUP TERRITORY

> The court had every conceivable deficiency. The baskets were hung against the end walls, which meant that those of us accustomed to using them mastered the art of dashing headlong at the wall, planting our right foot high against the planking, and vaulting upward toward the basket, ending high above the rim so that we could then dunk the ball downward. This was a shot fairly hard to stop by a bewildered defender who had never before seen such a court.
>
> The ceiling was unusually low, with a wide, heavy rafter right above the basket, and we became expert in speeding down the floor, and with maximum force slamming the ball vertically upward so that it caromed back down through the basket. This, too, was a shot difficult to stop if you were not accustomed to it.
>
> On this bizarre floor the Doyleston Boys' Brigade fielded teams with far more than normal skills. We once went for a period of three years without losing a home game, even though we played teams that had better reputations and much taller players. At the time I thought we were pretty good, but now, looking back on those years, I realize that even superlative opponents would have required about three-quarters of a game to familiarize themselves with our peculiar floor and its strange rules. (Michener, 1976, p. 4)

Territoriality represents a perception of proprietary rights over a physical space. Perceptions of territoriality contribute to group morale and individual satisfaction. Territoriality also provides a feeling of permanence and stability and, consequently, all groups work to establish their own territory. Team logos are placed in the stadium or rink, team mascots are very much in evidence, and special locker room areas, eating areas, and clearly identified practice fields are set out.

For many sport teams, the stadium, rink, soccer pitch, grounds, or court become so intertwined with the identity of the team that it is often difficult to separate one from the other. Yankee Stadium. Old Trafford. Wembley Stadium. Maple Leaf Gardens. Each of these venues brings to mind an image of its team.

The group's territory has an influence on both intra- and extra-group members. For example, the layout or physical structure of a team's territory can influence the interaction between fans and athletes. Roger Kahn's (1972) description of Ebbets Field, the former home of the Los Angeles (Brooklyn at the time) Dodgers, provides a good example:

> *Ebbets Field was a narrow cockpit, built of brick and iron and concrete, alongside a steep cobblestone slope of Bedford Avenue. Two tiers of grandstand pressed the playing area from three sides, and in thousands of seats fans could hear ball player's chatter, notice details of a ball player's gait and, at a time when television had not yet assaulted illusion with the Zoomar lens, you could see, actually see, the actual expression on the actual face of an actual major leaguer as he played. You could know what he was like! (p. xi-xii)*

As another example, the sport team's territory—its court, stadium, grounds, or rink—can provide it with advantages during the competition. In professional baseball, the "Green Monster," the left field wall in Boston's Fenway Park, continues to confuse visiting outfielders and intimidate visiting pitchers. In international cricket, Jamaica's cricket pitch, hardened from constant pounding by the sun and an absence of grass, produces these same sentiments of confusion and intimidation in visiting batters.

In amateur sport, the problems posed by the home team's territory can be even greater. Many facilities are built for multiple purposes—and sometimes sport wasn't one of them. Consequently, a home team's territory can often give new meaning to the phrase "home court advantage." The quote from James Michener (1976) used to introduce this chapter is an excellent example. There is no doubt that Michener's home territory was uniquely advantageous.

The Nature of Territoriality

Individual Territory

The earliest work carried out in social psychology on territoriality focused on aspects of personal distance. Edward Hall (1966) proposed that when interactions occur in dyads, four types of interpersonal distance zones are possible: intimate, casual-personal, social consultative, and public (see Table 4.1). An *intimate* zone extends from physical contact

Table 4.1
The nature of interpersonal distance zones (Adapted from Hall, 1966)

Type of Interpersonal Distance	Distance Zone	Characteristic Activities
Intimate	Contact to 18 in.	Intimate activities (e.g., kissing)
Casual-Personal	18 in. to 5 ft.	Close informal contacts (e.g., conversations among close friends)
Social-Consultative	5 ft. to 12 ft.	Formal social activities (e.g., conversations among casual acquaintances)
Public	Beyond 12 ft.	Formal interactions (e.g., lectures)

to 18 inches. As the name suggests, an intimate zone is associated with intimate interactions such as kissing—although combative sports like boxing, wrestling, judo, and so on also are carried out in the intimate zone. If there is such a thing as a fondness continuum, dyads that find themselves in the intimate territory are usually at either of the two extremes—very friendly or very unfriendly.

The relationship among individuals who share a *casual-personal* zone is still very personal since the zone runs from 18 inches to just 5 feet. Conversations among close friends and aggressive interactions are the characteristic activities of this zone. Coaches who adopt an in-your-face style of communicating, generally are at the close extreme of the casual-personal zone.

The *social-consultative* zone, which extends from 5 feet to 12 feet, is characterized by more formal activities such as conversations among acquaintances. A coach discussing defensive strategies with her team before practice would likely use the social consultative interpersonal distance zone.

Finally, the *public distance* zone extends beyond 12 feet. As the name suggests, it is the zone used for formal interactions. A team meeting in a classroom would be illustrative of this type of zone.

Group Territory

Group territory is different from individual territory in that a) groups have a greater tendency to establish a territory and defend it against invasion, and b) group territories are larger and less clearly defined (Shaw, 1981).

Irwin Altman (1975) pointed out that a spatial location does not become part of a group's territory until the group can exert some control over it over a period of time. The nature of the control and the length of time over which the group has control have a direct influence on the development and extent of the group's sense of territoriality (see Table 4.2).

Table 4.2
The nature of group territory (Adapted from Altman, 1975)

Type of Territory	Level of Group Control	Duration of Group Control	Sport Example Team locker room,
Primary	High and direct. Access by others restricted. High probability territory will be defended.	Long term and permanent. Ownership may be involved.	Stadium, or the park of professional teams.
Secondary	Moderate. Group is a habitual user and identified with territory.	Short term and temporary.	Practice fields, locker rooms and parks shared by more than one team.
Public	Low. Group has control only when using territory.	Control does not exist or is of minimal duration.	Public tennis courts, university gyms.

Primary territories are "owned and used exclusively by individuals or groups . . . [they are] clearly identified as theirs by others, are controlled on a relatively permanent basis, and are central to the day-to-day lives of the occupants" (Altman, 1975, p. 112). If a sport team has the exclusive use of a locker room, practice field, stadium, dormitory, or weight-lifting facility, this represents their primary territory. On some college campuses, the football team prevents all public use or student activity in its stadium, practice area, or weight-training room. A primary territory is actively controlled by the group, while access or use by non-group members is prevented. The group or the individual will defend a primary territory against invasion—as the quote in Box 4.1 illustrates.

Secondary territories are those "places over which an individual or a group has some control, ownership, and regulatory power but not the same degree as over primary territory" (Altman, 1975, p. 117). In high school sport, a number of teams may share the same facility—a locker room, gymnasium, or playing field. If they do so at the same time (e.g., by splitting the area in half), certain boundary markers become demarcation lines between the groups. These boundary markers might be very actively defended and any intrusion could be met with hostility and conflict.

This occurs in ice hockey and football, for example. The center line is a well-accepted boundary separating the territories of the two teams during the pre-game warm-up. No intrusion into an opponent's territory is permitted. In hockey, if a puck goes into an opponent's territory, it must be left there to be returned (or not) at the convenience of the opponent. Any player who ventures into the other team's territory risks a confrontation (see Box 4.1).

Full-scale brawls have been initiated because one player crossed over the red line into an opponent's zone during a pre-game skate. A highly publicized example of territoriality in hockey occurred in a 1987 NHL Stanley Cup Series between the Philadelphia Flyers and Montreal Canadiens. Some Canadien players stayed on the ice after Philadelphia had completed its warm up. They then "invaded" the Philadelphia territory and shot pucks into the open net for good luck. When they were spotted by a Flyer, both teams returned to the ice and a battle royal between the two teams resulted.

The third category, *public* territories, has a "temporary quality, and almost anyone has free access and occupancy rights" (Altman, 1975, p. 118). In university gymnasia, individuals or groups may arrive to play basketball. If other individuals or groups occupy the courts, the newcomers are able to join the game. In public tennis courts, it is universally understood that players should alternate on the courts after a set number of games or fixed period of time. Also, as the quote in Box 4.1 illustrates, right of occupancy of the batting cage in baseball is only temporary. In all of these instances, the individuals or groups have some occupancy rights and some control but these are only temporary.

Marking Group Territory

Signs and symbols are used to separate a home territory from the territory of other groups. In an early, classic study, William Whyte (1943) observed that different street gangs used graffiti on buildings, sidewalks, and signs to mark off their territory from their rivals. The amount of graffiti present increased with increasing proximity to a group's base.

In sport teams, the signs and symbols representing territoriality may consist of posters, names over lockers, ornaments, and slogans. They also may consist of trophies and flags

Box 4.1
Illustrations of primary, secondary, and public territories in sport

Type of Territory	Quotation
Primary	I walk towards the rear of the bus and, just past halfway, turn to the left . . . Others come on to the bus turning in right or left, apparently at random. But nothing is random. Just as it is in the dressing room, we each have a seat that is ours . . . we sit where we do because if we didn't, we might sit in a seat important to someone else. And sitting where we do as much as we do, gradually where we sit becomes important to us . . . . At training camp, and a few times each year when injuries bring two or three new players to the team, it can be a problem. For new players, unfamiliar with our habits, sit anywhere, and one person in the wrong seat means someone else in the wrong seat until a simple chain of confusion becomes a mess. While most of us hover near our occupied seats wondering what to do and where to go, not quite willing to admit that a particular seat matters to us, someone will usually come along and say something—"Hey, get the fuck outa my seat"—to straighten out the problem. (Dryden, 1983, pp. 112-113)
Secondary	We wheeled around in our half of the ice, the Flyers in theirs. There was no communication between the two teams; indeed, the players seemed to put their heads down as they approached the center line, sailing by within feet of each other . . . [Pettie] told me about a pregame warmup in one of the Soviet-NHL series, in which our teammate Wayne Cashman had spotted a Russian player coming across the center line to chase a puck; Cashman had intercepted the Russian and checked him violently into the boards. "Well, the guy was in the wrong place," Pettie said when I expressed my astonishment. "He should have known better." (Plimpton, 1978, p. 35)
Public	Once, a minor [baseball] leaguer was supposed to be in the batting cage, but one of the coaches yelled for [Michael] Jordan to get in.
	"Is that OK?" Jordan asked the kid somewhat sheepishly.
	"Sure," the kid replied. After all, Jordan did play golf in his spare time with the manager.
	"Asshole," the kid spat as Jordan took his swings. (Smith, 1995 p. 25)

symbolizing past successes. In their description of the Montreal Forum, the former home territory of the Canadiens, Chrys Goyens and Allan Turowetz (1986) outlined the impact of these types of symbols:

> *Unlike the teams that have made the Forum great, the building itself is squat and functional . . . Inside, the Forum is just another hockey rink at first glance. If you've visited any area of size in the National Hockey League, the impression here will be one of overwhelming sameness . . . it could be the Forum in Inglewood, California, or the Capital Center in the middle of nowhere between Baltimore and Washington. Second glance will uncover a series of visual clues that indicate the familiar and the fabled.*
>
> *The stylized CH will be the first reminder of what this building has meant to the sport. But that isn't the key to the Forum either . . . Where is the real Forum? Look up. Straight above your head, in the rafters. There you'll find the real Forum. There, high above the ice, they hang silently. To call them just pieces of cloth is like describing an Arras tapestry as just another wallhanging . . . Only the Forum holds twenty-three separate white panels on which these words are written in blue with red trim: "Montreal Canadiens, Stanley Cup Champions." (pp. 15-16)*

The signs and symbols marking territoriality are quite important individually and collectively. Laboratory and field studies have shown that group morale and individual satisfaction are higher, feelings of being crowded are reduced, and a territory is considered to be more pleasant when it becomes personalized through the use of signs and symbols (e.g., Baum & Valins, 1977; Edney & Uhlig, 1977).

The Size of Group Territory

Professional and college teams have clearly established facilities, the size of which is often dictated by budget considerations. In recreational and more informal groups, however, the size of the group's territory serves as a measure of its status. Territory represents dominance; the greater the status of the group, the greater the amount of territory it marks out (e.g., Durand, 1977). Group territory does not grow in direct proportion to group size, however. In fact, as groups grow in size, there is an increasing tendency for them to take over relatively less space per member (Edney & Jorden-Edney, 1974).

Also, with increasing group size, the boundaries for the group's territory become more permeable, less clearly defined (Edney & Grundmann, 1979). For example, soccer teams of 15 members might jealousy guard its one practice field. Intruders would be asked to leave. However, if that soccer team expanded to 45 members and used three fields, it would probably be easier for intruders to use a corner of one field. A pair of students might throw a baseball in one corner, sit and watch practice, or carry out individual exercises.

The Advantages of Home Territory

One aspect of territoriality that has received considerable attention in sport is what has come to be known as the *home advantage*. One indicant of this attention is the frequency of references made by coaches, competitors, fans, and the media. In fact, after conducting an informal content analysis of media reports, Edwards and Archambault (1989) stated that more references are made to the difficulty of defeating a home team than to any other single factor, including prior record, player talent, injuries, and momentum.

There seems to be little doubt that home territory is important consideration in team success. As early as 28 years ago, Schwartz and Barsky (1977), commenting on the importance of game location (i.e., being at home versus away) versus the relative ability level of the two teams stated,

> *Being at home . . . may be as decisive an element of play as being good. The reason for the caution with which this conclusion may be stated is that game location is a real dichotomy while team quality is not . . . Therefore, the conservative inference is probably the best one: game location and team quality are equally important determinants of performance. (p. 649)*

In 1992, Kerry Courneya and Albert Carron provided a formal definition of the home advantage: "the consistent finding that home teams in sport competitions win over 50% of the games played under a balanced home and away schedule" (p. 13). They also observed that the presence of a home advantage during regular season competitions is one of the most robust and replicable findings in sport psychology (home advantage in the playoffs may be another matter; this is discussed later in the chapter).

A Conceptual Model for the Home Advantage[1]

In 2004, Albert Carron, Todd Loughead, and Steven Bray set out a conceptual framework for examining the home advantage. This framework, which represents a slight adaptation to earlier work by Kerry Courneya and Albert Carron (1992), is presented in Figure 4.1.

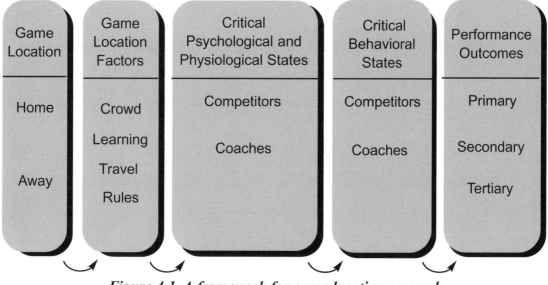

Figure 4.1. A framework for game location research
(Adapted from Carron, Loughead & Bray, 2005)

---

1. A large portion of the discussion which follows appeared originally in Courneya and Carron (1992) and Carron, Loughead, & Bray (2004).

As Figure 4.1 shows, five major components are considered important in understanding the home advantage: game location, game location factors, critical psychological states, critical behavioral states, and performance outcomes.

Game Location

The first component in Figure 4.1, *game location*, takes into account whether a team is competing at its home venue or at an opponent's venue. If there is an interest in determining whether a home advantage exists (and why), then *home* versus *away* are the only two considerations possible (i.e., competitions at neutral sites are irrelevant to the issue).

Harry Neale, a former coach in the National Hockey League, is reputed to have said, "We can't win at home; we can't win on the road. My failure as a coach is that I can't think of anywhere else to play." Recently, many leagues have experimented with a strategy that might have solved Neale's dilemma; on occasion throughout the season, competitions are scheduled for a neutral site where, of course, one of the two visiting teams is designated as the home team. However, the model illustrated in Figure 4.1 would not be pertinent to the analysis of these competitions.

The extent of the home advantage has been found to vary across sports (see Table 4.3). In baseball, home teams win approximately 54% of the games played—4% above chance. On the other hand, soccer teams win 69% of the time. Considered from an overall perspective, however, there is no doubt that

1. A home advantage is present in both professional and amateur team sports (Courneya & Carron, 1992, Schwartz & Barsky, 1977);
2. A home advantage is also present in individual sports (Bray & Carron, 1993; Gayton & Langevin, 1992; Irving & Goldstein 1990);
3. The home advantage is generalizable across gender (Courneya & Carron, 1992);
4. Competing in a home territory positively benefits countries in international competitions; host countries tend to win more medals at Olympic Games than they do in the immediately preceding or subsequent Olympic Games (Leonard, 1989); and
5. The home advantage is not a recent phenomenon; e.g., the extent of the home advantage in English soccer has remained relatively unchanged since 1888 (Pollard, 1986).

Table 4.3
The home advantage in major team sports (Adapted from Courneya & Carron, 1992)

Sport	Total No. Of Studies	Total Games	Winning Percentage
Baseball	6	23,034	53.5
Football	5	2,592	57.3
Ice Hockey	4	4,322	61.1
Basketball	8	13,596	64.4
Soccer	2	37,202	69.0

Researchers have also found, however, that there are moderators of the magnitude of the home advantage. For example, in their analysis of the number of medals won by competing nations in the Winter Olympic Games (1908-1998), Balmer, Nevill, and Williams (2001) found that when all events were combined, a significant home advantage was present. However, there were substantial differences across events with little or no advantage observed in a number of the events. A critical factor was the protocol for measuring performance; a significantly greater home advantage was present in judged events (e.g., figure skating) than in more objectively determined events (e.g., short track speed skating).

In some sports, time of season may have an influence on the extent of the home advantage. For example, Ward (1998) proposed "opening day in major league baseball represents a highly ritualistic and festive occasion" (p. 280). Given that this is the case, Ward felt that players and fans might be more strongly motivated to create a positive impression, and therefore, that the home advantage would be greater than it might be during the regular season and/or even the World Series and league championships. The findings were consistent with this expectation. The winning percentages in games played (a) on opening day versus (b) during the regular season in front of large crowds, versus (c) in "must win" World Series and league championships were 75%, 70%, and 57% respectively.

Studies by Bray (1999) and Clarke and Norman (1995) also show that the home advantage is not universal for all teams. For example, in his analysis of the performance of *individual teams* in the National Hockey League for the period 1974 to 1993, Bray found that teams won 17.3% more games at home than on the road. However, over that same period, 37.7% of the teams won fewer than 50% of their home games. Similarly, Clarke and Norman reported that 14% of the teams in English soccer in any given year in any one division had a negative home advantage.

Game Location Factors

Because of its importance and pervasiveness across sport, various authors have attempted to gain a better understanding of why home teams enjoy such an advantage. The best guess of Wright and House (1989)—based on Wright's experience as statistician for a major league baseball team and House's experience as a major league baseball player and coach—was that 5% of the home advantage is due to a psychological lift from the crowd, 5% results from the advantage of batting last, 10% is due to familiarity with the stadium, 10% is due to the ability of the home team to select and use personnel best suited to its home stadium, 30% is due to a regimen regularity, and 40% is due to an umpire bias that favors the home team.

Courneya and Carron (1992), drawing on the work of Schwartz and Barsky (1977), proposed that there are four principal factors resulting from the game's location and these, in turn, influence the home advantage. These four, illustrated in the second component of Figure 4.1, are

1. *crowd factors*—generally competitors at home have more support from spectators than do visiting competitors;
2. *learning/familiarity factors*—competitors at home are generally more familiar with their own venue and also have the opportunity to modify that venue temporarily in order to capitalize on their perceived strengths;

3. *travel factors*—visiting competitors generally must undergo the inconvenience of some travel; and

4. *rule factors*—in some sports the rules may favor the home team (e.g., last line change in ice hockey).

Crowd Factors. Teams competing at home have the potential to benefit from a supportive crowd—and they do (see Illustration 4.1). But, what is not as clear is what characteristics of the crowd provide for a maximum advantage. Is it the crowd's partisanship (i.e., unqualified support)? Type of behavior (i.e., booing versus cheering)? Absolute size? Density (i.e., percent capacity)? Intensity (i.e., noise level)?

Phil Jackson (1990), then a National Basketball Association coach with the Chicago Bulls, proposed that the *partisanship* of the crowd has a strong effect on players. In discussing why home teams seem to win more games, Jackson observed, "There's the basic influence of spectators' supporting and rooting that influences a club to play well" (quoted in Smith, 1990, p. 1).

Research seems to support Jackson's belief. Richard Pollard's (1986) study of "local derbies" is interesting in this regard. A local derby is any match played between the 13 first and second division soccer teams in the greater London area. Pollard found that the home advantage in these local derbies—where travel is not a substantive issue and crowd access is relatively equal for supporters from both teams—was 56.1%. When these teams played opponents traveling from outside London—opponents who had to travel and understandably would have had fewer supporters at the match—the home advantage increased significantly to 64.3%.

The nature of the crowd's *behavior* is also a consideration. The effect of antisocial crowd behavior—swearing, chanting obscenities, throwing objects on the floor, and fighting—was examined by Thirer and Rampey (1979). They recorded the number of infractions (fouls and turnovers) by home and visiting basketball teams for 5 minutes immediately following the onset of the antisocial behavior. These results were then compared with infractions by the home and visiting teams during normal crowd behavior periods. During the normal crowd behavior periods, the home team showed an advantage in that they committed fewer infractions. During periods where antisocial crowd behavior occurred, however, the visiting teams had an advantage; they maintained their same level of play whereas the home teams showed an increase in number of infractions.

Illustration 4.1. A home court advantage!

In a subsequent study, Greer (1983) examined the effect of basketball spectator booing that lasted longer than 15 seconds on points scored, turnovers, violations (fouls plus goaltending) and a composite measure of points scored minus turnovers and violations. As was the case with the Thirer and Rampey study, the home team was superior on all the performance measures. Contrary to the results of Thirer and Rampey, however, the home team's superiority became greater during episodes of booing behavior.

The results relating to the influence of absolute *crowd size* have been mixed with some studies showing that larger crowds do not improve the home team's advantage while others show that they do. For example, when Dowie (1982) compared the extent of the home advantage in four divisions of English Football League (soccer), he found that the home advantage did not differ from Division 1 to Division 4 whereas the average crowd size varied from 25,000 to 2,500 spectators. Also, Agnew and Carron (1994), using data from two seasons of competition in a Canadian Major Junior A ice hockey league, found that absolute crowd size was not at all useful as a predictor of game outcome.

Conversely, however, Allan Nevill and his colleagues found that absolute crowd size was positively related to the home advantage in English and Scottish soccer. Home teams had increased home winning percentages where crowd size was large, whereas, the home advantage was nearly absent in two leagues (i.e., G.M. Vauxhall League, Scottish Second Division) where crowd sizes were small.

The results pertaining to *crowd density* have been relatively consistent. For example, Agnew and Carron found that crowd density was a reliable predictor of the home advantage in ice hockey. Also, Schwartz and Barsky (1977), in a study of Major League Baseball, found that when the crowd's density was low (less than 20% of capacity), the home team's winning percentage was 48%. This winning percentage increased to 55% when density was moderate (20 to 39.9%) and then to 57% when density was high (greater than 40%). It might be argued that these results could reflect team quality—poor teams don't attract very many spectators so their home parks would be almost empty. Thus, ability, not density might be a logical explanation for the results. However, Schwartz and Barsky, recognizing this possibility, statistically controlled for ability and obtained similar results.

There is another aspect to the home advantage that is associated with the home crowd. Aamodt (1981) found that baseball fans tend to vote for players from their home team in All-Star balloting. Consequently, teams with the greatest home attendance have more players selected. Aamodt also examined whether these results were simply a result of the fact that the best players play well so, therefore, more fans come out to watch them and, therefore, they receive more votes. Aamodt found that home attendance correlated .52 with team wins. Thus, there is no doubt that fans do come out if the team is successful. However, home attendance was not significantly correlated with individual All-Star player statistics such as batting average (r = .03), home runs (r = .28), runs batted in (r = .19), or runs scored (r = .05). Thus, the better players don't always play in front of the bigger crowds.

Another line of study has been to examine the perceived influence of supportive behaviors by spectators. In their study, Steven Bray and Neil Widmeyer (2000) asked female collegiate basketball players to indicate which factors contributed to the home advantage. Over 25% of the athletes stated that support from the home crowd was an important factor in winning at home. Despite this belief among players, findings from field studies have shown that spectator support for the home team (i.e., cheering) is not related to greater home team success in either soccer, ice hockey, basketball (Salminen, 1993), or American football (Strauss, 2002).

The Home Crowd and Officiating Bias. The home crowd may also have an effect on refereeing decisions. Thus, for example, a noisy supportive audience could exert a subtle influence on officiating decisions. This was a point made by Phil Jackson when he was coaching the Chicago Bulls:

> *[the home advantage results from the] officiating . . . some of it has to do with human frailty. It's natural when 15,000 people are rooting for one team. That's a lot of noise and energy and basic influence. (quoted in Smith, 1990, p. 1)*

The research by Balmer and his colleagues (2001) that was discussed above seems to support the points made by Jackson. They found that in subjectively judged events (e.g., figure skating) in the Winter Olympics events host team athletes garnered a greater number of total medals compared to performances at other Olympic Games. No home advantage was found in objectively scored events (e.g., speed skating).

The home crowd also might influence officiating decisions by drawing attention to fouls committed by visiting teams (while remaining silent when the home team transgresses). Phil Jackson also commented on this possibility:

> *You don't get the same calls [on the road], which accounts for not shooting as well. Teams shoot about 10 percent higher at home than on the road. And there are close situations where the calls are going to go against you . . . You turn those around and some teams, like us, could have a winning road record. (quoted in Smith, 1990, p. 1)*

There is some research that supports Jackson's claim that visiting teams garner more fouls. For example, Sumner and Mobley (1981) found that in International Test Cricket, visiting teams are the recipients of more Leg-Before-Wicket decisions (LBW, the baseball equivalent of a strike out). Also, Smith (1990) reported that a great number of foul calls in the National Basketball Association were made against the visiting team 57% of the time and against the home team 31% of the time (in the remaining 11% of the games, the number of foul calls was equal). Further, Mohr and Larson (1998) found that in Australian football, in-state teams received 10% more free kick decisions when they played on their home (i.e., in-state) grounds than when they played on away (i.e., out-of-state) grounds. However, two studies have also found no evidence of officiating bias—Jones and his colleagues (2001) in English Club Cricket matches and Dennis and his colleagues in the National Hockey League.

Finally, Lehman and Reifman took a slightly different approach (1987). They examined the number of fouls called on higher- and lower-status professional basketball players (i.e., stars and non-stars) at home and away. They reasoned that officials might feel more pressure to be lenient with a team's star player. As was predicted, fewer fouls were called on star players at home than on the road; for the non-stars, there were no differences in the number of fouls called at home and on the road.

A number of authors have pointed out, however, that these types of findings do not necessarily support the conclusion that there is an officiating bias that favours the home team (e.g., Sumner & Mobley, 1981; Varca, 1980). Visiting teams may deserve more negative decisions because of their style of play.

In an attempt to test this possibility, Nevill and his colleagues (2002) conducted a laboratory study using experimentally manipulated crowd noise. They had two groups of qualified soccer referees record their officiating decisions of a videotape-recorded match under conditions of either crowd noise or silence. Although all referees, on average, scored the same match, 2.3 fewer fouls were called against the home team by those referees experiencing crowd noise compared to those who called the match with no noise present. Nevill and his colleagues also found that the same number of fouls was called against the visiting team regardless of noise condition, which helped substantiate their supposition that referees are more reluctant or uncertain when it comes to calling fouls against the home team.

Dennis, Carron, and Loughead (2002) analyzed videotapes of National Hockey League games to determine if incorrect officiating decisions (i.e., a penalty was called when no infraction occurred or an infraction occurred but no penalty was called) favored the home team. No evidence of officiating bias was observed; referees made an equal number of incorrect decisions towards both home and visiting teams.

Learning Factors. Learning factors (see Figure 4.1 again) is an umbrella term that is used to represent environmental considerations of two types: stable and unstable. The *unstable* types consist of those elements that can be manipulated to advantage by the home team. A good example is provided in a commentary on the 2004 National League Championship Series between the Houston Astros and St. Louis Cardinals:

> *For anyone who doesn't believe how much power [Roger] Clemens wields in his home ballpark, there were some subtle preparation moves in the moments prior to the game to create the perfect pitching environment for The Rocket. The ground crew hosed down the dirt in the infield for so long there were almost puddles in front of the plate. The effect, of course, is that ground balls don't scoot through quite as quickly and the Cards' swifter baserunners are slowed down slightly. (Griffin, 2004, p. E4)*

Is the manipulation of the home environment specific to baseball? Probably not. Another example of the potential importance of unstable learning factors on the home advantage is provided by Sam Smith (1995) from discussions he had with then Chicago Bulls' coach Phil Jackson:

> *Before the game, Jackson noticed the league-imposed seal that prescribes the uniform amount of pressure for backboards and rims was broken . . . He knows, as do NBA insiders, that home-court advantage comes less from all the nonsense about sleeping in your own bed, eating at home, and having a regular routine than from the way home teams can manipulate the equipment. Jackson had long suspected the Detroit Pistons of tampering with one basket during their championship years . . . to make it harder to shoot at that basket . . . [and] keep an offensive rebounding team on the floor under that supposedly tainted basket to get offensive rebounds.*
>
> *Likewise, Jackson also carried an air gauge with him to test the poundage of the game balls. Years ago, the Lakers, Jackson believed, used to sneak in inflated balls because Magic Johnson liked a high dribble,*

while teams with slower guards might remove some air from the ball to slow the Bulls' quicker guards. (pp. 197-198)

The *stable* types of learning factors are those idiosyncratic elements in the court, rink, or stadium with which the home team has become familiar and to which it has accommodated its play. The Green Monster in Boston's Fenway Park or the home court of the Doyleston Boys' Brigade described by Michener in the quote used to introduce this chapter are good illustrations of environmental considerations that have the potential to benefit the home team. In a close game, uncertainty and/or errors resulting from a lack of familiarity with the playing surface could prove to be decisive. Visiting teams simply do not have the same amount of experience with the home team's facility. Phil Jackson highlighted this point when he noted, "You know your bench won't play as well [on the road] . . . they won't get as many opportunities or the same feel for the court" (quoted in Smith, 1990, p. 1). Any research that has been done pertaining to learning factors has implicitly studied the stable types.

One such study was undertaken by Pollard (1986) who compared the home advantage of teams competing on atypical surfaces with that of teams competing on standard surfaces. He found that during the period of 1981-84, the two English professional soccer teams playing on the largest playing surface (i.e., 9401 sq. yds.) and the two playing on the smallest playing surface (i.e., 7700 sq. yds.) experienced a 65.6% home advantage. Also, the one club competing at home on artificial turf had a 63.9% home advantage. However, the home advantage enjoyed by these teams with atypical surfaces was not significantly different for that of teams in the rest of the league (64.9%).

More recently, Clarke and Norman (1995) reexamined this question but for a 10-year period between 1981 and 1990. They found a trend towards a higher-than-average home advantage when team quality was controlled; in short, teams playing on larger or smaller playing surfaces did have an advantage. Furthermore, both Clarke and Norman and Barnett and Hilditch (1993) reported that teams playing on artificial turf playing surfaces had higher home advantages than teams playing on natural grass.

Another strategy that has been used to determine the role that facility familiarity plays has been to compare the extent of the home advantage prior to and following a move to a new facility (Loughead, Carron, Bray, & Kim, 2003; Moore & Brylinsky, 1995; Pollard, 2002).

Pollard (2002) compared the home winning percentages for the entire season before and after a facility change using 37 teams that had moved to new venues between 1987 and 2001 from the National Basketball Association (NBA), National Hockey League (NHL), and Major League Baseball (MLB). For 26 teams, there was a decrease in the home advantage following a move, 10 teams showed an increase, and one team showed no change.

Using a slightly different approach, Loughead, Carron, Bray, and Kim (2003) compared home team game results from three time periods: (a) the block of games (i.e., ten) immediately prior to relocating to a new venue; (b) the block of games (i.e., ten) immediately after relocating to a new venue; and (c) the block of games (i.e., the next ten) when teams were more acclimatized to their new surroundings. The overall home winning percentage prior to moving to a new venue for the 57 teams that had relocated from the National Basketball Association (1991-2000), National Hockey League (1982-2000), and the English and Scottish Professional Football Associations (1988-2000) was 55.2%. The relocation did not produce significant changes in the home advantage. In the time period immediately after relocating, the home winning percentage was reduced to 53.9% and this remained virtually unchanged (53.1%) for the next time period. Loughead and his colleagues did find, however, that team quality is a moderating factor. High quality teams—teams with a home winning percentage greater than 50% prior to relocation—experienced a significant reduction in home advantage in the period immediately following relocation (from 70.6% to 59.2%). Conversely, low-quality teams—teams with a home winning percentage lower than 50% prior to relocation—experienced a significant increase (from 34.1% to 46.8%).

Loughead and his colleagues suggested that any one or all of three explanation might have accounted for these findings. One was that both high- and low-quality teams might have shown a statistical "regression toward the mean." Another was that high-quality teams might be better able to use facility familiarity to their advantage. The third was psychological in nature—low-quality teams might view a move as an opportunity for a fresh start while high-quality teams might experience reduced confidence because of reduced familiarity.

Travel Factors. As Figure 4.1 shows, another category of factors considered to contribute to a home team's advantage is the travel required by their opponents. Fatigue and the disruption of sleeping and/or eating routines are associated with travel. Also, distance traveled, travel in close proximity to game time, number of successive travels, and times zones crossed all have the potential to negatively influence the preparation of visiting teams (and, consequently, contribute to the home team's advantage). An anecdote by Allan Strachan (1988) about the influence of travel in the National Hockey League is illustrative of the role that travel is thought to play:

> *Former Flame coach Bob Johnson, who had to deal with it [travel problems] on a regular basis when he was in Calgary, said it was one problem he was unable to conquer. Everything else, from poor power plays to nutritional failings to peripheral vision, had a solution, Johnson said. But a means of overcoming jet lag eluded him. (p. 15)*

Much of the earliest research led to a conclusion that travel played only a minor or no role in the home advantage but more recently studies have led to a reevaluation of this perspective. Characteristic of the earliest research is a study by Schwartz and Barsky (1977) who felt that *time of season* might be a consideration. They reasoned that "if visitor fatigue is a significant determinant of home advantage, then one might assume that this advantage would be more pronounced as the season progresses and the effects of injuries and physical wear and tear accumulate and become aggravated by travel" (p. 65).

In their examination of the home advantage results from professional baseball, professional football, college football, professional hockey, and college basketball, Schwartz and Barsky found that there were no differences between the first versus the second half of the season. Subsequent research by Courneya and Carron (1991) with minor professional baseball teams, Pace and Carron (1992) with National Hockey League teams, and Agnew and Carron (1994) with Junior-A hockey teams produced identical results.

A similar approach was taken by Dowie (1982) in a study of English soccer matches. Rather than use the season as a frame of reference, however, Dowie compared goals scored in the first versus second half of a game. His rationale was that any fatigue in the visiting team resulting from travel would have its maximum effect in the second half of a match.

Dowie found, however, that the goal differential between the visiting and home teams remained constant throughout the match.

If there are disadvantages associated with travel, then the *distance traveled* might prove critical. However, the research evidence has provided mixed results. For example, in studies of professional soccer (Pollard, 1986), professional hockey (Pace & Carron, 1992), Junior-A hockey (Agnew & Carron, 1994), and high school, university, and professional basketball (Gayton &Coombs, 1995), no relationship was found between distance travel and visitor disadvantage. Conversely, other studies have reported a relationship (Snyder & Purdy, 1987)

Clarke and Norman (1995) proposed that methodological considerations might account for failures to find a visitor travel disadvantage relationship. They pointed out that a team could travel a short distance and compete with no disadvantage and a then long distance and compete with some disadvantage. When the magnitude of the disadvantage in these two competitions was averaged, the result could be either no disadvantage or a minimal disadvantage. When they controlled for this possibility statistically, Clarke and Norman found a significant correlation ($r = .07$, $p = .0001$) between distance travelled and the home advantage (i.e., visitor disadvantage). Although, the correlation is relatively small in magnitude, the number of observations ($n = 10,153$ paired matches) increases confidence in the effect.

Another study showing that distance travelled does contribute to visitor disadvantage was reported by Brown, Van Raalte, Brewer, Winter, and Cornelius (2002). They found that countries that had further to travel to compete in the 1998 World Cup scored fewer goals and had more goals scored against them.

Also, if there are disadvantages associated with travel, then the *duration of a road trip* could be important—the longer the trip the greater the visitor disadvantage. Again, however, the results have been mixed. For example, for minor league baseball, Courneya and Carron (1991) observed that home teams had a greater home advantage in terms of winning percentage later in their home stand (i.e., length of time they had been at home) as the duration of the visitors' road trip became longer. Conversely, Pace and Carron (1992) found that visiting professional hockey teams were less successful in the initial games on a road trip; as the trip progressed, they had more success. Finally, Smith, Ciacciarelli, Serzan, and Lambert, (2000) undertook research with professional hockey, basketball, and baseball. The duration of the road trip failed to predict home team success in either basketball or baseball. However, insofar as professional hockey was concerned, their findings were identical to those of Pace and Carron. That is, during initial games of the road trip, visiting teams had less success; however, as the road trip progressed, they had more success.

Although the results seem counter-intuitive, Pace and Carron (1992) offered possible explanations as to why there is a positive relationship between success and length of the visiting team's road trip. First, changes in routines would be greatest during the initial games of a road trip. Consequently, players may have trouble acclimatizing to these new routines at the beginning of a road trip. The second explanation may be related to the team's cohesiveness. As teams spend more time together over the course of a road trip, the players are more likely to interact and communicate more with each other. Interaction and communication are associated with increased cohesion

Another line of inquiry has been to examine the possible effects of travel across *time zones*. The severity of jet lag experienced by travellers and subsequent speed of recovery is a function of the number of time zones crossed and the direction of travel. Also, typically, the body readjusts faster after travel in a westward direction ("west is best"). Using archival data from three seasons in Major League Baseball (MLB), Recht et al. (1995) compared performance for teams based in the Eastern time zone and teams in the Pacific time zone (i.e., a three-hour time difference). The only significant finding was that home teams based in the Eastern time zone scored an average 1.24 more runs per game against visiting teams from the Pacific time zone who had just completed eastward travel. A similar finding also emerged in data gathered from the National Football League (NFL). Jehue et al. (1993) found NFL teams from the Pacific time zone lost more games when visiting teams from the Eastern and Central time zones.

Rules Factors. The category of rule factors acknowledges "the possibility that the rules in some sports may favor home teams (e.g., batting last in baseball, last line change in hockey)" (Courneya & Carron, 1992, p. 15). As was pointed out earlier, Wright and House (1989) estimated that 5% (out of 100%) of the home advantage in baseball is due to batting last.

It is difficult to test the effect of the rules on the home advantage, however, because in most situations scientific control is impossible. For example, in professional baseball, the home team not only bats last, it has crowd support, is most familiar with its park, and has not had to travel.

Courneya and Carron (1990) did have access to data from a situation where it was possible to assume that the only game location factor that varied for the two teams was their opportunity to bat last. Results were used from recreation slo-pitch softball leagues where the contests between the teams were double headers and home and visiting team status was alternated (i.e., last bat/first bat). The games were played at neutral sites which were equally familiar to both teams, equally accessible to both teams, and equally accessible to the small numbers of fans from both teams who chose to watch. Courneya and Carron found that batting last did not provide a home advantage.

Critical Psychological States

As the conceptual model presented in Figure 4.1 illustrates, it is assumed that the game location factors will have an effect on the psychological states of two groups of individuals who exert an influence on the outcome of the competition: competitors and coaches.

Competitors. Competitors' psychological states at home versus away have been examined using a variety of protocols including retrospective descriptions, hypothetical scenarios, and concurrent psychological assessment. In total, this body of research has yielded somewhat mixed results.

The studies using retrospective descriptions and hypothetical scenarios have supported a conclusion that athletes' psychological states are superior at home. For example, collegiate basketball players reported to Jurkovac (1985) that they had higher confidence and motivation when playing at home compared to away. Similar results were obtained in a series of studies by Bray and his colleagues (Bray, Culos, Gyurcsik, Widmeyer, & Brawley, 1998; Bray & Widmeyer, 1995, 2000). Female collegiate basketball players reported their teams had higher levels of collective efficacy and that they were less anxious, more motivated, and better able to concentrate when playing at home compared to away. Athletes also believed increased self-confidence played an important role in better performance when competing at home. Finally, when Bar-Eli and his colleagues (1995) presented athletes with home and away competitive scenarios, the athletes indicated that psychological crisis states were less likely to occur when competing at home.

Four studies that have directly examined athlete mood states prior to both home and away competitions have failed to observe differences (Bray & Martin, 2003; Duffy & Hinwood, 1997; Kerr & Vanschaik, 1995; Neave & Wolfson, 2003). Conversely, three studies have found differences (Bray, Jones, & Owen, 2002; Terry, Walrond, & Carron, 1998; Thuot, Kavouras, & Kenefick, 1998). In one of the most comprehensive studies of precompetition psychological states and home advantage, Peter Terry and his colleagues (1998) had male university and club rugby players complete measures of mood, cognitive and somatic state anxiety, and self-confidence prior to a pair of home and away matches. Results showed consistent game location effects across all variables. Cognitive anxiety, somatic anxiety, tension, depression, anger, fatigue, and confusion were all lower prior to the home match compared to the away match, while self-confidence and vigor were higher.

Coaches. The only study examining psychological states of coaches in relation to game location was carried out by William Gayton and his colleagues (2001). Male and female high school coaches from a variety of sports indicated that facility familiarity, travel, crowd support, officiating bias, and self-fulfilling expectancies all contributed to the home advantage for the teams and athletes they coached. Familiarity with the home venue was rated as the most influential factor, while officiating bias was believed to have the weakest effect.

Critical Behavioral States

As Figure 4.1 illustrates, the psychological states of coaches and competitors are assumed to influence their behaviors.

Competitors. The critical behaviors of athletes that could be influenced by game location include performance, aggressiveness, persistence, effort expended, and so on. Essentially, the home team receives more support from the crowd. This, in turn, contributes to heightened motivation. Barry Schwartz and Stephen Barsky (1977) stated that "while we cannot prove it directly, the bits and pieces of evidence we have been able to piece together suggest teams win more games at home because they play more aggressively in their home territories" (p. 646).

Schwartz and Barsky felt that this aggressiveness was manifested more in offensive behaviors. They found, for example, that in baseball, there were no differences in the defensive statistics of errors, double plays, walks, or strikeouts. But, the home teams were superior in the rate of runs scored (i.e., runs scored as a function of the number of times at bat), extra base hits, total hits, and runs as a proportion of hits. In hockey, home teams were superior in terms of shots taken, goals scored, number of assists, and number of assists per goal. And, finally, in basketball, while home teams obtained more rebounds (a defensive measure), they also took more shots and scored more points. Schwartz and Barsky also felt that the superiority of the home team on offense should be expected because *these are precisely the kinds of activities most likely to elicit the approval of a friendly audience. The most casual observation will show that local spectators everywhere reach their highest point of enthusiasm when the home team is at bat or in control of a basketball or puck. The mere possibility of offensive success is enough to excite a crowd. Superb defensive plays, on the other hand, only create a stir after they occur. (p. 652)*

A study by Phillip Varca (1980) also provides support for the view that the differences in success at home versus away can be attributed to factors such as greater aggressiveness, hustle, and intensity. However, Varca found that aggression on offense versus defense is not as important as whether the aggression is functional or dysfunctional. Functional aggression includes behaviors such as rebounds, steals, and blocked shots—skills which facilitate effective performance. On the other, hand, dysfunctional aggression includes fouls—behaviors which detract from effective performance.

The college basketball teams studied by Varca were considerably more successful at home than on the road with a winning percentage of 70% at home. Also, the home teams were more functionally aggressive. They had more steals, rebounds, and blocked shots. At the same time, they committed fewer fouls—the measure of dysfunctional aggression. These results are not inconsistent with the Schwartz and Barsky contention that increased aggressiveness on the part of the home team to secure the social support of the crowd is the basis for the home advantage.

Coaches. For coaches, the critical behaviors that could be influenced by game location include strategic and tactical decisions. For example, professional soccer teams and ice hockey teams often play cautiously and defensively initially when they are playing away from home (Pollard, 1986). Commenting on the approach taken by soccer teams on the road, Pollard (1986) noted that in European Cup competitions, teams adopt ultra-defensive tactics because a 1-0 defeat is considered to be a success.

Dennis and Carron (1999) carried out two studies to determine whether hockey coaches adopt different strategies depending on the location of the game. In Study 1, when National Hockey League and Major Junior-A League were interviewed, they reported using an assertive forechecking style more at home than on the road (81.1% versus 71.8% respectively). In ice hockey, assertive forechecking has specific behavioral characteristics. In the offensive zone, constant pressure is placed on the puck carrier by at least two of the three forwards. Also, the defense plays assertively, "pinching in" along the boards. This system results in the opposition passing the puck and clearing their zone under considerable pressure. The fundamental objective of an assertive defensive strategy is to force a turnover by the opposition in its own zone in order to create a scoring opportunity.

For Study 2, Dennis and Carron (1999) conducted a video analysis of 62 National Hockey League games to assess whether the coaches stated strategies were translated into team play. It was found that the degree of assertive forechecking was even more prevalent than the coaches had suggested (i.e., 90.0% at home versus 82.2% on the road).

Performance Outcomes

The final component in the sequence illustrated in Figure 4.1 reflects the fact that game location can have an effect on performance at a number of levels. The primary performance measures are the foundation for team success—errors in baseball, steals in basketball, shots on net in hockey, and so on. Thus, for example, a team may have more steals or penalties at home than on the road. The secondary performance measures reflect the scoring of the competition—points scored, goals allowed, and so on. It is possible, for example, for teams to score fewer points on the road and still win. Finally, the tertiary performance measures are the traditional outcome measures such as win/loss ratio or points obtained (i.e., two points for a win, one for a tie, and none for a loss). As the discussion above shows, all three levels of performance have been used in research to examine the home advantage.

Can Home Territory be a Disadvantage?

Evidence for a Home Disadvantage

In 1984, Roy Baumeister and Andrew Steinhilber published an interesting article which showed that there are times when competing at home could be a disadvantage—when support from partisan spectators could lead to "choking" by the home team. The Baumeister and Steinhilber analyses of playoff competitions in professional baseball and basketball stimulated considerable discussion, some controversy, and additional research with other professional sports. Eventually, the data for professional baseball and basketball were reexamined 10 years later. All of this is discussed subsequently. First, it may be beneficial to examine the original Baumeister and Steinhilber results and propositions.

In a seven-game championship series in baseball and basketball, Games 1, 2, 5, and 7 were played at the home of the team that had the superior record throughout the regular season. Thus, the home advantage summarized earlier in Table 4.3 might be expected to be even stronger in the playoffs since the stronger team plays more games at home.

For their analyses, Baumeister and Steinhilber excluded all four-game sweeps because it was assumed that they represent a clear superiority on the part of one team. They reasoned that any advantage from playing at home should appear in close competitions, not in one-sided mismatches. (Interestingly, of the ten 4-game sweeps in baseball, five ended with a home victory, five with a visitor victory. Of the seven 4-game sweeps in basketball, five ended with a visitor victory, two with a home victory.)

Games 1 and 2 in baseball and Games 1 to 4 in basketball were used as baseline measures in the two sports. This baseline measure of home team success was then compared with the winning percentage in the last game (which might have been Game 5, 6, or 7) as well as with the winning percentage in Game 7 for those series which went all seven games.

In the initial games (the baseline measure), the home team won 60.2% of the time in baseball and 70.1% of the time in basketball. This advantage in favor of the home team is comparable to results reported for the regular season for basketball but somewhat higher than for baseball (see Table 4.3 again). However, as the championship series progressed and neared completion, the home advantage seemed to reverse itself and become a disadvantage. When the final game was either Game 5, 6, or 7, the winning percentage for the home team dropped to 40.8% in baseball and 46.3% in basketball. When the championship series was tied at three games each, the home advantage virtually disappeared. The home team won only 38.5% of the time in both baseball and basketball.

SECTION 3

MEMBER ATTRIBUTES

Colorado has a superior blend of veterans and youth, dazzling offensive players and muckers, two fabulous lines . . . and the best playoff goalie of his generation. The Avalanche will repeat [as Stanley Cup Champions]. (Farber, 1996, p. 70)

Chapter Five

THE NATURE OF GROUP COMPOSITION

> During the 1950s the Jackie Robinson Brooklyn Dodgers were outspoken, opinionated, bigoted, tolerant, black, white, open, passionate: in short, a fascinating mix of vigorous men. (Kahn, 1972, p. xi)

During World War II, a series of conferences were attended by what was referred to as The Big Three: Franklin Roosevelt, Joseph Stalin, and Winston Churchill. The purpose of these meetings was to negotiate the terms of cooperation between the Allies in their war efforts and then, the terms for peace in Europe following the war. It is doubtful that any group could have had three more contrasting group members. They differed in personality, motives, political ideology, attitudes, and even in energy and physical health since Roosevelt's health was rapidly deteriorating by 1944. Differences also were present within The Big Three in the way in which they were able to get along with each other.

For example, Joseph Alsop (1982), Roosevelt's biographer, noted that Roosevelt and Churchill became very close personal friends and that that close friendship "was the cornerstone of the Western alliance throughout the war . . . a partnership of the war leaders of two great nations like no other one can think of in history" (p. 243). This type of close friendship between two group members has the potential to destroy a three-person group—particularly if the other dyadic relationships within the group are not as positive. And, in The Big Three, they weren't. The relationship between Stalin and Churchill was cool. They were cordial, they respected each other, but there was also mutual suspicion and no friendship in their relationship. Similarly, the relationship between Roosevelt and Stalin was also marked by cordiality and mutual respect but not friendship. Nikita Khrushchev (1970) pointed out in his autobiography that "Stalin was more sympathetic to Roosevelt than Churchill because Roosevelt seemed to have considerable understanding of our problems . . . in disputes during the working sessions in Teheran, Stalin often found Roosevelt siding with him against Churchill" (pp. 222-223). So, here was a group composed of men of completely different personalities and political ideologies who established interpersonal relationships that varied markedly in their friendship. As a group, they were responsible for establishing and maintaining the framework for cooperation between the superpowers and their Allies. Despite their personal differences and the differences in their interpersonal relationships, they operated as a cohesive, effective group. And, the fact that they did testifies to the complex nature of groups.

Although the Big Three could never be described as a typical group, it did have aspects in common with every other group including sport teams. Like every other group, it was composed of independent individuals. Like every other group, those individuals brought a wide range of attitudes, motives, abilities, previous experiences, and other characteristics to the group situation. The quote about the Jackie Robinson's Brooklyn Dodgers used to introduce this chapter highlights this aspect of group membership. Differences among the group members—such as were present in the Big Three or the Brooklyn Dodgers—can split a group. But, in both cases, they didn't. Not surprisingly, researchers have been intrigued by the effect of group composition and member characteristics on group effectiveness. What are the conditions under which personal differences are ignored or even used as elements to build a better group? What are the conditions under which these differences destroy the fabric of the group? In short, how does group composition influence group cohesion and group effectiveness?

Group Composition Defined

Initially, it may be helpful to look at what is meant by group composition and list the approaches that have been used to study it. Shaw (1981) defined it as "the relationships among the characteristics of individuals who compose the group" (p. 454). In a similar vein, McGrath (1964) defined it as "the properties represented by the aggregate of persons who are members of a given group at a given time" (p. 72). The properties referred to by McGrath also represent the resources of that group, the attributes that the group can draw upon to carry out its functions (see Illustration 5.1).

A group's resources—the attributes that the group can draw upon—include the group members' physical size and body type, mental and motor abilities, attitudes, aptitudes, motives, needs, and personality traits. In addition, group members can differ on social identifiers such as age, education, race, sex, and social status. One of the most frequently examined issues in group dynamics research has been the relationship between group composition and group effectiveness.

Illustration 5.1. Athletes bring a variety of resources to the team.

The Widmeyer and Loy Perspective

A frame of reference (see Table 5.1) for considering group composition in sport teams was proposed by Neil Widmeyer and John Loy (1981). They suggested that the properties of sport groups can be considered from three perspectives: in terms of the amount of a resource possessed by the average group member, in terms of the variability in resources present among group members, and in terms of the degree of compatibility between and among members.

With the first approach—looking at group composition in terms of the average amount of an attribute present in the group—the focus is on the *quantity* of the property present and its influence on group performance. Thus, one Davis Cup tennis team might consist of the 1st, 8th, 15th, and 40th ranked players in the world. Another Davis Cup team might consist of the 12th, 14th, 16th, and 22nd ranked players. The average of the individual rankings (which in this example is 16) would represent the amount/quantity of tennis ability present on both teams.

Interest in the amount of group resources is not restricted to ability. For example, a field hockey coach might be interested in determining whether the height and weight of her defense was related to their effectiveness. In order to answer this question, she could compute the average physical size of a number of defensive units and then compare those units for their relative effectiveness. Are larger defenses better? Or, are smaller and quicker ones more effective?

One example of research in which the average amount of a team attribute was studied to determine its relationship to group effectiveness was undertaken by Klein and Christiansen (1969). They focused on the personality trait of need for achievement in basketball players. Their results showed that the greater the amount of average achievement motivation present in basketball teams, the greater was the team's success.

Table 5.1

Three perspectives for considering group composition (Adapted from Widmeyer & Loy, 1981)

Component	Description
Amount of Group Resources	The focus is on the average or total amount of skills and attributes present. The fundamental question is whether the presence of more positive skills and attributes in more members produces a more effective group.
Variability in Group Resources	The focus is on the variability in the skills and attributes of the group members. The fundamental question is whether groups composed of individuals with similar or dissimilar attributes are more effective.
Compatibility of Group Resources	The focus is on the fit between group members in terms of their personal attributes and skills and/or on the fit between the individual's skills and attributes and the task requirements. The fundamental question is whether complementarity between individuals and/or between individuals and their tasks influences group effectiveness.

In the second approach mentioned by Widmeyer and Loy, the *variability* in the team resources is emphasized. In the two Davis Cup tennis teams cited as an example above, the spread among the players in ranking would represent the variability in ability present. What Davis Cup team might be expected to be more successful—the one with players ranked 1, 8, 15, and 40 (i.e., the team which is relatively heterogeneous in ability) or the one with players ranked 12, 14, 16, and 22 (i.e., the team which is relatively homogenous in ability)? When Widmeyer and Loy examined this general issue with female tennis players, they found that homogenous teams were generally more successful.

The third approach involves looking at the *compatibility* of the members in terms of some property considered to be important for group effectiveness. Shaw (1981) referred to this as the *assembly effect*, "the variations in group behavior that are a consequence of the particular combination of persons in the group, apart from the effects produced by the specific characteristics of group members" (pp. 211-212). In the two Davis Cup tennis teams, a doubles pair comprised of individuals ranked 8th and 15th would contain slightly more ability than a doubles team comprised of individuals ranked 16th and 22nd. However, if the higher ranked individuals had conflicting playing styles or did not like each other personally, they might not be effective as a doubles pair.

Carron and Garvie (1978) investigated the assembly effect in a study of international wrestlers. They were interested in determining whether coach-athlete compatibility in personality had any effect on the athlete's absolute performance (final placement) or relative performance (whether the final placement was better or worse than expected). The results revealed that performance success was only minimally related to coach-athlete compatibility in the personality traits of need for control, need for affection, and need for inclusion.

Each of these three approaches to the study of group composition has been used in research conducted in the general area of group dynamics and in the psychology of sport. The results of that research are discussed in Chapters 6, 7, and 8 respectively.

Chapter Six

THE AMOUNT OF GROUP RESOURCES

> Last week's injured Spurs trio of center David Robinson
> . . . and forwards Sean Elliott . . . and Dominique Wilkins
> have 18 All-Star Game selections among them. Their
> replacements, center Will Perdue and forwards Carl Herrera
> and Monty Williams, have none. The circumstances would
> suggest that San Antonio is a lock for a spot in June's draft
> lottery. (MacMullen, 1997, p. 88)

Teams are composed of individuals. And the skills, abilities, energies, and personal characteristics that those individuals bring to the group represent the amount of the team's resources. A team's resources can be represented by either the average or the summed total of the attributes of individuals in a group. The quote used to introduce this section on member attributes illustrates one instance in which a team's resources are predicted to lead to a championship; the quote used to introduce this chapter illustrates a situation in which the absence of a team's resources are predicted to lead to a poor finish. In the present chapter, group resources are considered from two perspectives: (a) the psychosocial characteristics of group members and (b) the ability of the group members.

Psychosocial Attributes of Members

On the basis of common sense or intuition, two contrasting conclusions seem plausible about the relationship between the amount of specific psychosocial attributes of group members and group effectiveness. On the one hand, it seems reasonable to expect that some personal qualities are beneficial to group functioning. Therefore, having a large amount of those qualities in a large number of group members should contribute to group effectiveness. Sociability, extroversion, achievement motivation, conscientiousness, enthusiasm, empathy, intelligence, and dominance are all potentially positive attributes for any group member. Conversely, timidity, suspicion, depression, jealousy, and a lack of self-control are all potentially negative attributes. Thus, it seems plausible that if a large number of members possessed the positive attributes (and in large amounts) and only a few members possessed the negative ones (and in small amounts), the team should be more effective (see Illustration 6.1).

On the other hand, however, it is also intuitively reasonable to expect that the psychosocial attributes of individual team members are unrelated to team performance. People are complex—they possess a large number of attributes in differing degrees and combinations.

Illustration 6.1. The amount of resources available can contribute to group success.

Kluckhohn and Murray (1949) emphasized this point when they observed that each individual is like all other people, like some other people, and like no other person. All of us are intelligent to some extent; we're like every other person in this regard. Some of us are even identical in intelligence. But, our intelligence in combination with all of our other traits makes us unique; we are like no other person. Also, we bring that uniqueness to the group.

The difficulty in determining the relationship of individual psychosocial attributes to team effectiveness was highlighted by Ivan Steiner (1972), who noted that

> *Any single individual may be regarded as a composite of many attributes. He possesses certain skills to a high degree and others in meager measure; he is well informed about some topics and ignorant of others; his personality involves a concatenation of interrelated propensities that may be patterned in myriad ways. Humans are multifaceted beings any two of whom may resemble one another with respect to one property but may be dissimilar with respect to another. For this reason, research dealing with group composition always requires a simplification of unmanageable complexities. (pp. 106-107)*

There is no doubt that the interrelationship of the group members' psychosocial attributes (as one aspect in group composition) is complex. However, one researcher who has attempted to simplify the unmanageable complexities mentioned by Steiner has been Marvin Shaw (1981). After conducting a comprehensive review of the available research for his classic book, *Group dynamics: The psychology of small group behavior,* Shaw concluded that the "personality characteristics of group members play an important role in determining their behavior in groups. The magnitude of the effect of any given characteristic is small but taken together the consequences for group processes are of major significance" (p. 208).

Social and Work Groups

Much of the earliest work on group resources was carried out with social and work groups, not sport teams. The most important attributes identified by Shaw (and their relationship to effectiveness in social and work groups) are presented in Table 6.1. As Shaw pointed out, the relationship is small but there seems to be little doubt that the presence of certain positive interpersonal attributes and the absence of other negative interpersonal attributes do contribute to group cohesion and group effectiveness. The most important interpersonal attributes for group effectiveness are an orientation toward people, social sensitivity, empathy, sociability, and good judgment. If more group members possess these in large degree, the more the group will be positively affected. Insofar as the negative interpersonal attributes are concerned, Shaw concluded that when group members are attracted to things (as opposed to people), it detracts from group cohesion and group effectiveness.

There are also a number of personal attributes that are associated in a positive way with activity within the group, the development of cohesiveness, and group effectiveness. These include intelligence, dependability, integrity, responsibility, self-reliance, personal adjustment, emotional control, and emotional stability. Conversely, a number of negative personal attributes detract from group effectiveness. These include a lack of conventionality, anxiety, neuroticism, and a tendency toward depression.

Finally, Shaw identified a number of attributes that are associated with involvement in leadership roles within the group. These are intelligence, authoritarianism, dominance, assertiveness, and ascendancy. In every instance, if group members possess these to a large degree, they are more active within the group and assume a more prominent role in the group's leadership.

Sport Groups

In the context of sport, there are two avenues of research that have indirectly or directly dealt with the effect of athlete psychosocial attributes on team effectiveness. One avenue, descriptive in nature, has been concerned with whether team and individual sport athletes

Table 6.1
The influence of various traits on group involvement (Adapted from Shaw, 1981)

Trait	Effect on Group Involvement
Members with high intelligence	Are more active and popular, less conforming, in leadership roles
Authoritarian members	Are more demanding and more conforming
Members with high social sensitivity	Are more readily accepted and enhance group effectiveness
Members interpersonally ascendant	More readily conform, assume leadership roles, are more popular, more frequently engage in group activities, contribute to group cohesion and have more impact on decisions
Members high in dependability	More readily become leaders and enhance group effectiveness
Members high in conventionality	Inhibit group effectiveness
Members high in anxiety	Inhibit group effectiveness
Members high in personal adjustment	Enhance group effectiveness

differ in personality. According to Walter Kroll, if there are differences between these two categories of athletes, two underlying mechanisms might be in operation (Kroll, 1967). One is that a process of natural selection is at work. Those athletes who have the personal qualities necessary to be effective members of a particular type of sport group select and stay (or are retained); the others leave. The second is that group experiences help to develop certain personal qualities within the athlete.

Obviously, any link between the personal characteristics of the athlete and the effectiveness of the group is indirect. But, if personal characteristics such as intelligence, social sensitivity, dependability, and so on are important for social and work group effectiveness, there is no reason to believe that the same or similar personal attributes are not equally important in sport groups.

Team and Individual Sport Competitors

Schurr, Ashley, and Joy (1977), in a comprehensive study, compared the personality traits of 1956 college male team sport athletes, individual sport athletes, and non-athletes. Athletes were categorized as participating in either team sports (e.g., basketball) or individual sports (e.g., golf). Major differences in personality were found between individual sport athletes and team sport athletes. Team sport athletes differed from the individual sport athletes in a number of qualities that should lead to increased team cohesion and improved team effectiveness. For example, team sport athletes were more extroverted, more dependent on others, and less sensitive. In addition, the individual sport athletes also possessed a number of qualities that should lead to more effective involvement in their groups such as independence and low anxiety. The key word in both cases, however, is should. While these traits are positive and, therefore, should lead to improved group effectiveness, there is no direct evidence to demonstrate this link.

Individual Orientations in Groups

A second avenue of research does permit more direct inferences to the group composition-group effectiveness issue. It is directly concerned with whether the individual orientation or motivation of group members influences team effectiveness. Motivation, a theoretical concept, is used to represent the selectivity, the intensity, and the persistence in behavior. Thus, for example, if one athlete chooses to train while a second does not, this choice (i.e., different selection) is considered to be a manifestation of motivation. Also, if two athletes are training and one works harder than the other, this effort (i.e., greater intensity) is also considered to be a manifestation of motivation. Finally, if two athletes are training and one continues after the other has stopped, this persistence (i.e., greater duration) is also considered to be a manifestation of motivation.

Motivation accounts for both the focus (selection) and the energy (intensity and duration) for behavior. Thus, theorists in group dynamics have assumed that it is possible to determine the nature and strength of a group's primary goals by examining the primary motivation of its individual members. Also, because a distinction is made in group dynamics research between individual motives and group motives, both of these perspectives have been examined.

Interpersonal motivation may even determine whether an individual will participate in team sports. Ryckman and Hamel (1992) examined female adolescents' intrapersonal motives related to involvement in organized team sports. They found that friendship formation or maintenance was one of the important reasons why girls participated in organized team sports. As well, they found that girls with more extensive involvement in sports were more achievement-oriented, suggesting that they like challenging tasks and strive to be successful. This may have implications for adherence to team sports. Girls who are motivated to form and maintain friendships may enjoy playing team as opposed to individual sports. Athletes involved in a sport they enjoy are more apt to remain in that sport.

Bernard Bass and his colleagues made one of the more important contributions relating to individual motivation in groups (Bass, 1962; Bass, Dunteman, Frye, Vidulich, & Wambach, 1963; Dunteman & Bass, 1963). Their work was based on the assumption that individual behavior in group situations is a product of the person's needs and motives. In fact, Bass and his colleagues (1963) even stated that the group is "merely the theatre in which certain generalized needs can be satisfied" (p. 102). In short, it was proposed that people get involved in group activities to satisfy their individual needs.

There are some slight differences in perception about the significant types of needs that individuals want satisfied in group situations. Hollander (1967), for example, has stated that two main clusters of needs are predominant: task motives and affiliation motives. The task motives are associated with the group's goals and objectives. When a group is engaged in activities that are task oriented (playing basketball, practicing with an elite team), the individual's task needs are fulfilled. The affiliation motives are associated with social needs and interpersonal relationships. Thus, when group members have an opportunity to socialize with one another before or after practice and to develop and maintain friendships through participation in sport, their social needs are fulfilled.

Bass and his colleagues proposed that in addition to a task and affiliation motive, group members also have a self-motive—an orientation toward personal rewards and goals. Again, by way of example, if the self-motivation of the members of a basketball team was predominant, it could be predicted that the athletes would be satisfied with good personal statistics even if the team was unsuccessful.

The influence of affiliation and task motivation on the success and satisfaction experienced by 1,200 college males participating on 144 intramural basketball teams was examined by Rainer Martens (1970). The task and affiliation motives of each athlete were assessed by a questionnaire administered prior to the season. The average response for the members of each team was then computed. On the basis of these average scores, the teams were categorized as low, moderate, or high in task motivation and affiliation motivation. Each team's win-loss record was used as the measure of success and the degree of team satisfaction was obtained by averaging the individual responses from a postseason questionnaire.

Martens found that the two motives were quite distinct in their effect upon performance and satisfaction. The teams that were high in affiliation motivation were less successful but were more satisfied than teams that were low in affiliation motivation (see Figure 6.1). Thus, when affiliation motivation (a concern with developing and maintaining warm personal relationships within a group) is relatively high for all of the members on a team,

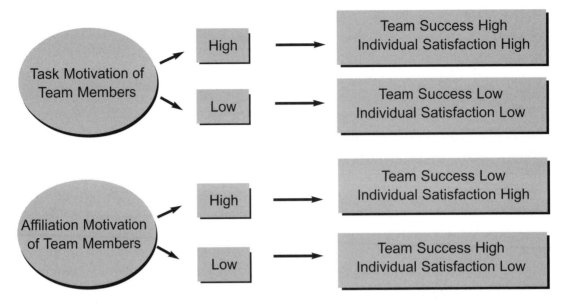

Figure 6.1. The effect of high task and affiliation motives in group members on team success and individual satisfaction (Adapted from Martens, 1970)

performance effectiveness and ultimate success suffer. From an individual perspective, however, this may be unimportant; the members are satisfied with their group experience.

Martens also found that teams that were high in task motivation were more successful and more satisfied than the teams that were low in task motivation. So, when task motivation—an orientation toward the group's performance goals and effective completion of the group task—is high on a team, that team's performance effectiveness and ultimate success benefits. Also, the individuals are more satisfied with their group experience.

A number of other authors have also examined the personal orientation of group members and its relationship to group effectiveness (see Table 6.2). For example, Cooper and Payne (1967) found a correlation of .72 was present in soccer teams between the high task motivation of coaches and trainers and team success. Subsequently, Cooper and Payne (1972) also reported that athletes on more successful soccer teams were more task-oriented and less self- and affiliation-oriented than athletes on less successful teams.

Sorrentino and Sheppard (1978) examined two affiliation motives of swimmers in individual versus group competition. They discovered that approval-oriented swimmers (i.e., motive to gain approval is greater than the motive to avoid social rejection) had faster swimming speeds in group versus individual competitions, whereas rejection-threatened (i.e., motive to avoid social rejection is greater than motive to gain approval) swimmers had slower swimming speeds in group than in individual competition. Thus, it may be more beneficial for teams to have athletes who are approval-oriented than rejection-threatened in order to maximize performance and minimize social loafing (see Chapter 3).

In summary, the results of the research outlined in Table 6.2 contribute to a suggestion that teams composed of players who are highly task-motivated, self-motivated, and approval-oriented are likely to perform better than teams comprised of individuals who possess lesser amounts of these qualities. Further, the Widmeyer (1977) study showed that the influence of these motives was mediated by other variables (e.g., group cohesion). Thus, when examining the effect of the quantity of group resources, several resources should be examined simultaneously using a multivariate approach (Widmeyer, 1990).

In an attempt to determine whether this startling reversal of the home advantage was due to the home team choking or to the visiting team excelling, Baumeister and Steinhilber analyzed individual performances in the baseline games and the seventh game. They chose errors in baseball as the measure of choking because, unlike pitching or batting, they are not directly influenced by the other team. An error, by definition, is a poor performance that, in the judgment of the official scorer, should have been handled successfully. In basketball, free throws were used. This is also an individual performance measure that is not mutually determined by the athlete and an opponent. Therefore, it is also a relatively good measure of choking.

It was expected that for all of these measures, the home team should have an advantage. In the World Series, for example, the home team is much more familiar with the playing surface and its idiosyncrasies. It has had a full season of games in the stadium whereas the visitors have only played three previous playoff games. In basketball, the home team isn't subject to the same harassment and distractions while shooting free throws. Nonetheless, despite these advantages, members of the home team performed more poorly in Game 7 than members of the visiting team. In baseball, for example, in the initial games (the baseline measure), the home team committed less errors than the visitors (.65 versus 1.04 per game) and had more errorless games (33 versus 18 games). But, in Game 7, the home team committed more errors than the visitors (1.31 versus .81 per game) and had fewer errorless games (6 versus 12 games).

In basketball, the home and visiting teams were approximately equal in the initial games (the baseline measure). The home team shot 72% from the free throw line, the visitors, 73%. In Game 7, however, while the visitors stayed about the same (74%), the home team dropped to 69%. On the basis of these results, Baumeister and Steinhilber concluded that the reversal of home advantage in Game 7 was primarily due to choking on the part of the home team, not improvement on the part of the visiting team.

According to Baumeister (1985), the underlying reason for the home team's choke is that athletes become preoccupied with what he referred to as self-presentation (i.e., they start to dwell on how they will perform, look to others, be perceived by others, be described by others). Everybody has self-presentation concerns. A young child in a race may simply want to avoid looking foolish; another may want to be first and be "the fastest in Grade 6." When an event increases in importance, concerns with self-presentation also increase. When there is an opportunity to claim a desired identity—"champion," "winner," "best," "smartest"—concerns with self presentation also increase. And, when there is an opportunity to claim a desired identity in front of a sympathetic, supportive audience, concerns with self presentation are maximal.

Baumeister suggested that as a result of the heightened concerns with self-presentation, athletes begin to pay too much attention to what they are doing and how they are doing it. Instead of performing their skills automatically, they begin to concentrate on a step-by-step execution. The result is that performance becomes poorer. Baumeister pointed out,

> *The pressure, the chance for self-redefinition and the audience all encourage choking by the home team. Most pro athletes are tough and experienced enough to cope with one or two of these factors during the season. But the combination of all three—found chiefly in championship play—is psychologically different from regular-season play. That may be why it is so rare for a team to win a championship the first time it qualifies for the*

playoffs. And, it is not surprising that even seasoned athletes become self-conscious and choke. (p. 52)

If this is the case, a question of interest is, is a home disadvantage present in the play-offs in other sports?

The Search for the Generality of a Home Disadvantage

The results from research with other sports have produced mixed results; some studies have found a home disadvantage during playoffs, others have not. One of the earliest studies published after the Baumeister and Steinhilber research was carried out by Gayton, Matthews, and Nickless (1987) with professional hockey (i.e., the National Hockey League). Using the same baseline measures as Baumeister and Steinhilber, they failed to find a home disadvantage. The home advantage in terms of winning percentage was 53.8% in the initial games, 52.5% when Games 5, 6, and 7 were considered as the last game, and 58.3% when the series went to a deciding seventh game.

Interestingly, in a subsequent study, Edward Wright and his colleagues (Wright, Voyer, Wright, and Roney, 1995) did report that a home disadvantage exists in National Hockey League playoff competitions. They used games 1 and 3 as their baseline measures and compared these baseline results against the last game in the playoff series (whether it was game 4, 5, 6, or 7). Unfortunately, they did not present percentage values so a direct comparison against the Gayton et al. results is not possible. They also failed to speculate on why their results were different from what Gayton and his colleagues had found.

Another sport in which a home disadvantage during playoff competitions has not been found is American football. Alan Kornspan and his colleagues (Kornspan, Lerner, Ronayne, Etzel, & Johnson, 1995) found that home teams have won 71% of the playoff games held in the two conferences of the National Football League—no support whatsoever for a home team choke.

Conversely, however, Wright, Jackson, Christie, McGuire, and Wright (1991) did find support for a home disadvantage in golf. They compared the scores of contending British (i.e., "home") golfers with those of contending foreign golfers from the first to final rounds of the British Open Golf Championship. It was noted that the scores of contending British golfers dropped off more during the course of the competition than those of foreign golfers who were also in contention.

Overview of the Home Disadvantage

Sport Research. So, what can we make of the above? Is it reasonable to conclude that teams choke in championship competitions played in front of home spectators? The jury seems to be out insofar as the results from sport research are concerned. That is, various authors have suggested that the conclusion that a home disadvantage is present in championship competitions should be questioned because of a) the small number of games on which that conclusion is based, b) the failure to find a home disadvantage in other sports such as football and hockey, and c) the failure to find a home disadvantage when perennially dominant teams are excluded from the analyses (Benjafield, Liddell, & Benjafield, 1989; Courneya & Carron, 1992; Heaton & Sigall, 1989).

A fourth compelling reason why the conclusion may be tenuous is that a reanalysis of basketball and baseball by Barry Schlenker and his colleagues—which also included playoff results over the past 10 years—casts doubt about the presence of a home-team choke in those sports as well (Schlenker, Phillips, Boniecki, & Schlenker, 1995). Schlenker and his colleagues observed that

> *there is no convincing evidence for a home-field championship choke that places the home team at a disadvantage in decisive contests. The home team has an advantage in all phases of a championship series. (Schlenker et al., 1995, p. 641)*

Schlenker et al. suggested that the home disadvantage found by Baumeister and Steinhilber could have been due to one aberrant period in the history of baseball—1950-1968. During that period, visiting teams won 9 of 11 World Series that went to a seventh game. Throughout the remaining history of the World Series (and League Championship games), home teams had a consistent advantage.

The last word, however, should probably go to Roy Baumeister (1995). In a rebuttal of the Schlenker et al. work, Baumeister pointed out that

> *despite using an imprecise, weak analysis strategy and including data that were confounded by rule changes (which they did not mention), Schlenker et al. (1995) still found results that did not differ significantly from those found by Baumeister and Steinhilber (1984). They merely found that the effect dropped below significance. This does not seem to justify a sweeping conclusion that the home-field disadvantage hypothesis is wrong. (p. 646)*

Laboratory research. Most importantly, Baumeister also noted that it is difficult to support or reject a hypothesis using archival data only. On the positive side, archival data provide the researcher with the opportunity to examine real-life phenomena in their natural context. On the negative side, however, archival data do not afford the researcher the same level of scientific control characteristic of research undertaken in the laboratory.

Moreover, research carried out in laboratory settings has shown that individuals do choke in exactly those self-presentation situations identified by Baumeister and Steinhilber—when the pressure is high and the individual has an opportunity for self-redefinition (Baumeister, Hamilton, & Tice, 1985; Baumeister, Hutton, & Cairns, 1990; Heaton & Sigall, 1991). So, while the jury seems to be out in terms of the results from sport research, evidence from non-sport contexts does provide support for the concept of a "championship choke."

> **Box 6.1**
> ***The amount of resources on a sport team***
>
> The Lakers already had some great veteran talent. Kareem Abdul-Jabbar was on his way to becoming the greatest scorer in NBA history. Point guard Norm Nixon was among the league leaders in steals and assists. Jamaal Wilkes averaged close to twenty points a game, and Michael Cooper was about to break onto the scene and become the greatest sixth man in the game. (Riley, 1993, p. 32).

of cohesion and ability to success in intramural basketball teams, Widmeyer and Gosset (1978) found that team member ability correlated .73 with team success.

In a third, more comprehensive report, Widmeyer and Loy (1989) had two independent raters judge the skill of eight female tennis players in the serve, volley, forehand, and backhand. Win-loss records were assessed for the 28 teams (i.e., the 8 players combined as teammates in all of the possible combinations). The results showed that the average ability of the two players was related to the team's effectiveness. The correlations for the individual components were .30 between the doubles team's forehand ability and team success; .42 for the doubles team's ability to serve and team success; .61 for the doubles team's ability to volley and team success; and .79 for the doubles team's backhand ability and team success. The correlation between overall individual tennis ability and team success was .77. The authors suggested that backhand ability was the best predictor of team success because of a greater variation for this stroke across all players than for any of the other abilities tested.

Another extensive investigation of the relationship of individual ability to team success was carried out by Jones (1974). He used individual statistics in professional tennis (singles rankings), baseball (runs batted in and earned run averages), basketball (points, assists, rebounds), and football (points for and against). These statistics were then correlated with team effectiveness as represented by rankings and win-loss records. Team effectiveness and individual skill and ability were correlated .70 in men's tennis, .80 in women's tennis, .91 in football, .94 in baseball, and .60 in basketball.

The fact that the highest relationship found by Jones was in baseball and the lowest was in basketball is consistent with what would be predicted from Steiner's proposition that actual productivity is a product of the potential productivity of a group minus the losses due to faulty group processes. Faulty group processes result primarily from the inability of group members to coordinate their efforts efficiently and effectively. In baseball, the amount of coordination required on offense and defense is relatively small so the potential losses due to faulty group processes in any team would be small. Consequently, the team with the best actual productivity (win-loss record) should most frequently be the one with the best potential productivity (i.e., the best players). In the Jones study, this was the case as reflected in the very high correlation of .94.

In basketball, greater coordinative team play is required on offense and defense. Thus, individual talent by itself (potential productivity) is not as strongly related to actual productivity. The ability to play well together (i.e., to minimize the process losses) is important. This was also reflected in the relatively lower correlation of .60 found by Jones. A summary of the relationships between members' ability resources and team performance outcome is presented in Table 6.3.

Table 6.3
The Relationships Between the Quantity of Members' Ability and Team
Performance Outcome (Adapted from Widmeyer, 1990)

Reference	Sport/Skill	Relationship to Team Performance
Jones (1974)	Women's Pro Tennis	r = .80
Jones (1974)	Men's Pro Tennis	r = .71
Jones (1974)	Pro Football	r = .91
Jones (1974)	Pro Baseball	r = .94
Jones (1974)	Pro Basketball	r = .60
Widmeyer & Gossett (1978)	Men's Intramural Basketball	r = .73
Spense (1980)	Women's Intramural Basketball	r = .78
Widmeyer et al. (1980)	Men's Club Tennis	r = .54
Widmeyer & Loy (1989)	Women's Tennis Forehand	r = .30
Widmeyer & Loy (1989)	Women's Tennis Backhand	r = .79
Widmeyer & Loy (1989)	Women's Tennis Serve	r = .42
Widmeyer & Loy (1989)	Women's Tennis Volley	r = .61
Widmeyer & Loy (1989)	Women's Tennis Overall	r = .77

Although the relationship between individual measures of ability and team performance are not perfect (i.e., a combination of the best individuals does not always produce the best team), there is sufficient strong evidence to support the view that coaches should always select on ability first. Diane Gill (1984) emphasized this point in her summary of the research on the relationship of individual ability to team ability:

> *Perhaps the most basic finding is that research supports our common belief*
> *in the general individual ability-group performance relationship; the best*
> *individuals make the best team. No evidence suggests any reason for select-*
> *ing any but the most skilled or capable individual performers. (p. 325)*

Further, there are a number of psychosocial attributes that contribute to effective group performance in social and work groups. Similarly, there are also a number of psychosocial attributes that detract from group effectiveness. Unfortunately, however, psychosocial attributes are partly a product of heredity and partly a product of daily social experiences and learning. Consequently, they develop (and change) very slowly over time. Thus, it's unrealistic to expect that a six-month or one-year athletic season can have a major effect on a team member's psychosocial attributes. It is possible, however, for a coach to emphasize the importance of behavior consistent with these specific attributes, reinforce the positive behaviors when they occur, and discourage any negative manifestations. In addition, it must be kept in mind that more successful sport teams seem to contain members who are high on task motivation. The task, the performance goals and objectives of the team, must be consistently emphasized through group goal-setting programs.

Chapter Seven

THE VARIABILITY IN GROUP RESOURCES

> At 35 he [Paul Coffey, defenseman for the Philadelphia Flyers of the National Hockey League] remains a defensive risk but a supreme offensive force, capable of adding dash to a miserable power play that through Sunday ranked 21st in the league. (Farber, 1997a, p. 54)

The variability of group resources—or homogeneity (i.e., composed of similar parts) versus heterogeneity (i.e., composed of dissimilar parts) as it is also called—has been the topic of considerable research and debate for a wide variety of groups. Depending upon the nature of the group and its task, variability has been considered to be beneficial, detrimental, or even both. As one example, Alvin Zander (1982), a psychologist who has extensively researched and written on groups, pointed out that homogeneity is beneficial to group development because it

> *encourages a group sense. Birds of a feather flock together, and create a more distinct entity when they do. People too form a better unit if they are alike, and an effective leader develops oneness within a set by encouraging likeness among members. To do this, she recruits persons who will interact well because of similar purpose, background, training, experience, or temperament. She pays special attention to their basic values (what they feel they should or should not do) because similarity in values plays a major part in determining who associates with whom and who remains within an organization. Persons whose beliefs do not fit together well have a hard time forming a strong group, as has been observed in school boards, management committees, or fraternities. (p. 3)*

Zander was referring to homogeneity in psychological attributes. Common sense indicates, however, that homogeneity in physical skills and attributes might not always be desirable. When World Cup or All-Star teams are selected for international competition, for example, heterogeneity of skill is considered an essential. The performance of sport teams is enhanced by the presence of different individuals who have the skills to play different roles. This is illustrated in the quote in Box 7.1 by former Los Angeles Lakers' coach Pat Riley. No soccer team, field hockey team, or basketball team could hope to be successful if each team member possessed identical skills.

If a basketball team was composed solely of guards, no matter how effective those guards were, the team would lack major resources when playing teams composed of athletes capable of playing the post position, the forward position, the guard position, and so

> **Box 7.1**
> *The variability in team resources*
>
> Earvin had both style and efficiency and knew when to let one dominate over the other. He quickly established himself as a dominant player, but he did it in a unique way. He was an avid student of all styles of basketball. Instead of crushing his team-mates under his greatness, he studied their styles and figured out how he, as the man controlling the movement of the ball, could help them get the most out of their abilities. He dealt to their strengths. (Riley, 1993, p. 33)

on. "The division of responsibility present on sport teams—setter and spiker in volleyball, blocking and pass receiving in football, playmaking and rebounding in basketball—requires heterogeneous skills if the team is to be successful" (Carron, 1981a, p. 250; see Illustration 7.1).

The quote used to introduce this chapter provides an example of how heterogeneity in the variety of skills enhances team effectiveness. The first responsibility of a defenseman is defense. However, National Hockey League Hall of Fame player Paul Coffey had a dimension in his game that few other defensemen who have played ice hockey have possessed—exceptional offensive ability. His offensive ability differentiated Coffey (i.e., made him heterogeneous) from other defensemen on his team and in the league and provided his team with offensive potential.

Social, Work, and Sport Groups

On the basis of their research in business and industry, Richard Hackman and Greg Oldham (1980), two industrial psychologists, provided several generalizations related to the relationship between group composition and group effectiveness. One generalization is that the group should possess both homogeneity and heterogeneity in the characteristics of its members. For example, homogeneity enhances communication while heterogeneity limits it. The link between homogeneity and communication represents the basis for the Hackman and Oldham proposition that some similarity among members will contribute to group effectiveness. At the same time, however, heterogeneity among group members

Illustration 7.1. Heterogeneity in the resources available can contribute to group success.

insures that varied perspectives, skills, and attitudes are brought to the group. These varied resources help the group—as long as the group members are able to work together.

The homogeneity versus heterogeneity issue has also been approached from the point of view of the group task (Steiner, 1972). Table 7.1 contains an overview. In *additive tasks* where the group product results from the combined efforts of the group members (e.g., track teams), the question of homogeneity versus heterogeneity is largely irrelevant. If one team has more competent members than another team, its output will be better; if it has more incompetent members, its product will be poorer. The variability among members is not an issue except to the degree that relatively incompetent members will drag the group down.

The issue of homogeneity versus heterogeneity is also largely irrelevant in *compensatory tasks*—tasks in which the group product is the average of the results from individual members. Judging in gymnastics or diving is an example. Ultimately an average score representing the pooled evaluations of the individual judges is used. So, as was the case with additive tasks, the important issue is the competence of all of the judges, not the variability among them.

Table 7.1

Steiner's task types and productivity when individual resources are homogeneous versus heterogeneous

Type of Task	Production Effects	Homogeneity versus Heterogeneity
Additive	Group product is the sum of individual products; e.g., tug of war	Homogeneity vs. heterogeneity is irrelevant
Compensatory	Group product is the average of individual products; e.g., judging in gymnastics	Homogeneity vs. heterogeneity is irrelevant
Eureka Disjunctive	Group product is an either-or solution; one individual's output is used; e.g., calculating batting averages	Heterogeneity is best because there is an increased likelihood that individuals with requisite skills will be available
Noneureka Disjunctive	Group product is a judgment solution; one individual's output is used; e.g., selecting an all-star team	Heterogeneity is best because there is an increased likelihood that individuals with requisit skills will be available
Unitary Conjunctive	Group product is the result of the combined efforts of all and no division of labor is possible; e.g., mountain climbing team	Homogeneity is best because no single group member will hold back the team.
Conjunctive (Divisible with matching to tasks)	Group product is the result of the combined efforts of all and a division of labor is possible; volleyball team.	Heterogeneity is best if individual skills can be matched to the task.
Discretionary (Variable)	Group output is the result of an autocratic, democratic, or delegative decision	Homogeneity vs. heterogeneity is irrelevant

Steiner has suggested that heterogeneity of ability has the tendency to establish higher levels of productivity when the task is *disjunctive* (Steiner's task typology is discussed in greater depth in Chapter 3). There are two types of disjunctive tasks. When a group of coaches is faced with a problem that involves an either-or solution, that task would be *eureka disjunctive*. Deciding which of two athletes to select in a professional draft would be an example. If that same group of coaches was faced with a problem that was more philosophical in nature (e.g., determining the team's defensive philosophy), the task would be *noneureka disjunctive*. For both eureka and noneureka disjunctive tasks, heterogeneity is better than homogeneity. Varied resources, different insights, and different approaches can be brought to bear on the same question. Consequently, there is a greater chance that somebody in the group will have the skill and expertise to solve the problem.

In the case of *unitary conjunctive tasks*, such as mountain climbing, all group members participate equally and contribute to the group product. Thus, the group is only as strong as its weakest link. Homogeneity is an advantage in this case "because it permits a high level of potential productivity and is less likely than heterogeneity to generate dissatisfaction among superior members of the group" (Steiner, 1972, p. 112).

Divisible conjunctive tasks are another case. These types of tasks require a specialized division of labor. The process of assembling any sport team is an example. Both offensive and defensive specialists, rebounders and playmakers are required. Consequently, heterogeneity in the team's membership increases the likelihood that individuals with more specialized resources will be available. Also, if the specialized skills of team members can be matched to the task demands, the group's performance is more effective.

Discretionary tasks evolve from leadership and/or decision-making situations. In any decision-making situation, there are a variety of ways in which the group can arrive at the solution to a problem (Forsythe, 1983). The four most frequently used—(autocratic, participative, consultative, delegative) are discussed in detail in Chapter 13 (see Table 13.4). Since one individual makes the decision for the group in the autocratic, consultative, and delegative approaches, homogeneity versus heterogeneity is irrelevant. The democratic approach is similar to the approach used in compensatory tasks. So, again, the issue of homogeneity versus heterogeneity is irrelevant.

In social and work groups, there is a high degree of flexibility in terms of the assignment of individuals to specific tasks. This same level of flexibility is not always present in sport teams; a coach usually works with the talent available. Possibly this is one of the reasons why the issue of heterogeneity versus homogeneity has received so little attention in sport research. The research that has been carried out has focused on the effect of differences in the depth of ability (i.e., the amount of skill group members possess) rather than the breadth of abilities (i.e., the variety of skills members bring to the group). Nevertheless, there have been some investigations of the effects of variability in sex, age, race, and certain social psychological characteristics in work settings and to a smaller extent in sport settings.

It is useful to examine the conditions under which heterogeneity and homogeneity are beneficial, detrimental, or unimportant on sport teams. The following section focuses on research on variability in the sport environment complemented by some examples from social and work groups.

Variability in Sex

Wood (1987) conducted a meta-analytic review of 52 laboratory studies that examined productivity and gender as a group composition variable. Wood found that when working in same sex groups, the performance of men's groups was superior to that for women's groups. It was suggested that this finding might be due to the nature of either the task or the setting—in many of the laboratory studies the tasks used favored men's interests and abilities over women's.

Wood also located 13 studies that examined mixed-sex groups. Comparisons between mixed-sex versus all-male or all-female groups showed that there is a tendency for mixed-sex groups to be superior in performance. It is unclear, however, what contributes to this effect. Hoffman (1965) stated that mixed-sex groups may be more effective than same-sex groups because of the diverse resources brought to the task by men and women. For example, the combination of men's and women's interaction styles in mixed-sex groups equips the group to be moderately effective both at tasks requiring task activity and at those requiring social activity. Conversely, a popular stereotype is that all-male groups are less effective than mixed-sex ones at tasks requiring social activity, and all-female groups are less effective at tasks requiring task activity.

Hare (1976), however, has argued that same-sex groups are more efficient than mixed-sex groups because same-sex groups spend less time on socio-emotional activities. Shaw (1981) suggested that the conclusion by Hare and Hoffman may both be correct; mixed-sex groups may be more effective than same-sex groups when the task solution requires differing perspectives, but mixed-sex groups may be less efficient if the presence of members of the opposite sex distracts from task performance.

Is the effect of sex as a group composition factor important in sport teams and physical activity groups? Widmeyer (1990) stated that this question has not been of great concern to researchers examining competitive sport because co-ed teams rarely compete against same-sex teams. Nonetheless, the question is important in that the answer may provide insight into the enjoyment of participants in co-ed recreational teams versus same-sex recreational teams. As well, the sex composition of exercise classes may influence participant's enjoyment and consequently their adherence. For example, Marshall and Heslin (1975) found that females preferred large groups to small groups when they were in a mixed-sex setting, but they preferred small groups to large groups when they were in a same-sex setting.

Variability in Age

The lack of research pertaining to the effect of variability in age in teams is largely the result of age restrictions imposed in sport. Would variability in age in sport and exercise groups have an effect on member satisfaction, performance, or adherence? McGuire (1985) did examine preferences for homogeneity versus heterogeneity in age with 223 seniors and 115 university students participating in various leisure activities. Seniors preferred older participants when they were engaged in sedentary activities such as leatherwork, flower arranging, needlework, sewing, cooking, and carpentry. On the other hand, the seniors preferred younger participants for more active "youthful" pursuits such as hiking, bicycling, football, waterskiing, swimming, and kite flying. These findings could have implications for exercise adherence of the elderly. If seniors have a preference for participating in exercise with younger companions, then programs aimed at exercise adherence for seniors may benefit from heterogeneity in age composition of the group.

Variability in Race

Research on the effect of race differences on group dynamics was heavily examined in the United States in the 1960s because of the substantial increase in the number of black-white groupings resulting from school desegregation, affirmative action, and other social reforms (Davies, 1994; Shaw, 1981). Today, racially mixed groups are common in the military, the work place, the school system, exercise classes, and athletics (Widmeyer, 1990) and research interest has declined.

In the sport environment, several researchers have studied the effects of racial heterogeneity on the performance of athletic teams (Anshel & Sailes, 1990; Jones, 1974; Klein & Christiansen, 1969). For example, Aamodt, Kimbrough, and Alexander (1983) examined the relationship between team racial heterogeneity and team performance in the starting lineup of college basketball teams. The teams were categorized on the basis of their degree of racial heterogeneity: homogeneous (all white or all black), slightly heterogeneous (four black and one white or four white and one black) and heavily heterogeneous (three white and two black or three black and two white). It was found that there were more homogeneous black teams than homogeneous white teams. Further, the slightly heterogeneous teams performed better than both the homogeneous teams and the heavily heterogeneous teams. Aamodt et al. (1983) noted that it is important to recognize that it is unlikely that race alone caused the differences in team performance. Other variables masked by race (e.g., personality, socioeconomic status, attitude toward school) could have had an effect.

Anshel and Sailes (1990) examined the psychological needs and perceptions of the sport environment of intercollegiate black and white athletes participating in basketball, football, baseball, and volleyball. It was noted that black and white athletes differed in their orientations toward white coaches. The black athletes tended to be less trusting and more distant from white coaches, were less receptive to negative information feedback from the coach, and perceived the coach to be too authoritative before competition. In regards to performance, black athletes made more internal attributions (i.e., took more responsibility) for winning and losing. These differences notwithstanding, white and black teammates tended to interact positively. Anshel and Sailes suggested that this was possible due to the similar attitudes toward competition among all athletes.

One aspect of race composition in team sports that has received a great deal of attention is the relationship between race and playing position. In 1970, Loy and McElvogue published their classic study on the racial composition of player positions in professional team sports. The authors' examined occupational discrimination in sport by comparing the racial makeup of the central and noncentral positions on professional baseball and football teams. The concept of centrality (which is discussed in greater depth in Chapter 9) is that those positions located closest to the physical center of the team's network (e.g., quarterback, pitcher, center) allow greater social interaction, require more leadership ability, and provide more prestige for the occupant. In short, the central positions are more important for team success. Loy and McElvogue found that central positions were occupied primarily by white players and that noncentral positions were over-represented by black players. Subsequent research in other sports has shown a similar pattern (see Table 7.2).

In discussing the question of why central positions seemed to be primarily occupied by white players and the noncentral positions primarily occupied by black players, White and Willits (1991) suggested that there is no conclusive evidence to support the view that assignment to position is explained by psychological or physiological difference between the races. Thus, relationship between race and playing position may reflect what Maguire (1987) refers to as "socially constructed racial discrimination."

Table 7.2
The Relationship Between Race and Playing Position

Author	Sport	Result
Ball (1973)	Canadian football	Overrepresentation of whites in central positions
Eitzen & Sanford (1975)	College football	Blacks were over-represented in one central position (offensive guard), and underrepresented in all other central positions. Blacks were overrepresented in the three non-central positions (wide receiver, running back, and defensive back).
Hallinan (1991)	Rugby	Black Aboriginal rugby players were over-represented in non-central positions.
Leonard (1977)	Professional baseball	White players were overrepresented in central positions (pitcher & catcher). Black players were overrepresented in non-central playing positions (outfield).
McGuire (1987)	Professional soccer	Black players were underrepresented in central positions.
Marsh & Heitman (1981)	College football	Black players underrepresented in all central positions except linebacker and overrepresented in non-central positions.
McGehee & Paul (1986)	College football	Black players were underrepresented in central positions of quarterback, center, and offensive guard.
Norris & Jones (1998)	Professional Soccer	Black players were underrepresented in certain positions (e.g., goalie) and overrepresented in other positions (e.g., central striker).
White & Willits (1991)	Male (amateur) soccer	Black players were more likely to occupy non-central positions.
Williams & Youssef (1975)	College Football	Black players were underrepresented in all central positions.

Variability in Social Psychological Characteristics

In regards to the homogeneity versus heterogeneity issue there is no simple generalization relating to social psychological group composition and group performance (cf. Widmeyer, 1990); findings have been inconsistent. Collins (1970) noted that, on the one hand, increased heterogeneity of personality can increase the group's problem solving potential because random errors are likely to be eliminated, constant biases are less likely, and more alternative solutions are available for consideration. On the other hand, however, increased heterogeneity of personalities in a group can increase the difficulties of establishing good interpersonal relations, which, in turn, can inhibit performance.

Jackson and her colleagues (1991) examined the effect in work groups of group homogeneity versus heterogeneity with respect to age, tenure, education level, college curriculum (i.e., undergraduate versus graduate), military service, college alma mater, and career experiences. Over a four-year period, 93 top management teams consisting of 939 employees in bank holding companies were observed. It was noted that birds of a feather do seem to flock together. Top-level executives were arranged in teams characterized by a greater homogeneity of personal attributes than would be expected by chance. Birds of a feather also were more likely to stay together; teams heterogeneous in attributes had higher turnover rates than homogenous teams. Also, executives who were dissimilar to their teammates were more likely to leave the firm than executives who were similar to their teammates.

Although few studies have examined the issue of psychological homogeneity versus heterogeneity in sport, Melnick (1982) suggested that there is some theoretical and empirical evidence supporting the view that psychological heterogeneity is a valuable group composition variable. Theoretically, the numerous and diverse roles that exist in any task-oriented small group argues for team members whose personalities differ on such traits as need for individual prominence, affiliation motivation, achievement motivation, and preferred action style. The 'special chemistry' that is thought to exist on successful teams may be nothing more than the effective meshing of a set of personalities. Melnick stated that all things being equal, teams composed of members with very similar needs (i.e., psychological homogeneity) will find it difficult if not impossible to successfully complete the social structures of the team. Wolff (1995) has provided a good illustration of this scenario:

> Consider how St. John's, the school on Utopia Parkway in Queens, N.Y., became the most woefully misaddressed team in college basketball last year. Freshman star Felipe Lopez arrived with such ballyhoo that he had appeared on the cover of SI [Sports Illustrated] and was profiled in The New Yorker before he had ever played a college game. There was only one problem: James Scott, a senior who had come in a year earlier billed as the best juco player since Larry Johnson, believed it was his turn to shine. (p. 42)

Research within the sport environment has found inconsistent results regarding the homogeneity versus heterogeneity issue of social psychological characteristics. For example, Klein and Christiansen (1969) found that for achievement motivation, heterogeneous teams were more successful than homogeneous teams. However, in studies of men's and women's tennis doubles teams, differences in the action styles of the athletes had no effect on the performance of the team (Widmeyer, Loy, & Roberts, 1980; Widmeyer & Loy, 1989).

Variability of Members' Ability

Research generally supports the notion that groups heterogeneous in ability are more successful than homogeneous groups (e.g., Goldman, 1965; Laughlin, Branch, & Johnson, 1969). In one study, Diane Gill (1979) tested female college students in the laboratory on a motor maze task in two experiments. The scores obtained by individuals practicing alone were used to form homogeneous and heterogeneous ability groups. For example, two individuals with poor scores were combined to represent a low ability category; when a person with a high score was partnered with a person of low ability they represented an average ability category; and, when two individuals with good scores were combined, they represented a high ability category.

These same categories of groups were examined from another perspective as well: in terms of the discrepancy in ability in the group. Thus, partners that were low-low and high-high in ability were homogeneous; they represented groups with a low discrepancy in ability. The low-high partners were heterogeneous in ability; they represented a group with high discrepancy. Also, the situation was manipulated by Gill in two experiments to insure that either cooperation or competition occurred.

In the first experiment, Gill found no relationship between the discrepancy in ability and group performance under cooperative or competitive conditions. Good and poor performance could not be explained by the fact that individuals were in groups that were homogeneous (low-low, moderate-moderate, high-high) or heterogeneous (low-high, moderate-low, moderate-high, etc.) in ability. However, in her second experiment that involved a cooperative task, Gill did find a correlation of .31 between discrepancy in ability and group performance. The groups that were heterogeneous in ability were more effective.

In a study by Widmeyer and Loy (1981) with female tennis players, homogeneity in ability was positively associated with team effectiveness. The number of team losses decreased as the discrepancy in the ability between the two partners decreased. This finding was most noticeable in the case of homogeneity in the ability to serve ($r = -.38$), followed by the volley ($r = -.38$), the backhand ($r = -.31$), and the forehand ($r = -.11$). The heterogeneous teams had a winning percentage of 45%; the homogeneous teams, a winning percentage of 55%.

Widmeyer and Loy observed that

> *many would predict the opposite finding arguing that the heterogeneous teams should do better because they have a high-ability person who can play the majority of shots. The results suggest that these female tennis players adopt a very egalitarian strategy when playing with their partners and thus their game is not marked by "poaching" or any other form of overplaying by the better players. It could also be that the homogeneous teams are directing the majority of their shots to the weaker player on heterogeneous teams. Support for these two assumptions lies in the fact that the total ability of the weakest player was more positively related to team performance outcome ($r = .74$) than was the total ability of the best player ($r = .49$). (p.27)*

A possible explanation for why heterogeneous groups might outperform homogeneous groups is a phenomenon referred to as a spillover effect. A spillover effect occurs when the stronger member of a heterogeneous group has a positive influence on the subsequent performance of the weaker individual (e.g., Dunnette, Campbell, & Jaastad, 1963; Goldman & Goldman, 1981; Silverman & Stone, 1972). The spillover effect seems to be due to both learning and motivation. The lower-ability person not only learns new strategies and techniques but the task is approached with renewed interest and energy.

A study by Florence Goldman and Morton Goldman (1981) helps to illustrate the spillover effect in a classroom context. High school students were tested on a problem-solving task in three sessions. In the initial session, the students worked alone and on the basis of their performance were categorized as high, medium, or low in ability. In a second session held two weeks later, the students either worked alone or in pairs. Every possible combination of ability group was included—high-high, high-medium, high-low, medium-low, etc. Then, in the third session held two days later, the students again worked independently.

Goldman and Goldman had initially expected that the experience of working in a group would be beneficial to the performance of all subjects. This wasn't the case. For high-ability and moderate-ability subjects, there was no difference between working in groups and working alone. In the case of the low-ability subjects, however, performance was better in the group situation. Also, when homogeneous and heterogeneous group involvement was contrasted with working alone, the low-ability subjects in the heterogeneous groups were the only ones to show a positive effect. Working with someone more knowledgeable was a benefit. Goldman and Goldman noted that "in general, students indicated that because of the peer-group experience they became aware of new arguments, details, and strategies and were helped to correct errors in their understanding . . . and that due to these sessions they may have had incentives to improve their performance" (p. 88).

In most sport situations, the division of responsibility required insures that heterogeneous skills are necessary if the team is to be successful. Volleyball involves blocking and setting; basketball involves playmaking, shooting, and rebounding; and football involves blocking, tackling, passing, running, and receiving. Each of these sports profits from having a division of labor that permits different individuals to focus on developing very specific skills and abilities (see Box 7.1 again).

Chapter Eight

THE COMPATIBILITY IN GROUP RESOURCES

> There have been a lot of quarterbacks stuck in bad coach-player relationships . . . When quarterbacks sit down together, those are the things we talk about; we recognize that we're not independent contractors. We try to coordinate things on the field, and if you don't have a guy off the field trying to do the same thing, it's a problem. (Steve Young, quoted in Silver, 1995, p. 86-88)

Essentially, compatibility reflects the ability of an individual to function effectively and in harmony with other people and/or in the situation. The quote used to introduce this chapter highlights the essence of compatibility. In compatible relationships, a mesh or fit is present in attitudes, personality, and/or skills. In sport groups as well as in other social situations, compatibility contributes to increased individual satisfaction and performance effectiveness. Shaw and Webb (1982) stated that "it is almost a tautology in group dynamics that compatible groups are more effective than incompatible groups" (p. 555).

Marvin Shaw (1981) emphasized this point when he noted that

> *when group members have personality attributes which predispose them to behave in compatible ways, the group atmosphere is congenial, the members are relaxed, and group functioning is more effective. On the other hand, when member attributes lead to incompatible behaviors, members are anxious, tense, and/or dissatisfied, and group functioning is less effective. (p. 238)*

Although compatibility is most often viewed as the fit between individuals, it is much broader than this. It is also the property of the relationship between an individual and the role he/she must play in the group, and between an individual and the demands of the task (Schutz, 1966). Thus, when the composition of the group is looked at in terms of the compatibility of the resources, the focus is on the fit between individuals, the fit between individuals and their role responsibilities, and the fit between individuals and the demands of the task. Compatibility is not simply similarity, however, as the quote in Box 8.1 illustrates. Individuals may be quite different and still be compatible with each other. Aikman and Turner, despite differences in opinion, had a relationship that elevated the team.

Box 8.1
Compatibility in sport teams

Troy Aikman remembers standing in the pouring rain, his passes and his composure slipping away. It was Halloween 1993 in Philadelphia, and Aikman was living in a quarterback's house of horrors. His Dallas Cowboys were clinging to a three-point lead over the Eagles, and Aikman's waterlogged throws were as accurate as Darryl Strawberry's income tax returns.

After watching yet another incomplete pass slide off his hands, Aikman stomped to the sidelines, picked up the telephone and began talking with his mentor, Cowboy offensive coordinator Norv Turner. During this crisis the bond between the two men was downright inspiring.

"What's the problem?" Turner asked from his perch adjacent to the Veterans Stadium press box.

"What do you mean?" Aikman shot back.

"You're throwing the ball like crap."

"Yeah, 'cause it's wet," Aikman explained patiently.

"Well, you're throwing it differently."

"I am *not* throwing it differently."

"Oh, hell, you're not even trying."

"——, yeah, I'm trying!"

Actually, the salty banter between quarterback and mentor spoke to the health of their relationship. Aikman and Turner, who is now coach of the Washington Redskins, fought through their frustration and forged ahead with the game plan. "He and I would yell at each other a lot of times, and that game was maybe the worst of them," Aikman says. "But we wouldn't take it to heart. We had the ability to truly tell one another how we felt, without having to worry about the other getting upset. (Silver, 1995, p. 85-86)

Incompatibility between an individual and a role could exist if a quiet, reserved, withdrawn individual was appointed team captain. The leadership demands in the role of captain might be overwhelming. Insofar as person-task compatibility is concerned, specific tasks require specific dispositions. The individual must possess these dispositions in order to be effective.

The following quote by Tretiak (1987), a former goal tender for the Soviet Union, is another example of compatibility between individuals:

> *It is impossible to talk about [Valery] Kharlamov without mentioning Boris Mikhailov and Vladimir Petrov. Valery's superb linemates helped him to discover his talents. It seems that they were born to meet and become the greatest hockey line in history . . . What distinguished this trio was their thirst for goals. They did not care who got the credit for a goal or an assist; the important thing was to score. They could not bear defeat . . . Each trusted his linemates as he would himself ... they were picky about their game. To play carelessly, not giving it their all, was not their style. They could not do it. (Tretiak, 1987, pp. 62-63)*

As well, Tretiak also highlighted that individuals can be quite different yet still be compatible with each other when he pointed out that Mikhailov "was not as talented as Kharlamov . . . not as powerful as Petrov" (p.62). Their talents complemented one another. In fact, an example that highlights complementarity is the nursery rhyme "Jack Spratt could eat no fat, his wife could eat no lean; so betwixt them both they licked the platter clean." The Spratt family, like the Kharlamov line, not only held some things in common; they possessed other attributes that served to complement one another.

Perspectives on the Compatibility in Groups

Groups with members who have compatible personalities are likely to be more cohesive, more efficient, and more productive than groups with members who have incompatible personalities. One reason for this is that, in incompatible groups, interactions among group members are disrupted or inhibited resulting in deleterious effects of task and socio-emotional activities (Davies, 1994; see Illustration 8.1).

A considerable amount of attention has been directed toward the question of whether compatibility—the fit between individuals—contributes to group effectiveness in social and work groups. It was pointed out previously that compatibility represents complementarity of needs. An individual who prefers to lead complements the preferences of an individual who prefers to be led. Not surprisingly, the general consensus is that the mesh or fit between people is important for group effectiveness. On the basis of his work, Argyle (1969) concluded that, "there are three results of incompatibility—the meshing is poor, the interactors do not enjoy the interaction or like each other, and task performance is poor" (p. 204).

Illustration 8.1. Incompatibility among team members can contribute to a poor interaction.

In the study of compatibility in sport teams, the principal focus has been on coach-athlete compatibility. Athlete-athlete compatibility has generally been considered under the topic of group cohesion (with interpersonal compatibility being one of the factors associated with the development of group cohesiveness). Sport is a unique activity in terms of the degree of control and power held by the coach. This is illustrated in the quote by NFL quarterback Steve Young that was used to introduce this chapter.

Thus, compatibility is often a matter of the athletes making a greater effort to conform to the needs and personality of their coaches. Many athletes, because of the nature or strength of their own personality, have difficulty doing so. Athletes who are incompatible with their coach or who don't conform often quit the sport (Pease, Locke, & Burlingame, 1971).

Ryckman and Hamel (1992), in examining female motives related to involvement in organized team sport, suggested that coaches who adopt the style of coaching of legendary football coach Vince Lombardi—"winning isn't everything; it is the only thing"—will be at odds with their female adolescent athletes who are oriented less toward the outcomes of athletic competition but more toward self-testing and learning.

Birrell and Richter (1994) have presented a strong case for the view that an inordinately heavy emphasis on a winning-is-essential perspective is at odds with adult females as well. A quote from a female softball player is illustrative:

Most women on the team wouldn't play for a man because it would just be another domination thing and win-at-all-cost attitude. The women on our team want quality, not quantity. (Birrell & Richter, 1994, p. 227)

Coach-athlete incompatibility is likely to produce strong dissatisfaction with the coach's style and with the athletic experience in general (Chelladurai, 1984; Horne & Carron, 1985). As Pease et al. (1971) noted, those athletes who do not adapt to the coaches style usually leave the sport.

Two main approaches have been used to study the nature and effects of coach-athlete compatibility. In the first approach, the fit between the specific behaviors of the coach and the athlete have been examined. In the second approach, the fit between the needs and personalities of the coach and athlete have been contrasted through the FIRO Theory (it rhymes with Cairo and means Fundamental Interpersonal Relations Orientation).

A Behavioral Approach

In the behavioral approach, the frequency with which specific behaviors occur in practices or games is tabulated by direct observation or through the use of videotapes. Some typical questions might be: Is the coach frequently critical? How often is praise used? Does the coach spend a great deal of time talking or do the athletes have frequent opportunities to practice? From a compatibility perspective, the relative frequencies of these various behaviors are then compared with athlete preferences, satisfaction, and performance. Typical questions in this regard are: Is the relative frequency with which a coach gives positive encouragement associated with athlete satisfaction? When the coach spends a great deal of time talking, does team performance suffer? The behavioral approach to the study of coach-athlete compatibility is discussed in detail in Chapter 13.

The FIRO Theory

One of the most influential analyses of group compatibility is Schutz's (1958, 1966) theory of interpersonal behavior. FIRO theory begins with the premise that *people need people*. Schutz pointed out that human beings have interpersonal (social) needs that are as important as their biological needs for sustaining health. These interpersonal needs are satisfied through the development and maintenance of compatible relationships with other people. The three principal interpersonal needs identified by Schutz are inclusion, control, and affection. Schutz also proposed that in interpersonal relationships, people not only need to express inclusion, control, and affection, they need to receive these from others. Thus, there are six components which make up the interpersonal elements in FIRO theory: expressed inclusion, wanted inclusion, expressed control, wanted control, expressed affection, and wanted affection. A description of the six behaviors is presented in Table 8.1.

Inclusion is a need that is manifested in such interpersonal behaviors as associating, mingling, joining, and communicating. It is a behavior that is fundamental to any interpersonal relationship; if the other person is not considered to be significant enough to be "included" (either psychologically or physically), then no interpersonal relationship is possible. Individuals high in the need to express inclusion actively seek out relationships, communicate freely, and indicate to others that they are significant and important. Individuals who are high on wanted inclusion behavior have a high need to be with others, to be considered significant and important, and to be included in the activities of others.

Table 8.1
Schutz's Fundamental Interpersonal Relations Orientation Theory (Adapted from Schutz, 1966)

Dimension	Type	Description
Inclusion: To belong, associate, mingle, communicate, join	Wanted Inclusion	The need to be included in others' activities, to associate with others, to be considered significant.
	Expressed Inclusion	The need to include others, to actively join and associate with others, and to indicate to them that they are significant.
Control: To exert power, leadership, authority, dominance	Wanted Control	The need to have others control, dominate, lead, influence, or handle authority.
	Expressed Control	The need to control others, to lead and influence them, to take charge, exert leadership.
Affection: To love, like, affiliate with others, cohere, be affectionate.	Wanted Affection	The need to be liked, loved, friendly with others, to have others provide affection.
	Expressed Affection	The need to give others love and affection, to be friendly with others.

Control is behavior associated with the decision-making process between people; it is reflected in power, authority, dominance, influence, and leadership. Individuals high in the need to express control are dominant in their behavior. They actively seek out leadership roles and positions of power and influence in interpersonal relationships and group situations. On the other hand, individuals who are high in wanted control have a strong preference to let others make the decisions, to follow the rules set out for them.

Finally, *affection* is behavior associated with feelings of love, affiliation, friendship, and cohesion. Individuals who are high in expressed affection actively show their love, liking, and friendship to others. On the other hand, those individuals who are high in wanted affection have a great need to be liked, loved, and/or friends with others.

It is possible for a coach or athlete to exhibit any one of four behavioral patterns insofar as the giving and receiving of inclusion, control, or affection is concerned. Schutz referred to these four behavioral patterns as receiver only, originator only, high interchanger, or low interchanger. A *receiver only* is a person who wants others to provide a specific behavior but does not express that behavior to others. An example of this is an athlete who looks to others for leadership on a team but declines any opportunity to lead. An *originator only* is a person who has a preference for expressing but not for receiving a behavior. An athlete who is comfortable leading but is uncomfortable when others are trying to exert influence or power illustrates this behavioral pattern. When a person has a high preference for both giving and receiving a behavior, they are referred to as a *high interchanger*. The person who wants and gives a great deal of affection illustrates this. Finally, the fourth behavioral pattern, a *low interchanger*, reflects behavioral isolation. This person has no desire to either express or receive a behavior. Track athletes who prefer to work out alone—they don't want other athletes to practice with them and they reject all invitations—are an example of a low interchanger for inclusion behavior. In the sections that follow, compatibility (using Schutz's FIRO theory as a basis for determining compatibility) is examined from the perspective of (a) compatibility with individuals, (b) compatibility of member's ability, (c) compatibility with roles, and (d) compatibility with the task.

Compatibility with Individuals

Personal. In one of his early studies, Schutz (1966) examined the relationship between interpersonal orientations and dyadic relationships in a fraternity. Sociometric questionnaires were administered to assess each individual's preferences for roommates and traveling companions. Also, each individual's behavioral preferences for inclusion, control, and affection were assessed (see Table 8.1 again). Because selecting a roommate involves a relatively long-term commitment, it was expected that compatibility in all three dimensions would be important. Schutz's results supported this prediction. Individuals compatible in their preferences for inclusion, control, and affection consistently selected one another in the sociometric questionnaire.

Selecting a traveling companion involves only a limited commitment that terminates within a short period of time. Consequently, Schutz expected that compatibility in the area of control would be most important. Again, the results supported this prediction. Individuals compatible in their preference for control consistently selected one another as a potential traveling companion.

Other research examining the FIRO Theory has found that compatibility is related to group cohesiveness (Yalom & Rand, 1966), reported hostility in groups (Smith & Haythorn, 1972), greater facilitation of learning (Shaw & Webb, 1982) and group effectiveness (Reddy & Byrnes, 1972). These studies suggest that compatibility does affect behavior in groups and generally supports the perspective that compatible groups are more effective than incompatible groups.

The importance of coach-athlete compatibility was illustrated by Silver (1995) who stated, "At its best, the relationship between a coach and his quarterback can elevate a team. At its worst, it can destroy an entire season" (p. 85). Carron and his colleagues have undertaken a number of studies to examine the sources of coach-athlete incompatibility (e.g., Carron, 1978; Carron & Bennett, 1977; Carron & Chelladurai, 1978, 1981; Carron & Garvie, 1978; Horne & Carron, 1985). These are summarized in Table 8.2. In the earliest study (Carron & Bennett, 1977), university coaches identified the athletes with whom they were most compatible and those with whom they were most incompatible. The compatible group was comprised of athletes who satisfied a gestalt definition of most coachable and least disruptive—who were furthest removed from being "problem athletes." The coaches were also asked to identify the athletes who caused the greatest problems, who were on the opposite end of the spectrum.

Table 8.2
Sources of Incompatibility in coach-athlete dyads

Authors	Group	Results
Carron & Bennett (1977)	College athletes & coaches from various sports	Affection and control were factors but inclusion was the most important contributor to coach-athlete incompatibility.
Horne & Carron (1985)	College athletes & coaches from various sports	Affection, control, and inclusion did not discriminate between compatible and incompatible coach-athlete dyads.
Carron (1978)	College students	Coaches were perceived to express high control but little affection or inclusion. Athletes were perceived to be recipients of control and to express little affection or control.
Pease, Locke, & Burlingame (1971)	Junior high school baseball players	Coach-athlete incompatibility was not associated with athlete decisions to leave the team.
Carron & Garvie (1978)	Olympic wrestlers	Coach-athlete compatibility in control, affection, and inclusion were not related to performance.
Carron & Chelladurai (1981)	High school wrestlers and basketball players	Coach-athlete compatibility in control, affection, and inclusion were not related to cohesion in wrestlers. Compatibility in control was related to cohesion in basketball players.

The results showed that although control and affection were contributors to compatibility, inclusion was the most important behavior differentiating compatible and incompatible coach-athlete dyads. The relationship in the incompatible dyads was characterized by relatively detached, withdrawn, isolated behavior (i.e., a lack of inclusion) on the part of *both* the coach and athlete. This result is consistent with the suggestion made by Tutko and Richards (1977) that if a coach has "an athlete who suffers from the same problem as the coach, there is a very high probability that the coach will be unable to handle the player successfully or communicate with him effectively" (p. 74).

In a later study by Horne and Carron (1985), the question of compatibility versus incompatibility was approached from the athlete's perspective. Intercollegiate athletes were asked to rate their overall relationship with their coach. None of the three behaviors (control, affection, inclusion) was a predictor of coach-athlete incompatibility. As well, Prapavessis and Gordon (1991) examined coach-athlete compatibility with elite tennis players. Similar to the results of Horn and Carron, the authors found that none of the three behaviors differentiated compatible from incompatible dyads.

Prapavessis and Gordon (1991) noted that athletes in incompatible dyads were dissatisfied with their coach's authoritarian style. The athletes wanted their coaches to encourage decision-making and to value their opinions. Prapavessis and Gordon emphasized that problems can develop if coaches approach elite players in an authoritarian manner.

The question of who holds the perception of incompatibility—the coach or the athlete—might be quite critical to continued involvement in sport. Pease, Locke and Burlingame (1971) pointed out that when athletes are cut from the team, it is the result of the coach's perception. When athletes quit a team, it is a result of their personal perception that the situation is unattractive. When Pease and his colleagues studied athletes who were cut from baseball teams, they found that compatibility with coaches in terms of inclusion, control, and affection was not a factor. In other words, the coaches did not center out those athletes with whom they were incompatible and cut them from the team. A different picture emerged, however, when athletes who quit the team were studied. Dropouts were found to be incompatible with their coaches in control and, to a lesser extent, affection.

Bryant Cratty (1983) has suggested that one way to capitalize on coach-athlete differences is to assign an athlete whose personality does not coincide with that of the coach to another coach on the same team. He also proposed that on individual sport teams different coaches with different psychological attributes (e.g., a tranquil versus an emotional coach) should be used to motivate athletes at critical times. The key ingredient seems to be flexibility—having the ability to adapt to different situations and different athletes. A summary of studies in sport which have used Schutz's FIRO Theory are presented in Table 8.2.

Compatibility of Member Abilities

There is no doubt that compatibility in ability is one important aspect of group success. The Kharlamov example discussed at the beginning of the chapter is one example. Good doubles teams in beach volleyball, badminton, and tennis are another. If the skills and attributes of one individual mesh and complement the skills and attributes of the other, the team is more successful. What is not clear across different sports is what similar skills the individuals should possess and what skills should be complementary. In some sports the answer seems intuitively obvious. On a hockey line, it is beneficial if all three of the individuals are similar in skating ability. A poor skater can't keep up with the two good skaters. But a line with three playmakers and no checker wouldn't be effective. So, complementarity in the skills of playmaking and checking are essential.

Another example of compatibility of ability is illustrated in the following quote regarding two NCAA basketball players:

> *A well-matched set of guards is often a critical component in creating good chemistry. Kansas coach Roy Williams is particularly high on his backcourt of Jerod Haase and Jacque Vaughn. "Jerod is a sort of reckless-abandon type, and Jacque takes a more intellectual approach," says Williams, "but when they agree on something, the rest of the team usually follows." (Wolff, 1995, p. 39).*

Two of the few studies to assess the relative importance of the fit of different abilities to team success were undertaken by Widmeyer and his colleagues (Widmeyer & Loy, 1989; Widmeyer, Loy, & Roberts, 1980; Widmeyer, 1990). They compared the importance of compatibility in the serve and volley versus compatibility in the forehand and backhand using men's and women's doubles tennis teams. Compatibility in the women's forehand and backhand was more important (r = .78) for team effectiveness than in the serve and volley (r = .51). In contrast, among men, serve-volley compatibility was a better predictor of performance outcome (r = .72) than was forehand-backhand compatibility (r = .48). The authors cautioned that this result could have been particular to the populations tested. The women players who were tested had a tendency to play at the baseline rather than to come to the net in a serve and volley style whereas the men frequently engaged in a serve-volley style.

Compatibility with Group Roles

Another aspect of compatibility concerns the relationship between the dispositions of individual group members and the roles they must fill in the group. A number of examples serve to illustrate this aspect. A young basketball player was told that he would have to be the "enforcer or policeman" on the team if he hoped to play regularly. He didn't want this role. Moreover, he saw himself as a potential scorer. So he left that team. As a second example, an outgoing, people-oriented athlete was asked to help two first-year athletes make the transition from high school to university. She took on this responsibility and successfully provided a complete orientation for both first-year athletes. As a final example, an outstanding basketball player in her senior year was approached by her coach and asked to assume more of a leadership role because the rest of the team was very young and inexperienced. Although the athlete tried, she was always uncomfortable directing and encouraging others. Also, her own play seemed to suffer. The time and energy spent trying to fill the leader's role detracted from her concentration.

Liddell and Slocum (1976) reported a laboratory study that illustrates the importance of person-role compatibility. The participants were selected on the basis of the control dimension (see Table 8.1 again) of Schutz's FIRO Theory. They were then assigned to groups of five people to solve communication problems. The task was set up as a wheel network whereby one person occupied a central position (in the hub of the wheel) while the remaining four people were in peripheral positions. The people in the periphery had to direct their communications through the hub, they couldn't communicate directly with each other. Thus, the person in the central position had a very dominant role with a considerable amount of control; the people in the peripheral positions had passive roles with minimal control.

Three groups were created: compatible, moderately compatible, and incompatible. In the compatible group, an individual with a high need for control was placed in the central position and four individuals with a low need for control were placed in the peripheral positions. Thus, all group members occupied a role that was completely compatible with their personalities. In the incompatible group, a person with a low need for control was placed in the central position and four individuals with a high need for control were placed in the peripheral positions. In this case, all group members occupied roles completely incompatible with their personalities. Finally, in the moderately compatible group, the hub and each of the four peripheral positions were occupied by a person randomly selected (in terms of control). Thus, from the perspective of person-to-role compatibility, this group fell between the other two.

Liddell and Slocum found that the compatible group arrived at decisions faster and made fewer errors than both the moderately compatible and the incompatible groups. The moderately compatible group was the next most effective. They arrived at decisions faster and made fewer errors than the incompatible group (see Table 8.3).

When the high status individual in the group assumes or is assigned the leader role, the group is more effective. For example, Slusher, Van Dyke, and Rose (1972) found that when the most technically competent among the nine leaders of a group of thirty engineers rejected the role of leader, the group's productivity was not as effective. Similarly, Shaw and Harkey (1976) found that problem-solving groups were more effective when more socially dominant individuals were assigned to leader roles.

Another way of looking at person-role compatibility is to determine whether all of the individuals in a group are in agreement in terms of the appropriate role behaviors for a position. Carron (1978) adopted this strategy when he asked participants to indicate the appropriate role behaviors for coaches and athletes. He found that both coaches and athletes perceived that the coaching role involves exerting a high level of control and being passive in terms of initiating interactions with athletes and developing warm personal

Table 8.3
Person-role compatibility and group performance (Adapted from Liddell & Slocum, 1976)

Occupant of Central Position	Occupants of Peripheral Positions	Person-role Compatibility in Group	Group Performance
High need for control	Low need for control	Highly compatible	Fastest performance Fewest errors
Moderate need for control	Moderate need for control	Moderately compatible	Medium performance Moderate errors
Low need for control	High need for control	Highly incompatible	Slowest performance Most errors

friendships. The athlete's role was perceived to involve very little control and also to be passive in terms of initiating interactions or establishing a friendship with the coach.

These perceived role behaviors could contribute to coach-athlete incompatibility. If both the coach's and the athlete's roles involve being passive in terms of initiating inter-actions and developing friendships, the athletic situation would be cold and impersonal. It must be kept in mind, however, that interpersonal relationships are a product of both the personality of the individuals and the nature of the situation. Early in a group's develop-ment, the situation has the strongest influence on interpersonal interactions. Both the coaches and the athletes could be expected to behave in a manner consistent with their role expectations. As the group develops, the personal dimension and the personalities of the coaches and athletes assume more importance. Consequently, in well-established teams, incompatibility would more likely be the product of differences in personality rather than differences in appropriate role behaviors.

Compatibility with the Task

One area in which the relationship of person to task compatibility and individual effec-tiveness has been tested is personnel selection. The rationale for matching individuals to jobs on the basis of their personality dispositions was highlighted by Schutz (1966), who later found support for his expectations in a number of studies:

> jobs may be classified according to their interpersonal require-ments . . . For example, the essence of a salesman's job, ordinarily, is wide and frequent contact with people, or high inclusion. The politician's role involves high control in that when in office he exercises power over a large number of constituents, but he also may be voted out by them; therefore his constituency has a kind of collective control over him. The expectations for a military officer as far as his relations to subordinates is concerned, may be described as low affection, exemplified by the "no fraternization" dic-tum interposed between officer and enlisted man. (p. 67)

Mood states. In sport, skill is the ultimate criterion. Nonetheless, there has been a longstanding interest in whether specific psychosocial attributes are associated with ath-letic success. Early work by William Morgan and his colleagues (Morgan, 1979; Morgan & Johnson, 1978; Morgan & Pollack, 1977; Nagle, Morgan, Hellickson, Serfass, & Alexander, 1975) contributed to the belief that it might be possible to differentiate suc-cessful from unsuccessful (or less successful) athletes on the basis of mood states.

Typically, Morgan and his colleagues assessed the mood states of athletes prior to major competitions using a psychological inventory called The Profile of Mood States (POMS, which measures six moods: tension, depression, anger, vigor, fatigue, and confu-sion). After the competition, the more versus less successful athletes were then compared on their pre-competition mood states. Morgan and his colleagues found that, in contrast to unsuccessful (or less successful) performers, more successful performers exhibited what now has come to be known as an *iceberg profile*. That is, the more successful performers scored above the 50th percentile on vigor and below the 50th percentile on the other five moods. The iceberg profile is illustrated in Figure 8.1.

As a consequence of the ability of Morgan and his colleagues as well as other researchers (e.g., Silva, Schultz, Haslam, Martin, & Murray, 1985) to predict athletic

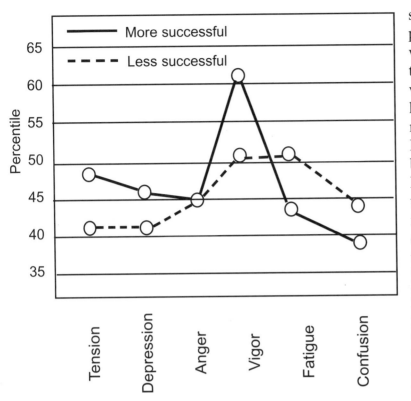

Figure 8.1. The iceberg profile (Adapted from Morgan, 1979)

success from pre-competition mood states, it was popularly assumed that the iceberg profile was a prerequisite for high-level sport achievement (Morgan, 1980). More recently, however, both Terry (1995) and Renger (1993) have urged caution in accepting this assumption. For example, Terry pointed that in a number of studies, with sports such as basketball (Craighead, Privette, Vallianos, & Byrkit, 1986), football (Daiss, LeUnes, & Nation, 1986), and marathon running (Frazier, 1988), mood states failed to differentiate between athletes of varying achievement levels. It was also noted that in other studies, the most desirable mood state for success was not vigor. For example, in karate and cross-country running, anger has been found to be associated with success. It was concluded by Terry that, "the mood profiling process is both individual and sport dependent" (p. 321).

What value does mood state have as a basis for "personnel selection" in sport teams? Probably very little. Nonetheless, there is certainly some value in using POMS in applied sport psychology to monitor individual athletes. As Terry observed,

> *Having utilized mood profiling with hundreds of international performers, it is notable to me that almost all performed best when their profile was iceberg shaped. Superior performance was (almost always) associated with high vigor scores, occasionally with above average levels of tension or anger, but rarely with above average depression, fatigue, or confusion. On those rare occasions when athletes performed well with high depression, fatigue, or confusion scores, they invariably concluded that they succeeded despite their mood and not because of it. It should equally be emphasized that there are also many occasions when athletes perform below expectations even though they exhibit the iceberg profile. This suggests that any claim that mood profiling is the "test of champions" (Morgan, 1980) is misleading. (Terry, 1995, p. 321)*

Support for Terry's (1995) suggestion that mood profiling does not always predict performance was found in a recent study of soccer players. Hassmen and Blomstrand (1995) examined the mood states of nine elite female soccer players from the same team. The players completed the POMS before, immediately after, and two hours after each game during a season. They found that game outcome affected the players' mood states—tension, depression, anger, and confusion scores were lower, and vigor was higher when the team won. However, prior to the games, only minor differences in POMS scores were detected, regardless of the outcome of the game. Thus, Hassmen and Blomstrand concluded that pre-performance mood states did not (a) predict the outcome of a soccer game and (b) distinguish between a successful and a less successful performance, at least not at the team level.

Psychosocial attributes. A number of other studies have also examined elite athletes including gymnasts (Mahoney & Avener, 1977), racquetball players (Meyers, Cooke, Cullen, & Liles, 1979), wrestlers (Highlen & Bennet, 1979), and divers (Highlen & Bennett, 1983). Although there were slight differences from one study to the next, some similarities also emerged across the studies. The elite athletes were superior in self-confidence, were less anxious, used positive performance imagery to a greater extent, and were better able to block out negative thoughts. Although personnel selection in sport based on the presence of positive personality traits is intuitively appealing, the evidence available isn't sufficiently conclusive to permit this.

SECTION 4

GROUP STRUCTURE

The [National Football League Jacksonville Jaguars] . . . reached the AFC title game in 1996 and '99 but a series of poor drafts and costly free-agent mistakes, along with coach Tom Coughlin's grating management style, combined to create lousy teams and a disgruntled fan base . . . Eyebrows shot up when owner Wayne Weaver tapped Jack Del Rio, Carolina's defensive coordinator . . . to make over the team. The Jaguars started last season 1-7 and seemed destined to be defined by Del Rio's decision to place an axe and a tree stump in the center of the locker room to symbolize his blue-collar philosophy . . . But he maintained his focus on building . . . the improvement on both sides of the ball was so substantial that in the off-season Jacksonville became a trendy Super Bowl pick." (Elliott, 2004, pp. 57-58)

Chapter Nine

THE ELEMENTS OF GROUP STRUCTURE

> First Epler [Stephen Epler, founder of 6-man football] decided how many players to put on each side of the ball. He chose six because he figured he could count on rounding up the five players who started on the basketball team, all of them good-sized, athletic boys. Also, with six, you could put three on the line and three in the backfield . . . All players are eligible to receive a forward pass, but the quarterback can't run the ball unless a teammate handles it first. (Bradley, 1996, p. 70)

In Chapter 2, the focus was on group development. Group development is fundamentally associated with the emergence of group structure. As the term suggests, group structure is a term used to represent the fact that groups establish an organization and become stable. Thus, for example, the structure of a house—its walls, floors, ceilings, and windows—provide that house with stability and permanence. The structure of a group serves the same purpose.

Physical Structure of the Group

The structure of a group can be viewed from many different perspectives. One perspective concerns a group's *physical structure*. The physical structure of a group is associated with its composition and organization—the number of members, the formal reporting networks, the formal leadership hierarchy, and so on. In many instances, such as in army units or organized sport teams, individuals come into a situation where the specific organizational structure is in place. The size of the team, its organizational format, its rules of conduct, the nature of its leadership structure (e.g., one captain, three co-captains), are established through the rules or through tradition. In some other instances, such as new sport franchises, ad hoc committees, and social alliances, individuals are faced with a situation in which no pre-existing physical structure is present. Consequently, one must develop.

The quote that was used to introduce this chapter illustrates the scenario where a physical structure had to be established. The inventor of 6-man football, Stephen Epler, was in a town—Chester, Nebraska—which didn't have a sufficient number of students to field an 11-person football team. So he developed a new game composed of 6 people. Athletes who now play 6-person football do so within the constraints of the physical structure developed by Epler.

Psychological Structure of the Group

A group also can be viewed from the perspective of its *psychological structure*. Immediately upon group formation, individual members begin to interact and communicate. With that interaction and communication, differentiation among individuals appears and the four components that most clearly reflect the presence of a psychological structure emerge. Those four components of psychological structure are group position, status, norms, and roles.

Group *position* refers to the place or location of the individuals in the group. Thus, for example, in a family, members will typically sit in the same chair for meals. That location would constitute a position. As another example, in basketball, hockey, and football, the term center refers to a position occupied by one of the athletes during competition. Box 9.1 contains a quote in which the three key *positions* involved with the field goal in football are discussed: the kicker, the ball holder, and the center (snapper). Different sports have different positions. Thus, the positions on a hockey team differ from those on a basketball team and both differ from those on a soccer team. Anyone attempting to describe the unique characteristics or structure of these particular sport groups might begin by describing their positions.

A second element that makes up the psychological structure of a group is *status*. Status has been defined as "the amount of importance or prestige possessed by or accorded to individuals by virtue of their position in relation to others" (Jacob & Carron, 1994, S67). The members of any work group, army platoon, or sport team vary in terms of their status—their power, prestige, and importance to the group. The essence of status is illustrated in Box 9.1 where Don Cherry, a former coach of the Boston Bruins hockey club, discusses Bobby Orr, a member of the National Hockey League Hall of Fame. Orr's preeminence was acknowledged, not only on his own team, but by athletes around the league.

Status can be related to the location (i.e., position) that a group member occupies. For example, in the quote in Box 9.1 pertaining to position, John Madden suggested that the center who snaps the ball is more important than the holder. Later in his book, Madden also stated that, "In the NFL, quarterback is still the most important position. If you don't have a quarterback, your team won't be a winner" (Madden & Anderson, 1986, pp. 35-36). Despite these two quotations from Madden, it is important to bear in mind that status and position are not always related. The person with the highest status on one field hockey team could be the goal tender; on another, a forward. The positions that individuals occupy on a team can provide them with status but status is not determined by position alone. The antecedents of status are discussed more fully in Chapter 10.

A third element that makes up the psychological structure of a group is a *role*. A group role is a generalized expectation for the behavior of an individual who occupies a specific position. Teams (or subgroups within teams such as the snapper, holder, and kicker in football), work groups, social groups, organizations, corporations, and societies in general establish behavioral expectations for the occupants of different positions.

Although the quote in Box 9.1 illustrates a social (i.e., as opposed to a group) role, it highlights nonetheless the fact that a role represents a generalized expectation. Jambor and Weekes undertook a case study of a 36 year-old female long-distance university track athlete, married with two children. The athlete occupied a number of roles—athlete, teammate, university student, mother, daughter, wife—all of which included specific

Box 9.1
Illustrations of the four aspects of psychological structure in sport teams

Factor	Illustration
Group Position: The place or location of the individual in the team	No matter how good a kicker is, he's no better than his holder and snapper. It takes all three. The holder needs sure, quick hands He's got to be able to catch the snap without bobbling it, then get the ball down quickly, spotting it with the index finger of his rear hand while getting his front hand out of the kicker's way. The snapper, the center who snaps the ball back, is even more important than the holder . . . Every good snapper knows where to position the laces in his grip so that the rotation will bring the ball into the holder's hands with the laces away from the kicker. (Madden & Anderson, 1986, pp. 170-171)
Group Status: The amount of prestige or importance possessed by or accorded to an individual	Even his own players would bug him. Before a game other players would send him sticks to be autographed for their fans or their uncles or cousins . . . working with [Bobby] Orr, for me, was like being a museum curator [with an] extremely valuable piece of art. (Don Cherry, in Cherry & Fischler, 1982, pp. 166-167)
Group Role: An expectation for the behavior of an individual occupying a specific position	My mother doesn't understand what I do or why I do it. She can't even understand why I went back to school after so long, let alone started running. I think she wishes I was more like her, or at least just get my degree and get a job. It's hard to talk about what I do on the track team with her. (Female track athlete quoted by Jambor & Weekes, 1996, p. 151)
Group Norm: An expectation for the behavior considered appropriate for team members	Male coaches try to treat you like a male. They want you to act the same way. We might be serious about playing, you know, and we might be cracking jokes, dancing around ... I had a male coach who did not like that kind of behavior. He said, you know, 'You are acting like a bunch of women out there'. That's what we are, you know, and we are serious. We don't have to walk around with our jaws jutted out, feeling our biceps and strutting into the park. You don't have to do those things. It's just not part of us. (Female athlete quoted by Birrell & Richter, 1994. P. 227)

expectations for behavior. Her mother failed to understand either the need for or demands of all of these roles.

A group *norm* is the fourth element that makes up the psychological structure of the group. Norms are the standards for the behavior that are expected of members of the group. Norms reflect the organization's (or group's) consensus about what is considered acceptable. Box 9.1 contains a scenario in which a male coach had developed an expectation for what he considered the appropriate (normative) behavior for individuals who occupied the role of athlete on his team. The female athletes did not share that expectation; as a group, they had developed their own norms.

The interrelationship of group positions, status, roles, and norms to group structure can be illustrated by the example of a group of fraternity members who decide to establish an intramural basketball team. Even though the individuals are all members of the same fraternity, a specific structure will emerge within the basketball team. Part of that structure will be represented by the positions that the different individuals hold; e.g., center, guard, forward. The position that each person holds in the fraternity is unrelated to the position held in the team.

Part of basketball team's structure also will be represented by the roles filled by different individuals. These might include the "coordinator," who acts as liaison between the team and the central administration for intramurals, the "task specialist(s)," who introduces the offensive and defensive systems to the team, and the "social director," who serves as a catalyst for the social activities after the game.

Another part of the team's structure will be represented by the fact that the various team members will have different status, prestige, and importance. If the team considers task success to have the highest priority, the outstanding players and/or task specialist might have the highest status. If, on the other hand, the team considers having a good time to have the highest priority, the social director might have the highest status. It is also, possible of course, that during the game, the outstanding players would have the highest status whereas after the game, the social director would have the highest status.

Finally, norms will slowly evolve for the behavioral standards group members consider appropriate. These norms may revolve around attendance at practices and games, the amount of effort expected during games, the number of shots any one person can reasonably be expected to take, and so on.

Chapter Ten

GROUP POSITION

> From the outset the offensive line has been the main target of [Arizona Cardinals' coach Dennis] Green's displeasure . . . "Four of the six highest paid guys on the team were offensive linemen," Green said, "but I thought it was our least productive group." (King, 2004, 80).

As was pointed out in the previous chapter, group position refers to the place or location of the individuals in the group. As such, it represents a geographic location. The phrase "being in the right position at the right time" serves to illustrate the commonly held belief that our geographic location can be important. What about our position in groups? Sports differ in the positions occupied by various participants—catcher and outfielder in baseball, goaltender and forward in soccer, center and defenseman in ice hockey, and so on. Further within a given sport, baseball for example, over the course of different seasons and even in different teams within the same season, the individuals who occupy the positions of catcher and outfielder vary in ability, the roles held on their teams, their team status, and so on. Is it possible that irrespective of season, team, and even the individual, that one position better satisfies the expression "being in the right position at the right time" than another?

The Importance of Positions in Groups

Not surprisingly, therefore, group dynamics theoreticians have frequently examined the impact that position in the group has on individuals and on group processes. They have found evidence that supports the commonly held belief that position does make a difference. As one example, Strodtbeck and Hook (1961), in a comprehensive study of jury selection, found that a foreman was more frequently chosen from one of the two persons seated at the ends of the table. As another example, Steinzor (1955) found that if people happen "to be in a spatial position which increases the chances of . . . being more completely observed, the stimulus values of [their] . . . ideas and statements increase by virtue of that very factor of [their] . . . greater physical and expressive impact on others" (p. 349). This relationship between physical location and psychological impact has come to be known as the *Steinzor effect*.

The cause-effect nature of group position and social impact is not clear. It may be that more dominant individuals gravitate to more dominant positions. It is also possible that more dominant positions generate more dominant impressions on the group. There is evidence to support both views. For example, Hare and Bales (1963) found that the occupants of more prominent seats had more dominant personality profiles. Also, Sommer (1969) observed that when individuals were selected to lead small group discussions, they more frequently selected seats at the head of the table. So it is likely that the certain individuals do seek out certain positions.

However, in some studies, the effect of individual differences in personal attributes has been controlled by rotating individuals among different positions while holding the content of their opinion constant. The value attached to an opinion was found to vary with the position of the speaker (e.g., Steinzor, 1955). In short, some positions have the potential to make a greater impact on the group—no matter which individuals occupy them.

Importance of the Positions in Sport Teams

In sport, a frequently examined question has been whether the general formal structure of a team and the specific location of different positions are associated with different status, prestige, importance, or reward for the sport participant. One question of interest, for example, has been whether there is a greater likelihood that individuals will be nominated as the MVP of a team if they are catchers versus outfielders in baseball, goaltenders versus defensemen in hockey, forwards versus guards in basketball, and setters versus spikers in volleyball.

Oscar Grusky (1963) reported one of the earliest studies concerned with this question. He began with the following premises:

- the formal structure of an organization establishes major offices or positions and the primary responsibilities for the occupants of the positions;
- the positions in a group vary according to their spatial location, the type of task the occupant performs, and frequency of interactions with other positions; and,
- certain positions, because of their responsibilities and the behaviors required, increase the likelihood that the occupant will develop leadership skills and assume a leadership role.

According to Grusky, "all else being equal, the more central one's spatial location, (1) the greater the likelihood dependent or coordinative tasks will be performed, and (2) the greater the rate of interaction with occupants of other positions" (p. 346). In short, he felt that organizational positions can be distinguished on the basis of whether they are central, high-interaction positions or peripheral, low-interaction positions. He also felt that the occupants of central, high-interaction positions would be more frequently selected as most popular, more respected, and more frequently promoted to executive positions in the organization.

Baseball, the sport that Grusky studied, can be used as an example to illustrate these points. The formal structure of the game dictates that there are nine positions: catcher, pitcher, first base, and so on. The responsibilities for each of these positions are well established. Pitchers pitch, catchers catch, the centerfielders are in the outfield between the other two fielders, and so on. The position of catcher differs from the position of right fielder in a number of significant ways: proximity to the main flow of activity, amount of involvement in the play on every pitch, and opportunity to interact verbally and/or engage in coordinated team play with other team members (see Illustration 10.1). Consequently, the opportunities to provide leadership, to assume a leadership role, and to learn leadership skills are also different.

Grusky proposed that in the organization of baseball, individuals in central, high-interaction positions as players would more likely be recruited as managers. In order to test his proposition, he examined the backgrounds of all of the field managers of major league baseball teams for the periods 1921-41 and 1951-58. The central, high-interaction positions were defined as catchers and infielders, the peripheral, low-interaction positions as pitchers and outfielders. Grusky found that the majority of managers (76.9%) were recruited from central, high-interaction positions rather than from peripheral, low-interaction (23.1%) positions. The highest percentage was former catchers (26.2%) followed by shortstops (14.0%) and third basemen (13.1%).

A number of other studies replicated or extended Grusky's work into other areas and other sports. Some of the areas examined included the recruitment of college coaches, the selection of team captains in high school and university, and the selection of most valuable players. Other sports examined included football, basketball, field hockey, and ice hockey. Essentially, the results of these other studies were consistent with those reported by Grusky (see Table 10.1). One exception was a study by Tropp and Landers (1979) that was concerned with leadership, team captaincy, and interpersonal attraction in field hockey. Tropp and Landers suggested that their results might be explained by the fact that centrality is not a useful concept in highly dynamic sports.

As Table 10.1 shows, Breglio (1976) found that individuals in peripheral positions in baseball were more frequently recruited to umpiring positions. Nonetheless, he considered his results to be consistent with Grusky's propositions. The task demands of umpiring require the individual to be independent and aloof. These characteristics are more likely to be developed in the peripheral positions. Therefore, if the responsibilities and behaviors

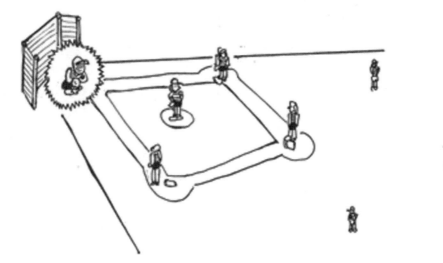

Illustration 10.1. The centrality of the catcher's position allows for more leadership opportunities.

Table 10.1

The relationship between position in sport and organizational rewards

Sport	Results	Reference
BASEBALL		
Professional	Managerial recruitment was greatest from the high-interaction positions (76.9%).	Grusky (1963)
Professional	Recruitment of umpires was greatest from the low-interaction positions.	Breglio (1976)
College	Selection was greatest from the high-interaction positions for team captains (69%), most valuable player awards (54%), and managerial recruitment (72%).	Sage, Loy, & Ingham, (1970)
High School	Selection of team captains was greatest from the high interaction positions (93%).	Loy & Sage (1968)
BASKETBALL		
Professional	Recruitment of coaches was greatest from the central positions (71%).	Klonsky (1975)
FOOTBALL		
Professional	Recruitment of coaches was approximately equal from the central and peripheral positions.	Massengale & Farrington (1977)
College	Selection of team captains was greatest from the central positions (51%).	Sage (1974)
College	Recruitment was greatest from the central positions for head coaches (65%) and from the peripheral positions for assistant coaches (51%).	Massingale & Farrington (1977)
ICE HOCKEY		
Professional	Recruitment was greatest from the central positions for general managers (67%), coaches (74%), captains (76%), and co-captains (78%).	Roy (1974)

acquired during competition serve to prepare the individual for other positions in the organization, then umpires are more likely to come from the peripheral positions.

Overall, it seems reasonable to conclude that position in sport does make a difference. Being in a high-interaction, central position enhances a player's chances of being selected team captain, being selected as the most valuable player, and being recruited into a management position.

An Alternate Perspective

The concept of centrality does not necessarily refer to a geographical location in the middle of the total group—the hub in the center of the wheel. For example, Hopkins (1964), in a discussion of how influence works in groups, argued that "centrality designates how close a member is to the 'center' of the group's interaction network and thus refers simultaneously to the frequency with which a member participates in interaction with other members and the number and range of other members with whom he interacts" (p. 28). In Hopkins view, centrality is viewed as the center of the interaction network, not the physical center of the geographical boundaries of the group.

Hopkins' perspective makes sense. In the case of an army, the command post is the hub of activity (i.e., central) but it is not in a geographical location midway between command and the front line. In short, in a wide variety of situations, the most central location in terms of interaction, leadership, and criticality is at the extreme of the physical boundaries of the group or organization. Feld (1959), in a study of command responsibility in military organizations, stated that "the wider the responsibility, the more remote the post ... In so far as command responsibility increases, the proper station will be progressively to the rear" (p. 17-18). Adams and Biddle (1970) also pointed out that "the teacher's spiritual and temporal home seems to be the center front of the room."

On the basis of this general line of reasoning, Chelladurai and Carron (1977) proposed an alternate model to account for the importance of different positions in sport. This model contained two dimensions: propinquity and task dependence. The first dimension, *propinquity*, consists of the combined attributes of (1) *observability,* which is the extent to which a position provides its occupant with knowledge of ongoing events, and (2) *visibility,* which is the degree to which the occupant of the position is seen and watched by individuals in other positions (including opponents).

Thus, for example, catchers in baseball are in a position to observe everything that happens on the playing field; everything occurs in front of them. So, the position of catcher is highly observable. Baseball catchers are also high in visibility: they are located in a position that insures that they are in the focus of a large number of other players on the playing surface. Consequently, the position of catcher would rate high in the propinquity dimension even though it is not geographically central.

It would seem that outfielders also are in a position to observe everything that happens on the playing field; everything occurs in front of them. However, unlike the catcher, they are not high in visibility. Consequently, they would rate lower than catchers in the propinquity dimension.

The second dimension, *task dependence*, refers to the degree of task interdependence required by the position, the extent to which the occupant of the position interacts with the occupants of other positions. A catcher in baseball would be rated high in task interdependence; an outfielder, low. Catchers control the play on the playing surface and interact continuously with other positions.

When the positions of baseball are classified according to these two dimensions, a catcher would be rated high in task interdependence and propinquity, infielders moderate in both, and outfielders relatively low in both (see Figure 10.1). When Chelladurai and Carron (1977) reanalyzed the data reported in the previous studies of baseball (see Table 10.1), they found that leadership, status, and rewards were highly related to the degree of propinquity and task dependence present in a position. A summary is presented in Table 10.2. Catchers, who are highest in these two dimensions, were also highest in team captaincy, MVP, and recruitment to management positions. Outfielders, the lowest in these two dimensions, were least frequently the recipients of these organizational rewards.

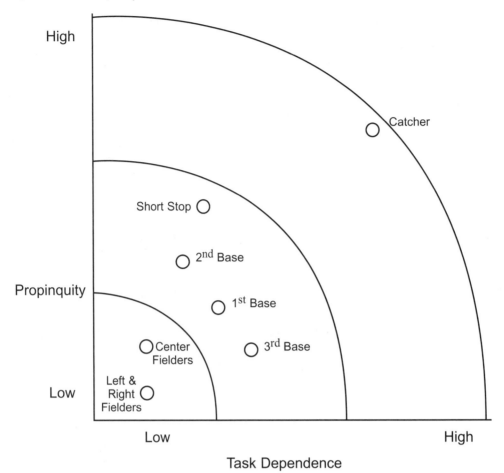

***Figure 10.1. The interaction of propinquity and task dependence
(Adapted from Chelladurai & Carron 1977)***

Positional Segregation by Race/Ethnicity

In 1970, in a classic study, Loy and McElvogue examined whether race/ethnicity is related to the likelihood that an individual will occupy a geographically central or non-central position on a sport team. Their results were unequivocal; blacks were most likely to be found in non-central positions and whites to be found in central positions. This phenomenon came to be known as *stacking*.

Subsequent to the Loy and McElvogue publication, other authors became interested in determining if there was any generality in the findings (e.g., Berghorn, Yetman, & Hanna, 1988; Curtis & Loy, 1979; Jones, Leonard, Schmidt, Smith, & Tolone, 1987). As a consequence, research was undertaken with other types of sports, such as soccer and rugby, in countries other than the United States, such as Australia, New Zealand, and Great Britain, and with other ethnic groups, such as aborigines (cf. Hallinan, 1991; Hayman, 1981; Lavoie, 1989; Maguire, 1988; Melnick, 1988; Melnick & Loy, 1996). Consistently, the pattern of results observed by Loy and McElvogue remained unchanged; whites were found to have a greater probability of occupying a spatially central position, while other ethnic groups were found to have a greater probability of occupying spatially non-central positions.

Table 10.2

The recruitment of managers/coaches and the selection of team captains and most valuable players on the basis of playing position (Adapted from Chelladurai & Carron, 1977)

Factor	Catchers	Infielders	Outfielders	Reference
Managers[1]	26.2%	12.2%	5.3%	Grusky (1963)
Coaches[2]	27.0%	11.0%	1.8%	Sage et al. (1970)
Team Captains[3]	27.3%	16.7%	2.2%	Loy & Sage (1968)
Team Captains[2]	15.5%	13.3%	6.4%	Sage et al.(1970)
MVP[2]	12.9%	10.4%	6.4%	Sage et al. (1970)
Average of all Studies	21.8%	12.7%	4.4%	

1. Professional
2. College
3. Interscholastic

The general consistency of the results led Hallinan (1991) to advance what he referred to as an *Anglocentric hypothesis*. The essence of this hypothesis is that in countries where stacking by race/ethnicity occurs, "there is a strong Anglo heritage as well as histories of structural inequalities resulting in discrimination for certain populations" (Hallinan, 1991, p. 76).

Much of the earliest research on stacking was undertaken with male athletes. Thus, a number of authors have been interested in determining whether the tendency for whites to occupy central positions is also present in female sport teams. In college basketball teams, the findings have been mixed with some studies finding support for the stacking of Afro-Americans while others have not (Berghorn, Yetman, & Hanna, 1988; Leonard, 1987; Yetman & Berghorn, 1993).

The findings across other sports have also been mixed. For example, Eitzen and Furst (1989) observed that in college volleyball, Afro-Americans were statistically over-represented in the hitter position and underrepresented in the setter position. Conversely, Melnick (1996), in a study of New Zealand netball teams, found that Maori women were not statistically underrepresented at either the center position (the most central, highest interacting position) or goal defense (the most tactically important playing position). In discussing his results, Melnick (1996) suggested that

> *Racial segregation by playing position in Anglocentric societies may be directly related to the salience of race as a categorizing variable in a particular society. Unlike the American preoccupation with race for classifying people and explaining individual differences, New Zealanders seem far less impressed with the construct. This is probably due in no small measure to the considerable amount of interracial marriage and the resulting interchange of genes that have taken place over the last century. For many New Zealanders, the establishment and reinforcement of racial boundaries is utter nonsense. (pp. 270-271)*

Melnick also suggested that an important consideration for interpersonal relations and group dynamics on sport teams is the proportional representation of majority and minority members on a team. Thus, in a team composed of 90 percent minority players, stacking is not likely to occur. "It seems intuitively correct to suppose that stacking and racial stereotyping are most likely to be present on teams where minority team members are numerically outnumbered, not where they are in the majority or in the same proportion as the majority" (Melnick, 1996, p. 267).

Group Position and Group Processes

The positions individuals occupy in relation to each other can also influence the nature and amount of their interaction and communication. For example, Sommer (1969) has shown that specific seating arrangements are closely associated with certain activities (see Figure 10.2). Individuals in competitive situations prefer a face-to-face or distant (i.e., across and at the opposite end of the room) arrangement. On the other hand, individuals engaged in cooperative activities prefer a side-by-side arrangement. Co-acting individuals—those working on the same task but independent of one another—prefer to be seated in a distant position.

The pattern of interpersonal dynamics identified by Sommer and illustrated in Figure 10.2 does have implications for sport. On the one hand, on a sport team, little attention is usually paid to locker room arrangements. For example, John Feinstein (1987), in his account of a season in which he followed the Indiana basketball team, provided the following description: "The locker closest to that door is Alford's [Steve, a dominant member of the Indiana Hoosiers]—a coincidence, since players inherit empty lockers the way they inherit empty chairs at pregame meal" (p. 74). In short, little attention is paid generally to geographical factors.

On the other hand, it might be useful for coaches or trainers to consider the pattern of interpersonal dynamics identified by Sommer in such decisions as locker room assignments. For

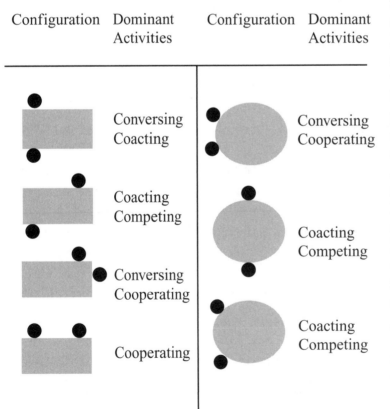

Configuration	Dominant Activities	Configuration	Dominant Activities
	Conversing Coacting		Conversing Cooperating
	Coacting Competing		Coacting Competing
	Conversing Cooperating		Coacting Competing
	Cooperating		

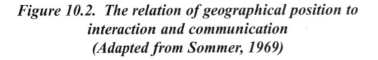

Figure 10.2. The relation of geographical position to interaction and communication (Adapted from Sommer, 1969)

example, if teammates are in competition—for a scoring title, the same position on the team, or leadership roles—and that competition has the potential to destroy the cohesion of the team, it would be beneficial to assign them lockers in close proximity. This might not eliminate the competitiveness entirely but it would increase their interaction and communication. Moreover, a distal arrangement only serves to contribute to or maintain the competitive orientation.

Group Position and Group Cohesion

As the results in Tables 10.1 and 10.2 clearly show, geographical location does have an impact on the benefits that an individual group member receives. Individuals who are in positions that are central, are more likely to be voted team captain and recognized as the most valuable player, and, eventually, to coach or manage. In short, individuals in central positions benefit more from team involvement than individuals in non-central positions.

It is not clear whether individuals in more central positions perceive that they play a more important role or that they have a greater sense of belonging. There is a difference in perceptions of the group between athletes in starting positions versus athletes on the reserve team, however. When Joseph Gruber and Gary Gray (1982) compared the reserves and starters of elementary, junior high, senior high, small college, and large college basketball teams, they found that in comparison to nonstarters, starters were more satisfied with their own performance, were more task conscious, had a greater desire to affiliate, and valued their membership to a greater extent.

Also, in a study examining football players from a medium-sized high school, a large-sized high school and a Division III university, Granito and Rainey (1988) observed that athletes in starting positions were more task-cohesive than nonstarters.

On the basis of his research, however, Kevin Spink (1992) suggested that performance factors could play a role in the perceptions of cohesion in starters and nonstarters. When he examined elite female and male volleyball teams, Spink found that while there were no differences in social cohesion on the less successful teams, the starters were more task-cohesive than nonstarters. On the more successful teams, however, there were no differences in either task or social cohesion. It is possible that on more successful teams, winning serves to keep the team united; even those individuals who are competing less frequently are motivated to identify with the group's accomplishments. On the other hand, when the team is less successful and the athlete is not competing, she or he may not wish to identify with the lack of accomplishment and may psychologically withdraw from the group.

Chapter Eleven

GROUP STATUS

> You know, those two little words, The Man, have wrecked a lot of teams—teams that couldn't decide who The Man was, teams where the wrong man became The Man. I've seen it happen, and it won't happen here. Grant Hill is The Man, and he wears it well (Detroit Pistons' Joe Dumars, quoted by McCallum, 1996, p. 48).

It was pointed out in Chapter 9 that the amount of prestige possessed by or accorded to group members by virtue of their standing within the group is referred to as status (Jacob & Carron, 1994). When individuals come together in a group and begin to interact, differences among them become evident; not all group members possess the same attributes to the same degree.

Status differences exist in groups and teams (as well as society generally) because people hold different beliefs, perceptions, and/or evaluations about the importance of various attributes. These beliefs, perceptions, and/or evaluations influence the expectations and interactions among group members. For example, age is a characteristic perceived (believed, evaluated) to be associated with higher status in some cultures. As another example, in some cultures, different occupations are accorded more status; e.g., judges, medical doctors. So in a group context, older individuals (or judges or medical doctors) likely would be accorded greater status.

Perceptions of greater status influence the dynamics of the group. For example, group members who have higher status are both the initiators and recipients of more communications within a group (Driskell & Mullen, 1990). Thus, in the case of a group where an older individual has more status, he/she likely would be the hub of the group's communication network. In addition, the value of a viewpoint or perspective is associated with the status of the individual who holds it; communications from group members of higher status are given greater credibility within the group. Consequently, in groups where age is associated with higher status, an opinion advanced by a younger member likely would not receive the same level of attention, respect, or acceptance as the same opinion advanced by an older member.

The Nature of Status

Personal Attributes Associated with Status

There are a wide variety of personal attributes that are perceived to be prestigious. Jacob and Carron (1996, 1998) noted that in research with small social and work groups, 17 attributes have been identified which have the potential to contribute to the status of an individual group member. These include an individual's *age, experience, role* (e.g., team captain), *performance/skill/ability, education* (both the type and amount), *position* (e.g., quarterback in football), *social class, language, place of residence* (e.g., residing in a large city versus a small town), *occupation, income, marital status, ethnic background, parent's occupation, parent's income, parent's education*, and *religion.*

Jacob and Carron also pointed out that various researchers have felt that many of these 17 individual status attributes share common characteristics or features. Consequently, they have been organized into what has been considered to be conceptually similar categories. For example, Joseph Berger and his colleagues (Berger, Fisek, Norman & Zelditch, 1977) proposed that one meaningful way to consider status would be on the basis of an attribute's relevance to the task at hand. Thus, a *specific* status attribute would be one that is directly relevant to the function of the group. In the list of 17 attributes presented above, ability, experience, and role would be directly relevant to a sport team's task in most situations. The other 14 attributes might or might not be viewed as specific depending upon the circumstances. For example, in marital counseling groups, marital status likely would be viewed as a specific attribute whereas in sport groups, it likely would not.

Attributes possessed by the individual that are not directly relevant to the functioning of the group are labeled *diffuse*. Parent's education and parent's income would in all likelihood be viewed as diffuse attributes in most work groups, social groups, or sport teams. It is easy to imagine situations where any of the other 15 attributes listed above could be viewed as either diffuse or specific depending on the situation. A good example might be the status attribute of religion. In most instances, it would likely be a diffuse status attribute; it is not directly relevant to the task of a work group, military unit, or sport team, for example. However, in a study group that focuses on the religion of Islam, a Muslim could reasonably be expected to have greater status than a Christian.

Another intuitively appealing classification was proposed by Marshall (1963), who subdivided the status attributes into *ascribed* and *achieved* on the basis of the degree of personal effort involved in their attainment. Achieved attributes are those sources of status that require some effort to attain. Performance, experience, education, role, ability, and position would be classified as achieved status attributes. Ascribed sources of status are those possessed by the individual independent of personal effort. Thus, religion, age, parent's income, and language would be classified as ascribed sources of status.

In newly forming groups where there is an absence of achieved sources of status such as role, ability, experience, the ascribed sources of status will likely contribute to the development of perceptions, beliefs, and expectations about competence at the task. In contact sports, new recruits who are unknown to the team will likely be given some status immediately if they possess exceptional size. If their subsequent performance doesn't meet with early expectations, that status will vanish. Similarly, an unknown, well-dressed male who enters a poolroom with his own pool cue will likely be treated with deference and respect—at least initially.

Ascribed characteristics can sometimes also cause the group to expect very little of the individual in terms of competence in the task—they can lead to a loss of status. A quote from Ken Stabler (1986) on the training camp of the Oakland Raiders illustrates this point:

> One rookie came into camp with a huge jigsaw puzzle. That guy might as well have posted a sign that read: I AM NOT RAIDER MATERIAL. (Stabler & Stainback, 1986, p. 4)

Situational Characteristics and Status

A number of characteristics within the situation are also associated with status. Spatial position is one. As Brown (1965) pointed out, "for Americans the spatial positions of above and in front of clearly imply superiority of status" (p. 78). In short, individuals elevated on a platform or in front of an audience usually have higher status than others in the situation. Also, in Chapter 10, it was pointed out that some team positions, such as the catcher in baseball, for example, have more status than others.

Symbols are another type of situational characteristic associated with status. Team jackets, crests, pennants, uniforms, and titles are all symbolic; and, all can serve the purpose of conferring status (see Illustration 11.1). Goyens and Turowetz (1986) emphasized this point in their commentary on the status attached to certain team uniforms:

> Whether it be the Yankee pinstripe . . . or perhaps the Kelly green with white trim of the Boston Celtics . . . there is something instantly recognizable about the uniform colours of a special team in a particular sport. Few will argue that Yankee pinstripes represent baseball at its finest over the twentieth century. The same glory is attached to the Boston green and white in professional basketball. In professional hockey it is . . . the red-white-and-blue of [the Montreal Canadiens]. (pp. vi–vii)

The status attached to various symbols can increase or decrease over time and according to circumstances. For example, the more successful sport franchises at any given time are readily identifiable by the number of young children wearing replicas of their jersey. With team success, its jersey becomes fashionable and prevalent; with a lack of team success, the jersey almost disappears. As another example, the value of an autograph from very incompetent professional athletes may have little value when they are still participating, but may increase in value after their retirement.

Status Rank

It was pointed out above that status exists because people hold different beliefs, perceptions, and/or evaluations about the importance of various attributes. Depending on the nature of the group, different combinations of the 17 status attributes identified earlier would be considered important. In an academic study group, age, education, position (e.g., university administrator), and language might be relevant. Consequently, the individual who possessed more of these attributes would be accorded higher status. Similarly, in a

Illustration 11.1. High status has its rewards!

sport team, experience, group role (e.g., team captain), performance (skill, ability), and position on the team would be directly relevant to the group's task. As a result, the overall status of the individual—which is referred to as *status ranking*—would be based on a combination of these attributes.

Status Congruency

The presence of differences in status ranking does not necessarily detract from group effectiveness. What can detract from group effectiveness is a discrepancy in group members' perceptions about where they lie in the status hierarchy relative to where they perceive they belong. Research has shown that a lack of consensus on status ranking within a group contributes to conflicting expectations, feelings of injustice, and discomfort (Bacharach, Bamberger, & Mundell, 1993; Zimmerman, 1985).

In the quote used to introduce this chapter, Joe Dumars highlighted the problems associated with a lack of consensus on status ranking in sport teams. According to Dumars, many teams have been destroyed because of conflicts over who should be "The Man"; who is at the top in the status hierarchy, who takes the initiative in critical situations, who is the hub of media attention, and so on. Dumars emphasized that his Detroit Pistons team would not be the site of a power struggle between Grant Hill and him to be The Man—the person at the top of the status hierarchy. As the following quote illustrates, such was not the case in a more recent power struggle between Shaquille O'Neal and Kobe Bryant of the Los Angeles Lakers professional basketball team:

> *This couple keeps playing "He Said, He Said," Shaq insisting he's the Man, Kobe suggesting that he's the Man. "Constant one-upping can be a real issue in all relationships," says Dr. Brenda Shoshanna, a psychologist and couples counselor based in New York City. "It goes on with parents and children, with office workers. The Lakers need to understand that each person is a Man, working toward a common purpose. And when*

that happens—when a team is like five fingers on a hand—they will be unstoppable." (Rushin, 2003, p. 21)

Bernard Bass (1980) also discussed a situation where the degree of congruency between an organization's (or group's) formal and informal status structures could influence the dynamics of the situation. A person who is elected or appointed team captain has a position of higher rank in the formal organizational structure. For the purpose of the present discussion, this can be referred to as *formal status*. Vikki Krane, Christy Greenleaf and Jeannine Snow (1997) provided an anecdote from an elite gymnast elected captain of her team that provides a good example of formal status:

> *I was always a leader in everybody's eyes. . . . Kids always coming up to me asking for my autograph. And here I was. I wasn't that great. But to them I was and that made me feel like, hey, I am special. And I do mean something to them. So I would drive myself harder to, to keep going and to maintain my status. (p. 61)*

In the hierarchies illustrated in Figure 11.1, any differences in status associated with being a team captain versus a co-captain versus a team member are a product of the formal structure.

As Bass pointed out, another more informal hierarchy may develop in the group based on the esteem members have for specific individuals. This esteem could be the result of exceptional ability. In sport teams, the most competent athletes in the group are generally held in high esteem. Similarly, in social groups, the most outgoing, gregarious individuals are generally held in high esteem. For the sake of the present discussion this is referred to as *esteem status*.

Group effectiveness is influenced by the degree of congruence between the formal status hierarchy and the esteem status hierarchy (e.g. Haythorn, 1968; Shaw & Harkey, 1976). The group will be more effective if the individuals with high formal status are also those individuals who hold high esteem status in the group. Conversely, a lack of congruency between the formal status and esteem status hierarchies can produce conflicts and detract from group effectiveness. According to Bass (1980),

> *This is readily explained. The tendency to lead is greater among those of higher [formal] status as well as those of higher esteem [status]. Suppose that the person of higher esteem [status] in a group is not the same as the member with highest [formal] status. The occurrence of two or more individuals with equal leadership potential is likely to promote conflict in interaction. For instance, the higher status of the foreman of a department permits him to serve as a leader. But if the most esteemed member is someone other than the foreman, this other member of the department also has the potential to influence the team. As long as the foreman and the most esteemed department member agree on the solutions to the group's problems, no conflict occurs. But if disagreement arises between these two members, both of whom have power to influence the department, conflict is likely. (pp. 470-471)*

Two possibilities can exist in teams in regard to the formal status and esteem status hierarchies. The first is that they are congruent; the same person has the highest formal status and esteem status. The second possibility is that there is incongruency: one person has the highest formal status, another the highest esteem status.

Also, high esteem status in a team can result from two different sources. One general source is the individual's positive personal attributes that contribute to group effectiveness. Ability would be an example of a positive personal attribute. A second general source of high esteem status is the individual's negative personal attributes—attributes that detract from group effectiveness. Group members who are notorious for being "party animals" or eloquent "club house lawyers" might be held in high esteem by their teammates. However, the attributes that contribute to their esteem status do not contribute to the team's performance.

These four possibilities taken in combination are illustrated in Table 11.1. The implications for group effectiveness and the most appropriate course of action for a coach or team leader are different for each of the four possibilities. For example, the upper left hand box reflects a situation in which there is congruency between the esteem status and formal status hierarchies and the basis for the esteem status is a positive personal attribute. This scenario would be present, for example, if the captain (formal status) was held in the highest esteem (esteem status) because of exceptional ability (positive personal attribute). In this case, the status quo represents the best possible scenario and, therefore, shouldn't be disturbed.

The situation illustrated in the lower left hand box also

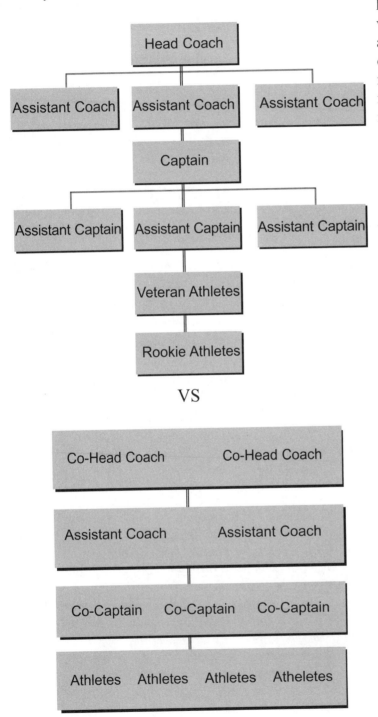

Figure 11.1. An example of a status hierarchy in two sport groups

Table 11.1

*The consequences of congruency in formal status
and esteem status hierarchies in teams*

| | Congruency in Formal Status and Esteem Status | |
	Congruent	Not Congruent
Positive Personal Attributes	Highly Desirable: Retain the Status Quo	Moderately Desirable: Recruit the High-Esteem Status Person into the Leadership Process
Negative Personal Attributes	Highly Undesirable: Remove from Formal Leadership and/or Team	Undesirable: Remove the High-Esteem Person from the Team

reflects a situation in which there is congruency between the formal status and esteem status hierarchies. However, the basis for the esteem status is negative personal attributes. An example of this combination would be a team captain (formal status) held in high esteem (esteem status) because of his capacity for carousing. This combination represents the worst possible scenario. One solution might be to remove the individual from the team. If this isn't possible, at a minimum, the team captaincy should be removed.

The upper right hand box reflects a situation in which the basis for the esteem status is positive but there is lack of congruency in formal status and esteem status. That is, one individual has high formal status (i.e., team captain) while another has high esteem status (i.e., best player). In this case, it would make sense to include the high esteem status individual in a leadership role or to include him/her in the leadership process.

The final possibility, the bottom right hand box in Table 11.1, represents a negative scenario. In this case, there is a lack of congruency between the formal status and esteem status hierarchies and the esteem status results from qualities that are detrimental to effective team performance. The best solution might be to remove the individual from the team—even if that individual also happens to possess high ability. The negative behavior coupled with the position of high esteem could have a negative impact on the behavior and attitudes of other team members.

Sources of Status in Sport Teams

A comprehensive program of research was undertaken by Jacob and Carron (Jacob, 1995; Jacob & Carron, 1996, 1998) to determine which attributes, alone or in combination, provide members of sport teams with status. In one investigation (Jacob & Carron, 1996, Study 1), Canadian intercollegiate sport athletes were required to rate the degree of importance within their team of the 17 status attributes identified in research with social and work groups. As was pointed out above, these attributes are age, experience, role in the group, performance/skill/ability, education, position in the group, social class, language, urbanity, occupation, income, marital status, ethnic background, parent's occupation, parent's income, parent's education, and religion. The athletes identified experience as the most important source of status.

Wolff (1995) provided an interesting commentary on the importance of experience as a contributor to status within a team:

> *In Al McGuire's system at Marquette, during the Warriors' heyday in the 1970s, players from Maurice Lucas to Bo Ellis to Butch Lee fell in line as underclassmen until it was their turn to shine as seniors. Then most of the shots—on the floor and in the media guide—came their way. But during the 90s, blue-chip recruits have become more and more determined to reach the NBA within two years. Thus they expect to take over their teams by the end of their freshman seasons, and that only exacerbates tensions with upperclass teammates. (Wolff, 1995, p. 42)*

Jacob and Carron found that following experience, role on the team (i.e., captain or co-captain), performance/skill/ability, and then age were the major factors associated with status. With the exception of age (which is undoubtedly associated with experience on sport teams), these attributes are what is referred to as achieved sources of status (the athletes possessed them through personal effort), not ascribed sources of status. In fact, not surprisingly possibly, the athletes did not rate the ascribed sources of status (i.e., language, religion, parent's income, parent's occupation, parent's education, and so on) as at all important for status on their teams.

In an attempt to determine if the culture in which a sport team exists influences the importance of various attributes as a source status among team members, Jacob and Carron (1996, Study 2) then repeated their research with semi-professional athletes from India. The authors felt that India was a good location to determine impact of status because, among other factors, India

> *is noted for the diversity of status attributes deemed to be important . . . there is an inequality in society based on gender . . . there are 3,000 or more castes (social sections) . . . 1,652 languages as mother tongues and 15 of these are considered to be a major language . . . [and] there has been a steady rural to urban migration over the past three decades (Jacob & Carron, 1996, Study 2, p. 375).*

Three of the four primary sources of status endorsed by Canadian athletes (experience, performance/skill/ability, and age) were also singled out by the Indian athletes. The fourth status attribute rated highly by the Indian athletes was education. It was concluded that "in sport teams, culture seems less critical than the situation . . . even though sport teams are considered to be microcosms of society, the sources of status prevalent in society and sport are not the same (Jacob & Carron, 1996, Study 2, p. 379).

Jacob and Carron (1998) also undertook an investigation with Indian and Canadian high school and intercollegiate athletes to examine the relationship between the importance attached to status attributes and task cohesion as well as level of status congruency and task cohesion. Status congruency was measured as the discrepancy between the athlete's perception and teammates' perceptions of the athlete's status ranking within the team.

Surprisingly, status ranking and task cohesion were not correlated. However, there was a relationship between the importance attached to status and cohesion. The higher the athletes' perceptions of task cohesion, the smaller the degree to which they attached importance to status. It may be that athletes who have a perception of their team as highly united have a desire to downplay any conditions that might be divisive.

One caveat to the above literature examining status in sport teams is that it was based on status attributes (e.g., age, experience, etc.) that were borrowed from studies conducted on social and work groups. More recently, Jacob-Johnson (2004) continued her line of work on status in sport by having athletes from Canada and India identify, in an open-ended format, the sport-specific status attributes they considered important (i.e., athletes were asked to indicate the conditions associated with having importance/prestige among other team members). The responses for both Canadian and Indian athletes fell under four general categories. The first, *physical attributes*, indicated that status could be gained through attributes associated with (a) performance, (b) experience, (c) appearance, (d) role on team, and (e) position. The second category highlighted attributes that reflect *psychological attributes* at both the individual (e.g., positive attitude) and group (e.g., team spirit) level. The third category contained *demographic attributes*, such as age and family status. The final category was labeled *relationship with external others*, and indicated sources of status associated with the athlete's relationships to individuals who are not teammates. Jacob Johnson concluded by noting that this open-ended approach demonstrated "different and generally more important [status attributes] that the attributes identified in earlier studies" (p. 62). Further, she suggested that the examination of status in relation to other important variables (e.g., cohesion, leadership, etc.) is critical for a greater understanding of group dynamics.

The Correlates of Status

A number of terms have often been used interchangeably with status. Some of the more popular include authority, power, and social influence. These are not simply synonyms for status, but are other elements in the group's structure that are closely associated with status differences. Further, they not only contribute to status, they also emerge as a result of status differences. For example, individuals in authority positions in the team (e.g., an elected captain), are generally accorded higher status than other team members. Similarly, individuals with high status (e.g., a team member with exceptional ability or experience) are generally elected to positions of authority.

Authority

The hierarchy for authority (and associated status) varies from one team to the next. Consider, for example, the two hierarchies illustrated in Figure 11.1. In the upper example, the pyramid is steeper and the status of the head coach is clearly greater than that of the three assistants, who have equal status. Greater coaching authority, prestige, power, and importance lie in the hands of that one person—the head coach. Similarly, among the athletes, the pyramid is also quite steep with differentiation existing between the one captain and three assistant captains. There are also differences in status between veterans and rookies.

In the lower example, the pyramid is relatively flat for both the coaches and the athletes. The two co-head coaches have equal status, power, authority, and prestige. (One might be responsible for the offense, the second for the defense.) There are two assistant coaches with equal status. Among the athletes, three co-captains share the leadership role and no distinction in status is made between veterans and rookies.

An authority hierarchy seems to develop in all task groups—whether they have formalized leaders such as coaches and captains or not. Berger and his colleagues have referred to this as a status organizing process (Berger, Fisek, Norman, & Zelditch, 1977). They suggested that a status hierarchy—the organization of the group according to status differences—results logically from members' expectations for future performances. Those individuals who are expected to contribute the most to the group's effectiveness are accorded the greatest status.

In Chapter 9, an example was used of a group of fraternity members who decided to establish an intramural basketball team. It was pointed out that even though the individuals were all members of the same fraternity, a specific structure would evolve within the basketball team that was specific to that group. Part of that structure would result from a status organizing process. If the group wanted to be successful, its members would most likely accord the greatest status to those individuals expected to contribute the most to future performances. If the group wanted to have a good time socially, the individuals with the greatest social skills would be accorded the greater status and authority.

It is preferable for the formal status hierarchy (e.g., captains, co-captains) to be identical with the informal status hierarchy (e.g., the most competent group members). Otherwise, group effectiveness suffers (e.g., Haythorn, 1968; Slusher, Van Dyke, & Rose, 1972). For example, in the hierarchy illustrated in the top half of Figure 11.1, the one head coach has greater authority than the three assistant coaches. But, if one of those assistant coaches was held in considerably higher esteem because of ability and contributions than the head coach, there could be resistance to the head coach's decisions among the assistant coaches and the athletes. Similarly, if one veteran player not in a formal leadership role was held in much greater esteem than the captain or co-captains, the team's effectiveness could suffer.

Power

Power is "the capacity to produce intended and foreseen effects on others" (Wrong, 1979, p. 21). As is the case with other correlates of status, power both contributes to and results from status. Individuals who have status in the group—coaches, captains, outstanding players—have the capacity to influence other group members. Also, possessing power in the group leads to status.

In a comprehensive analysis by John French and Bertram Raven (1959), it was assumed that there are five sources of power in small groups (see Box 11.1). *Expert* power results from knowledge, expertise, and competence at the task. Group members are influenced and will more readily follow the directions of more competent group members. In a sport group, the coach is generally the most knowledgeable. In the quote in Box 11.1 that is used to illustrate expert power, Kareem Abdul Jabbar commented on the expertise of his former UCLA basketball coach, John Wooden, and the impact that this expertise had on the team's confidence. Holding expert power made it easier for Wooden to lead.

Another source of power associated with status in a group is called *coercive*. It results from threats, the possibility of having a reward withheld, or a punishment applied. If a group member has the potential to inflict some penalty on other group members, that power can help to produce desired outcomes. In the example presented in Box 11.1, the

---

Box 11.1
The French and Raven sources of power in coaching situations

Focus	Quote
Expert Power: Results from knowledge, competence, and expertise at the task	[Coach John Wooden] used his mind and he understood the game totally. The best he could do was the best there was . . . our confidence in him never wavered. (Abdul Jabbar & Knober, 1983, p. 152)
Coercive Power: Results from threats, warnings of danger, and punishment	No one would call Northwestern's Randy Walker a player's coach—not on the field, anyway. His drills are famous for their toughness and precision, and he once described practice as something akin to Pavlovian training. "You give them positives when they run that maze the right way and find the cheese," he said. "You shock their asses when they don't." (Price, 2001, p. 81)
Reference Power: Results from affection and being liked	More than anything else the assistant coach has to be respected and liked by the players in his group. The rapport is important . . . he's got to wear it well. If he doesn't, he'll turn off the players. They'll stop listening to him. (Madden & Anderson, 1986, p. 208)
Legitimate Power: Results from rank or position	Control was the operative word. [Coach Monte] Clark had control of the 49er operations, which meant drafting, trading and coaching . . . Thomas wanted control of the first two . . . Monte refused to give up his power. He knew what he was doing. Thomas fired him. (Plunkett & Newhouse, 1981, pp. 144-145)
Reward Power: Results from the control of rewards and payoffs	[Coach Scotty Bowman] works them hard in practice, watching them, telling the press how hard and well they are working, making them feel they are earning their place on the team. Given a chance, usually at home, they give back an inspirational game. (Dryden, 1983, p. 41)

quote by Northwestern football coach Randy Walker (cited in Price, 2001) highlights a coaching philosophy based on coercive power.

Reference power exists when an individual is well liked and respected by other group members. In the quotation presented in Box 11.1, Coach John Madden emphasized the need for assistant football coaches to have the affection and respect of the group of athletes they coach. Without it, the players will not respond to the coach's leadership.

In the status hierarchies illustrated in Figure 11.1, those individuals at the top of the pyramid have the greatest power; the organization has appointed them to be in charge. When power exists because of rank or position, it is referred to as *legitimate*. Legitimate power is strongly associated with status—the greater the legitimate power, the greater the status and influence. In the quotation presented in Box 11.1, Jim Plunkett, another former National Football League quarterback, discussed a struggle between the head coach of the

San Francisco 49ers, Monte Clarke, and the general manager, Joe Thomas. As the quotation illustrates, Thomas had more legitimate power, and Clarke had to leave.

The fifth source of power that comes from and contributes to status is referred to as *reward*. As the name suggests, it is power which results from control over rewards and payoffs. If an individual has the power to reward other group members, he/she will have a major impact on the group. In the final quotation in Box 11.1, Ken Dryden outlined how his National Hockey League coach, Scotty Bowman, used praise and public recognition as a motivator for the fringe players on the roster.

In all of the examples used above, the focus is on coaches. In any sport team, they generally have the greatest status and the greatest power. However, high-status athletes on the team also may possess these same sources of power. In fact, in some instance, a high-status athlete may have more power within the group than the coach.

Sport Involvement and Social Status

One approach to the study of the relationship of status and sport has been to examine the impact that being involved in sport has on the social status that individuals possess among their peers. It has become apparent that gender differences are present. That is, traditionally sport involvement has been a primary source of social status for males but not for females. In the case of females, James Coleman (1961) reported in his classic study that being a leader in activities was the most important factor associated with social status in high school. Subsequent research over the next 25 years by a number of other authors has shown that the importance of leadership in high school activities is still preeminent for females (Feltz 1978; Kane, 1988; Thirer & Wright, 1985; Williams & White, 1983).

Even for elementary school females, sport is not the most important criterion for social status among a student's peers. In 1976, when Hugh Buchanan and his colleagues (Buchanan, Blankenbaker, & Cotton, 1976) examined the sources of social status among female students in Grades 4 to 6, they found that having good grades was most important. Sport involvement ranked second and was followed by being good looking and having money.

Melissa Chase and Gail Dummer replicated the Buchanan et al. study in 1992. They found that, for females in Grades 4-6, social status resulting from sport involvement had remained unchanged in relative importance. Sport ranked second with being good-looking ascending to first place. The importance attached to grades was ranked above having money.

As indicated above, sport plays a considerably different role in the achievement of social status for males. In fact, sport has been *the most important* source of peer status for at least the last 35 years. In one of the earliest studies focusing on this question, Abraham Tannenbaum (1960) examined the attitudes of high school juniors toward different types of male students (cited in Coleman, 1961). He found that the rankings from the most to least acceptable were

1. Brilliant nonstudious athlete
2. Average nonstudious athlete
3. Average studious athlete
4. Brilliant studious athlete
5. Brilliant nonstudious nonathlete
6. Average nonstudious nonathlete
7. Average studious nonathlete
8. Brilliant studious nonathlete

In his classic study, Coleman (1961) found that sport was the most important source of social status for high school males—followed by being in the leading crowd, being a leader in high school activities, having good grades, and coming from the right family. When Coleman's study was replicated 15 years later by Eitzen (1976), an identical pattern was still present. Sport was the most important source of status for high school males, followed by friendships, high school activities, grades, and family background.

For males, the importance attached to sport starts early. In their study with boys in Grades 4-6, Buchanan and his colleagues (1976) found that sport was ranked first, followed by grades, appearance, and money. When Chase and Dummer (1992) examined this same issue 16 years later, they found that sport still remained first in importance. However Chase and Dummer noted that grades had fallen in importance to third place, while appearance had increased in importance and was ranked second.

Why do differences exist in the role that sport plays in determining status for females versus males? Differences in opportunity would not seem to be the answer in the United States. As Chase and Dummer pointed out in their discussion of this issue, with the passage in the mid-1970s of the legislation referred to as Title IX, increased opportunities were made available for girls and women to participate in athletics. With these increased opportunities, changes in societal views about participation in sport might have been expected. Given that this was not the case, Chase and Dummer (1992) speculated that

> the lack of importance of sport as a social status determinant for girls may be that, in many case, Title IX still involves only one generation. The women who would have been affected by Title IX are just reaching the age at which they could be the parents of children in elementary school. As parents, these women could influence their children to have more favorable attitudes towards women's participation in athletics, and then changes may occur. (p. 422)

Periodically, research replicates the work that began with Coleman (1961). It is possible that in future research examining Chase and Dummer's proposition, sport will be shown to have increased in importance for social status among female students. However, it is also equally plausible that sport will have declined in importance among male students. As early as 1975, Eitzen felt that a trend was emerging whereby sport involvement was diminishing as a prerequisite for male social status. In fact, a more recent study by Holland and Andre (1999) showed that while males were slightly more likely than females to want to be remembered as a star athlete and slightly less likely to want to be remembered as a brilliant student or activity leader, these results were not statistically significant. Furthermore, the characteristics that were associated with those individuals who wanted to be remembered as an athlete, student, or leader, were similar for both genders. Both these results seem to support the notion that differences in perceptions of athlete status between the genders are diminishing.

Overall, with increased technology, increased competitiveness for enrollment in professional schools, problems in funding scholastic sport, and an increased variety of leisure-time options, it is possible that competitive sport will decrease in its social importance. If that is the case, the factor determining social status could also change.

Chapter Twelve

GROUP ROLES

> I never felt I was playing in [Wayne Gretzky's] shadow . . . I had a responsibility on the team that was different from Wayne's. Everyone had his role, and I felt great about mine. So did many others about theirs. If we won, and won often, we knew everyone would get respect. (New York Rangers' Mark Messier, quoted in Swift, 1996, p. 60)

A role is the pattern of behavior expected of an individual in a social situation. A role arises from the combined influence of the individual's position in the group, status in the group, and/or assigned or assumed responsibilities. In role theory, the individual who occupies a role is referred to as the *focal person* while the other principals in the social situation are referred to as *role senders* (Kahn, Wolfe, Quinn, Snoek, & Rosenthal, 1964; King & King, 1990). In role theory terms, the team captain on a sport team would be the focal person and team members would represent one category of role sender while management would represent another. Individuals who occupy the role of captain perceive the expectations arising from their teammates and from management. Often the two sources (teammates and management) hold similar expectations for individuals occupying the role of captain. However, it is possible that they might not.

In the quote used to introduce this chapter, hockey player Mark Messier highlights the nature of a role. There is a direct parallel between a role on a sport team and the role in a drama production. Whatever the individual's talents—and there are good actors and poor actors just as there are good athletes and poor athletes—each actor must operate within a system, a production, or an overall plan and carry out the requirements of his or her role. Some personal interpretation is always possible, but the individual's behavior must be generally consistent with what is prescribed by the role. Otherwise, the overall group performance suffers.

Types of Group Roles

Formal vs. Informal Roles

Within every group, there are two general categorizations of roles. The first is related to the degree of formalization of those roles (Mabry & Barnes, 1980). *Formal roles* are those that are directly established by the group or organization. Many of the formal roles within a sport team are the result of the way in which the leadership hierarchy is set out. For example, Figure 11.1 in the previous chapter illustrates two different hierarchical models insofar as the formal leadership roles of a coach, assistant coach, team captain, and assistant captain are concerned. The expectations of both coaches and the team for the behavior of the coaches in the two hierarchies illustrated in Figure 11.1 would be quite different.

There are also a number of formal performance roles in a sport team which result from the specific offensive and defensive systems used. Examples include the setter and spiker in volleyball and the power forward, point guard, and small forward in basketball. Every sport team, as an organization, requires specific individuals to carry out these types of specific roles. The roles are so important to the success of the group that individuals are either trained or recruited to fill them.

The *informal roles* in a team evolve as a result of the interactions that take place among the group members. Some examples of the informal roles that often emerge on a sport team include leader (which may or may not be the team captain), policeman or enforcer, social director, and team clown. The expectations of behavior for individuals who occupy these types of informal roles are not as well established as formal roles but they are present. The role of policeman (or enforcer) on professional hockey and basketball teams is interesting in that it can be either a formal or an informal role. Athletes most suited to the role often inherit the responsibility. However, if it is assumed that a team can't be successful without someone in the policeman's role, players will be specifically recruited to carry out this responsibility. The following provides a good illustration from professional sport:

> *Former Stars coach Ken Hitchcock, now the Flyers' coach, had difficulty finding ice time for enforcers, so he went without them the last three seasons. Mike Modano believes he and the top players on the Stars were knocked around because other teams didn't have to answer to a player such as [Aaron] Downey . . . "It was time to stop turning the other cheek," [General Manager Doug] Armstrong says. "We needed a player who knows that role. I believe that when you have a tough guy like Aaron, the toughness filters down the lineup." (Wharnsby, 2002, p. 61)*

The role of a "policeman" in hockey is often an informal role. Individuals best suited to the demands of the role assume its responsibilities. Whether they occupy an informal team role or a formal one, athletes very quickly become aware of their role and carry out its requirements. The degree to which role performance is successful helps to explain why groups are more or less effective.

Task vs. Social Roles

Another general categorization of roles is related to their fundamental focus. Bales and Slater (1955) noted that roles could be considered from either a task or a social perspective. *Task roles* are those that are primarily concerned with accomplishing the group's stated purpose (e.g., performing as a team, winning the competition) while *social roles* are those that are concerned with producing greater group harmony and cohesion.

Roger Rees and Mady Segal (1984) carried out a study designed to assess who the task specialists and socioemotional specialists are on sport teams. The *task specialist* in a group is that individual who assumes a leadership role in the achievement of the group's goals. Task specialists influence, support, organize, and direct other group members toward the accomplishment of the group's task. This is often referred to as an instrumental role because the task specialist serves as an instrument for team success.

The *socioemotional specialist* in a group is that individual who is influential in promoting group harmony and integration. The task specialists often produce stress and tension because of their preoccupation with performance, productivity, and achievement. The socioemotional specialist helps to diffuse some of the tension by providing support, promoting team unity, and emphasizing the importance of team cohesion.

Rees and Segal found that the task leaders on the football team came almost exclusively from the first string players while the socioemotional leaders were equally balanced between first and second string. Interestingly, considerable role integration was present— 55% of the individuals who were listed among the top 10 individuals as task leaders were also listed among the top 10 socioemotional leaders. All of the athletes who occupied both roles were first-string players (see Table 12.1).

When Rees and Segal looked at the effect of experience on role involvement, they found that task leaders were drawn from the total spectrum of the team: senior (33%), junior (56%), and sophomore (11%). On the other hand, the socioemotional leaders were almost exclusively the senior players on the team (90%). When individuals were listed in both roles, they were generally seniors (73%). It seems that ability is the most important qualification for a task leader on a sport team. Being on the first string is essential; years of experience on the team is not. On the other hand, years of experience are an essential prerequisite to be a socioemotional leader. Being on the first string is not as important as being a senior.

Despite the existence of formal leadership roles such as captain, co-captain, and assistant captain, interactions within the group lead to the emergence of the task specialist and socioemotional specialist. From a group dynamics' perspective, the most desirable outcome is if (a) the same person or people occupy both roles and (b) they are in formal leadership roles. In this case, the status and esteem hierarchies discussed in Chapter 11 are in agreement (see Table 11.1 again). If the task specialists do not have a formal leadership

Table 12.1
Characteristics of individuals in leadership roles in sport teams
(Adapted from Rees & Segal, 1984)

Team Tenure	Task Leaders	Socioemotional Leaders	"Great Man" (Both Task & Social Leaders)
Starting Status			
First String	100%	50%	100%
Second String	0%	50%	0%
Team Experience			
Senior	33%	90%	73%
Junior	56%	10%	18%
Sophomore	11%	0%	9%

role (e.g., captain or assistant captain), they should either be given one or be included in the leadership process.

Although the socioemotional specialist may seem to be unimportant or irrelevant in task-oriented groups such as a sport team, this is not the case. The socioemotional specialists play a valuable role in diffusing some of the tension and stress that develop as the team works toward its goals and objectives. They enhance task and social cohesion and, as is pointed out in Chapter 16, both are strongly related to team success.

How Roles Develop

Emergence of Roles

The emergence of roles in work groups has been studied extensively by Robert Bales (1966). He observed that certain behaviors are associated with the appearance of different group roles within task-oriented groups. The three general types of behaviors identified by Bales were *activity*, *task ability*, and *likability*. Behavior directed toward standing out from others is referred to as activity. On a basketball team, for example, speaking out frequently in the dressing room, encouraging others, and encouraging teammates during a game are some examples of activity behavior. Task ability is behavior that helps the group achieve its goals. As the name suggests, task ability, is synonymous with expertise. Finally, likability is behavior directed toward the development and maintenance of socially satisfying relationships. Arranging group parties, coordinating social activities, and acting as a peacemaker are some examples of likability behavior.

According to Bales, the relative degree to which individuals exhibit these three behaviors has an influence on their roles within a group (Table 12.2). Although group members generally fill the roles of task and socio-emotional specialist, many sport teams also try to insure that they have coaches who carry out both of these roles. Usually (but not always) the head coach is the task specialist—person most strongly oriented to the task concerns of productivity and performance. Then one of his or her assistants is the social specialist who provides the social support and diffuses the stress and tension that inevitably arise. This is an effective combination. One anecdote that illustrates the task and socioemotional coaching roles was provided in John Feinstein's (1987) account of an incident in which Bobby Knight criticized one of his athletes:

Table 12.2
Behaviors associated with role development in task-oriented, problem-solving groups

Group Role	Activity	Task Ability	Likability
Task Specialist	High	High	Low
Social Specialist	High	Low	High
Leader	High	High	High
Underactive Deviant	Low	Low	Low
Overactive Deviant	High	Low	Low

Knight walked out onto the floor. He was drained. He turned to Kohn Smith. "Go talk to Daryl [Thomas]," he said. Knight knew he had gone too far with Thomas, and undoubtedly he had regretted many of the words as soon as they were out of his mouth. But he couldn't take them back. Instead he would send Smith, who was as quiet and gentle as Knight was loud and brutal, to talk to Thomas. (p. 7)

The original research on role differentiation and leadership led to the conclusion that only two informal roles—task specialist and socioemotional specialist—emerge as the group develops (e.g., Bales & Slater, 1955). Initially, it was thought that these two roles were viewed as incompatible with each other. It was felt that because the preoccupation of the task specialists with performance produced tension and stress, socioemotional specialists emerged to insure that the group wouldn't disintegrate.

On the basis of a reanalysis and review of earlier research concerned with group leadership and role differentiation, however, Lewis (1972) concluded that the two roles are often integrated. And, when one person fulfills both the task specialist and the socioemotional specialist roles, he or she has an overall *leadership role* in the group (see Table 12.2 again). When this occurs, leadership within the group is more effective. Individuals who occupy both the task and social roles simultaneously are considered to be exceptional leaders.

The final two roles in Table 12.2 are the *overactive deviant* and the *underactive deviant*. Individuals who are chronic complainers in the locker room, who exhibit high activity behavior but low task ability and likability behaviors, occupy the role referred to as the overactive deviant. The underactive deviant is low on all three behaviors. It seems likely that there is a very low prevalence of this type of individual in sport teams.

Communication of Role Responsibilities in Sport

While roles emerge naturally within groups (i.e., informal roles), quite often responsibilities associated with individual roles are communicated (successfully or unsuccessfully!) by people in positions of power or influence. As noted at the beginning of this chapter, those who communicate role responsibilities (typically the coach but also, in some instances, teammates, parents, fans, etc.) are referred to as *role senders* while the person who occupies the role is referred to as the *focal person* (typically the athlete).

Eys, Carron, Beauchamp, and Bray (in press) adapted a framework from Kahn et al. (1964) to illustrate how role responsibilities are communicated and what factors might influence how well this communication process takes place. As can be seen in Figure 12.1, the communication process consists of a cycle of five events. Consider a typical situation in sport where a coach attempts to outline role responsibilities to an athlete: Event 1 occurs when the coach generates expectations responsibilities to the athlete. Event 2 occurs when the coach, through his/her verbal or nonverbal communications, exerts pressure on the athlete to perform those responsibilities follows. The third event occurs when the athlete perceives that the coach has expectations for him or her. The response (Event 4) follows. Typically, in sport, this response is the proper execution of the role responsibilities (which is positive). However, other responses are possible. For example, if the coach's communication is unclear, the athlete's response might be dissatisfaction, frustration, and/or confusion (which is negative). Finally, Event 5 highlights the fact that the coach makes judgments about how the athlete has responded to the role expectations. Overall, there are a number of elements involved in this process that could influence how well the role is communicated, the nature of the response to role expectations, and how effective the athlete performs his or her role. These elements are highlighted in the subsequent sections.

The Nature and Correlates of the Elements of Role Involvement

Role Performance

Role performance represents the *behavioral* aspect of role involvement and is typically what the role senders evaluate when expectations are communicated. On any team, there are a variety of roles that must be performed. The diversity of those roles and their importance to team success is illustrated in a quote presented in Box 12.1. Yvan Cournoyer, a small but highly effective goal scorer for the Montreal Canadiens' hockey team, pointed out that someone was needed to fill the role of policeman or enforcer.

Role Clarity

In order for any team to be successful, each focal person must carry out his/her role consistent with the expectations of the role senders. As Figure 12.2 illustrates, the relationship between individual roles and team effectiveness is influenced by the presence of specific conditions. One of these is *role clarity,* which is one cognitive aspect of role involvement. Each athlete must clearly understand the responsibilities associated with his or her role. A quote by Bobby Clarke, a former captain of the Philadelphia Flyers, illustrates role clarity (see Box 12.1).

When role clarity has been examined in both sport and work groups, it is usually under the label of *role ambiguity* that, of course, represents the

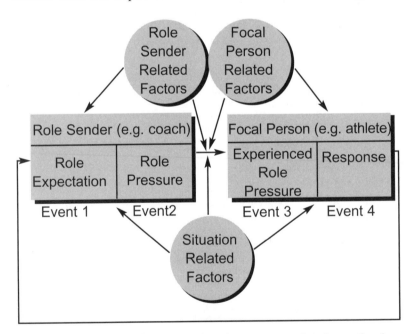

Figure 12.1. A framework for the communication of role responsibilities (Eys et al., in press).
Note. Adapted from Organizational Stress: Studies in Role Conflict and Ambiguity (p. 30), by R.L. Kahn, D.M Wolfe, R.P. Quinn, J.D. Snoek, and R.A. Rosenthal, 1964, New York: Wiley

Box 12.1
The dimensions of role responsibilities in sport teams

Role Dimension	Illustration
Role Performance: Behavior which is consistent with role expectations	We all have our jobs on a hockey team . . . And we respect a player who does his job because he is bringing something special to the team. John [Ferguson] was a rough and hard hockey player because the Montreal Canadiens needed a player like that. Without him, and guys like Terry Harper and Ted Harris on defense, we would not have been as good as we became. (Montreal Canadiens' Yvan Cournoyer, quoted in Goyens & Turowetz, 1986, pp.200-201)
Role Clarity: The degree to which the individual understands what behavior is expected	Everyone knew his job . . . We were a big, strong team that was not very mobile, so Freddie gave us a system that would work for us. It wouldn't have worked for Montreal or one of the more skilled teams, but it did for us. He used to say, "Give a guy a small job and make him do it very, very well." (Bobby Clarke, quoted in Swift, 1987, p. 97)
Role Conflict: The lack of sufficient ability, motivation, or time to achieve that goal.	A part of [Kobe Bryant] . . . wants desperately to be in the group, to enjoy the camaraderie of his teammates . . . But there is another part of Kobe, which often wins out, a part that wants, perhaps needs, to be isolated from the group. To have it both ways is simply not possible. (Phil Jackson, quoted in Jackson & Arkush, 2004, p. 44)
Role Efficacy: The degree to which the individual believes that he or she has the capabilities to perform formal role functions	So what the Heat has is a sweet kid with a sweet game. It also has three strong personalities—Shaq, [Eddie] Jones and [Damon] Jones—who allow [Dwyane] Wade to stay comfortable in his role as the quiet young star, the object of everyone's affection. "Being a leader is one thing I've never felt comfortable with," says Wade. "Even in high school and college I wasn't the guy firing everyone up. It's not in my nature, and I sure don't have to be outspoken around here." (quoted in McCallum, 2005, p. 58)
Role Acceptance: The degree to which the individual agrees and has similar expectations for his or her role responsibilities as the role sender	Anchoring the second unit will be Derek Fisher . . . [who] also puts the team first. This season I'm asking for his biggest sacrifice yet. For Fish, a starter the last two years, going back to the bench will feel like a demotion, which, unfortunately, comes at the most inopportune time, the option year of his contract . . . The transition can be difficult, but if a player fully commits to his revised role, he can be effective. I'm convinced Fish will make it work. (Phil Jackson, quoted in Jackson & Arkush, 2004, p. 29).
Role Satisfaction: The degree to which the individual is satisfied with his/her role responsibilities	Just 48 hours after righthander Jaime Navarro arrived at the [Chicago] White Sox training headquarters . . . he was summoned into manager Terry Bevington's office. You're my Number 1 guy," Bevington told Navarro. You're my Opening Day starter. I'm counting on you." . . . Navarro relished the opportunity. "I'll be ready," he told Bevington. "Give me the ball." (quoted in Tim Crothers, 1997, p. 107)

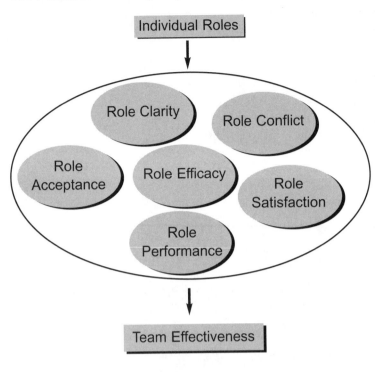

Figure 12.2. The relationship between individual roles and team effectiveness

flip side of role clarity. Kahn and his colleagues (1964) identified two major types of role ambiguity. One major type is referred to as *task ambiguity,* which represents uncertainty resulting "from lack of information concerning the proper definition of the job, its goals and the permissible means of implementing them" (Kahn et al., 1964, p. 94). A second major type is referred as *socioemotional ambiguity.* Socioemotional ambiguity represents the uncertainty that the individual possesses about the consequences to herself, to the organization, and/or to the role as a result of carrying out expected responsibilities.

Beauchamp, Bray, Eys, and Carron (2002) developed a conceptual model (see Figure 12.3) of role ambiguity for interactive sport teams based on the work of Kahn and colleagues. Interactive sport teams, such as hockey, basketball, soccer, are those where athletes interact with both their own teammates and their opponents. As the model depicted in Figure 12.3 illustrates, on both offense and defense athletes need to understand four aspects associated with their role. One aspect pertains to the scope of their responsibilities. For example, a basketball player might have a number of general roles that he or she is required to perform including, perhaps, the point guard position and the role of captain.

The second aspect is related to the manner in which the responsibilities of a role should be carried out (i.e., the behaviors necessary to carryout role responsibilities). For example, how does a captain behave? A young inexperienced athlete just elected captain might wonder about the degree to which she should be vocal/critical/supportive with her teammates or whether she should consult with the coach about potential problem areas or athletes. A young captain may not have the answers to these questions.

A third type of role ambiguity that might be present is an uncertainty regarding how role performance is being evaluated. An individual playing a point guard role may not know whether the evaluation criteria for his/her position is based on statistics (e.g., points scored) or by more subjective criteria, such as the leadership displayed on the court. Also, a captain may not understand whether the criteria he or she should be concerned about originates with the coach or teammates (i.e., who does he/she represent?)

Finally, the fourth type of ambiguity arises from uncertainty about the consequences of not successfully fulfilling role responsibilities. Thus, for example, the young team captain discussed above could worry that her behaviors in her role might distance her

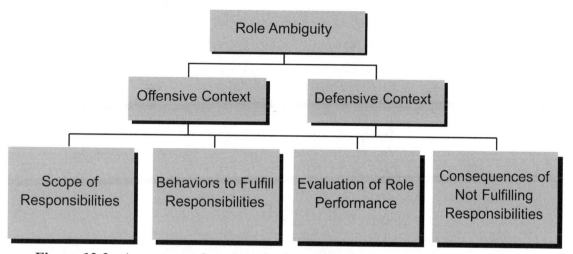

Figure 12.3. A conceptual model of role ambiguity for interactive sport teams (Adapted from Beauchamp et al., 2002)

socially from her teammates or possibly diminish the prestige associated with being a team captain.

It was pointed out earlier that formal roles are those established by the group or organization whereas informal roles evolve as a result of the interactions which take place within the team. There is generally a greater probability that role clarity will be present in the case of formal roles. Nonetheless, even in the case of formal roles, the specific responsibilities associated with a role must be clearly spelled out. This insures that there are no misunderstandings. However, in reality, misunderstandings exist and result in individuals not understanding their roles as well as they should. In an effort to understand why role ambiguity exists, Eys and colleagues (in press) undertook a study to determine what athletes believed were potential sources of role ambiguity. The results of this study demonstrated that athletes perceived a number of different causes of role ambiguity, which are summarized in Table 12.3. Generally, it is possible that the athlete (i.e., the focal person), the coach (i.e., the role sender), and the situation can play a part in role ambiguity being present for the role incumbent.

The importance of understanding roles in a sport environment can be demonstrated by a concise overview of recent research that has been conducted. Most importantly, the greater the athlete understands his or her role, the more likely he or she will perform the role successfully (Beauchamp et al., 2002). In addition to better role performance, role clarity is also related to individual cognition and affect. For example, greater role clarity has been found to be related to decreased perceptions of competitive state anxiety (Beauchamp, Bray, Eys, & Carron, 2003), increased perceptions of athlete satisfaction (Eys, Carron, Bray, & Beauchamp, 2003), and increased task cohesion (Eys & Carron, 2001).

Task cohesion is the degree to which the group is united in the pursuit of its goals and objectives. When there is consensus on the group goals and how to achieve them, when there is a strong general commitment to the group task, considerable pressure is placed on individual members. That is, there is greater group pressure on individual members to clearly understand their responsibilities, to accept those responsibilities, and to carry them out effectively.

Table 12.3
Sources of Role Ambiguity in Interactive Sport Teams
(Eys, Carron, Beauchamp, & Bray, in press)

Source	Potential Causes
The Role Sender (typically the coach)	The coach does not have sufficient expertise or knowledge to communicate role responsibilities. The coach does not communicate with his or her athletes. The coach communicates with athletes but communication is unclear. The coach communicates with athletes but sends conflicting information (e.g., be an enforcer on the ice but don't get penalties).
The Focal Person (typically the athlete)	Athlete is not attending team functions or not paying attention to task instructions (e.g., in practice). Athlete is not informing the coach that he/she does not understand his/her role responsibilities (e.g., lack of initiative). Athlete lacks expertise in sport to be able to comprehend role expectations. Athlete believes role responsibilities to be different from those the coach communicates.
The Situation	Complexity of the sport (e.g., athlete moves from a high school environment to the university level) Prior experiences of the athlete (e.g., athlete is new to the sport) Lack of practical application for the athlete (e.g., a bench player or injured athlete)

Finally, it is important to remember that not all athletes or group members react similarly to ambiguous situations. For example, prior research has shown that role ambiguity perceptions differ for starters and non-starters (i.e., starters experience less role ambiguity than non-starters; Beauchamp et al., in press) as well as veteran and rookie team members (i.e., veteran players typically experience less role ambiguity than first year players; Eys et al., 2003). Also, some individuals have a higher *need for clarity*. Bray and colleagues (2004) found that the negative relationship between role ambiguity and athlete satisfaction was more pronounced for athletes who had a higher need for their roles to be clear.

Role Conflict

Role conflict exists when, despite the presence of consensus about role responsibilities between a role sender and a role occupant, the role occupant (i.e., focal person) doesn't have sufficient ability, motivation, or time to achieve that goal. Role conflict is another *cognitive* component of role involvement. Every coach wants his or her athletes to do a good job, to help the team, to contribute to team success. This is constantly conveyed directly and indirectly to the athlete. But, an athlete may lack the necessary skills, or may be confused because the behaviors considered to be associated with "doing a good job" may vary either between coaches or from one instance to the next.

Kahn and his colleagues (1964) identified a number of different types of role conflict. One, called *intrasender conflict*, exists when the role occupant feels incongruent expectations from a single member of a role set. This is clearly illustrated in Box 12.2 in the anecdote relayed by Don Cherry, a former coach of the Boston Bruins. Harry Sinden of the Boston Bruins (the only role sender) indicated that Al Secord was to be aggressive. At the same time, however, Secord was criticized for receiving penalties, a logical consequence of being aggressive. So from the same source, he felt pressures to both engage and not engage in the behaviors consistent with his role.

A second type of role conflict identified by Kahn and his colleagues is *intersender conflict*. Intersender conflict is present when the role occupant feels incongruent expectations from two or more members of a single role set. Box 12.2 provides an illustration from work by Susan Birrell and Diana Richter (1994) in which they discussed the feminist transformation of sport using softball as a frame-of-reference. They pointed out that the feminist solution to low skill level is "to offer opportunities for women with little sport experience to learn the sport in a supportive environment" (Birrell & Richter, 1994, p. 235). However, the softball player quoted in Box 12.2 experienced intersender conflict. On the one hand, her role as a member of the team involved playing to her capabilities. On the other hand, lesser talented individuals also sent messages that put her under pressure because her skill level was considered to be too high at times.

Person-role conflict, a third type of role conflict identified by Kahn and his colleagues, is present when a role requires certain behaviors that the person doesn't have the motivation or ability to carry out. The examples of person-role conflict in sport are numerous. Box 12.2 contains a quote by Louie DeBrusk, a hockey player who had difficulty fulfilling the role expectations associated with being his team's enforcer. Another example arises from baseball. In 1987, George Bell of the Toronto Blue Jays was the American League Most Valuable Player. When he arrived at spring training in 1988, the Blue Jays indicated they intended to use him in the designated hitter role (DH). He was extremely unhappy with his new role and his motivation suffered. As his agent Randy Hendricks pointed out,

> *I guess the best way to describe it is that he feels a big arrow has been shot into his ego . . . The designated hitter is generally regarded as one-half of a player . . . it's a blow to George's pride. I could see if this thing gets out of hand that the Blue Jays might want to trade him. ("Gillick talks," 1988, C2)*

Athletes in amateur sport who experience person-role conflict often quit the sport (Volp & Keil, 1987) while professional athletes often demand to be traded or, as George Bell did, they air their grievances with the team in the media.

The above three types refer to what is termed *intrarole conflict*, or conflict that is experienced within one role set (e.g., conflict having to do with being a member of a sport team). However, it is possible to experience conflict that arises when there are incongruent expectations from two or more different role sets (e.g., being a member of a sport team *and* being a student). This is termed *interrole conflict*. The quote in Box 12.2 from

Box 12.2
Examples of role conflict in sport

Role Dimension	Illustration
Intrasender Conflict: Incongruent expectations for behavior from one member of a role set	Sinden always liked fighters, which is why I couldn't understand why Secord didn't make a hit with him. After I left the Bruins, I ran into Al one day in Boston and he was really depressed. "I don't understand what the Bruins are doing to me," he said. "I'm on the bench. I asked why I wasn't playing and they told me, 'Because you're not playing your game, you're not playing aggressive and not hitting.' So naturally, I go out and be aggressive and start hitting and naturally I get a few penalties. Then they bench me again. I say, 'Why aren't I playing?' They say, 'Because you're getting too many penalties.' My head is all screwed up." (Don Cherry, former coach of the Boston Bruins, quoted in Cherry & Fischler, 1982, p. 193)
Intersender Conflict: Incongruent expectations from different individuals from one role set	I got criticized for being too good, because if I threw a ball too hard to someone it was oppressing them. Just bullshit, absolute bullshit. And, I'll never forget this one woman, she came up to me at a party one time and she said, "You know, you really oppress me because you're so good at softball." It's like people were struggling with that whole feeling of how women are discouraged from sport, and how people who weren't good at it are put down in phys. ed. in grade school, and (they were) dumping all that confusion on people who are good athletes. (Softball player quoted in Birrell & Richter, 1994, p.237)
Person-Role Conflict: Role requirements are in conflict with individual's motives or values	The fact that I am a fighter on the ice and the difficulties I've had with that job definitely brought me to drink a few times. I'd go out after the game, and all I could think of was the pressure I had on me during the game. Maybe I didn't fight. There'd be guilt that I didn't fight, the feeling of worthlessness, I guess. Then I'd go out and drink myself into oblivion, and maybe I'd get into a fight later. I have been advised by people who have helped me in rehab not to go back to my job. (Edmonton Oilers' hockey player, Louie DeBrusk, quoted in Farber, 1997b, p. 68).
Interrole Conflict: Incongruent expectations from two or more role sets	The whole week my son was sick, I hardly trained at all. It was hard on both of us because I wanted to go out for a run, but he felt too sick for me to leave him. I would have to wait until my husband came home from work, but sometimes he would work a double shift so I would get no running in. So not only is my training hurt, but I missed several classes because I had to stay home with him [my son]. (36-year old college distance runner quoted in Jambor & Weekes, 1996, p. 150).

a nontraditional college athlete—a 36-year old married female with two children who was interviewed by Jambor and Weekes (1996)—provides a good example. There are responsibilities associated with being an athlete, a mother, a wife, and a student. As the quote in Box 12.2 clearly shows, the pressures associated with these various roles can produce interrole conflict.

One generalization well supported by research is that role conflict has a bearing on an individual's commitment to the organization. When role conflict—in any of its manifestations is high—the individual's commitment to the organization is reduced. The story of Paul Mulvey, an NHL player, is extreme but it does serve to illustrate the point. Mulvey hesitated for what he estimated to be 20 seconds when he was ordered to leave the bench and enter a fight on the ice. Between periods his coach, Don Perry

> *started screaming that Mulvey wouldn't stick up for his teammates. Mulvey got undressed—and never again put on an NHL uniform. "Those 20 seconds," Mulvey says, "probably cost me a million dollars." (quoted in Farber, 1997b, p. 72)*

In addition to commitment, role conflict is negatively related to satisfaction (Jackson & Schuler, 1986), the degree to which individuals believe they have the capabilities to carry out their role functions (i.e., role efficacy; Beauchamp & Bray, 2001), and is positively related to burnout (Capel et al., 1987).

Role Efficacy

When role clarity ambiguity and role conflict are minimal or absent, the role occupant is more likely to believe that he or she can successfully carry out expected responsibilities. An athlete's belief in his or her capabilities to perform role responsibilities is termed *role efficacy* and reflects a third cognitive component of role involvement. Strictly speaking, role efficacy is "a distinct construct representing a player's perceived capabilities to perform formal role functions in an interdependent team environment" (Bray, Brawley, & Carron, 2002, pp. 661-662). Similar to self-efficacy—the belief "in one's capabilities to organize and execute the course of action required to produce given attainments" (Bandura, 1997, p.3)—role efficacy is directly determined by the types of mastery experiences an athlete has acquired. For example, Bray and his colleagues (2002) found that those athletes who had greater playing time and were starters on their respective teams also had higher perceptions of their ability to perform their roles. The importance of role efficacy was demonstrated in separate studies by Beauchamp and colleagues (2002) and Bray, Balaguer, and Duda (2004). They found positive relationships between role efficacy and role performance in British rugby and Spanish soccer players respectively.

Role Acceptance

A final cognitive component of role involvement is role acceptance. Role acceptance reflects "the degree to which an athlete perceives his or her own expectations for role responsibilities as similar to, and agreeable with, the expectations for role responsibilities determined by his or her role senders" (Eys, Beauchamp, & Bray, in press, p. 36). Typically, role acceptance has been thought of as the degree to which an athlete is satisfied with a role. However, it is possible for an athlete to accept role responsibilities but not be completely satisfied with them (see Illustration 12.1). For example, an athlete who typically does not see a lot of playing time may be dissatisfied with her position on the bench but, for a variety of reasons, agrees to occupy that role and be a contributing member of the team by trying hard in practice and encouraging other members who are in the playing unit. Sage (1998) provided two suggestions that would be applicable to account for the cognitions and behaviors of individuals in this situation. First, athletes might accept potentially unsatisfying role responsibilities because of other benefits in the situation; for example, recognition for being a member of a popular sport group, attending team parties, and traveling to new places all might be secondary benefits. A second suggestion that is applicable to this situation is that throughout the course of their athletic careers, athletes are conditioned to conform to the demands of the coach or other authority figures and, thus, will agree to attempt to perform roles that may be dissatisfying. Overall, the degree to which all athletes on a team accept and attempt to perform their role responsibilities (regardless of the prestige associated with the role) is absolutely vital to the proper functioning of the group as a whole. It is likely that this element of role involvement is the most critical in terms of how well the group performs together.

Role Satisfaction

Another link in the relationship between individual roles and group effectiveness is *role satisfaction*—the affective aspect of the role dimension (see Illustration 12.1). Locke's (1976) definition for job satisfaction is equally applicable to role satisfaction: "pleasurable emotional state resulting from the perception of one's [role] as fulfilling" (p. 1342). The quote used to introduce this chapter also provides an illustration of role satisfaction. Former New York Rangers' captain Mark Messier pointed out that when he was a member

Illustration 12.1. Role acceptance does differ from role satisfaction!

of the Edmonton Oilers, he had a role that was different from the one played by teammate Wayne Gretzky and that he was happy with that role. Box 12.1 contains another example of role satisfaction. In the quote, Jaime Navarro, a Chicago White Sox pitcher, expresses satisfaction with his role within the team.

In an attempt to determine what aspects of a role are associated with satisfaction, Genevieve Rail (1987) tested 60 administrators and coaches involved in amateur sport programs. She found that no matter what level the individuals worked at—local, provincial, or national—the same four conditions were critical for satisfaction. One of these is the *opportunity to use specialized skills or competencies* in the role.

Thus, for example, an athlete might be required to fulfill a defensive specialist role on the team and that role initially might seem unattractive; the skills required to be a defensive specialist might not appear to require high ability or competency. Consequently, satisfaction with that role might be low. If the role occupant can be led to the understanding that playing outstanding defense requires specialized skills and competencies, there is an increased likelihood that role satisfaction will be enhanced.

Another contributor to role satisfaction is *feedback and recognition*. The defensive specialist is often less visible than other members of the group. When feedback and recognition are provided to the role occupant, satisfaction is increased; when they are not, satisfaction diminishes.

A third, related factor mentioned by Rail was *role significance*. If the role is critical or perceived to be critical to team success, the occupant is more satisfied. In the quote in Box 12.1, Yvan Cournoyer outlined the importance of John Ferguson's role as a policeman on the Montreal Canadiens. Ferguson knew that his role was viewed as significant and important for team success, as the following quote illustrates:

> It was really important to me that the guys felt that way. One year the Canadiens veterans voted me the most valuable player and that was the year Cournoyer led the team in scoring. What impressed me was that in the Canadiens' scheme of things you could be a leader not only as a goal scorer but also as an aggressor. (Quoted in Goyens & Turowetz, 1986, p. 201)

The fourth condition identified by Rail was *autonomy*—the opportunity to work independently. It may be possible that autonomy isn't as important for role satisfaction in athletes as it was for the administrators and coaches studied by Rail but, this seems unlikely. In 1980, Richard Hackman and Greg Oldham developed a conceptual model in an attempt to account for the motivation, satisfaction with personal growth, satisfaction with job responsibilities, and work effectiveness of individuals in achievement situations. Three critical psychological states identified by Hackman and Oldham were (1) the perceived meaningfulness of the work, (2) the perceived personal responsibility for the outcome, and (3) the knowledge of results available. Autonomy directly influences perceptions of personal responsibility for the outcome.

Enhancing Role Performance

Coach. Athletic Director. Student. Counselor. Mother. Daughter. One person could play each of these roles (and others) simultaneously. Humans are social animals and, consequently, involvement in a large number of groups is inevitable. And equally inevitable is the assumption of different roles in these different groups. William Shakespeare probably expressed it best in his play *As You Like It:*

> *All the world's a stage. And all the men and women merely players. They have their exits and their entrances. And one man in his time plays many parts. (Act II, Scene 7)*

Unfortunately, the general behaviors considered appropriate for each of the roles listed above can be quite different. Consequently, a number of challenges are associated with performing any one role successfully—for example, the role occupant may not have sufficient ability, motivation, time, or understanding of the role to produce the behaviors expected. The last chapter of this book highlights some team-building strategies that may be effective. However, some general suggestions can be found below regarding enhancing role execution.

First, an effective goal-setting program at both the team and individual level can improve both role clarity and role acceptance. Goal setting serves four important functions: it directs the individual's attention and actions toward appropriate behaviors, it motivates the individual to develop strategies to achieve the goal, it contributes to increased interest in the activity, and it leads to prolonged effort (Locke, Shaw, Saari, & Latham, 1981). All of these contribute to role clarity and role acceptance.

With regard to role conflict, some approaches suggested from other problem areas in sport have relevance. For example, Andreas Volp and Udo Keil (1987) observed that one effective means of dealing with intrapersonal conflict is through cognitive restructuring. An underlying assumption for engaging in cognitive restructuring is the need for cognitive consistency. As Volp and Keil noted,

> *All organisms prefer to live in a state of equilibrium, a state of cognitive balance. Whenever this equilibrium is threatened, cognitive inconsistency or dissonance arises, which is perceived as tension or conflict . . . This is always the case when elements within a cognitive field are inconsistent with each other. The individual then takes steps to reduce conflict and restore the equilibrium. (p. 359)*

In the process of cognitive restructuring, two strategies are possible. An individual can devalue one of the roles. Thus, a coach might reduce the importance (i.e., relevance) of her teaching role if the behaviors in that role are in conflict with her coaching. An individual can also bring different roles into balance (i.e., harmony) by decreasing the differences among the component parts of each role. Thus, a coach might emphasize the fact that his coaching is teaching, that elite athletes are similar to elite students (i.e., graduate students), that recruiting in athletics is like recruiting in graduate programs, and that scholarships for outstanding athletes are comparable to scholarships for outstanding students. This altered perspective would help to reduce conflict between the two roles.

When Volp and Keil compared elite athletes with medium- and lesser-skilled athletes, they found that elite athletes exhibited the least intrapersonal conflict. The elite athletes also made the greatest use of cognitive restructuring strategies, particularly by increasing the harmony among potentially conflicting elements. On the basis of their results, Volp and Keil suggested that *competing successfully at a high level requires the athlete to cognitively restructure incoming information to reduce conflict that might otherwise be an obstacle to performance . . . A successful athlete seems able to align himself or herself with the demands of the sport. The harmonization of conflicting cognitions seems to be a functional method of coping with contradictions inside the cognitive field . . . that might otherwise impair motivation and performance. (p.372)*

There are other techniques in addition to cognitive restructuring, which might be useful for reducing role conflict. For example, in his discussion on alleviating athlete burnout, Keith Henschen (1986) suggested (a) scheduling time-outs, (b) increasing participation in decision-making, (c) assuming control of outcomes, and (d) planning mental practices. Each of these might be used to deal with role conflict.

Scheduling time-outs involves setting up periods away from the situation. A coach may feel overwhelmed by the pressures and stresses associated with teaching and coaching simultaneously; with planning and attending practices; with meeting athletes, the media, parents, and other coaches. It could be beneficial to have his or her major teaching load scheduled in a term after the end of the season. Another strategy might be to timetable in a specific day, or a morning or evening, or even a period away from the concerns of the role. A time-out can vary in type, timing, and duration depending on the constraints of the situation. There are no fixed prescriptions except that time away from a role does help reduce role conflict.

Increasing the participation of others in decision-making can also help to reduce role conflict resulting from overload. Since role conflict arises because the role occupant doesn't have sufficient ability, time, motivation, or understanding, the recruitment of others to fill these gaps can alleviate some of the problem. Increased participation may be accomplished in either of two ways: by sharing responsibilities among available group members or by increasing the number of group members. As was pointed out in Chapter 3, increasing the group's size produces increases group resources.

A third possibility is to attempt to assume greater control over outcomes. Role expectations evolve from both the individual (the role occupant) and the group or organization (role senders). By attempting to gain greater control, the role occupant can insure that the behavioral demands (either self-imposed or from others) for the role are not beyond his or her capabilities. One way to gain greater control is by negotiating compromises. For example, an athlete could attempt to have the coach alter the factors producing the greatest stress or pressure. Similarly, a coach might negotiate with the administration to reduce some responsibilities producing role conflict.

Chapter Thirteen

GROUP NORMS

The Club de Hockey Canadien did not immediately stand the NHL or the sports world on its ears. The Fabulous Flying Frenchmen were just one of many teams, no more, no less. But they were an organization that would eventually develop . . . a winning tradition by stressing the importance of success. One would assume that most work organizations naturally generate such strong beliefs and commitments among their employees. The truth is that these qualities take years to cultivate. In the case of the Canadiens, those athletes and administrators not willing to commit themselves to the degree considered necessary for success were selectively eliminated from within the organization. (Goyens & Turowetz, 1986, p. 28)

The nature of group norms is clearly illustrated in the quote used to introduce this chapter. Norms are the standards for behavior that are expected of group members. As Table 13.1 shows, norms are descriptive, evaluative, informal, unobtrusive, internal, flexible,

Table 13.1
The Nature of Norms (Adapted from Forsythe, 1983)

Characteristic	Description
Descriptive	Norms represent the standards for behavior in a group.
Evaluative	Norms establish priorities for different behaviors, marking some out as more valuable than others.
Informal	Norms are not formally adopted by the group but result from a gradual change in behavior until a consensus in reached in the group.
Unobtrusive	Norms are taken for granted and only become an important issue when they are violated.
Flexible	Minor deviations from norms are generally permitted.
Internalized	Norms are internalized by individual group members. Adherence results primarily from satisfaction produced rather than fear of sanctions.
Stable	Norms develop slowly over time and are very resistant to change.

and stable (Forsythe, 1983). Insofar as their descriptive function is concerned, norms outline the group's beliefs about the standards for behavior considered appropriate.

In terms of their evaluative function, norms put a priority on the values or standards that govern the behaviors of a wide cross section of different individuals who have membership in the group—independent of position occupied, status possessed, and/or role responsibility. As such, group norms represent the organization's or group's consensus about what is considered acceptable. Norms are also informal and unobtrusive; they are not specifically or overtly set out by the group. Gradual changes in individual behavior occur over time until a consensus is achieved about what is appropriate. Because they are not specifically set out as rules or laws, norms are most evident when they are violated. Nonetheless, individual group members internalize norms so that adherence occurs primarily because of the satisfaction this produces rather than the fear of sanctions. Some flexibility is also present and minor deviations from a norm are acceptable. Finally, norms are stable; they emerge slowly over time and are resistant to change.

Because norms reflect existing group values, the group evaluates individual behavior on an ongoing basis and judges it to be acceptable or unacceptable, satisfactory or unsatisfactory. Acceptable behavior is rewarded or approved through verbal appreciation, elevated prestige, increased group acceptance, and recognition. On the other hand, unacceptable behavior is sanctioned by verbal criticism, ostracism, physical abuse, or even rejection from the group (Crosbie, 1975). The sanctioning of unacceptable behavior is illustrated in a quote regarding a gymnastic team coached by Bela Karoyli (see Box 13.1).

Groups emerge in a sport setting. For example, as the structure of an intramural basketball team emerges, group norms develop around such behaviors as the average number of

---

Box 13.1
Sanctioning of Unacceptable Behavior

Erika Stokes, a former elite American gymnast, "rarely ate in front of people, a behavior instilled by Karolyi. During the summers, she and the other members of Karolyi's elite team lived at the coach's 53-acre ranch north of Houston. Karolyi ran gymnastics camps for youngsters from across the country while also training his elites. After practicing from 7 a.m. until late morning, the girls would hit the kitchen in the cabin where they stayed under the supervision of an adult. None ate breakfast before working out, so they were starving. They grabbed cereal or fruit, then plopped down in the living room to watch "The Price is Right," listening for the tires of Karolyi's four-wheel drive. The coach stopped by every day to announce the rest of the day's schedule. Whenever they heard him approaching, they stashed the food. Karolyi equated eating with sloth and weakness.

One day, arriving on foot, he was almost to the door before anyone spotted him. "Oh my God, here he is!" The girls lunged toward the kitchen, slamming the cereal boxes behind cabinets. They shoved their bowls under the couch. But Erika sat calmly eating her peach. How could Karolyi mind her eating a peach?

Karolyi took one look at the peach and exploded. "You're so lazy!" he bellowed. "You're so fat! You just come in and pig out after workouts. All you think about is food."

That night, Karolyi made the team train an extra two hours for Erica's transgression. (Ryan, 1995, p. 74-75)

shots taken by any one player in a game. Also, pressure is placed on individual members to conform to this group norm. If a team member violates the norm—(e.g., continually taking more shots than is deemed appropriate), he or she will be sanctioned. The sanctions might take the form of criticism or ostracism. Other team members might begin using a derogatory nickname such as "Gunner" to try to relay their irritation or they might stop passing the ball. Depending on the persistence of the behavior, its seriousness, and the cohesiveness of the group, the norm violator might even be rejected from the team.

Types of Team Norms

Four general types of norms have been identified by Mott (1965). These are summarized in Box 13.2. A *prescribed norm* serves to specify which behaviors are considered appropriate for group members. The norm for productivity—the concept of a fair day's work— would be one example of a prescribed norm. In Box 13.2, Dave Poulin, a former captain of the Philadelphia hockey team, illustrates the norm for productivity.

The expectations that emerge around behaviors not considered appropriate are referred to as *proscribed norms*. Essentially, they represent the flip side of a prescribed norm. For example, being unshaven and poorly groomed—(behaviors used as examples in Box 13.2) are sometimes considered inappropriate behaviors. As well, in coed softball, proscribed norms define the game as less serious than same-sex softball. In coed softball, men are expected to "tone down" the aggressiveness of the play they exhibit in male softball. Some

Box 13.2 *Illustrations of Various Group Norms*	
Type of Norm	**Quotation**
Prescribed Norm	When a kid comes to camp and sees what's expected of him . . . he thinks, 'I've got no choice'. It's a lot easier to assimilate someone into that than to start it from scratch. (Philadelphia Flyer captain Dave Poulin, quoted in Swift, 1987, p. 99)
Proscribed Norm	I want our boys to look like the All-American boy . . . the All-American boy is clean shaven and his hair is in order. That is how I expect them to look. (Former Tennessee basketball coach Ray Mears, quoted in Eitzen & Sage, 1982, p. 71)
Permissive Norm	We're always looking at an advantage-disadvantage situation . . . Did the person do something illegal to create an advantage for himself or put his opponent at a disadvantage? If he did, then, it's a foul. If not . . . that's a foul we wouldn't call. (NBA official Darrell Garretson, quoted in Montville, 1987, p. 68)
Preference Norm	I play without officials on the playground . . . I never call a foul. You call a foul and then you have your 10 minutes of arguing and then maybe five minutes of fighting before you can start playing again. It's not worth it . . . unless, of course, the score is 9-9 and the game is 10. Then you call everything and go ahead with the fight. (former Detroit Piston player Isiah Thomas, quoted in Montville, 1987, p. 69).

of the proscribed norms for males include "not throwing the ball hard to a female team-mate, not sliding hard into an opposing female infielder, and regulating language" (Snyder & Ammons, 1993, p. 6).

It is important to bear in mind that norms are expectations that exist in the minds of group members. They provide guidelines about what group members should do, ought to do, and are expected to do (Homans, 1950). As was pointed out in the introduction to this chapter, they are not laws or formalized rules. Thus, if a team had a rule relating to cur-few—"anyone missing curfew will not be on the roster for the next game"—it would not be considered a norm. Norms do emerge around rules and regulations, however. The norm, the expectation of the group, might be that the rule about curfew is unimportant.

As Box 13.2 shows, there are also *permissive norms:* patterns of behavior that are permitted but not required. This type of norm is illustrated in Darrel Garretson's statement that the norm for officiating in the NBA evolves around the principle of advantage. Behaviors for which a foul might be (or should be) called are ignored if no advantage is gained or if no disadvantage to an opponent results.

Another place where permissive norms exist is baseball. David Rainey and Janet Larsen (1988) demonstrated empirically that baseball umpires use a strike zone that differs from what is set out in the rulebook. They had 16 high school/college level umpires describe the official rule-book definition of the strike zone. The umpires were then required to reproduce the strike zone by drawing lines across a picture of a batter's body. Finally, they were asked to draw two more lines showing the upper and lower boundaries of the strike zone they actually used.

A significant deviation was found between the top of the actual strike zone and the line umpires used. The umpires reduced the size of the strike zone by lowering the top boundary. The reasons given for not following the rule book fell into five general categories: (a) positioning problems (with a low stance behind the catcher, it is difficult to call the high pitch), (b) others' expectations (the coaches and players expect a lower strike zone), (c) major league influence (the high pitch is not called in the major leagues), (d) convenience (the letters on a player's jersey are a better reference), and (e) discretion (provide the batters with a better opportunity to hit).

The final type of norm presented in Box 13.2 is the *preference norm*—behaviors preferred but not required by group members. The quote by Isaiah Thomas provides a good illustration. Fouls could be called constantly in a playground basketball game. But, players prefer not to call them because they disrupt the flow of the play. However, in a close game, a foul likely will be called if an advantage/disadvantage results.

Emergence of Team Norms

If a norm is a behavioral standard, how does it develop? One essential prerequisite is team *interactions*. The contacts members have with each other help to clarify the standards that are acceptable for behavior. As Victor Vroom (1969) pointed out, "interaction among persons tends to decrease the variance in their behavior, and, in the extreme, can produce highly standardized behavioral patterns" (p. 223). The influence of group interaction on the development of norms was demonstrated by research conducted by Michelle Colman and Albert Carron (2001). They examined the prevalence of norms in *independent* sport teams, such as swimming, track and field, and wrestling. While many of these athletes consider themselves members of a team, they compete individually and, thus, have less interaction in games and practices than their counterparts participating in sports such as basketball, hockey, or soccer. Not surprisingly, Colman and Carron found little support for the presence of norms on individual sport teams.

A second essential prerequisite is *reinforcement*. The behaviors that the vast majority of team members find acceptable are reinforced; unacceptable behaviors are discouraged. Consequently, each individual comes to understand the standards (norms) deemed appropriate.

The role of interaction and reinforcement in the emergence of group norms is illustrated by an example. When a bridge club forms, a wide range of differences are possible in issues such as punctuality, the amount of "coaching" permissible during the bidding, the amount of social conversation appropriate during the play, and even the type of food and beverages served. Through interactions and reinforcement, a general understanding develops within the group; the range of behaviors considered permissible by the group decreases. The general standards that develop help the group operate smoothly. Similarly, as sport teams develop, and team members interact frequently, differences in the amount of effort they expend at practices, the type of clothing they wear on road trips, and so on, gradually decreases.

The Function of Team Norms

Describing their influence, Armstrong stated, "Norms exert very powerful pressure on behavior" (p. 207). Researchers (Armstrong, 2001; Jones, 2001; Wheelen, 1999) have noted that norms perform important functions within the industrial/organizational domain in that they tell people what they should be doing, saying, and believing. By providing group members with general prescriptions for appropriate behavior and implicitly outlining the limits for permissible deviations from those prescriptions, norms serve two general functions within the team (Kiesler & Kiesler, 1969). One of these is *informational*. Norms help the individual gain insight into the group; they provide a standard against which a new member can validate his/her opinions, attitudes, and behavior. Norms also insure that the individual's opinions, attitudes, and behavior don't deviate dramatically from other team members. Dave Poulin illustrated the informational function of team norms in the quote presented in Box 13.2. He pointed out that Philadelphia Flyer rookies came to camp, saw how the veterans were working, and saw what was expected to be successful. This information helped to insure that their opinions, attitudes, and behaviors were consistent with what was expected of the Flyers.

The second, related function of team norms is *integration*. The individual who understands and accepts the team norm is drawn into the group; the individual who does not is rejected or removed from the group. When team norms are accepted, team goals can be successfully pursued and the continuation of the group is insured. The integrative function of team norms is illustrated in an anecdote pertaining to a novice shooter:

> *It is expected that the novice shooters will seek advice from the experts. The failure to do so is a clear violation of informal rules, and results in ostracism. In one incident, a novice was put into a squad to shoot. Because*

of his dress and expensive weapon, he was assumed to be familiar with the sport. After flagrant violations of an established safety rule (leaving the breech closed while changing positions), he was chastised by an expert shooting in the squad. This resulted in subsequent gossip in the clubhouse and exclusion of the shooter while paying for his second round of trap. The novice departed after two rounds. (Guy, 1995, p. 35)

Partridge and Stevens (2002) outlined four specific benefits that emanate from the integrative and informational functions of norms: (a) positive norms (e.g., a strong work ethic) can facilitate performance, (b) the behavior of team members who adhere to team norms can be anticipated and others can respond accordingly, (c) embarrassing problems can be avoided through the presence of norms (e.g., being late and missing the bus), and (d) the values of the group are promoted (e.g., a disciplined and proud group of high school football players may decide to wear ties to school). Overall, conformity to the team norms helps to contribute to the unity of the team. Deviance from the norms breaks down this unity.

The Stability of Norms

Once team norms are established, they are slow to change. In a typical study on conformity to group standards, Jacobs and Campbell (1961) had groups of four subjects judge the distance a light moved. Initially, three of the four group members in each group were confederates (accomplices) of the experimenter; they all reported that the light had moved 15 to 16 inches. The naive subjects in the group correctly perceived (and reported) that the light had moved approximately 4 inches. However, after a series of trials in which the confederates continued to endorse an incorrect standard, the naive subjects also began to report that the light had moved 15 to 16 inches. When this incorrect norm was well established, the composition of the group was changed so that naive new members replaced existing group members over a series of "generations."

With each generation, the new group member (a naive subject) reported that the light had traveled about 4 inches. The three established group members (who were no longer confederates of the experimenter) continued to adhere to the incorrect standard and report that the light had moved approximately 15 to 16 inches. After a series of trials, the new naive group member adopted the group norm. Although each generation showed a tendency to move closer to the correct standard, it took four to five generations before this was accomplished (see Figure 13.1).

What this demonstrates of course is the stability of group norms. There is always the question, of course, whether a laboratory study has specific application in the "real world." People associated with work and sport organizations know that it does. An applicable case study is the Toronto Raptors of the National Basketball Association:

[New head coach Sam] Mitchell's greatest obstacle isn't [players Vince] Carter and [Jalen] Rose. It's an ingrained acceptance not just of losing, but of the Raptors' unique brand of constant, unrelenting craziness . . . Randall Becker . . . president of . . . a Toronto-based management consultant firm that helps to take the teeth out of poisonous workplaces [stated,] "It takes a long time to change culture, particularly a culture that has

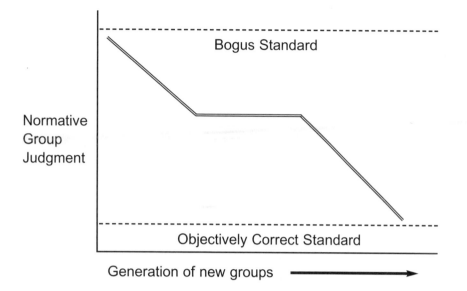

Figure 13.1. Schematic representation of the stability of norms over successive generations within a group (Based on research by Jacobs & Campbell, 1961)

> been in place a long time . . . if you're looking at fine tuning, it could be accomplished in a year or two. But if you're looking at a wholesale culture change, like say the [Toronto] Maple Leafs during the (Harold) Ballard era, it can take 10-15 years to turn the organization around." (Ulmer, 2004, pp. D1-2)

If a team develops negative norms such as abusive behavior toward officials or other team members, a poor work ethic, or an emphasis on individual rather than team goals, these can persist over a number of seasons (i.e., generations)—long after the individuals primarily responsible for their development have left the team. A common, ongoing practice for a number of sport teams is to initiate new members; a practice sometimes referred to as *hazing*. A recent quote pertaining to a hazing incident in a high school football program illustrates the stability of group norms:

> It was understood that they would endure their humiliation without complaint, and by the time they returned home [from camp] . . . they would have standing as official members of the team. And besides, they could take some comfort in knowing that someday they would be the ones leading the initiation. (Wahl & Wertheim, 2003, p. 68)

At the same time, positive norms are also transmitted to succeeding generations. This is the essence of any good team or organization, a point E.M. Swift (1987) continually emphasized in an article about the development of the Philadelphia Flyers over a 20-year period. Through a series of quotes (which are presented in Box 13.3), Swift illustrated the stability of a work ethic over three successive generations. (It may help the reader appreciate the transition from one generation to the next if it is understood that, initially, Bob Clarke was a rookie, then a team captain, and then the general manager).

It was pointed out previously that norms develop slowly in a team. But when they are present, they are also changed slowly. It is irrelevant whether a norm is positive or negative, correct or incorrect (as was the case in the Jacobs and Campbell study). Once it develops, it will take a number of generations before it is changed.

Conformity to Group Norms

When you rise from your seat to cheer a goal during a soccer game, is this an example of conformity? After practice, when you run three miles with your teammates, are you conforming? When you and your teammates agree not to lift weights because it is believed that there are no benefits for performance, are you conforming? The answer is that it depends upon whether your behaviors and beliefs would be similar or different if you were not in a group. Would you rise to cheer the goal if you were the only fan in the stands? Would you run after practice even if the rest of the team did not?

Conformity is not just behaving as other people behave; it is being influenced by how they behave. Conformity is defined as a change in behavior or belief as a result of real or imagined group pressure (Kiesler & Kielser, 1969). There are two distinct types of group conformity: compliance and acceptance.

Compliance occurs when people conform without completely believing in what they are doing. Compliance is, thus, publicly acceding to social pressure while privately disagreeing (Myers, 1990). Compliance was evidenced in a cheerleader who learned to binge and vomit—behaviors she considered appalling—because everyone on the squad did it (Squire, 1983, cited in Crandall, 1988).

Also, however, that same cheerleader believed that binge eating and vomiting were acceptable prior to cheerleading competitions. She explained that "everybody does it then, so it doesn't seem like the same thing" (Squire, 1983, p. 48, in Crandall, 1988). Her behavior in this latter regard can be referred to as *acceptance*—both acting and believing in accord with social pressure (Myers, 1990). There are times when we genuinely believe in

---

Box 13.3
Stability of Work Ethic

"'Guys like Ashbee and Dornhoefer set a standard of performance that the young players had to match,' says Pat Quinn . . .

Says Clarke, 'Those guys had played a long time in pro hockey and understood the commitment it takes to play this game. They understood the importance of playing as good as they could all the time. . .'

'Clarke set the standards at the team level,' says Snider . . .

The standards are higher in Philadelphia than anywhere in hockey this side of the Montreal Forum. 'I talk to Davey Poulin all the time,' says Clarke. 'I've told him, by rights you shouldn't even have a bad practice, never mind a bad game. The one demand we can make of our players is that they work hard. . .'

Work hard, don't back down, and win. That attitude has been assimilated from Ashbee's Flyers to Clarke's to Poulin's . . . there has never been an extended period when the Flyers didn't play like the Flyers" (Swift, 1987, pp. 94-99).

what the group has exerted pressure on us to do. You may purchase the same basketball shoes as the rest of your teammates due to a team consensus that they will help you jump higher.

Social Norms

The majority of the research that has examined the factors influencing the development of group norms has been undertaken in laboratory research on conformity. In one classic study, Muzafer Sherif (1936) examined whether the emergence of a social norm could be observed in the laboratory. He used an illusion known as the autokinetic effect. With this illusion, a stationary single light is shown in a darkened room. The light appears to move (sometimes erratically) because there are no reference points, no frame of reference within which to place it. When Sherif had subjects estimate the amount of movement of the light alone and in groups, he found that the presence of others made a considerable difference in individual judgments.

First, he showed individual subjects a single pinpoint of light in a dark room and asked them to judge how far the light moved. When individuals made judgments alone, they established their own idiosyncratic pattern in which the estimates of movement varied erratically from 1 to 10 inches. However, when the individuals were brought together as a group with one or two other naive subjects, group norms developed. Subjects in the group setting were asked to continue estimating the light movement and to announce their estimates so that the other group members could hear. The estimates of the group members converged so that after a period of time each person reported that he saw approximately the same amount of movement as the other group members (see Figure 13.2). It was as if a funneling effect had occurred—from divergence and discrepancy to convergence and consensus.

Subjects in the autokinetic experiment were faced with an ambiguous reality, one with no obvious correct answer. Solomon Asch (1951) suspected that intelligent people would not conform in situations where they could readily see the truth for themselves. To test this hypothesis, Asch (1951), in another classic study, used confederates to influence the judgment of participants concerning the length of a line. Participants were asked to compare the length of a standard vertical line with three other lines. They were then asked to choose the line which best matched the standard line. The confederates gave their selection first and unanimously chose an incorrect line in 12 of the 18 trials. Each participant, in turn, provided a personal choice of the line that best matched the standard line in length. Thus, the naive participant

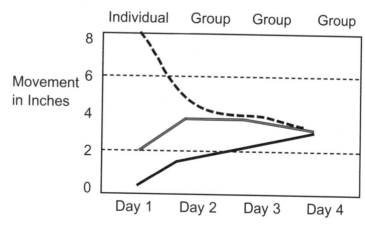

Figure 13.2. Sherif's study on norm formation (Data from Sherif & Sherif, 1969, p. 209)

was confronted with the choice of selecting either an incorrect option (thereby remaining in agreement with the group), or the correct option (thereby being in opposition to the group).

Asch found that 33 percent of the subjects adopted the group norm (the incorrect judgment) on 50 percent or more of the incorrect trials. Only 25 percent consistently maintained an independent (correct) judgment. Interestingly, those who answered alone gave the correct response 99 percent of the time.

Asch's procedure became the standard for hundreds of later experiments. In 1996, Rod Bond and Peter Smith conducted a meta-analytic review of 97 conformity studies conducted in the United States that used an Asch-type procedure. The review revealed that conformity was highest when the size of the majority was large, when the proportion of female participants was greatest, and when the majority did not consist of out-group members. As well, they found that the levels of conformity had steadily declined since Asch's original studies in the 1950s. The authors suggested that the decline in conformity might be due to the "changing cultural climate of Western societies" (p. 124).

In the research that followed these early classic studies, the focus was on identifying the conditions which influenced conformity to social pressure and group norms. Essentially, two classes of conditions have been identified: *personal* factors and *situational* factors (Carron, 1980).

Personal Factors

Two of the personal factors that are associated with conformity to the group's norms are personal status and idiosyncrasy credit. Individuals with greater status have a greater effect on the development of group norms. Influential team members—team leaders, the most competent athletes, individuals with the greatest status in the group—have a greater role in setting and enforcing the standards adopted by the group (e.g., Hollander, 1961). There is also less pressure on them to conform strictly to these norms.

Status and conformity to the group norms over an extended period of time contribute to the development of what has been referred to as idiosyncrasy credit (Hollander, 1971). High-status individuals more readily build up idiosyncrasy credit and are given more latitude in the degree to which the group requires them to conform to group norms. Thus, the team leaders may help to establish a norm in which the team lifts weights everyday in the off-season. After this norm has been well established, the team leaders might miss occasionally. There would be less pressure exerted on them by the group if this occurred than if low-status individuals missed occasionally. The following anecdote about the release of baseball player Ruben Rivera after he stole, and then subsequently returned, the glove and bat of teammate Derek Jeter, illustrates idiosyncrasy credit:

> There is a sign in many baseball clubhouses that says, WHAT WE SAY HERE, WHAT YOU SEE HERE, LET IT STAY HERE, WHEN YOU LEAVE HERE. It's not about keeping the opposing team from learning the game plan. It's about avoiding embarrassment over the foolish things that go on in a clubhouse. So why did the story get beyond the locker room? If there really was such a thing as the sanctity of the clubhouse, it should have protected Rivera. But it didn't, for the simple reason that Rivera is a marginal player. Imagine if Jeter had taken Rivera's glove and sold it . . .

Would Jeter have been kicked off the team? Fuhgeddaboudit. Some player or coach would have pointed up and said, "Boys, that's why we have that sign." (Bouton, Kim, & Kennedy, 2002, p. 25)

Another important personal factor associated with conformity to group norms is gender. Many of the earliest studies found that women were more likely to conform than men (cf. Worchel, Cooper, & Goethals, 1991). Nord (1969) summarized this early research very well when he concluded that, "it has . . . been well established, at least in our culture, that females supply greater amounts of conformity under almost all conditions than males" (p. 198). These results were often explained by reference to sex roles in that men were expected to be independent while women were expected to be more reasonable and sensitive to others. While this explanation fits many of the earlier results, it does not explain subsequent findings.

More recently, it has been suggested that these results might be due to the fact that the tasks used have favored the masculine sex role. Conformity is greatest in situations of high uncertainty, a situation that would exist if a female was performing a task more appropriate to the masculine sex role. When Sistrunk and McDavid (1971) included neutral, masculine-type, and feminine-type tasks, they found that conformity was greater by females in the masculine-type tasks, greater by males in the feminine-type tasks, and the same in the neutral tasks. In support of this, Alice Eagly and Linda Carli (1981), in a meta-analysis of studies examining conformity differences in males and females, found that gender alone does not determine conformity; gender interacts with the situation to determine conformity.

Although it seems intuitively obvious that some personality characteristics will more naturally be associated with conformity to group norms than others, the evidence is very weak. In contrast to the power of situational factors (described below), an individual's personality characteristics do not strongly predict his/her conformity behavior. Researchers, however, have found that slightly greater adherence to group norms is exhibited by individuals who are more authoritarian, less intelligent, more conservative, and more extroverted (Shaw, 1981).

Situational Factors

One important situational factor associated with conformity to group norms is group size—both the number of supportive others and the number of individuals in opposition. Insofar as the former is concerned, when the number of supportive others increases, resistance to the group norm also increases. Individuals who want to behave in a way contrary to the group norm more readily do so as the number of people supporting their position increases. In this situation the group is not able to exert as much pressure.

Similarly, when the number of people forming the opposition increases, there is a tendency for conformity to the group norm to increase. Studies on conformity behavior have shown, however, that there is a limit to the group's influence. At some critical point, further increases in the size of the opposition no longer have any social impact. This failure of increasingly larger groups to continue to exert influence on their members has been attributed to two related factors. First, a large opposition of 50 individuals could be perceived as a single unit, not 50 units. Second, a large number of opponents who are in agreement could be considered to be in collusion (Carron, 1980).

Not surprisingly, another situational factor that influences conformity is the degree of ambiguity present in the group norm (e.g., Nordholm, 1975). Consider for example, two regulations that might be established by management and eventually adopted as team norms: a curfew and an acceptable standard of dress for public appearances. If the curfew is set at midnight, a team norm could develop to "adhere to the curfew." Further, there is no ambiguity about midnight, no uncertainty. Consequently, team member's deviations would be obvious.

It is more difficult to establish fixed standards concerning what is acceptable in the case of a dress code (see Illustration 13.1). There is the cliché that "beauty is in the eye of the beholder." So too is any norm for "an acceptable standard of dress"—there is some ambiguity, some uncertainty about what is acceptable. A norm might develop in which a suit coat is the team standard, but considerable latitude could appear around this criterion. Thus, adherence to the team norm might not be very good.

Cohesion also is associated with conformity to group norms. The relationship between conformity to group norms and group cohesion is reciprocal (Widmeyer, Brawley, & Carron, 1985). More cohesive groups exert greater pressure on their members to adhere to the group norms. In turn, greater adherence to the group norms leads to a more cohesive group.

The leadership structure of the group also influences conformity behavior (Shaw, 1981). When the group leadership is centralized (i.e., autocratic) and resides almost exclusively in the hands of one individual, there is less conformity than when it is decentralized (i.e., democratic). In short, when a number of individuals are involved in the decision-making process and have leadership responsibilities, there are more individuals to exert pressure on other members to adhere to group standards.

Illustration 13.1. Pick out the athlete who violated the norm for the dress code!

The Nature of Group Norms in Sport Teams

Prapavessis and Carron (1997) conducted a study to pertaining to the question, "What types of norms typically develop in sport teams?" After athletes on elite cricket teams were provided with a definition of a group norm, they were asked to list the norms present in their team. The most frequently cited norms were being punctual at practices and competitions (23.4%), staying focused on the field (18%), adhering to the dress code (14.6%), providing support to teammates (11.4%), and giving maximum effort during training (10.6%).

The same issue was pursued in a more comprehensive study undertaken by Krista Munroe and her colleagues (1999). A sport team can develop expectations for individual behavior in at least four specific situations: during competitions, at practices, in social situations, and during the off-season. Munroe and her colleagues had athletes from different sports list the important group norms for each of these four situations. Table 13.2 contains an overview of the four most frequently cited norms for each situation.

The strongest team norms are associated with work output; teams put pressure on their membership to work hard. As Table 13.2 shows, *giving effort* was the most frequently mentioned norm for competitions, *training* was the most frequently cited norm for the off-season, and *productivity* was the second most frequently cited norm for competitions. Further evidence of the importance of the task (performance) to sport teams is the norms that develop for the off-season. In addition to training, *working on skills* and *playing* (i.e., staying involved with the sport) are considered important.

Groups either cease to function well or cease to exist if members do not attend group functions. Consequently, it is not surprising that *attendance* or *punctuality* were also frequently cited in all four situations (see Table 13.2). Groups also may cease to exist or to function well if the interpersonal relationships among members are not courteous and respectful. Consequently, it also is not surprising that *respect* was among the most frequently cited norm in competitions, practices, and social situations. It's uncertain why respect is not a team norm in the off-season. Norms only develop around matters of importance to the group. Since contact among team members is reduced in the off-season, it is possible that other matters become more critical—maintaining contact, training, and so on.

Table 13.2
The nature of the group norms that develop in sport teams
(Adapted from Munroe, Estabrooks, Dennis, & Carron, 1999)

Team Norms for Competitions	Team Norms for Practice	Team Norms for the Off-Season	Team Norms for Social Situations
Effort (16.3%)	Punctuality (23.6%)	Training (60.1%)	Attendance (16.5%)
Support (13.0%)	Productivity (22.3%)	Contact (8.7%)	Respect Others (15.9%)
Punctuality (8.9%)	Attendance (13.6%)	Skill Development (8.2%)	Attitude (15.2%)
Respect (8.9%)	Respect (8.3%)	Healthy Lifestyle (4.9%)	Consumption (15.2%)

Team Norms and Rule Violations

Rule Violations by Athletes

Normative expectations emerge around adherence to the formal rules of sport. Formal rules proscribe specific behaviors in order to insure that the competition between teams is fair. There is considerable evidence, however, that under certain circumstances it is not only legitimate for athletes to break these rules, it is expected. The "good foul" in basketball and soccer, the "good penalty" in hockey are some examples.

John Silva (1983) has suggested that the norms surrounding rule violations in sport—the necessity of committing the good foul in critical situations—have "become so important that participants in many sports must learn not only the written rules, but the unwritten or normative rules of their sport in order to be successful" (p. 438). Some support for this suggestion is available from a study by McIntosh (reported in Silva, 1983). When he asked soccer players whether a player in a good position to score should be brought down unmercifully, 70% of the professionals and 54% of the amateurs agreed.

In his study, Silva presented male and female college students with seven slides depicting rule-violating behavior in baseball, basketball, hockey, and football. The participants were required to rate the acceptability of the behavior on a four-point scale that varied from "totally unacceptable" to "totally acceptable." Silva's results showed that males perceived rule violations to be more acceptable than females. Also, the perception that rule violations are an acceptable part of the game was strongest in males who had the most sport experience, who were participating at the highest levels of competition, and who were involved in sports with the greatest amount of physical contact. These findings have subsequently been supported in a study by Tucker and Parks (2001), who found that female athletes are less accepting of aggressive acts than males and that "participants in contact and noncontact sports are less accepting than participant in collision sports" (p. 410). Interestingly, however, Tucker and Parks did note overall that none of the groups examined in their study considered aggression to be legitimate in sport.

Shields, Bredemeier, Gardner, and Boston (1995) examined leadership, cohesion, and team norms regarding cheating and aggression in college and high school baseball and softball players. They asked athletes to estimate how many of their teammates would violate a rule and would deliberately hurt an opponent if it would help their team win. The athletes were also asked to indicate if their coach would want them to cheat or injure an opponent if it would help the team win.

Shields and colleagues revealed that perceptions that cheating and aggression are acceptable were generally greater in male athletes, college level athletes, older athletes, and athletes with greater training in the sport. With regards to leadership and team norms, female athletes who had a female coach felt that teammates were less likely to cheat or aggress and their coaches would be less accepting of such behaviors than female athletes who had a male coach.

Rule Violations by Officials

In the officiating of sports, norms have emerged on how to a call the game. Rains (1984) described how National Hockey League (NHL) officials are expected to be fair and consistent in their calls, even at the expense of enforcing the rules. It appears that it is not the correctness of a call (or non-call) that is the concern, but the fairness of a pattern of discretionary calls (Rains, 1984)—as the quote in Box 13.4 regarding NHL official Kerry Fraser illustrates.

Norms pertaining to officiating have emerged in nonprofessional sports as well. Eldon Snyder and Dean Purdy (1987) surveyed 689 high school officials in regards to enforcement of rules within basketball games. The authors found that 35% of the officials agreed with the principle of "no harm, no foul." This indicated that at least a third of the officials disregarded rule violations in game situations. As well, 77% agreed that officials try to balance up a call after they have made a bad call against a team. Finally, 73% endorsed the statement, "I believe that consistency in one's officiating is more important than the rules to the letter."

The authors concluded that rule enforcement is elastic, and officials may adhere strictly to the rules in one segment of the game, typically in the early phase, or when the game becomes too physical, then ease up later. For example, the authors noted basketball officials frequently ignore blocks, holds, illegal picks, and rule infractions in the final minutes of a game.

Performance Norms

As was pointed out above, not only do groups develop norms concerning social behavior, they also develop normative expectations for performance and productivity. Performance norms refer to attitudes shared among group members about how high a level of performance the group should achieve (Misumi, 1985). The development of productivity norms is extremely prevalent in settings where the task is a major concern. Industry and sport are two good examples. A standard is established for performance and pressure is exerted on group members to adhere to this standard.

An example of productivity norms (and the associated group pressures) is contained in a discussion by Roethlisberger and Dickson (1975) dealing with the concept of a fair day's work. Roethlisberger and Dickson carried out research at the Western Electric Company, a telephone assembly plant. Management had introduced an incentive scheme in an attempt to increase production. This incentive plan was the object of considerable discussion because it came into conflict with the norm for that had emerged in the group over a long period of time. Roethlisberger and Dickson presented the following discussion between two workers:

W4: (to W6) "How many are you going to turn in?"

W6: "I've got to turn in 6,800."

> **Box 13.4**
> **_Norms in Officiating_**
>
> Fraser has called a penalty shot against Detroit when a Vancouver player in control of the puck and over the red line was tripped from behind by a Detroit player. The call itself was less remarkable than the circumstances in which it was made. The penalty shot was called against Detroit with only 30 seconds remaining in the game, it was the second penalty shot called against Detroit that period, and it was called against Detroit when Detroit was leading Vancouver by only 1 point (the score was 4-3). Because Vancouver then scored on the penalty shot, the outcome of the game was altered in the last 30 seconds from a win for Detroit to a tie. Fraser, along with linesmen Stickle and Pare, reportedly needed police protection to leave the Detroit arena . . .
>
> The fact that Fraser made an unpopular call against Detroit in Detroit, and needed police protection to leave the arena, dramatizes his absence of bias for the home team and the extent to which his decisions were unaffected by a partisan crowd. The fact that he called penalty shots against Detroit twice in the same period dramatizes his fidelity to game events and the rules rather than to a more diluted version of fairness: he did not "even up" the distribution of penalties to "look" fair. The fact that he called a penalty in the last 30 seconds of a close game dramatizes his disregard for the score and for the effect that the penalty itself might have on the outcome of the game. And the fact that he could have called a lesser acceptable penalty dramatizes his ability to make a tough rather than a cheap call. (Rains, 1984, p. 150-151)

> *W4: "What's the matter—are you crazy? You work all week and turn in 6,600 for a full day, and now today you're away an hour and a quarter and you turn in more than you do the other days."*
>
> *W6: "I don't care. I'm going to finish these sets tomorrow."*
>
> *W4: "You're screwy."*
>
> *W6: "All right, I'll turn in 6,400."*
>
> *W4: "That's too much."*
>
> *W6: "That won't make any difference. I've got to do something with them."*
>
> *W4: "Well, give them to me."*
>
> *W6: did not answer. (p. 92)*

Adherence to performance norms seems to depend on various group properties. As indicated above, the level of cohesion present in the group is one important consideration. For example, in an often-cited study by Schachter, Ellertson, McBride, and Gregory

(1951), high- and low-cohesive groups were examined in a laboratory experiment on a task that involved cutting cardboard squares. It was observed that the high-cohesive groups conformed to the norm more than the low-cohesive groups independent of whether the norm was for high or low productivity. Subsequent research has supported these findings for industrial groups (Mikalachki, 1969), military crews (Berkowitz, 1956), laboratory groups (Berkowitz, 1954), and business students (Miesing & Preble, 1985).

The implications seem clear; as Quadrant 1 of Table 13.3 illustrates, if group cohesion is high and the norm for productivity is high, performance will be high. However, if cohesion is high but the norm for productivity is low, performance will be poor (Quadrant 4); a strike or a work slow-down in a business context is a good example. In the situations outlined in Quadrants 1 and 4, the strong unity in the group would result in a great deal of pressure being exerted on members to adhere to the norm.

The two intermediate positions are represented by those situations where cohesion is low and the norm for productivity is either high (Quadrant 2) or low (Quadrant 3). The more desirable of these latter two situations would be Quadrant 2—a high norm for productivity with low cohesion. A general expectation would be present in the group to maintain a good work ethic. Because of the low cohesiveness, however, less pressure could be placed on those individuals who deviated from the norm than would be the case in Quadrant 1.

To test the above propositions, Gammage, Carron, & Estabrooks (2001) devised a laboratory experiment. They asked participants in the study to respond to one of eight written scenarios by indicating how much effort the main character in the scenario would be likely to expend training in the off-season. In the eight scenarios, the description of the group's cohesion, its norm for productivity, and the actor's potential to be observed by other group members (identifiability) were systematically varied from high to low. The Gammage et al. results supported the general pattern of interactions illustrated in Table 13.3. That is, the combination of a high norm for productivity and high cohesion was associated with the greatest amount of effort expended.

Myung-Soo Kim has conducted several studies examining performance norms in Japanese teams (Kim, 1992a, 1992b, 1995, 2001; Kim & Cho, 1996) that have implications for the both the team and the individual athlete. From an individual perspective, higher performance norms are related to higher self-monitoring (Kim, 1996) and greater satisfaction with the sport (Kim, 2001). From a group perspective, Kim (1995) found that teams that advanced to the semi-finals in a basketball tournament had higher performance norms than teams that were disqualified in the preliminaries. As well, Kim (1992a) found that teams with

Table 13.3
The Interaction of Cohesion and the Group Norm for Productivity
(From Carron, 1986. Used with Permission of the publishers)

		GROUP COHESION	
		HIGH	LOW
NORM FOR	HIGH	Best Performance (1)	Intermediate Performance (2)
PRODUCTIVITY	LOW	Worst Performance (4)	Intermediate Performance (3)

high performance norms at midseason also had high performance norms at post-season. In comparison, teams with low performance norms during midseason had a decline of performance norms at post-season. And finally, Kim (1992b) found that the team leadership affected the performance norms of sport teams. Specifically, performance norms were the highest under leaders with a goal-achievement and group-relations orientation.

Modification of Team Norms

Occasionally, an inappropriate team norm is established. For example, consider the following anecdote from the New Jersey Nets of the National Basketball Association:

> *"Well, whoop-de-damn-do. I miss practice [said Derrick Coleman].* *Dwayne (Schintzius) misses practice. Chris (Morris) misses practice. It's* *no big deal." We're guessing that this is not the attitude the Nets had in* *mind when they named Coleman co-captain in November 1993. "My miss-* *ing shoot arounds and practices doesn't make us lose games," he has said.* *"Some players are just practice players. They step on the court and don't* *do ——. I come out and bust my butt every night." (Taylor, 1995, p. 18)*

Is it possible to change this generalized expectation (i.e., this norm) concerning attendance at practices? How can it be changed? These are very real issues for coaches, managers, and/or team captains who have an interest in persuading high-status individuals and/or a majority of team members to change their views on what behaviors are appropriate and/or inappropriate?

Changing Attitudes

Essentially, a norm reflects the group attitude; thus, changing group norms involves changing attitudes. A considerable amount of research has been carried out in social psychology examining the factors influencing attitude change. Steven Penrod (1986) has summarized the research results into three general categories: the source of the communication, the nature of the communication, and the nature of the target.

The source of the communication. What is it that makes one communicator more persuasive than another? The personal characteristics of the individuals attempting to change a team norm—the coach, team captains, team members—will have an impact on their effectiveness. Experience and competency in the group situation also are certainly important. Derek Fisher, a former member of the Los Angeles Lakers spoke to this point in a discussion with Donovan Vincent (2005) about his transition to the Golden State Warriors:

> *Early on I was trying to fit in myself. We had a number of guys who had* *been on this team together for a few years, so it wasn't my place to come* *in and rearrange things . . . Working hard every day, playing hard in the* *games, as time goes on it gives me leeway to say something to a guy, chal-* *lenge him, maybe get in his face a little bit. But you have to put that work*

in and get it on your résumé before you can start challenging guys vocally. (p. B 12)

Individuals who are more credible, better liked, similar, attractive, or powerful possess greater powers of persuasion. This profile of characteristics might be expected because it is also associated with status. And, of course, individuals with high status play a significant role in norm development and maintenance.

On a team, the coaching staff or management might be interested in modifying existing norms. If a choice is available among different coaches, the best individual might not necessarily be the head coach (although he or she is certainly the most powerful). The coach who is perceived to be most credible by the athletes (in terms of trustworthiness and expertise on the specific issue), more similar, attractive, or better liked would be more effective.

Style of speech is another factor that has an effect on the degree to which a target group is influenced by a communicator. For example, the effectiveness of an argument increases if it is developed in the form of rhetorical questions—questions to which an answer is already known. For example, consider the following presentations to a team:

We do want to become better as a team, don't we? A tired athlete doesn't play as well, right? Don't you think it would be better if we established a minimum curfew for the night before the game?

Versus

If we are going to play better as a team, we have to be better rested. So a curfew has been established for the night before a game.

The first argument appears to involve a cooperative decision; the second represents a demand. The first is more persuasive than the second.

Another element in style of speech that influences persuasion is speed. Individuals who communicate in a relatively rapid manner as opposed to a slow, more deliberate fashion are more effective. James MacLachlan (1982; MacLachlan & Siegel, 1980) has illustrated the effectiveness of speed in persuasion by increasing speaker speed on radio and television commercials without altering the original pitch, inflection, and intensity of the speakers' voices. When speech speed of different speakers was increased by 25 percent, listeners comprehended the message just as well and also rated the speakers as more knowledgeable, intelligent, and sincere, and found the messages more interesting. In fact, normal (i.e., 140-to-150-word-per-minute) speech can be almost doubled before comprehension begins to drop abruptly (Foulke & Stichit, 1969).

The nature of the communication. Not surprisingly, persuasion is affected not only by who says it, but also by what that person says. According to Penrod's review, a number of elements in the communication itself can also influence reception by the target audience. One of these is the amount of discrepancy between the viewpoint being advanced and the position held by the team. For example, the members of a team might strongly believe that going out for drinks after every practice is good for team unity and morale. If the coaching staff attempted to persuade the team that complete abstinence during the season was better, the discrepancy between these two positions could produce considerable resistance.

Both the quality and quantity of the arguments advanced influence the effectiveness of the persuasion. Communications that are novel, have many points to support a particular position, and present both sides of the issue are more effective. Thus, any attempt to persuade athletes to abstain from alcohol during the season might be more successful if a physiologist was brought in to present research evidence on both sides of the issue.

Persuasion is greater when the communicator comes to a conclusion and presents it to the target group. Consider the above example in which rhetorical questions were used to advance the case for a curfew. The third question, "Don't you think it would be better if we established a minimum curfew for the night before the game?" is a conclusion. It's also essential to the case. If it was left out, the total argument would not be as persuasive.

The evidence on the effectiveness of fear as a persuader is mixed (Penrod, 1986). Sometimes messages that highlight the negative consequences of a behavior are effective. Advertisements on drinking, smoking, and driving without seat belts have used this approach to their advantage. Dawn Wilson and her colleagues (1987, 1988) had doctors send either a positively framed message (i.e., quit smoking and live longer) or a fear-framed message (i.e., continue to smoke and you will likely die sooner) to their patients who smoked. Only 8 percent of the smokers who received a positively framed message tried to quit smoking. In comparison, 30 per cent of the smokers who received a fear-framed message tried to quit.

However, messages that highlight fear are not always effective. For example, the destructive consequences of substance abuse (e.g., cocaine, anabolic steroids) have been repeatedly outlined. Yet, many professional athletes continue to be victims.

The nature of the target. Despite a good communicator and an effective communication, changes in norms still might not occur. The target group is the third factor in the equation. Penrod identified a number of characteristics of the target person or group that influence the degree to which a persuasive message is accepted.

The perception that there is freedom of choice is important. People who feel coerced into adopting an attitude show more resistance than those who feel that they have had a choice. One factor that increases resistance to a new perspective is ego-involvement. It is more difficult to change the attitudes of targets who are more highly ego-involved with an issue. In the quote presented above concerning the lack of attendance of New Jersey Nets players at practice, for example, a general discussion on the benefits of practice would probably have little effect on Derrick Coleman.

Also, it is possible for inoculation to occur if the initial argument is weak. This happens in much the same way that resistance to diseases develops. As a result of an inoculation with a weaker strain of bacteria, the body builds its resistance to stronger strains. Initially, if a weak argument is presented for discontinuing steroid use, for example, the target audience could develop effective counter arguments. When a better case is presented later, these counter arguments would be used to resist the persuasion.

Forewarning the target group that a new perspective will be presented is often effective. Again, however, it depends on the initial level of resistance in the target group. If resistance is high, forewarning may simply provide opportunities to prepare counter arguments against the new perspective. Freedman and Sears (1965) illustrated the difficulty of attempting to persuade individuals who have high resistance to a message. They forewarned one of two groups of high school seniors that they were going to listen to a speech titled, "Why teenagers should not be allowed to drive." Students that were forewarned were barely persuaded by the speech; however, students that were not forewarned were persuaded.

There is also evidence that people who are resistant to a new viewpoint are selective in the information they pick out of a presentation. If both sides of an argument were presented for why team members should attend practices consistently, for example, an individual who was strongly opposed would probably retain most of the negative content but little of the positive.

Using the Team as an Agent-for-Change

Teams develop expectations and teams can be used effectively to change inappropriate expectations (norms). A series of team-building strategies that can be used to modify group norms is outlined in Chapter 21.

Chapter Fourteen

GROUP LEADERSHIP

> "The captaincy in hockey is so important because of the history of it," [Glen] Sather says. "It's like knighting someone. The captain is the one who carries that team crest, the leader on and off the ice, the one who has the respect of the players, the one on whom the performance of a team might rest, the one who has as much, or more influence, than the coach." (quoted in Farber, 2000, p. 82)

No discussion of group structure is complete without dealing with group leadership. It is probably the group role most closely associated with group effectiveness. In Chapter 12, two types of group roles were discussed: informal and formal. The informal roles are those that emerge as a result of the interactions and communications that take place among group members. The group acknowledges and is influenced in its actions by those individuals who are most dominant, assertive, and competent. Because these individuals emerge from the group to occupy leadership roles, they are referred to as *emergent leaders*.

Formal roles, on the other hand, are those that are specifically prescribed by the organization or group. Consequently, individuals who occupy formal leadership roles are referred to as *prescribed leaders*. Coaches and managers of professional sport teams are one example of prescribed group leaders—they are the occupants of a formal group role. They possess what John French and Bertram Raven (1959) referred to as legitimate power, expert power, coercive power, reward power, and sometimes, referent power (see Box 11.1 again). In this chapter, the focus is on the formal leadership role and prescribed leaders.

Leaders who occupy formal group roles in sport, in education, in industry, and in the military are quite dissimilar in the sense that they engage in a variety of very different behaviors. Nonetheless, they are also similar; there are parallels among them. The major source of that similarity lies in their fundamental responsibilities. Every formal leader in every type of group has two identical responsibilities.

The first is to insure that the demands of the organization are satisfied, that the group is effective in terms of the goals and objectives of the organization. Typically for coaches at the professional level, the primary demand is to ensure a successful season by winning games. If the team is unsuccessful, it is usually the leader (i.e., the coach) who is held accountable as the following quote illustrates:

> *The Flyers scored just two goals in the series against Ottawa, and their playoff streak of 320 minutes, 36 seconds without a regulation goal . . . set an NHL record for futility. Given the club's $55 million payroll, changes*

are imminent. The first casualty could be coach Bill Barber, whose leadership was privately questioned by his players as the regular season wound down and whose inability to kick-start a woeful power play was symptomatic of his failing to wring the best from his players. (Habib, 2002, p. 80)

For the general manager of a professional sport team, effectiveness might mean increased attendance, a positive winning percentage, or both. This is well illustrated in a discussion by Michael Farber (1997c) of Cleveland Indians General Manager, John Hart:

Hart will keep looking ahead so that the Indians can make money while making good on the unwritten guarantee that with every season ticket goes a pennant race. That is baseball's clairvoyant: a prophet with his eyes on profit. (p. 89)

Every organization has different goals and objectives and a leader must reach those to be considered effective.

The second responsibility of every leader is to insure that the needs and aspirations of group members/subordinates are fulfilled. Phil Jackson, former coach of the Los Angeles Lakers of the National Basketball Association, alluded to this responsibility when he pondered about what he would miss about coaching. Using a previous hiatus as a benchmark, Jackson noted, "I missed the joy of the journey, of watching the guys I coached grow to become better players, and better men" (Jackson & Arkush, 2004, p. 270). When team member aspirations are met and the team is successful, the coach or manager of a sport team is considered to be an effective leader. However, a leader that is ineffective or utilizes an approach that is inconsistent with the needs of his or her team can be a source of stress for athletes (Fletcher & Hanton, 2003). While this seems to be fairly intuitive, it apparently isn't because there are still more questions than answers about leadership. In fact, James McGregor Burns (1978) noted that leadership is "one of the most observed and least understood phenomena on earth" (p. 2).

A Typology of Leadership Theories

Leadership has been approached from a number of different perspectives. In an attempt to aid in the classification of leadership theories, Behling and Schriesheim (1976) provided a typology that is presented in Table 14.1. The Behling and Schriesheim typology is an acknowledgment of the fact that on the one hand, some leadership theories have focused on what traits leaders possess while others have focused on what behaviors they exhibit. Furthermore, the frame of reference in which leader traits and/or behaviors have been examined has also differed. Some leadership theories focused on leadership in general (i.e., a universal approach) whereas others focused on leadership in specific situations (i.e., a situational approach). As Table 14.1 shows, the result has been four main types of approaches to the study of leadership: universal trait, situational trait, universal behavior, and situational behavior.

The *universal trait* approach is one of the oldest perspectives advanced about leadership. The predominant focus in this approach is on the personality traits of leaders. Did Winston Churchill, Mahatma Gandhi, Martin Luther King, and John Kennedy have similar personality characteristics? Are there some traits that naturally contribute to the emergence

Table 14.1

A typology of leadership theories (Adapted from Behling & Schriesheim, 1976)

	Traits	Behaviors
Universal	*Universal Traits* The Great Person Theory Description of the Personality Traits of Coaches	*Universal Behaviors* Coaching Behavior Assessment System
Situational	*Situational Traits* The Contingency Theory of Leadership	*Situational Behaviors* The Path-Goal Theory The Multidimensional Model of Leadership

of leaders in a group? The search for a universal set of personality traits in leaders is the main objective of the universal trait approach.

In the *situational trait* approach, the focus is on both the traits of the person and the characteristics of the specific situation. History has shown that all of the individuals mentioned above (Churchill, Gandhi, King, and Kennedy) generally were effective leaders. Assume for a moment that they were fundamentally different from each other in personality. And, also take it as a given that the situations in which they had to operate were also fundamentally different. Is it possible that each had a personality that was right for a specific situation? At other times or in other places, they might not have been as effective. In the situational trait approach, the focus is on identifying the characteristics of specific situations where specific personality traits will be most effective.

In the *universal behavior* approach, interest shifts from the search for general traits to the identification of the general behaviors in leaders. Thus, for example, Churchill, Gandhi, King, and Kennedy might have been completely different in personality. Nonetheless, they might have behaved in a very similar fashion when they were involved in leadership—directing, training, representing, facilitating, nurturing, and so on. In the universal behavior approach, the focus is on the identification of general behaviors exhibited by all leaders.

In the *situational behavior* approach, interest shifts from the identification of specific traits that are effective in specific situations to the identification of specific behaviors that are effective in specific situations. When Winston Churchill and John Kennedy were in the process of exerting political leadership, what did they do? Were they similar? John Wooden of UCLA, Pat Summit of Tennessee, and Adolph Rupp of Kentucky are the three most successful college basketball coaches in terms of national championships won. What did they do (or, in the case of Summit who is still coaching, what does she do)? In the situational behavior approach, the focus is on identifying the specific behaviors characteristic of different leaders in different situations.

In the sections that follow, each of these four approaches is discussed from the perspective of sport. This does represent a slight departure from the Behling and Schriesheim model. When they referred to a universal approach, they were referring to a broad spectrum of situations (e.g., sport, industry, the military, politics) and not simply a broad spectrum of sport situations.

Universal Trait Approach: The Great Person

Work Groups

It was pointed out above that the universal trait approach is one of the oldest approaches to the study of leadership. It has sometimes been referred to as The Great Person Theory of Leadership because it is based on the assumption that human progress has been the result of the accomplishments of great people. A considerable amount of research was carried out in management science and industrial psychology in order to determine what common personality traits helped outstanding leaders become successful.

This research met with limited success. No consistent pattern of traits was found for successful leaders. In the late 1940s, on the basis of his review of 124 studies, Stogdill (1948) concluded that there was no support for the universal trait perspective, that there are no specific personality traits associated with either the assumption or performance of leadership. Following Stogdill's review, the search for the universal traits in leaders received less attention. Researchers began to concentrate on better understanding the traits of leaders in specific situations, such as sport, the military, and industry.

Sport

In sport, George Sage (1975) outlined the rationale for the universal trait approach when he noted that "the notion of occupational-specific personality types is rather common. Thus, we have the stereotype of "the 'absent-minded' professor, and many more" (p. 408). Sage then quoted Jack Scott (1969) on the typical stereotype held for a coach:

> The typical . . . coach is a soulless, back-slapping, meticulously groomed, team-oriented efficiency expert—a jock's Robert MacNamara . . . Most coaches have as much concern for the welfare of their athletes as a general has for the soldiers he sends into battle . . . for most college coaches, the athlete is significant only to the extent that he can contribute to a team victory . . . For every relaxed, understanding coach . . . there are one hundred rigid, authoritarian coaches who have so much . . . character armor that they rattle. (p. 7)

A number of studies have tried to determine if Scott's stereotype is accurate for coaches. One test that received a considerable amount of use in this type of research was the Machiavellian Scale developed by Christie and Geis (1970). Its name is derived from the infamous Prince Machiavelli, who believed that cunning, duplicity, and bad faith were acceptable for manipulating the behavior of others. The research with coaches clearly showed that they are not any different than the average person in Machiavellianism (e.g., Sage, 1972; Walsh & Carron, 1977).

Testing of coaches has also been carried out using more general personality tests such as Cattell's 16 Personality Factor Questionnaire (e.g., Hendry, 1968). Again, however, no consistent pattern of traits has emerged that distinguishes more successful coaches from less successful coaches. In fact, no consistent pattern of traits has been found that distinguishes coaches from society in general. The conclusion that must be drawn from research is that there is no general (universal) pattern of personality traits characteristic of coaches as leaders.

Situational Trait Approach: Contingency Theory

A situational trait approach has its origins in the assumption that some personality types will be more effective in some situations than in others. For example, an authoritarian, dogmatic coach might be highly effective in the early part of the season when organizational concerns are critical. There are simply too many things to do to consult others or to use a democratic approach. This same coach might be less effective later in the season when the affairs of the team are running more smoothly. Similarly, an authoritarian, dogmatic coach might be highly effective with less mature athletes in high school but relatively ineffective with more mature athletes in professional sport.

One of the best-known situational trait approaches is the contingency theory of leadership developed by Fred Fiedler (e.g., Fiedler, 1967; Fiedler & Chemers, 1974). A contingency relationship is the cornerstone of Fiedler's theory. According to Fiedler, leadership effectiveness—defined as group performance and member satisfaction—depends equally (i.e., is contingent) upon the leader's style of interacting with the group and the favorableness of the situation.

Style of Interaction

A leader's style of interacting is considered by Fiedler to vary along a continuum from *task-oriented* to *person-oriented*. Task-oriented individuals derive their greatest satisfaction from the group's performance, productivity, and successful task completion. On the other hand, person-oriented individuals derive their greatest satisfaction from social contacts, affiliation, and successful interpersonal relationships.

These two interaction styles represent a hierarchy of preferences within the leader. Both orientations are present in every leader. That is, every leader is interested in both outcomes—people and productivity—but the importance attached to satisfying people versus being productive varies. Essentially, a task-oriented leader says, "If we can successfully carry out this task, we'll feel very good about one another and get along well." On the other hand, a person-oriented leader essentially says, "if we get along well, we'll be more effective on the job." The quote in Box 14.1 by Bill Parcells (quoted in King, 2003) helps to illustrate the priorities placed on task and person concerns. In Parcells' quotation, the task-oriented style is more dominant. But, from the quote, it is also evident that he feels that getting to know players on a personal level is important.

The quote by Arizona Wildcats' head coach Mike Stoop in Box 14.1 (King, 2004) illustrates a circumstance in which a person-oriented style had a high priority. In this quote, Stoop notes the importance of having an open-door policy and a willingness to listen to players. Overall, as was pointed out above, the important point about the contingency theory is the assumption that either a person-oriented or a task-oriented leader can be effective depending upon the situation.

Box 14.1
Illustrations of the various dimensions of
Fiedler's Contingency Theory of Leadership

A. LEADER'S STYLE OF INTERACTING

Task-Oriented: Major satisfaction is derived from the successful completion of the group task.	Parcells will immediately make his presence felt in Dallas. He'll work the weight room every morning, bantering with players, getting to know them. He will not prop them up with false encouragement. After a tough loss in his first season with the Patriots, he chastised the players, telling them they should not be satisfied with merely trying to win. "You get paid to try," he told them. "Don't tell me you tried hard. You've got nothing to be proud of when you lose." That's the kind of tough talk that Woodson wants to hear. Last week he was asked if he thought a majority of his teammates would be in favor of the new coach's my-way-or-the-highway approach. "In favor?" Woodson said, chuckling. "They're not going to have any choice." (King, 2003, p. 53)
Person-Oriented: Major satisfaction is derived from the development of harmonious interpersonal relationships	Stoops made it a point to learn why veteran players had felt so alienated under the previous regime. "It's important for guys to see the human side of coaches," says Stoops. "From Day One I made sure my door was open." The result is a renewed energy. (King, 2004, p. 165)

B. FAVORABLENESS OF THE SITUATION

Power Position of the Leader: The degree of authority and control; the amount of organizational support	A few weeks after Christmas holidays, Bear Bryant resigned as Maryland football coach . . . What had happened was the one thing he would not tolerate, not then, not ever, not from anybody. Curly Byrd had stuck his nose into Bryant's football business. Twice. (Herkowitz, 1987, p. 53)
Leader-Member Relations: The quality of the personal relationship between a leader and subordinates.	Buddy [Ryan] was hard on his [Chicago] Bear players. That was his way of motivating them. And it worked. His players hated him at first, but they grew to love him. (Madden & Anderson, 1986, p. 210)
Task Structure: The degree to which the task is structured, goals are clarified, and procedures are clear.	Before he came to Detroit . . . [Jacques] Demers had already had a reputation as one of the premier coaches in the league . . . "Our system is just discipline," Demers says. "You know what tight-checking is? It's a system. It's hard work. It's not complicated, but we have specific things we want our players to do." (Klonke, 1988, p. 8).

Favorableness of the Situation

What makes a situation favorable for a leader? One of the elements is the *power position* of the leader. If the leader is clearly in control, has authority, and possesses the support of the organization, he or she is in a powerful position to influence and direct the group. Conversely, if the group perceives that the leader's power position is not very strong, that the leader doesn't have the support of management, it will be more difficult to lead.

A quote in Box 14.1 is concerned with the circumstances surrounding Paul (Bear) Bryant's decision to leave his coaching job at the University of Maryland. Dr. D. H. (Curly) Byrd, the president (and a former football coach) of the university had reinstated an athlete suspended by Bryant and had fired one of Bryant's assistant coaches—without consulting Bryant. From a leadership perspective, Bryant considered his power position to be unacceptable so he quit his job—his first head coach position—after only one year.

A second element that contributes to situational favorableness is *leader-member relations*. If the group likes the leader, it will more readily follow the leader's directions, work harder, and make sacrifices. In addition, because the situation is favorable, it's easier for the leader to carry out the responsibilities of leadership. The quote in Box 14.1 concerning Buddy Ryan's relationship with his athletes illustrates a case of good leader-member relations.

The third element in situational favorableness is the *task structure*. In some tasks, the goals and objectives are clear and the steps necessary to achieve them are readily apparent. This makes it easier for the leader because there are only a limited number of possibilities or options present. In general, sport tasks are relatively structured but there are subtle differences among different sports. For example, open team sports are those in which the athlete must continually adjust to constantly changing conditions in the situation. Hockey, basketball, and soccer are some examples. On the other hand, closed individual sports are those in which the athlete is faced with a relatively fixed and unchanging environment. Track, archery, and bowling are examples. Closed sports are somewhat more structured and, therefore, would be more favorable from a leadership perspective. In the quote in Box 14.1, Jacques Demers, former coach of the Detroit Red Wings, pointed out how he likes to develop a highly structured situation for his athletes.

The Contingency Theory

The specific relationship proposed by Fiedler, for the leader's style of interacting and the favorableness of the situation, is illustrated in Figure 14.1. The favorableness of the situation can be rank-ordered into eight octants that vary from highly favorable on one end to highly unfavorable on the other. The most favorable situation for a leader is present when his/her power position is strong, the task is highly structured, and leader-member relations are high. In these types of situations, a task-oriented leader is more effective than a person-oriented leader. As Figure 14.1 illustrates, a task-oriented leader is also more effective in the most unfavorable situations—when his/her power position is poor, the task is unstructured, and leader-member relations are poor. In short, it is expected that Octants 1, 2, 3 and 8 represent situations where the task-oriented leader will be more effective. According to Fiedler, a person-oriented leader is more effective in situations that are moderately favorable. The moderately favorable situations are represented by Octants 4, 5, 6, and 7.

William Straub (1978) has used the case of Forest Gregg, a former coach of the Cleveland Browns, to illustrate some of the principles of the contingency theory. Gregg, who used a task-oriented style of interacting, was the Associated Press National Football League Coach of the Year in 1976. A year later, he was fired. Straub pointed out that after getting off to a good start in the season, the Browns began to lose. Gregg's relationship with the owner, Art Modell, and his players began to deteriorate. In short, his power position deteriorated and leader-member relations were poor. Since the task of football is relatively structured, the favorableness of the situation would be represented in the sixth column. And, consequently, a person-oriented style of interacting would be suggested within Fiedler's model. According to Straub, however, Gregg became even more forceful and autocratic in his style and the results were disastrous.

Much of Fiedler's initial work in developing his theory was conducted with basketball teams. Subsequently, a number of researchers have used the contingency theory to examine leadership on sport teams (e.g., Bird, 1977; Danielson, 1976; Inciong, 1974). Their results have provided only limited support for the model. However, it is difficult in sport situations to systematically vary the situational factors that are such an integral part of the model. And, "in the absence of differences in the situational parameters, Fiedler's model cannot be adequately tested" (Chelladurai & Carron, 1978, p. 29).

Schriesheim, Tepper, and Tetrault (1994) did examine the validity of the contingency theory using research from industrial psychology. Although they located 147 studies, only 10 of those studies contained sufficient data to adequately test the predictions of contingency theory. These 10 studies had tested 1282 groups, however. In their meta-analysis, Schriesheim and his colleagues found that the contingency theory was a better predictor of leader performance than three other rival theories.

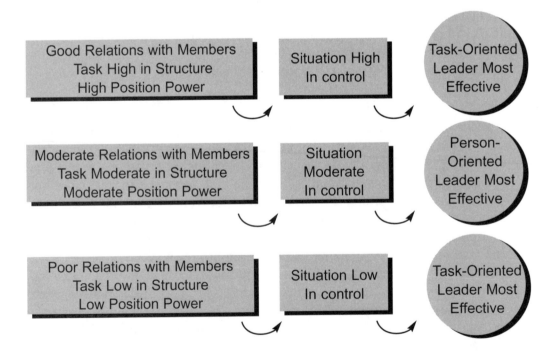

Figure 14.1. A schematic illustration of Fiedler's contingency theory of leadership

Universal Behavior Approach: Assessing Coaching Behavior

A behavioral approach concentrates on what people do rather than on more abstract concepts like their personality, orientation, or motivation. Thus, for example, Tharp and Gallimore (1976), intrigued by the success of John Wooden (who coached the UCLA Bruins to 10 NCAA basketball championships in 12 years), systematically recorded his behaviors during 30 hours of practice time. Of the 2326 behaviors charted, 50.3% were directed toward instruction (what to do and how to do it) while commands to hustle, to intensify activity made up 12.7%. The other behaviors observed included scolding and reinstructing (8%), praising and encouraging (6.9%), and simple declarations of displeasure (6.6%). When Wooden demonstrated—which usually occurred during patterned offensive drills and half court scrimmages—he modeled the correct way first then showed the incorrect way that had been used by the player. His demonstrations rarely lasted longer than 5 seconds.

As another example of research examining universal behaviors, Laios, Theodorakis, and Gargalianos (2003) summarized what they believed were behaviors coaches should engage in to be effective leaders. These included (a) developing interpersonal skills, (b) working toward a cohesive team, (c) listening well, (d) making strong decisions and being accountable for those decisions, (e) being an active and direct problem solver, (f) creating standards for performance, (g) recognizing and rewarding generously, (h) conveying enthusiasm, (i) teaching relevant skills, and (j) using punishment as the last resort but making those punishments clear beforehand. While these previous two studies highlight what might be thought of as *desirable* behaviors for coaches, these are not the only ones displayed by coaches at all levels. The subsequent sections contain discussions of approaches to the assessment of coaching behaviors as a whole.

Coaching Behavior Assessment System

The most comprehensive program for analyzing coaching behaviors was undertaken at the University of Washington by Ron Smith, Frank Smoll and their colleagues (Curtis, Smith & Smoll, 1979; Smith, Smoll, & Hunt, 1977; Smoll, Smith, Curtis, & Hunt, 1978). As Table 14.2 shows, in their Coaching Behavior Assessment System (CBAS), 12 behaviors (B1 - B12) considered to be typical of coaches in athletic situations are identified. Using the CBAS, an observer can record the ongoing behavior of a coach and assess the frequency of various types of behaviors. The twelve behaviors included in the CBAS fall into two classes: reactive and spontaneous. Reactive behaviors are responses to something the athlete has done such as a good or bad performance. Spontaneous behaviors are those initiated by the coach; they are not the result of prior activity by the athlete.

The reactive behaviors are further subdivided into three categories: reactions by the coach to desirable performances by the athlete, reactions by the coach to an athlete's mistakes or errors, and reactions by the coach to misbehaviors on the part of the athlete. When the athlete's performance is effective or desirable, it can be positively reinforced by the coach (B 1, or Behavior 1) or ignored through non-reinforcement (B 2). A mistake or error by the athlete can be reacted to with encouragement (B 3), with instruction about the correct technique (B 4), with punishment (B 5), with both punishment and instruction on the correct technique (B 6), or the mistake can simply be ignored (B 7). Finally, misbehaviors on the part of the athlete can lead to coaching behaviors associated with keeping control (B 8).

The spontaneous behaviors of the coach are subdivided into two categories: game related and game unrelated. When a coach exhibits a spontaneous behavior during the game, it either involves providing instruction on techniques (B 9), giving general encouragement (B 10), or organizing and administering the team (B 11). Finally, the spontaneous behaviors that are irrelevant to the game represent general communications on the part of the coach (B 12).

Smoll and his colleagues (Smoll, Smith, Curtis, & Hunt, 1978) used the CBAS to chart the behavior of 51 Little League coaches during the season. An average of 1,122 behaviors was recorded for each coach. Almost two thirds of these coaching behaviors were from three categories: positive reinforcement (B1), general technical instruction (B 9), and

Table 14.2

***The Smith, Smoll, Curtis, and Hunt Coaching Behavior Assessment System
(Smith, Smoll, & Curtis, 1979; Smith, Smoll, & Hunt, 1977)***

Stimulus Event	Coaching Response	Description
CLASS 1. General Reactive Behaviors		
Desirable Performance	B 1. Positive Reinforcement	Verbal or nonverbal reaction to an athlete's behavior
	B 2. Non-reinforcement	Failure to reinforce an athlete's behavior
Mistake or Error	B 3. Mistake-Contingent Encouragement	Encouragement following an athlete's mistake
	B 4. Mistake-Contingent Technical Instruction	Instruction to an athlete following a mistake
	B 5. Punishment	Verbal or nonverbal negative reactions to an athlete's mistake
	B 6. Punitive-Mistake Contingent Technical Instruction	Combination of negative reaction and instruction following a mistake
	B7. Ignoring Mistakes	Failure to respond in any way to an athlete's mistake
Misbehaviors	B 8. Keeping Control	Responses designed to maintain order and control
CLASS 2. Spontaneous Behaviors		
Game Related	B 9. General Technical Instruction	Communication to an athlete on technical instruction
	B 10. General Encouragement	Spontaneous encouragement to the athlete
	B 11. Organization	Communication of an administrative nature
Game Irrelevant	B 12. General Communication	Interactions unrelated to the sport or game

general encouragement (B 10). The behavior of the Little League baseball coaches was positive and directed toward instruction and teaching.

Interviews were also conducted with the athletes involved to assess their perceptions of their coaches' behaviors. A total of 542 players were included which represented 83 percent of the athletes. Interestingly, the athletes overestimated the amount of time that their coaches had spent keeping control (B 8). This behavior occurred very infrequently but it had such an effect on the athletes that they perceived that it occurred much more frequently. Maybe this is typical of all coach-athlete relationships—amateur and professional. Coaches exert control and this produces a strong negative reaction in athletes.

Smoll and his colleagues also found that being negative while providing instruction after a mistake (B 6) occurred only infrequently—2.8% of all of the behaviors recorded. (An example of this behavior might be "you dummy, keep your head down"). Nonetheless, it also had a significant effect on the athletes in that they were very accurate in their perception of its frequency.

Changing Coaching Behaviors

On the basis of this early research, Smith, Smoll, and Curtis (1979) then developed a set of behavioral guidelines for effective teaching and coaching. These guidelines were designed to emphasize positive behaviors and produce a better competitive environment for the young athlete. A group of 18 Little League coaches were then introduced to the guidelines and trained in the use of positive behaviors. Throughout the season feedback was also given on their actual coaching behaviors. Another set of 13 coaches who were not given the training program or exposed to the behavioral guidelines was used as a control group. The actual behaviors of the two groups were then observed throughout the season. In addition, the attitudes of the athletes playing for the trained and untrained coaches were compared.

The differences between the two groups of coaches were quite dramatic—particularly if it is remembered that the untrained coaches weren't poor coaches. They were probably typical of every coach involved in youth sports—fathers, mothers, older brothers or sisters, individuals interested in coaching young athletes. The group that was trained provided more reinforcement (B 1). They were also perceived by their athletes as better, more knowledgeable coaches who provided more reinforcement, more encouragement, and more instruction. The untrained coaches were perceived as providing more punishment and being less sensitive to good performances.

The athletes who played for the trained coaches were more satisfied with their experiences, felt that the team atmosphere was better, and had a greater desire to play for the same coach in the future. One of the most interesting findings was in the changes in self-esteem. The athletes who played for the trained coaches had scored slightly lower in an early measure of self-esteem. However, when they were assessed following the season, they showed an increase. On the other hand, the athletes who played for the untrained coaches showed a decrease. Smith and his colleagues concluded that "training programs designed to assist coaches, teachers, and other adults occupying leadership roles in creating a positive and supportive environment can influence children's personality development in a positive manner" (p. 74).

It is important to note that the CBAS measures *actual* coaching behaviors. However, the preceding paragraphs highlight that it is also essential to assess how athletes react to those behaviors. This point was raised by Williams and colleagues (2003), who noted, "The CBAS has proven effective at measuring actual coaching behaviors, but it does not assess athletes' evaluative reactions to the behaviors" (p. 18). Williams et al., assessing an evaluative tool called the Coaching Behavior Questionnaire (CBQ; Kenow & Williams, 1992), found that there were moderating factors, such as trait anxiety, state anxiety, and self-confidence, that influenced how athletes viewed their coaches' behaviors. Specifically, those who exhibited more trait anxiety, more state anxiety (cognitive and somatic), and less self-confidence were more likely to view their coaches' behaviors negatively.

Reinforcing Athlete Behavior

The work by Smith, Smoll, and their colleagues clearly supports the view that a positive coaching approach not only is preferred by athletes, it leads to positive changes in social psychological factors such as self esteem. The importance of a positive approach is so important that Smoll and Smith (1979) have suggested that coaches should

> *Be liberal with reward. Look for positive things, reward them . . . praise the little things that others might not notice . . . Have realistic expectations and consistently reward players when they succeed in meeting them. Reward positive things as soon as they occur. (pp. 6-7)*

Care must be taken, however, to insure that a wide variety of verbal rewarding behaviors are used. In a study undertaken with an experienced 32 year-old male swimming coach, Brent Rushall and Kenneth Smith (1979) found that the coach had a very limited repertoire of rewarding words—"good" tended to be the predominant word used. After Rushall and Smith introduced a training session, however, both the quality and the quantity of the coach's verbal reinforcers were increased substantially. It is likely that the most experienced coaches habitually use the same words or phrases—thereby diminishing their effectiveness.

Although positive reinforcement is preferable, there are qualifications. For example, Phil Jackson, the former coach of the Los Angeles Lakers, pointed out,

> *According to the Positive Coaching Alliance, which trains coaches in youth sports, the ideal is a 5-1 ratio of praise to criticism. I'm the national spokesman for the alliance, but I can tell you that at the professional level it can be nearly impossible sometimes to come up with five positives for every negative. What possible reinforcement can I offer to a player who committed five turnovers in the fourth quarter and failed to guard his man? "Way to make that layup?" (Jackson & Arkush, 2004, p. 54)*

Jackson did go on to offer additional insight:

> *Choosing my words carefully, I try to make the players understand that I'm criticizing their performance, not their personality. If, for example, a player has begun to lose sight of his teammates, I don't tell him, "You're*

being selfish by shooting the ball too much." The use of the word "selfish" would indicate something fundamentally wrong with him as an individual, which would only cause resentment. Instead I'll say, "You were a little thirsty out there, weren't you?" . . . The player is much more likely to absorb the criticism and modify his behavior. (Jackson & Arkush, 2004, p. 54)

Another qualification was offered by Daniel Kirschenbaum and Robert Smith (1983). They pointed out that there are sound reasons for interpolating some negative feedback along with positive feedback:

- conformity research has shown that when opinions are expressed in a highly consistent (rather than variable) fashion, the individual's social influence decreases;
- research on interpersonal attraction has shown that individuals who provide only positive feedback are not as well liked as individuals who change the sequence of their feedback from negative to positive; and,
- research on interpersonal influence has shown that both a positive-negative and a negative-positive sequencing of feedback are effective. If a positive approach is used initially, it can decrease defensiveness to later negative feedback. And, if a negative approach is used initially, it can increase the effect of later positive feedback.

Kirschenbaum and Smith had college students take basketball free throws in two blocks of trials under the supervision of an experimenter who served as a coach. The feedback within each block was positive-positive, negative-negative, positive-negative, or negative-positive. Continuous positive and continuous negative feedback produced the same result—a linear decrement in performance from the initial baseline measure. Similarly, the individuals experiencing a positive-negative and a negative-positive sequencing of feedback also had the same result—a linear positive improvement from the initial baseline measure.

Kirschenbaum and Smith emphasized that these results should not be interpreted to mean "that coaches should abandon the regular use of positive feedback. These findings merely suggest that continuous positive feedback, in the absence of any critical comments, may, under some conditions, produce some of the same adverse effects as continuous negative feedback. Clearly, the use of incessant criticism seems much more definitely ill-advised" (p. 340).

An approach that might be best involves the frequent use of positive reinforcement coupled with the use of feedback on correct performance. The former is behavior described as Positive Reinforcement (verbal or nonverbal positive reaction to the athlete's behavior) in the Coaching Behavior Assessment System (see B 1 in Table 14.2). The latter would be the behavior described as Mistake-Contingent Instruction (B 4, technical instruction to the athlete after a mistake). The combination of these two would represent the positive and negative feedback necessary.

Situational Behavior Approaches

Life Cycle Theory

In the situational behavior theories of leadership, it is assumed that particular coaching behaviors are more effective in specific situations. The life cycle theory, which was proposed by Hersey and Blanchard (1969, 1977), is a contingency-based approach to leadership. The basis of the life cycle theory is the proposition that leader effectiveness is a joint product of the leader's behavior and the level of maturity of subordinates. It was pointed out above that a contingency is something that is dependent on something else; it is characterized by a qualifying statement such as "if A then B." The contingency in the life cycle theory resides in the belief that as subordinates become more mature, the nature of the leader's behavior should change. That is, for immature subordinates, one approach is prescribed; for more mature subordinates, another leadership approach is prescribed.

As is the case in all other leadership theories, the two leader behaviors emphasized in the life cycle model are task and relationship behaviors. For *task behavior*, the leader's focus is on performance, productivity, and task success. For *relationship behavior*, the focus is on establishing and maintaining warmth, trust, and good interpersonal relationships with subordinates. It is assumed that while they are in a leadership role, all leaders will engage in both task and relationship behaviors (see Illustration 14.1).

Hersey and Blanchard viewed maturity of subordinates as people's ability and willingness to assume responsibility for the management of their own behavior. It is believed to be derived from a number of factors including the capacity to *set high but attainable goals*, willingness and ability to *take responsibility*, *education*, and level of *experience* in the job. Thus, for example, a young athlete being introduced to a new sport could not be

Illustration 14.1. Coaches will engage in both task and relationship behaviors.

expected to have the knowledge, skill level, or experience in the sport to set reasonable goals. On the other hand, an athlete competing at the professional level would. Thus, Hersey and Blanchard believe that the behaviors of a leader should reflect the fundamental differences in the maturity of these two sets of subordinates.

As Table 14.3 shows, when the maturity of subordinates is low, a *telling approach* is called for on the part of the leader. That is, the leader must provide considerable direction and, therefore, task behaviors are high. Also, because of the immaturity of subordinates, the relationship-oriented behaviors of the leader are reduced.

As the maturity of subordinates increases into the low to moderate range, the leader can adopt a *selling approach*. That is, the leader concentrates on persuading subordinates about the correct way of carrying out their responsibilities. As Table 14.3 also shows, with subordinates who are low to moderate in maturity, the leader's task behaviors must be high but relationship-oriented behaviors can also be increased.

When subordinate maturity is in the moderate to high range, a *participating approach* is prescribed. An emphasis is placed on discussing the approach to be taken with subordinates. Consequently, the leader's task-oriented behaviors can be low and relationship-oriented behaviors can be high.

When subordinates have high maturity, they have the education, skill, and/or experience to operate independently. Consequently, a *delegating approach* can be used by the leader and both task and relationship behaviors can be reduced.

Chelladurai and Carron (1983) assessed the validity of the life cycle theory of leadership for a sport context. Maturity was operationally defined through a combination of age and basketball experience. Basketball players competing at midget high school (14 to 15 years), junior high school (15 to 16 years), senior high school (17 to 18 years), and university (19 to 23 years) levels indicated how much social support (i.e., relationship-oriented) behavior and training and instruction (i.e., task-oriented) behavior they wanted from their coaches.

Table 14.3
The life-cycle theory of leadership
(Adapted from Hersey & Blanchard, 1969, 1977, 1982)

Maturity Level of Subordinates	Leader Style	Leader Behavior
Low	*Telling* The emphasis is on directing subordinates.	High Task with Low Relationship
Low to Moderate	*Selling* The emphasis is on persuading subordinates.	High Task with High Relationship
Moderate to High	*Participating* The emphasis is on discussion with subordinates on the approach to be taken.	Low Task with High Relationship
High	*Delegating* The emphasis is on allowing subordinates to choose.	Low Task with Low Relationship

The results were not consistent with the life cycle theory. Life cycle would predict that the preferences for social support would follow an inverted-U pattern (see Table 14.3 again): low in midget, high in both junior and senior high school, and then low in university. The results showed that there was a steady increase from midget to university basketball players in amount of social support preferred. Similarly, life cycle theory would predict high preferences for task behavior in midget and junior that would fall off in high school and university (Table 14.3). However, a U-relationship was found; preferences for task-oriented behavior were high in midget and university but reduced in junior and senior high school.

Multidimensional Model of Leadership

The model. Possibly the most extensively examined theoretical model used to investigate coaching behavior has been Chelladurai's multidimensional model of leadership (Chelladurai, 1978, 1990). A schematic summary of the model is presented in Figure 14.2. The essence of the multidimensional model is that antecedents such as the nature of the athlete, the nature of the coach, and situational characteristics have an effect on the coach's behavior and, in turn, the coach's behavior has consequences for athlete satisfaction and both individual and team performance.

As Figure 14.2 shows, a coach's behavior can be viewed from three perspectives: the behavior that is preferred by the athlete (Box 6), the behavior that is required (prescribed) by the situation (Box 4), and the actual behavior of the coach (Box 5). Preferred leader behavior is directly influenced by member characteristics (Box 3). It is not unreasonable to expect that athletes differing in age, experience, culture, and competence—to name but a few member characteristics—will differ in the degree to which they prefer their coaches to control training, show affection, allow for input into decision making, and so on. A very young athlete, for example, might be much more sensitive to criticism than an older, more experienced athlete. Or, older, more experienced athletes might like more input into the development of their training programs than novices.

The behavior required of a coach (Box 4) is strongly influenced by the

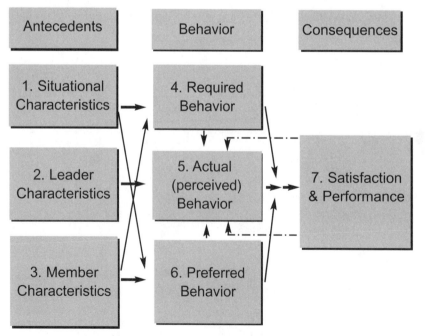

Figure 14.2. The multidimensional model of leadership (Adapted from Chelladurai, 1990)

demands of the situation (Box 1). For example, at the beginning of the season when 150 athletes are present, a democratic approach (where coaches and athletes jointly make decisions) wouldn't be effective. Chaos would result. Thus, an autocratic approach by the coach is prescribed by the demands of the situation. In addition, member characteristics (Box 3) also influence the coaching behaviors required. For example, a democratic approach would be ineffective for a group of seven-year olds at the first session of a learn-to-skate program. An autocratic approach would be required.

A coach's actual behavior (Box 5) is directly influenced by his/her personal characteristics (Box 2) including personality, age, experience, ability, and so on. Also, however, a coach's actual behavior is strongly influenced by the demands of the situation (Box 4). Two coaches of different age, ability and experience would exhibit similar behavior in their first meeting with a group of 150 athletes. The situation requires an autocratic approach and argues against providing social support to individual athletes. A coach's actual behavior is also influenced by the preferences of athletes (Box 6).

Chelladurai proposed that athlete satisfaction and more effective performance (Box 7) result when there is congruence between the coach's actual behavior, the behavior required (prescribed) by the situation, and the behavior preferred by athletes. Although there are other possible consequences of participation—for example, absenteeism and adherence—performance and satisfaction are considered to be the most important. Are the athletes satisfied with their experience? Are individual performance and team performance as effective as they could be?

Performance and satisfaction are considered to be related. As Chelladurai and Carron (1978) noted, "insofar as the subordinates (athletes) are oriented toward task accomplishment, and insofar as the leader (coach) meets these preferences, *both* satisfaction and performance are enhanced. That is, both are direct results of leader behavior" (p. 71).

The Leadership Scale for Sports (LSS) was developed by Chelladurai to assess five main behaviors considered characteristic of coaches-as-leaders (Chelladurai & Saleh, 1978; Chelladurai & Carron, 1981). These include the degree to which the coach provides *positive feedback,* gives *social support, trains and instructs* the athletes in the skills of the sport, uses a *democratic* approach, and is *autocratic* (authoritarian). Chelladurai's model has been tested in a number of studies and the links between the various elements in the model have been examined.

A distinction that has been made with regard to leader behavior that has relevance to the multidimensional model of leadership is whether that individual engages in transactional or transformational leadership activities (Bass, 1985). Transactional leadership is characterized by the exchange of reward (or decrease of punishment) for effort. For example, a coach who motivates athletes to work hard in practice by threatening to make them run sprints would be engaging in transactional leadership. By contrast, a coach engaging in transformational leadership inspires athletes to give effort for more idealized reasons such as the good of the team, the development of their skills, or the achievement of performance standards beyond their expectations. Bass (1985) noted that a transformational leader would utilize a combination of three behaviors. One of these is *charismatic leadership*. Charismatic coaches display confidence and assertiveness, promote their beliefs or vision for the team, and demonstrate a high level of confidence in the athletes. A second is referred to as *intellectual stimulation* whereby the coach involves and stimulates athletes in decision making. Finally, *individualized consideration* involves behaviors that would demonstrate the coach is considerate of the personal development of each athlete.

Member characteristics and coaching behavior. One important link that has received attention has been between member characteristics (Box 3 of Figure 14.2) and the type of leader behavior preferred (Box 6 of Figure 14.2). Two member characteristics that have been shown to influence preferences for leader behavior are the *sex* and the *experience* of the athlete. Male athletes have a greater preference for autocratic behavior, training and instruction behavior, and social support behavior. Conversely, female athletes like greater input into decision-making; they have a greater preference for democratic behavior (Erle, 1981; Chelladurai & Saleh, 1978).

The more *experience* athletes have in a sport, the greater is their preference for social support behavior from their coach (Erle, 1981; Chelladurai & Carron, 1982, 1983; Weiss & Friedrichs, 1986). Chelladurai (1984) has suggested that this is almost inevitable. As athletes increase in ability, they must pay increasingly higher costs for additional increments in ability. These costs include the time, effort, and energy devoted to training and the sacrifice of social contacts outside of athletics. Consequently, as the athlete increases in ability, the sport environment becomes increasingly more important as a source of social support. Thus, it's probably not surprising that athletes of higher ability show higher preferences for more social support behavior from their coach.

Also, more experienced athletes have a greater preference for autocratic behavior (Chelladurai, 1978; Chelladurai & Carron, 1982; Chelladurai & Saleh, 1978). This is probably a result of social learning. Athletes come to learn that the athletic environment is essentially autocratic. With time and experience, they also come to expect that the coach will make the majority of decisions. Eventually, the autocratic approach is preferred by the athlete.

It should be noted that the autocratic approach is not necessarily better. Commitment to a decision is enhanced if the athlete is involved in the decision. This perspective was highlighted by Phil Jackson, the former coach of the Los Angeles Lakers, who noted,

> *"I always prefer when players come up with a new wrinkle on their own. Feeling a greater degree of ownership, they will invest more effort in the strategy's outcome." (Jackson & Arkush, 2004, p. 46)*

Also, the opportunity for personal growth is enhanced. Again, Jackson spoke to this point when he argued against a coach's tendency to use

> *"timeouts as a defensive weapon to halt the opponent's momentum. I don't subscribe to that philosophy and I know it's one of my unconventional tendencies that infuriates my critics to no end. They see a run by the other team, and figure I'm the one who ought to stop it. I figure that my players are the ones who ought to stop it. Only by stewing in the mess that they created can they be subjected to its full embarrassing outcome, and only by discovering on their own how to extricate themselves can they be adequately prepared for the next time they lose their rhythm." (Jackson & Arkush, 2004, p. 59)*

Some athletes prefer more autocratic behavior than others. Horne and Carron (1985) found that the coach-athlete relationship was rated as incompatible by the athlete when the coach was perceived to be more autocratic than was preferred. This finding is not inconsistent with the studies that have shown that the preference for autocratic behavior increases systematically as athletes gain in experience. In the Horne and Carron study, the important point was not that the athletes didn't want autocratic behavior, only that the amount given by the coach was higher than was preferred.

Situational characteristics and coaching behavior. The situation also has an influence on the preferences that athletes have for different leader behaviors (the link between Boxes 1 and 7 in Figure 14.2). Peter Terry (1984) was the first researcher to look for the impact of *culture* on preferences for coaching behavior. He failed to find any differences among athletes from Canada, the United States, and Great Britain. Terry proposed that this might have been a result of the fact that the athletes he studied "all share similar cultural backgrounds and sporting ideologies" (p. 206).

In another examination of the influence of culture on preferences for coaching behavior, Chelladurai and his colleagues did find differences (Chelladurai, Malloy, Imamura, & Yamaguchi, 1987). Physical education students from Canada and Japan were tested. The Japanese students were subdivided according to whether they were participants in traditional sports (i.e., judo, kendo) or modern sports (i.e., basketball, volleyball). In comparison to the Japanese students in traditional sports, the Canadian students preferred less social support, less autocratic behavior, and more positive feedback. In comparison to the Japanese students in modern sports, however, the Canadian students preferred less democratic behavior and social support. Chelladurai and his colleagues concluded that while culture might influence preferences for coaching behavior, type of sport has a moderating effect.

Other situational variables that influence the athlete's preference for leader behaviors include the *type of organization* and the *nature of the sport*. In intramural sports, where the primary emphasis is on participation and enjoyment, athletes don't want as much training and instruction, social support, or positive feedback as athletes on intercollegiate sport teams (Erle, 1981). Also, athletes in team sports such as basketball prefer more training and instruction than athletes in individual sports such as track and wrestling (Chelladurai & Carron, 1982).

One conclusion that emerges from the discussion on leadership is that the nature of the situation is an extremely important consideration insofar as understanding leader effectiveness is concerned. Individual behavior is a joint product of the personality of the individual and the nature of the situational demands. Research focused on the universal trait approach to leadership has clearly shown that there is no single "coaching type." Coaches are different, not identical in their personalities. In a quote presented earlier, Jack Scott (1969) claimed that coaches are authoritarian and uninterested in the welfare of their athletes. If it can be assumed for the moment that coaches have behaved in a manner similar to Scott's stereotypical description, then the reasons for this must lie largely in the situation, not in the coaches' personalities. What is it about the athletic situation that causes a large number of individuals who are different in personality to behave in a relatively similar manner? Some factors that have been identified include the size of the group, the type of group task, the nature of the organization, and the age and maturity of the group.

Consequences of coaching behaviors. As Figure 14.2 shows, the consequences of coaching behavior are satisfaction and performance. In a comprehensive test of Chelladurai's model, Maureen Weiss and Warren Friedrichs (1986) tested athletes and coaches from 23 basketball teams participating in the National Association of Intercollegiate Athletics in an attempt to determine which coaching and situational variables were associated with athlete satisfaction. Weiss and Friedrichs assessed the size of the school, the percentage of the coach's workload devoted to basketball, the size of the team's budget, the amount of scholarship money available, and the tradition of success in the school. The only situational variable found to be important was *institutional size*—athletes from larger institutions expressed greater overall satisfaction than athletes from smaller institutions.

Weiss and Friedrichs also included a number of coaching characteristics, including the coach's playing experience, coaching experience, age when hired, and prior win/loss record as a head coach (see Box 2 of Figure 14.2). Then Weiss and Friedrichs had the athletes evaluate their coach's perceived behavior (Box 5) and indicate their satisfaction with supervision, playing conditions, teammates, amount of work, kind of work, and school identification (Box 7). The coaches who had less playing experience, had a better prior record, and were hired at a younger age had athletes who were more satisfied. Also, those coaches who more frequently provided positive feedback, provided more social support, and used a more democratic style had the more satisfied athletes.

Gender and Leadership

In business and industry, the number of females who are leaders and managers at upper levels is low (Bergman, 1986; Nieva & Gutek, 1981; Powell, 1988, 1990). In sport, a similar picture exists. The 2003 Racial and Gender Report Card (Lapchick, 2003) published by The Institute for Diversity and Ethics in Sport highlighted the current situation for men and women in athletics. Specifically, this report summarized that

> *Title IX has been the single most powerful tool to create opportunities for women in sport, including athletes, coaches, and staff. Yet, even more than 30 years after the advent of Title IX, 45 percent of head coaches in women's collegiate sports are women (p. 1).*

In addition, the report demonstrated an underrepresentation of women in a variety of leadership positions, including

(a) owners (e.g., 4 women had majority ownership of a professional team across all sports),

(b) head coaches of women's teams (e.g., 45% of collegiate sports and 7 of 24 teams during the 2002 season of the Women's National Basketball Association had female coaches),

(c) head coaches of men's teams (3% of collegiate men's teams head coaches were female during 2000-2001 season),

(d) assistant coaches of women's teams (approximately 50% of assistant coaches were female across Division I, II, and III of the NCAA), and

(e) top management (3 women were in the CEO/president role of men's teams).

Questions surrounding the involvement of females and males in leadership roles have intrigued social scientists in both sport and industrial psychology. Is the preponderance of males in leadership roles a function of superior qualifications? Are women as likely as men to emerge as leaders in leaderless groups? Do males and females have similar leadership styles? Does the gender of leaders have an influence on their evaluation by subordinates? In sport, there is some research that provides insight into these issues. However, in industrial psychology, a substantially larger body of research has made it possible to use meta-analysis to statistically answer these questions.

Gender and Emergence into a Leadership Role

Differences in the qualifications of male and female coaching applicants have been one explanation used to account for the increased likelihood that males are hired rather than females. Mimi Murray and Betty Mann (1993) argued, "The use of 'qualified' is, of course, prejudicial. It is often assumed in sport that males, regardless of training or experience, are more qualified than females" (p. 89). Murray and Mann then pointed out that research has shown that (a) hiring standards are lower for males coaching female teams than for males or females coaching same-sex teams, and (b) female coaches typically have a physical education degree whereas male coaches of female teams are primarily from other areas in education.

What about non-sport situations? Alice Eagly and Steven Karau (1991) undertook a meta-analysis to statistically summarize the research from 58 studies which had examined the emergence of male and female leaders in initially leaderless groups. Eagly and Karau suggested that the issue of emergence of leaders is practically and theoretically significant because it can provide insight into (a) why leadership roles in natural settings are occupied considerably more often by men than women, and (b) whether men emerge into leadership roles in small groups because they exhibit certain types of behaviors more frequently than women or because they carry out those behaviors differently.

The types of leadership measured in the 58 studies examined were either task-oriented, socially-oriented, or general in nature (although in other studies, the type of leadership was not specified). Eagly and Karau found that both males and females tend to emerge as leaders in groups that are initially leaderless. However, men are more likely to emerge as task leaders or general leaders whereas women are more likely to emerge as social leaders. It was suggested that "the fact that sex differences were equally strong for these two classes of measures suggests that men and women not only are treated differently in group settings but also behave differently . . . the tendency to choose men may . . . reflect a tendency to define leadership in terms of task-oriented contributions" (Eagly & Karau, 1991, p. 701).

Eagly and Karau did find that a number of factors have an influence on the tendency for men to emerge as task-oriented leaders. First, the longer the period that the group interacts before the leadership position is filled, the greater is the tendency for women to emerge as leaders. Thus, if a leader is chosen quickly, gender may play an important role in the selection process. When the opportunities to interact are increased prior to the selection of a leader, however, more information may be available on task-relevant competence. Consequently, there is an increased probability that gender will play less of a role.

The type of task is also important. In situations where the group task requires relatively complex social interactions—negotiations and the extensive sharing of ideas, for example—there is an increased likelihood that women will emerge as group leaders. Possibly the social contributions of women to the group become more apparent (and more obviously important) through prolonged group discussions and, consequently, the likelihood that they will emerge as the group's task leader increases.

In addition to what type of behaviors (i.e., task vs. interpersonal) are necessary to successfully complete the task, the degree to which the task is stereotypically oriented toward men or women influences leader emergence. Ridgeway (2001) summarized studies examining this phenomenon and noted that for tasks that were gender neutral or typically masculine in nature, men would initiate speech more often, spend more time talking, and use assertive gestures. When the task was more feminine in nature, women displayed these task-oriented behaviors to a greater degree.

The relative number of males and females in the group also plays a role in who will ultimately become the task leader. The tendency for males to emerge as the group's task leader is greatest when the number of males and females in a group is equal. When either females or males are in a majority in the group, the chances increase that a woman will emerge as the leader. Eagly and Karau suggested that cultural changes present in society might be the explanation for these intriguing findings. That is, a greater emphasis now exists toward achieving equality of the sexes. Thus, when women are in a minority, men may refrain from expressing dominance. Conversely, when men are in a minority, women may refrain from ceding leadership.

Fourth, group size has an influence. Males are more likely to emerge as leaders in smaller groups—especially dyads. Eagly and Karau felt that dyads are a special case and that specific social norms may have a major effect on the relations between men and women in dyads.

Finally, Eagly and Karau noted that their results were dependent on both the year of the study and the age of the subjects. That is, the tendency for males to emerge as leaders was more pronounced in earlier publications and for groups with older subjects. "Perhaps social change has created conditions more conducive to female leadership" (Eagly & Karau, 1991, p. 704).

Gender and Leadership Behavior

As was pointed out above, two types of leadership behavior are emphasized in all theories of leadership: *task orientation,* where the leader's focus is on organizing and directing subordinates toward productivity, performance, and task achievement; and *interpersonal orientation,* where the leader's focus is on the development and maintenance of morale and good relationships. It was pointed out earlier in the discussion of Fiedler's contingency theory that these two orientations represent a hierarchy of preferences for the leader (Fiedler, 1967; Fiedler & Chemers, 1974). Task-oriented leaders have high productivity as their first priority with the expectation that good interpersonal relationships will follow from task achievement. On the other hand, interpersonal-oriented leaders have good interpersonal relationships as their first priority with the expectation that high productivity will follow from good morale.

Are there differences between women and men in the tendency to be task oriented versus interpersonal oriented? A stereotypical belief does exist in business and industry that there is a masculine mode of management, which is characterized by a task orientation, and a feminine mode of management, which is characterized by an interpersonal orientation (Eagly & Johnson, 1990; Loden, 1985). Alice Eagly and Blair Johnson (1990) argued, however, that

> *behavior may be less stereotypic when women and men who occupy the same managerial role are compared because these organizational leadership roles, which typically are paid jobs, usually provide fairly clear guidelines about the conduct of behavior. Managers become socialized into their roles in the early stages of their experience in an organization . . . In addition, male and female managers have presumably been selected by the organization (and have selected themselves into these roles) according to the same set of organizationally relevant criteria. (p. 234)*

Eagly and Johnson (1991) then tested their predictions using meta-analysis on 370 comparisons from 162 studies in social psychology and industrial psychology. Consistent with their expectations, Eagly and Johnson found that in studies undertaken in *organizational settings*, there was no evidence that men lead using a task orientation and women lead using an interpersonal orientation.

Gender and the Evaluation of Leadership

Research on the preferences of athletes for coaches shows that both male and female athletes show a bias toward male coaches (George, 1989; Parkhouse & Williams, 1986; Weinberg, Reveles, & Jackson, 1984). Why this is the case is difficult to determine because of the relatively sparse number of studies concerned with this issue. Is it because males and females coach differently? Is it because females coach in a stereotypical male way—an approach that is incongruent with gender-role expectations? Is it because of an inherent bias in favor of males in a leadership role?

Research in social and industrial psychology does offer an opportunity to gain some insight into the general issue of the evaluation of female and male leaders. Typically the research has used one of two paradigms in laboratory settings. With the first paradigm, subjects are given a written vignette in which a manager responds to a problem. In the vignette, the gender of both the manager and the subordinates is varied systematically. Thus, for example, in half of the questionnaires, the manager is called Pat and references indicate he is male. The gender of the subordinates is changed systematically so that in a third of the questionnaires Pat supervises males, in another third, females, and in the final third, a mixed group of females and males. For the other half of the questionnaires, the manager is again called Pat but references indicate she is female. The subjects then rate the manager on various characteristics.

In the second paradigm, both a male and female confederate are trained by the experimenter to lead subordinates in an identical fashion. The participants, the subordinates in the study, then evaluate the leader on a number of characteristics.

The advantage in these two paradigms is that tight experimental control is present. The characteristics of the leader are held constant and the only factor that varies is their sex. Thus, any differences that emerge are a product of bias.

Eagly, Makhijani, and Klonsky (1992) located 61 studies concerned with the evaluation of male and female leaders. When they conducted a meta-analysis on the results from these 61 studies, they found that the tendency to evaluate female leaders less favorably than male leaders is small. However, the degree of bias increases under certain circumstances. When women occupy roles that are dominated by men, and when the subordinates are men, the bias against women increases. Also, when female leaders use a stereotypical masculine leadership style that involves autocratic or directive behavior, the bias increases.

Carli (2001) pointed out that there is evidence to suggest that women who wish to utilize assertive, directive behaviors can reduce resistance and increase influence by tempering "their competence with displays of communality and warmth" (p. 725) such as smiling, nodding, showing support, and expressing agreement. The obvious detriment to this approach is that it reaffirms past stereotypes of men and women in terms of how they (should) display leadership.

Leader Decision Styles

The Nature of Decision Making

One important aspect of leadership is decision making. Leaders must continually process information, weigh the alternatives, and then come to a decision. What offensive and defensive systems should be used? What training schedules are best? What athletes work best together? What time should practice start? How long should it last? Although the list of examples where decisions have to be made in sport seems endless, the process of decision making involves four basic approaches. The major difference among them is in the relative amount of involvement or influence by the leader and his/her subordinates.

When an autocratic decision style is used, the leader makes the decision alone. Consequently, this approach involves the greatest amount of independence by the leader. The example in Box 14.2 helps to illustrate this point. Alvin Dark portrayed Charlie Finley, the owner of the Oakland Athletics, as a man completely in control.

A consultative decision style is similar to the autocratic approach in that the leader makes the decision alone. A difference between the two, however, is that the leader initially consults with subordinates to obtain their input. This input may or may not be used when the decision is made but subordinates do have some involvement. The example in Box 14.2 describes professional indoor soccer coach Tatu's inclusion of players in the decision-making process but also his recognition that the ultimate decision rests with him.

A delegative decision style is also similar to the autocratic approach in that the leader again makes the decision. But, this time, however, the leader's decision involves handing over the responsibility to subordinates or to the group who then make the decision independently. The quotation in Box 14.2 is an illustration of the result of this approach. Quarterback Trent Dilfer presents a fairly positive opinion of his coach Mike Holmgren based on the perception that he delegates a lot of decision making to his player representatives.

The participative or democratic approach involves the greatest amount of involvement by the group in the decision-making process. The group (which could include the coach) jointly comes to a decision with the coach having no more influence than any other group member. Greer (2002) included participative decision making as a method of creating an

Box 14.2
Illustrations of the various decision styles in the process of leadership

Decision Style	Illustration
Autocratic: The leader arrives at the decision alone.	In discussing [owner] Charlie Finley, "master" is precisely the right word. If he's your boss, he has to own you, from the first warm-up of the spring to the last putout of the fall. Every minute, every day (Dark & Underwood, 1980, p. 6).
Consultative: The leader comes to the final decision after consulting one or more subordinates.	Things have worked out fine. In Tatu's first year as coach Dallas won the 1998 WISL [indoor soccer] championship, and last year it lost in the final . . . Tatu has succeeded, to a certain extent, by including his players in the decision-making process. "We're a family," the coach says. "We have a lot of opinions. But the buck stops at my lap" (Bechtel, Kim, & Mravic, 2000, para. 7).
Delegative: The leader delegates the decision to one or more subordinates.	"A lot of people perceive Mike [Holmgren] to be a high-ego, credit-seeking type of guy. I see a guy who delegates a lot of authority and relies a great deal on his captains. I honestly feel he'd be happier if he didn't get the credit, but maybe that's because I just played for the ultimate egomaniac" (Quarterback Trent Dilfer quoted in Silver, 2001, p. 42).
Participative: The group and the leader jointly make the decision.	"'We don't all agree with what the union stands for,' says [Dallas Cowboys player representative Doug] Cosbie, 'but we believe in the collective bargaining process. Collectively, we can improve working conditions'" (Lieber, 1987, p. 42).

"environment that will stimulate motivation and help elevate a team's achievement level" (p. 40). When the National Football League players went on strike in 1987, it was a decision that was arrived at through the democratic approach. The example in Box 14.2 presents the viewpoint of one of the player representatives, Doug Cosbie. Cosbie pointed out that, essentially, while not everyone agreed with the action taken, the strike represented a collective decision.

Decision Making in Sport

Chelladurai and Arnott (1985) and Gordon (1988) undertook an analysis of the decision styles preferred by athletes and/or used by coaches with male and female basketball players and with male soccer players. Their findings are summarized in Table 14.4. It is apparent that both coaches and athletes view the athletic situation as generally autocratic in nature. On the average, the coaches make decisions using an autocratic approach 82.9% of the time. In some instances, this is done after consultation (38%) but in the majority of cases, decisions are totally autocratic (44.9%). The participative style is used very infrequently (15.5%), whereas the delegative style is almost nonexistent (1.6%).

A major discrepancy between what coaches do and what players prefer lies in the use of a participative decision style. Male athletes prefer almost twice as much participation (29.5% versus 15.5%) and female athletes three times as much participation (46.9% versus 15.5%) as coaches provide. The delegative style is not only used infrequently, it is not wanted by either male or female athletes.

Chelladurai (1993) provided one interesting way of looking at the amount of involvement and influence by coaches and team members in the various decision styles. This is illustrated in Figure 14.3. He suggested that the coach's influence falls along a continuum ranging from 100%, when the autocratic approach is used, to 0%, when the delegative approach is used. As would be expected, with the participative approach, the coach's influence is in between at a moderate level. Chelladurai also suggested that the influence of team members is maximal when a participative approach is used. However, both the autocratic and the delegative approaches exclude them from participating in the decision.

At the management level, the delegative approach can be effective when it is clearly understood who is in command. An athletic director, general manager, or owner who hires a coach and then constantly interferes in the day-to-day leadership of the team reduces the coach's effectiveness. The sentiments expressed by Whitey Herzog are typical of the view held by most coaches: "The smartest people are those who hire good people and then just get the hell out of the way" (Herzog & Horrigan, 1987, p. 12). The delegative approach is ineffective when it is unclear who is in command. One example of this occurred in the 1988 National Basketball Association season. The Sacramento Kings hired former coach and player, Bill Russell, to coach the team. But after only nine months on the job

> the Kings finally acknowledged that Russell, though a legendary player, is
> no longer capable of being a successful NBA coach . . . "I'd say the effort

Table 14.4
Decision styles used by coaches and preferred by athletes (Adapted from Chelladurai, 1993, based on data from Chelladurai & Arnott, 1985, and Gordon, 1988)

Group	Autocratic	Consultative	Participative	Delegative
Coach's Decision Styles				
Coach's Choice	46.3	33.3	18.5	1.9
Coach's Perception of other Coaches' Choice	45.5	41.2	12.5	0.8
Athlete's Perception of Coaches' Choice	43.0	39.6	15.4	2.0
Average	44.9	38.0	15.5	1.6
Male Athlete's Preferences for Coach's Decision Style				
Soccer Players	31.2	41.9	24.9	2.0
Basketball Players	38.9	25.8	34.1	1.2
Average	35.1	33.8	29.5	1.6
Female Athlete's Preferences for Coach's Decision Style				
Basketball Players	33.0	18.1	46.9	2.0

was adequate," said [King's president and general manager Joe] Axelson. "Bill delegated a lot of authority, but he was always there." The fact remains: The Sacramento system, in which Russell acted as an "executive" head coach who gave many of the everyday coaching duties to assistants Willis Reed . . . and Jerry Reynolds . . . only left the players confused. "It was obvious that there was no direction on that team," said an assistant coach of a Western Conference team. (McCallum, 1988, p. 15)

Gender and Leader Decision Making

The work of Eagly and Johnson (1991) on leader behaviors was introduced earlier. It was pointed out that their meta-analysis was carried out on 162 studies (encompassing 370 comparisons) that focused on differences in leadership behavior between females and males. It was observed that in organizational settings women use a more democratic (participative) than men. Eagly and Johnson speculated on two possible reasons for these differences in decision making. The first possibility was that men and women who ultimately become leaders in organizations might have different personalities and behavioral tendencies. Consequently, even though women and men would face the same pressures associated with achieving organizational objectives and insuring task success, the personal skills of women would cause them to carry out their managerial duties differently; to increase subordinate input into decision making.

The second possibility, which was also highlighted previously from the work of Carli (2001), was that women might adopt a more democratic approach to placate peers and subordinates resistant to having women in a leadership position. Eagly and Johnson (1991) pointed out that, "to the extent that women leaders have internalized to some degree the culture's reservations about their capacity for leadership, they may gain confidence as leaders by making collaborative decisions that they can determine are in line with their associates' expectations" (p. 248).

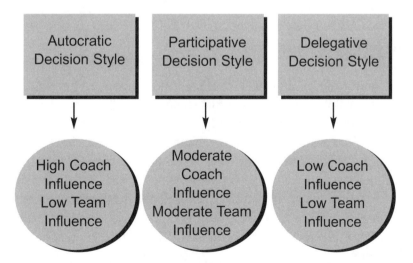

Figure 14.3. Coach's and athletes' relative influence in three decision styles (Adapted from Chelladurai, 1993)

There is no way to determine directly which of these two possibilities is closer to the truth. However, the results presented in Table 14.4 provide strong support for the first possibility—that women are inherently different in personality and behavioral tendencies. In turn, these inherent differences in personality and behavioral tendency cause women to favor a democratic approach more than men. As Table 14.4 shows, even when women are in subordinate roles, they have almost a 40% greater preference for a participative decision style from their coaches (i.e., 46.9% versus 29.5%). Whether in leadership or subordinate positions, women are more prone toward participation in decision making than are males.

Type and Level of Sport and Decision Making

A study by Beam, Serwatka, and Wilson (2004) examined preferred leadership behaviors of athletes in the National Collegiate Athletic Association (NCAA) Divisions I and II in relation to gender, task type, and competitive level. From a gender perspective, their results seemed to support the above research that men and women have different preferences for leadership behavior. They found that men preferred coaches to utilize an autocratic decision-making style to a greater degree than women. In addition, they also found that athletes participating in *individual sports* had different preferences for leader decision making than those participating in *team sports*. Specifically, individual sport athletes had a higher preference for a democratic decision-making style than their team sport counterparts. While no explanations were put forward for this result, it is possible that those in individual sports are considerably more responsible for the outcome of their performance and likely share a closer bond to their coach than team sport athletes. Thus, individual sport athletes are more involved in the decisions that are made. Additionally, decisions in team sports may differ in nature and quantity (i.e., greater in number and affecting more people). Consequently, an authoritarian approach may be more appropriate. Finally, the authors found no differences in leadership preferences between the two competitive levels (i.e., NCAA Division I and II). However, it is highly likely that more diverse competitive levels would show differences in decision-making preferences (e.g., recreational vs. intercollegiate sport).

Cohesion and Team Decision-Making

Brawley, Carron, and Widmeyer (1993) examined the influence of athlete involvement in team decisions on team cohesion and the athlete's understanding of and commitment to the decision. Female and male members of highly competitive, elite teams were asked to indicate the percentage of team members who had been involved in setting team goals for practice and competition. The athletes were then asked to rate how clear the goals were and what level of influence those goals had on team behavior (i.e., effort, persistence). Those athletes who had had greater participation in team goal setting possessed a stronger sense of task and social cohesion. Also, greater participation in setting team goals led to greater clarity (understanding) of those goals as well as a belief that the goals had a greater influence on team behavior.

Brawley and his colleagues suggested that the interactions that occur within a team when its members act together to arrive at a collective decision, encourage common perceptions about the group. These common perceptions include beliefs about the importance of team success, the degree of task and social unity present, and the level of satisfaction present. Also, collaboration in decision making increases the clarity of team goals and helps to insure that those goals have a greater influence on behavior.

More recently, Turman (2003) examined how different coaching techniques influence athlete perceptions of cohesion and concluded that strategies designed to incorporate a more democratic style of decision-making/leadership and social-support behavior are valuable in the pursuit of making a team more cohesive.

The Effectiveness of Decision Styles

Work Groups

The question of what form of decision making is better for productivity and satisfaction has intrigued researchers. The earliest work clearly showed that laissez-faire leadership clearly results in unproductive groups and dissatisfied group members (Lewin & Lippitt, 1938). However, the question of whether autocratic or participative (democratic) decision making is superior has produced discrepant answers in different research studies. In an attempt to reconcile this issue, John Gastil (1994) carried out a meta-analysis on 37 studies from organizational psychology.

Gastil's analysis led him to two generalizations. First, there is no difference between an autocratic versus a democratic leadership style for productivity. However, a democratic approach appears to be more effective in natural settings (but not laboratory or field studies). Second, there is a small relationship between a democratic leadership style and satisfaction.

The Normative Model of Decision Making

Chelladurai and Haggerty (1978) took a different approach to the question of what decision style is more effective in groups. They proposed a normative model of decision making (a contingency-based view) in which the nature of the situation is assumed to play a significant role in determining what decision style was most appropriate. It was pointed out in Chapter 13 that a norm is a standard that provides the individual with guidelines for behavior in specific situations. This is what the normative model does for leaders in decision-making situations. According to Chelladurai and Haggerty, seven situational factors have an influence on what type of decision style normally would be most effective. The first situational variable is *time pressure*. The amount of time available to deliberate, weigh alternatives, and consult with other people varies from one situation to another. In turn, this has a direct influence on the type of decision style that is most appropriate.

A second situational factor that has an effect on the type of decision style used is *quality requirement*. In some instances, the coach may be satisfied with any one from a number of equally good alternatives. Thus, the quality requirement in that situation is low. The decision concerning which individual to select as team captain is an example. It's not an unimportant issue but if the coach is satisfied with all the potential candidates, the quality requirement in the situation is low. On the other hand, the coach may feel that the selection of the final two or three players on the roster is important to assure maximum flexibility. An optimal decision must be made so the quality requirement of this decision is high.

A third situational factor is *information location*. Decision making involves the processing of information and the weighing of alternatives. Thus, it makes good sense that those individuals who possess the best information on an issue should be involved in the decision. If the coach has the best information, he/she should make the decision; if not, a consultative, delegative, or democratic approach should be taken.

Problem complexity is a fourth situational variable. Problems are complex if they involve a series of interconnected steps—where one decision has an influence on every subsequent decision. Picking the athletes for an Olympic basketball team is one example. A coach who has picked her best five might be faced with the dilemma of filling out the roster with a poor defensive player who is an outstanding 3-point shooter versus a versatile athlete who can play more than one position.

The fifth situational factor, *group acceptance*, is an acknowledgment that acceptance by team members may be critical for the successful implementation of a decision. A coach might autocratically decide to introduce a full-court press in basketball. If the athletes are convinced that they don't have the ability to make it work, their effort might be poor.

Another situational factor that influences the type of decision style that is most effective is the *coach's power*. When coaches possess the five sources of power outlined by French and Raven (1959)—expert, coercive, reference, legitimate, and reward—compliance by athletes with the decisions is virtually assured. On the other hand, if a coach doesn't possess expert power, the group could resist the decision.

The final factor is *group integration*, which refers to the level of task and social cohesiveness present. Thus, for example, a participative decision style could be used effectively with a highly cohesive team. It wouldn't be as effective with a non-cohesive group.

The role that the seven situational factors play in decision making is illustrated in Figure 14.4. The top branch of the decision tree is useful to illustrate the normative model in action. The first question encountered is whether there is restricted time pressure. If the answer is "no," the lower branch is taken and other situational issues become relevant. If the answer is "yes," however, then the upper branch of the decision tree is taken and only one other question is relevant: Does the coach possess relevant information? If the answer is "yes," an autocratic decision style is prescribed. On the other hand, if the answer is "no," the coach (normally) should delegate the decision to a group member who possesses the relevant resources.

Thus, the answer to the question of what decision style is more effective is, it depends upon the situation and the circumstances. The athletic situation and the circumstances under which sport occurs seem to be primarily autocratic in nature. Coaches are highly autocratic in their approach. Whether this is due to the fact that it is simply the best approach possible or that coaches (and athletes) have come to expect this approach through a process of social learning isn't clear. There is a strong preference by male and female athletes for greater participation in the decision-making process.

There are a number of advantages and disadvantages in providing athletes with more participation (Chelladurai, 1993). One advantage is that in discussions associated with group participation, alternative solutions and/or approaches to the problem can surface. As a result, a higher quality decision is possible. Also, when the group participates in a decision, there is a greater sense of "ownership" in the outcome. Consequently, there is also

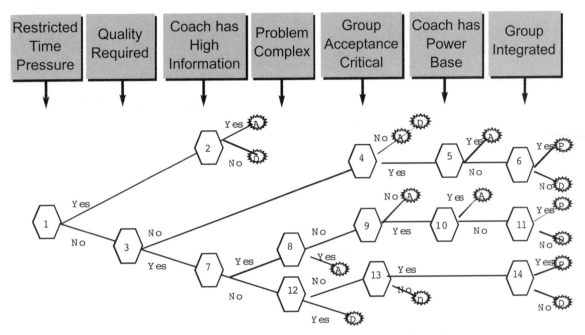

***Figure 14.4. A normative model of decision-making in sport
(Adapted from Chelladurai & Haggerty, 1978)***

greater motivation to insure that the decision is accepted and acted upon. The sense of ownership that will result from member input is illustrated in the case of Fontbonne College in St. Louis. The basketball coach, Lee McKinney, initiated a policy whereby

> *his players vote to select the starting lineup before each game . . . McKinney says his players not only pick the best lineup but also perform more intensely. "When it's not just one guy deciding your fate, everything changes," says sophomore forward Doug Davinroy. "You have to prove yourself all the time." (O'Brien & Hersch, 1997, p. 24)*

A third advantage of member participation in decision making is that it contributes to the personal growth of the athlete. Fourth, group unity is positively affected. Also, as a result of the discussion that leads to the group decision, group members become better informed and more knowledgeable about what the group is trying to achieve.

One disadvantage of a participative approach is that it is more time consuming. Introducing alternatives, discussing them, and arriving at a compromise solution takes time. Competitive sport situations don't often provide enough time for full participation in decision making. Participation also has limitations if the problem is complex—if it involves a number of interrelated alternatives. An example used earlier was the selection of an Olympic basketball team. One alternative influences a number of other interrelated alternatives. The greater the number of individuals involved, the greater the number of perspectives advanced. Consequently, one highly competent individual such as a coach is as effective as a group operating democratically. And, finally, a participative approach is not very effective if the team is not cohesive. Rivalry and competition between individuals or cliques could produce solutions which are not in the best interests of the group as a whole.

SECTION 5

GROUP COHESIVENESS

At the airport, the discrepancies in their lifestyle would disappear; they became an entity. They dressed similarly, in slacks and well-tailored sports jackets, or well-cut suits . . . Even their baggage was alike . . . the sense of pack that characterized them in airplanes was not confined to the road. The team was the nucleus of their lives. The rest of the world that spun around it—trainers, coaches, agents, writers, and at the very outside, fans—was extrinsic. Even their families sometimes seemed less important to them than their playmates. After a trip of several days, during which they had traveled, eaten, dressed, drunk, played hockey, and roomed with one another, they were liable on their return to forsake their women and children and congregate in one of the . . . watering holes they favored. Friendships were between the player and the team as a whole, rather than between individuals. (Gzowski, 1981, pp. 14 -16)

Chapter Fifteen

THE NATURE OF COHESION

> The most deadly of basketball viruses, a disturbing lack
> of chemistry and complaints about playing time, threaten to
> sink this stink bomb [the 2004 U.S. men's Olympic basket-
> ball team] as one of the all-time American disgraces in
> Olympic competition. (Mariotti, 2004)

In newspaper articles and radio and television discussions, a variety of terms and expressions have been used when commentators try to convey the idea that a team is cohesive; e.g., "highly united," "very close," "stick together," "great teamwork," "like a family," "chemistry." All of these terms and expression do reflect the construct *cohesion*; the word is derived from the Latin word *cohaesus,* which means to cleave or stick together. In his comprehensive review, Kenneth Dion (2000) pointed out,

> *in physics and chemistry, cohesion refers to the force(s) binding molecules*
> *of a substance together. In psychology and the social sciences, a similar*
> *metaphor applies, with the term cohesion or cohesiveness describing the*
> *process(es) keeping a small group or larger social entity (e.g., military*
> *unit, business organization, ethnic group, or society) together and united to*
> *varying degrees. (p. 7)*

The sticking together of group members is not literal, of course, as Illustration 15.1 seems to suggest. Groups are social units composed of two or more individuals. Cohesion reflects the strength of the social and task-related bonds among the members of the group. It is so fundamental to the development and maintenance of groups that it has been suggested that "there can be no such thing as a non-cohesive group; it is a contradiction in terms. If a group exists, it is to some extent cohesive" (Donnelly, Carron, & Chelladurai, 1978, p. 7). Obviously, however, different groups can vary in their level of cohesiveness—in the strength of social or task-related bonds that are present.

In the quote that introduced this section, Peter Gzowski (1981) described the presence of a very strong bond in the Edmonton Oilers hockey team. According to Gzowski, the team was the primary focus of the players' lives. The team as a whole became the basis for friendships. Team members dressed similarly. The team looked and acted as an entity and outsiders—trainers, coaches, agents, fans, writers, and even family—were excluded.

On the other hand, in the quote that introduced this chapter, Jay Mariotti (2004) decried the lack of cohesion in the heavily favored United States men's Olympic

Illustration 15.1. Cohesion means sticking together!

basketball team. Mariotti's comments were prophetic in that the defending Olympic champion U.S. team was only able to obtain a bronze medal.

In order to make sense out of group cohesiveness and understand its impact on team effectiveness and other important team and personal factors, it is necessary first to examine its nature. This is the focus in the present chapter. In Chapter 16, the correlates of cohesiveness—the factors found to be related to presence and absence of cohesiveness—are examined.[1]

Definition of Cohesion

The study of group cohesion has had a long, rich tradition in such areas as sport psychology, social psychology, military psychology, organizational psychology, counseling psychology, and educational psychology. It is not surprising that numerous authors in these various disciplines have attempted to define cohesion in slightly different ways. These definitional differences reflect different perspectives on this complex construct and illustrate the difficulty in defining any theoretical construct—which by definition is an abstraction and, therefore, not directly observable. For example, Festinger, Schachter, and Back (1950, 1963) defined cohesion as *the total field of forces causing members to remain in the group.* They also proposed that there are two general types of forces: the attractiveness of the group (which essentially represents the social and affiliative aspects of a group) and means control (which essentially represents the task, performance, and productive concerns of the group).

The Festinger et al. viewpoint focuses on the impetus underlying participation and involvement with the group—the primary reason why individuals join a group. This is illustrated in Figure 15.1a. If a large number of forces draw individuals to a team and

---

1. Much of what is discussed in the present chapter (and Chapter 16 for that matter) has also been presented elsewhere (e.g., Carron, 1980, 1982, 1984a, 1986; Carron & Brawley, Carron, Brawley, & Widmeyer, 1998; Carron & Chelladurai, 1981; Carron, Widmeyer, & Brawley, 1985; Paskevich, Estabrooks, Brawley, & Carron, 2001; Widmeyer, Brawley, & Carron, 1985). It will be obvious to even the most disinterested reader that the majority of the above citations are multi-authored. We are deeply appreciative to these co-authors for their generosity.

each of these forces is strong—for example, the team contains good friends, good coaching, good trips, a chance to win a championship— its attractiveness is high. Consequently, the level of cohesiveness would be high.

Gross and Martin (1952) felt that it makes more sense to define cohesion as *the resistance of the group to disruptive forces*. This perspective is illustrated in Figure 15.1B. Thus, if a college rugby team is highly cohesive, it would be

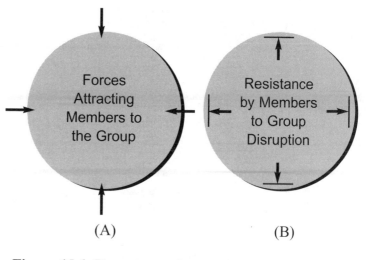

(A)   (B)

Figure 15.1. Two perspectives on group cohesiveness (Adapted from Carron, 1980)

able tolerate a great deal of negativity arising from the occurrence of unfavorable events, such as losing games, receiving criticism in the media, having a verbally abusive coach, possessing poor training facilities, and so on. The cohesiveness that binds the group into an entity also helps it resist all the pressures that can tear it apart. Also, of course, the reverse is true; if a team is not cohesive, minimally disruptive factors can cause members to begin leaving.

In order to understand cohesiveness—the factors that draw members to the group and/or help the group to resist disruptive forces—it is necessary to understand the group's goals and objectives. Every group has reasons for existing and these are interwoven into its development and maintenance. For example, social clubs, work crews, delinquent gangs, fraternity basketball teams, counseling groups, army platoons, and professional sport teams are all different. But, they are also all similar in the sense that they exhibit cohesiveness. The members of these different groups stick together because they all endorse some underlying common purposes. An outsider who is unaware of these purposes would be unable to comprehend the bases for the cohesiveness. Similarly, an insider (a group member) who either is unaware, unappreciative, or unaccepting of the bases for cohesiveness would either choose or be forced to discontinue involvement with the group.

A useful definition that has had the general acceptance of theoreticians in group dynamics (e.g., Cota, Evans, Dion, Kilik, & Longman, 1995; Mudrack, 1989) is that cohesion is "a dynamic process which is reflected in the tendency for a group to stick together and remain united in the pursuit of its instrumental objectives and/or for the satisfaction of member affective needs" (Carron, Brawley, & Widmeyer, 1998, p. 213). The value of this definition is that it serves to highlight four main characteristics of cohesion (see Box 15.1).

One characteristic of cohesion that must be kept in mind in order to fully understand the construct is that it is *multidimensional*. What this means is that there are numerous factors that cause any group to stick together and remain united and these factors can vary from group to group. For example, a synchronized swimming team may be highly united around its task objectives (e.g., achieving performance goals) and yet lack social unity (e.g., athletes don't like each other). Conversely, a second apparently similar synchronized

---

Box 15.1
The nature of group cohesion in sport teams

Aspect of Cohesion	Quotation
Cohesion is multidimensional.	As the New York Yankees wrapped up dress rehearsals and took their sideshow north for the opening of the 1988 campaign, all of your favorite characters were in midseason form . . . yes, sports fans, another season of mudslinging and enmity is here . . . [however] the Yankees —and this has been overlooked amid all the lovely verbiage—went 22-10 this spring and are confident that this is their year . . . "What irks me is we've got really good chemistry on this team," says [player Dave] Winfield. (Swift, 1988, pp. 36-38)
Cohesion is dynamic.	The chemistry of that team is something that will never go away . . . The next year wasn't the same. We were looking for a leader, and we were thinking about our individual stats and the NBA. The chemistry wasn't what it was during that championship season. (University of Lousiville basketball player, Jerry Eaves, quoted in Wolff, 1995, p.43)
Cohesion is instrumental.	We met and said we had to stop caring who scored and who got credit and who got attention . . . If not, we knew we were going to be remembered as one of the worst teams in Carolina history. You could tell that things just clicked after being put into perspective like that. (North Carolina center, Serge Zwikker, quoted in Wolff, 1997, p. 39).
Cohesion has affective aspects.	Sometimes coaches create tribulation just for cohesion's sake. An example occurred at Oklahoma last season. No one expected the Sooners to go 23-9, least of all new coach Kelvin Sampson, who noticed soon after the taking the job that his players didn't seem to like each other. So beginning right after Labor Day, he had them running at 6:30 each morning. "I wanted these kids to suffer together, to have a common bond," he says. "Three or four kids didn't make it . . . but those who did had a newfound respect for each other." (Wolff, 1995, p.39)

---

swimming team may be very cohesive socially but completely lack task unity. The first scenario is highlighted in a study by Hans Lenk (1969). Lenk's study examined the 1960 German gold medal rowing eight and the 1962 German world champion rowing eight. These teams were highly successful despite open conflict. It could be argued that the teams displayed high task cohesion yet lacked social cohesion.

A second important characteristic of cohesion is that it is *dynamic*. Cohesion in a group can change over time and the predominant factor(s) binding the group together early in its history may or may not be critical when the group is well developed. The quote in Box 15.1 serves to illustrate the changes in cohesion in a college basketball team from one season to the next.

A third characteristic of cohesion, one that was discussed above, is that it is *instrumental* in nature. That is, all groups form for a purpose. Sport groups, work groups, and military units form for task-oriented reasons. Even groups that may be considered purely 'social' in nature have an instrumental basis for their formation. Thus, for example, acquaintances that decide to form a social club to develop or maintain better friendships are cohering for instrumental reasons. As the quote in Box 15.1 illustrates, the instrumental basis for cohesion helps to account for team success.

Fourth, cohesion also has an *affective* dimension. Social relationships among group members may be present in a group initially and/or they might evolve over time. But, even in highly task-oriented groups—work crews, sport teams, military units—social cohesion generally develops as a result of member task and social interactions and communications.

The Measurement of Cohesion

Another way of understanding the nature of cohesion is to examine the approaches taken to measure it—the operational definitions used. Measurement helps to give precise meaning to theoretical constructs by showing how they are manifested in everyday situations. If cohesion is defined as the binding substance in groups, for example, this might seem reasonable. But, if cohesion is then measured by assessing the amount of time athletes spent together in the locker room after a game, this might seem unreasonable. Factors such as the availability of transportation, the length of the coach's post-game analysis, the comfort of the facility, and so on would contribute to the length of time athletes spend in the locker room. These factors are unrelated to friendships and affiliative needs (i.e., social cohesion), or to commitment to the team goals and objectives (i.e., task cohesion).

Work and Social Groups

Historically, three general approaches have been taken to the measurement of cohesiveness in social and work groups. These are summarized in Table 15.1. Possibly the most frequent approach has been to assess the degree of interpersonal attraction in the group. One implicit underlying assumption in this approach is that a major force attracting and maintaining individuals in a group is the presence of friends. A second implicit underlying assumption is that if the group contains a large number of individuals who are good friends, it will stick together and strongly resist disruption.

As Table 15.1 shows, a second approach has been to assess the level of attraction members feel for the group. For example, Bovard (1951) asked students to indicate how much they liked their class as a whole. The underlying assumption in this approach is that if a large number of group members view the group as attractive (prestigious, enjoyable, successful), there will be a strong tendency for them to stick with the group. That is, there will be a stronger force drawing members to the group and that group will be better able to resist the negative impact of disruptive events.

The measurement of cohesiveness through the use of some measure of attraction has been the subject of some criticism (Escovar & Sim, 1974). One of the reasons for this is that attraction underrepresents the concept of cohesiveness. Friendships, for example, are one type of interpersonal attraction. However, the number of friends in a work group,

Table 15.1

Approaches taken historically in the assessment of cohesion in social and work groups

General Category	Examples	References
Interpersonal Attraction	The presence of friends in the group	Dimock (1941)
	The number of reciprocal sociometric choices	Deep, Bass & Vaughn (1967)
Individual Attractions to the Group	Attractions to the group as a whole	Bovard (1951)
	Sense of belonging to the group	Indik (1965)
	Value of having membership in the group	Schachter (1951)
Commitment to the Group	Desire to maintain the group.	Schachter (1951)
	Resistance to moving to other groups	Seashore (1954)
	Ratio of within to outgroup choices	Dimock (1941)

social group, or sport team is never the sole basis (or even the most important basis) for individuals sticking together and remaining united in the pursuit of the group's goals and objectives. A second, related criticism is that measures of attraction don't explain why groups stick together when there is extreme conflict, tension, or disagreements. In the Lenk (1969) study of the German gold medal rowing team, discussed above, the team stuck together despite high conflict and a lack of friendship. If cohesion equals friendship, how can we account for the rowing team's resistance to disruption?

A third criticism is that attraction—either interpersonal attraction or attraction to the group as a whole—is not necessary for group formation and development. Ten strangers could sign up for intramural volleyball, be assigned to the same team, and attend practices and games regularly. The team might lose every game. Friendships might not develop. Also, the team might not be distinguishable from any other team in terms of value of membership and prestige. Yet, those ten people might continue to stick together. Measures of attraction would have a difficult time accounting for this behavior.

A fourth criticism is statistical in nature. The correlations between various measures of attraction are quite low. Research supports the view that cohesion is multidimensional and attraction is only one of the forces binding members to the group (e.g., Rumuz-Nienhuis & Van Bergen, 1960).

As Table 15.1 shows, the third approach to the measurement of cohesiveness involves the assessment of the group members' commitment to the group. Thus, for example, in research in a factory situation, Schachter (1951) asked workers if they would like the chance to persuade other workers to stay if it appeared that sufficient members might leave and the group might disband. If low cohesion was present, very few members would express an interest in persuading others to stay in the group. Conversely, if a high cohesion were present, a large number of members would be interested in keeping the group together.

Sport Teams

Table 15.2 provides an overview of the various studies in which an attempt has been made to measure interpersonal relations and/or cohesion in sport teams. Historically, scholars at the University of Illinois—Fred Fiedler, Albert Myers, Joseph McGrath, Rainer Martens, Dan Landers, John Loy, and Neil Widmeyer—have played a dominant role. Fiedler (1954), working with high school basketball teams, assessed interpersonal relationships within the team through measures of assumed similarity. That is, each athlete initially indicated which statement in a block of statements was most and least characteristic of himself. Then, the process was repeated with the athlete describing the characteristics most and least characteristic of the person with whom he cooperated best and the person with whom he cooperated most poorly.

Both McGrath and Myers carried out research in 1962 with recreational rifle teams at the University of Illinois. Myers assessed relationships within the teams by having team members indicate their esteem for teammates, their perception of their acceptance by

Table 15.2

Approaches taken historically in the assessment of cohesion sport teams

Measure	Reference
Assumed similarity—a measure of liking and personal warmth	Fiedler (1954)
Esteem for teammates Perceived acceptance by teammates Attribution of responsibility	Myers (1962)
Positive interpersonal relations—subjects rated teammates	McGrath (1962)
Perceived group task integration on each play of a football game	Stogdill (1964)
Sociometric social and leadership choices. Participant observation of social relationships	Lenk (1969)
Attraction to the group.	Klein & Christiansen (1969)
Friendship Value of membership Enjoyment Influence/power Sense of belonging Closeness Teamwork	Martens, Landers, & Loy (1972)
Team performance satisfaction Self performance satisfaction Value of membership Task cohesion Desire for recognition Affiliation	Gruber & Gray (1981, 1982)

teammates, and the degree to which they attributed failures to themselves, their teammates, or the other team.

In McGrath's (1962) study, he used one sociometric question and four behavioral items to assess interpersonal relationships. For the sociometric question, the individual indicated whether any of his teammates had helped him stay calm and relaxed. For the four behavioral items, the individual rated the degree to which each teammate was warm, standoffish, disruptive, and attentive.

One of the most novel approaches to the study of group dynamics in sport teams was taken by Stogdill (1964). During the six home games of the Ohio State football team, he had four judges sitting at different places in the stadium rate how integrated the team was on each play.

In the Lenk (1969) study that was discussed earlier in this chapter, group unity was assessed through sociometric social and leadership choices and by participant observation of social relationships.

Klein and Christiansen (1969) carried out their research with members of 3-on-3 basketball teams. To measure interpersonal relationships within each team, they had individuals rate the attractiveness of their unit prior to competition.

From a historical perspective, the cohesion inventory that has had the most significant effect on research in sport psychology has been the Martens, Landers, and Loy (1972) Sport Cohesiveness Questionnaire (SCQ). It was the first inventory to have a specific sport orientation and, possibly because of this, it stimulated considerable research on issues associated with cohesion in sport teams. The SCQ contains seven items that yield ratings of friendship (interpersonal attraction), personal power or influence, enjoyment, closeness, teamwork, sense of belonging, and perceived value of membership. These seven items have been used independently by researchers (Arnold & Straub, 1972) as well as in combination (Carron & Chelladurai, 1981). For example, the friendship and power items represent a category that can be referred to as *individual-to-individual* attraction—each team member's perceptions of his/her relationship with every other group member. The assumption is that if there are good individual-to-individual relationships among a large number of team members, high cohesiveness is present.

The questions that evaluate value of membership, sense of belonging, and enjoyment represent a category that can be referred to as *individual-to-group* relationships. With these questions, the individual evaluates his/her personal relationship and involvement with the group as a totality. It is assumed that if a large number of group members possess a strong sense of belonging to the group, value their membership in the group, and enjoy their involvement, the level of group cohesion is high.

The last category contains two questions relating to teamwork and closeness, and involving an assessment of the *group as a whole*. Each individual team member is required to step back and answer, *What are we like as a team in terms of teamwork and in terms of closeness?* If the overall ratings are high, the team is considered to be cohesive.

Another measure of cohesion, developed by Gruber and Gray (1981, 1982), consisted of 13 items used frequently in research on cohesion. When the athletes' responses were analyzed, it was found that these 13 items formed into six categories (or factors) representing different manifestations of cohesiveness. These six were called *team performance satisfaction, self-performance satisfaction, task cohesion, affiliation cohesion, desire for recognition*, and *value of membership*.

The Multidimensional Sport Cohesion Instrument (MSCI), the inventory developed by David Yukelson and his colleagues (Yukelson, Weinberg, & Jackson, 1984), evolved from the belief that cohesion in sport teams reflects "factors associated with the goals and objectives the group is striving to achieve, as well as factors associated with the development and maintenance of positive interpersonal relationships" (Yukelson et al., p. 106). Initially, 41 questions pertaining to cohesion were generated from other cohesion instruments, from definitions proposed by theoreticians, from pertinent research in industrial and organizational psychology, and by interviewing coaches and social scientists. This original questionnaire was then administered to 16 male and female basketball teams and the results were statistically analyzed. Twenty-two items measuring four categories (factors) of cohesion were identified.

One of the factors, *quality of teamwork*, is a measure of how well teammates work together to achieve group success. The second factor, *attraction to the group*, represents the degree to which individuals are attracted to and satisfied with group membership. The third factor, *unity of purpose*, is composed of items that assess commitment to the group's norms, rules, and goals. The last factor, *valued roles*, is a measure of the degree to which there is identification with group membership.

Both the Gruber and Gray (1981) and the Yukelson et al. cohesion inventories were a valuable contribution to the measurement of team cohesion because they were the first sport-related questionnaires to explicitly acknowledge that cohesion is multidimensional, containing both task and social bases.

The Group Environment Questionnaire (GEQ)

The Group Environment Questionnaire (GEQ, Carron, Widmeyer, & Brawley, 1985; Widmeyer, Brawley, & Carron, 1985) was developed on the basis of a conceptual model that emanated from social cognitive theories of human behavior, group dynamics theories pertaining to levels of analysis in groups, and the group dynamics perspective that groups serve both a task function and a social function.

A social cognitive basis for cohesion. Social cognitive theories are based on the premise that humans are rationale beings who consistently evaluate, form judgments about, organize, and interact in and with their environment (cf. Bandura, 1986; Kenny & Lavoie, 1985; Levine & Moreland, 1991; Schlenker, 1975). Using a social cognitive perspective, Carron, Brawley, and Widmeyer (1998) advanced five assumptions associated with the belief that cohesion can be assessed through perceptions of individual group members. The first is that a group has clearly observable properties. In the quote used to introduce this section, Peter Gzowski (1981) commented that the Edmonton Oilers "dressed similarly, in slacks and well-tailored sports jackets, or well-cut suits . . . Even their baggage was alike . . . the sense of pack that characterized them in airplanes was not confined to the road" (p. 14). Group properties may be readily apparent to an outsider observing the group but they are superficial relative to the group properties familiar to group members. For example, if members of the Oilers were asked, they would undoubtedly respond, "We may look alike but that's not what makes us a team." Members of any group are aware of the fact that there are differences among them in status, leadership, and role responsibilities and that general expectations exist for their behavior in the group. Also, group members are aware of the fact that their interactions and communications are different from those experienced in other groups.

The second, third, and fourth assumptions which follow directly from the first are that a) group members experience the social situation of their group, are socialized into it, and develop a set of beliefs about the group, b) these beliefs are a product of the member's selective processing and integration of information about the group, and c) the perceptions about the group held by a member reflect the unity characteristic of the group. We constantly come to conclusions about the groups in which we are members—about their effectiveness or ineffectiveness, about good and bad aspects of team membership.

The commentary in Box 15.1 by Jerry Eaves of the University of Louisville basketball team provides a good example of the three assumptions in operation. To use the language introduced above, Eaves and members of the University of Louisville basketball team were socialized into a common social situation (i.e., the team) and developed a belief about it (i.e., the presence of high chemistry). This belief that high chemistry was present undoubtedly evolved as a result of observations (i.e., selective processing and integration of information) of team member actions. As a result, Louisville team members held the belief that the team was highly unified.

A final assumption advanced by Carron, Brawley, and Widmeyer was that the social cognitions that members have about their group and its cohesiveness can be measured through a paper and pencil questionnaire.

It may seem at first glance that this belief and these assumptions are relatively straightforward and not too difficult to accept. However, the theoretical perspective advanced by Carron and his colleagues could be at odds with other theoretical perspectives advanced to understand human behavior. For example, a theoretician adopting an extreme behaviorist approach might argue that only behavior can be measured, that cognitions are not reliable or valid indices for behavior. Thus, a behaviorist interested in studying cohesion might record the amount of time group members converse, or the degree of cooperation they exhibit.

As a second example, there are theoreticians in group dynamics who would argue that if the focus is on a group construct, then the group and not individual members should be assessed. How could you assess a team to determine its cohesiveness? The approach taken by Stogdill that was discussed above would be one example (i.e., observers recorded the degree to which the Ohio State football team was integrated on each play). The team has a common goal or experiences a common fate and a single measure is used to represent that goal or fate. Cohesion, determined by summating the responses of individual group members, does not satisfy this requirement (see Chapter 1 again for the discussion on the reality of groups).

The individual and group bases for cohesion. In Chapter 1, the importance of distinguishing between the individual and the group was discussed. This has been a frequent theme in research in group dynamics. For example, Cattell (1948, 1953) pointed out that a group could be described at three different levels. At the first level, which Cattell referred to as the *population level*, the focus is on the individual group members—their personalities, aspirations, motives, attributes, and so on. The research that was discussed in Chapter 6 is an example of this approach. What is the personality of team versus individual sport athletes? What are the predominant motives (orientations) of athletes on intramural basketball teams? In order to answer these questions, it is necessary to evaluate the characteristics of individual team members.

At the second or *structural level*, the focus is on the member-to-member interactions. The research that was discussed in Chapter 8 illustrates this orientation. What are the factors contributing to coach-athlete compatibility? This question is answered by examining the specific interactions and relationship between the coach and the athlete.

With the third level, referred to by Cattell as *syntality*, the focus is on the group as a whole. What was the final ranking of nations in the 2004 Union of European Football Associations (UEFA) football championship? That question can only be answered at the group level.

Not surprisingly, the need to distinguish between the individual and the group has also been emphasized by a number of authors in the area of group cohesion. Table 15.3 provides an overview. The distinction made by Van Bergen and Koekebakker (1959) between individual attractions to the group (ATG) and cohesion is typical. Cohesion was the label used for the group property that Cattell referred to as the syntality level. ATG was the label used for the individual property that Cattell described as the population level.

The task and social aspects of cohesion. It was pointed out above that the specific objectives of social groups, delinquent gangs, fraternity basketball teams, army platoons, and so on can vary. Also, there are also differences in the specific goals and objectives of groups within the same category. For example, not every fraternity basketball team has the same reason(s) for forming and staying together. In one case, the opportunity to meet weekly and socialize may be predominant; in another, winning the university intramural championship may be most important.

Despite this diversity, it has usually been assumed that the goals and objectives that dominate the activities of all groups can be classified into two categories. The first is represented by the activities associated with the development and maintenance of social relationships; the second, by activities associated with task accomplishment, productivity, and performance (Fiedler, 1967; Hersey & Blanchard, 1977). Historically, cohesion has also been considered to be composed of these two elements—although the specific terminology used has varied from one author to another (see Table 15.4).

Table 15.3

The labels used to describe individual and group levels of cohesion

Individual Level Terminology	Group Level Terminology	Reference
Individual Attraction to the Group	Cohesion	Van Bergen & Koekebakker (1959)
Individual Attraction to the Group	Cohesion	Evans & Jarvis (1980)
Individual to Group Cohesion	Group as a Unit Cohesion	Carron & Chelladurai (1981)
Attraction to the Group	Quality of Teamwork	Yukelson, Weinberg, & Jackson (1984)
Valued Roles	Unity of Purpose	
Individual Attractions to the Group	Group Integration	Carron, Widmeyer, & Brawley (1985)

Table 15.4
***The Labels Used to Describe the Task and Social Aspects of Cohesion
(Adapted from Iso-Ahola & Hatfield, 1986)***

Social Cohesion Terminology	Task Cohesion Terminology	Reference
Attractions to the Group	Means control	Festinger, Schachter, & Back (1963)
Intrinsic Attraction	Instrumental Attraction	Enoch & McLemore (1967)
Social Cohesion	Task Cohesion	Mikalachki (1969) Gill (1977) Nixon (1977) Widmeyer & Martens (1978) Carron, Widmeyer, & Brawley (1985)
Attraction to the Group	Quality of Teamwork Unity of Purpose Valued Roles	Yukelson, Weinberg, & Jackson (1984)

For example, it was pointed out above that Festinger and his colleagues assumed that two major fields of forces cause members to remain in the group: attraction-to-the-group and means control. The former represents the social basis for remaining in the group; the latter represents the task basis. Also, Enoch and McLemore (1967) viewed cohesiveness as attraction to the group, which in turn, was assumed to be composed of an intrinsic (social) dimension and an instrumental (task) dimension. And, finally, Mikalachki (1969) advocated that cohesion be subdivided into two components—social cohesion and task cohesion.

A conceptual model for cohesion in sport teams. On the basis of the views of the group and of cohesiveness—the distinctions made between task and social dimensions and individual and group orientations—Carron, Widmeyer, and Brawley (1985) proposed a conceptual model for cohesion in sport teams. It is illustrated in Figure 15.2.

In the model, cohesion in sport teams is considered to be composed of group integration-task and social and individual attractions to the group-task and social. The *group integration* scales assess a member's perceptions of the group as a totality. Thus, the focus is on issues such as, how close are we as a group? Do we stick together socially? Are

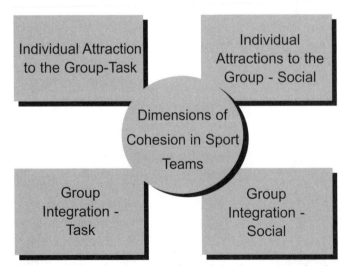

***Figure 15.2. A conceptual model of group cohesion
(Adapted from Carron, Widmeyer, & Brawley, 1985)***

Table 15.5

A sample of statements from the Group Environment Questionnaire used to assess perceptions of cohesion in sport teams (Adapted from Widmeyer, Brawley, & Carron, 1985)

Cohesion Scale	Example Statement
Interpersonal Attractions to the Group-Task	I do not like the style of play on this team.
Interpersonal Attractions to the Group-Social	Some of my best friends are on this team.
Group Integration-Task	Our team is united in trying to reach its goals for performance.
Group Integration-Social	Members of our team would rather go out on their own than get together as a team.

we unified in what we are trying to achieve? Are we united in how we are trying to achieve it?

The *individual attractions to the group* scales assess a member's personal attractions to the group. Thus, the focus is on issues such as: Am I happy with the challenges this group provides? Is the group attractive to me personally? How well do I fit in with the group? Does the group use performance strategies that I like? Both the group integration perceptions and the individual attractions to the group perceptions help bind members to the group.

As Figure 15.2 illustrates, the member's perceptions of the group as a unit as well as their perceptions of the attractiveness of the group personally are centered on two concerns. One of these is the group's task. On sport teams, members are concerned with personal performance issues and team performance issues. Concerns about the task help to bind the team together into a cohesive unit. A second element is the social aspects of the group. On sport teams, members are concerned with personal relationships as well as the togetherness, closeness, and affiliation within the team as a unit. Although other aspects of cohesiveness have been discussed in the literature, Carron, Widmeyer, and Brawley assume that the four manifestations presented in Figure 15.2 account for most of the reasons for cohesion in sport groups.

Some sample items for each of the four scales illustrated in Figure 15.2 are presented in Table 15.5. Some of these items are positively worded. Consequently, if a member felt that the team was highly cohesive, he/she would strongly endorse the statement. Also, some of the items are negatively worded. In the case of these items, if a member felt that the team was highly cohesive, he/she would strongly reject the statement.

Chapter Sixteen

CORRELATES OF COHESION IN SPORT TEAMS

> The secret of football, and of team performance, is harmony. True harmony is equivalent to perfection, to beauty. Think of the movement of a champion gymnast, or the perfect synchrony of a whole symphony orchestra playing together. Harmony can be everywhere: in music, in the mind and the body, in a football team's will to succeed; and it's the perfect understanding, this combining of forces that makes winning possible. Harmony in a team means everybody playing together and thinking as one. In the end it's all about getting the ball in the back of the net, about having the perfect touch when you have possession. This can only come from the combined efforts of all players. (Cantona & Fynn, 1996, p. 33)

One of the founders of the science of social psychology, Kurt Lewin (1935), suggested that there are two fundamental processes characteristic of all groups: maintenance and locomotion. Maintenance is represented by activity designed to keep the group intact, to help it maintain its unity, integrity, and stability. In short, cohesion is a desirable state, prized by all groups from marriages to work groups to sport teams. In the quote used to introduce this chapter, Eric Cantona of the Manchester United soccer team (i.e., the term *soccer* is used in North America to describe the game that the rest of the world refers to as *football*), highlighted the prevalent belief about cohesiveness when he stated, "True harmony is equivalent to perfection, to beauty" (Cantona & Fynn, 1996, p. 33).

Locomotion, the second fundamental process is represented by activity designed to facilitate the promotion or achievement of the group's goals and objectives. Later in this chapter, evidence that shows that cohesiveness is positively related to group locomotion is discussed. In the above quote by Cantona, the relationship of cohesion to locomotion is also highlighted when he pointed out that, "Harmony in a team means everybody playing together and thinking as one" (Cantona & Fynn, 1996, p. 33).

Thus, cohesion is a factor that directly contributes to group maintenance and facilitates group locomotion. It plays such an important role in the dynamics of all groups that some social scientists have called cohesion the most important small group variable

(Golembiewski, 1962; Lott & Lott, 1965). Because cohesion is so important, gaining an understanding of the variables associated with it has been an important research objective for social scientists in sport psychology, social psychology, industrial psychology, military psychology, and sociology. In this chapter, selected research from the area of sport psychology is examined. In order to organize that research into a more coherent package, the framework illustrated in Figure 16.1 is used.[1]

Figure 16.1 is based on the understanding that a large number of factors are positively related to group cohesion. Some of these factors are present in the *situation*, others are in the attitudes and characteristics the *individual* brings to the group, others are associated with aspects of *leadership*, and still others build within the *team as a unit*. The relationships between cohesion and the situational, individual, leadership, and team variables discussed in this chapter are most likely circular in nature. For example, cohesion influences performance success and

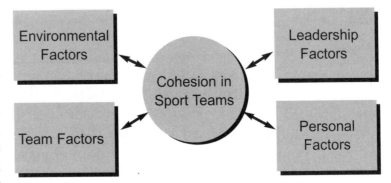

Figure 16.1. A general framework for examining the correlates of cohesion in sport and exercise groups

performance success influences cohesion. As another example, cohesion influences role acceptance and role acceptance influences cohesion. Consequently, while it is often convenient to discuss the relationship between cohesion and other variables in a causal fashion (e.g., cohesion contributes to role acceptance), it is important to bear in mind the dynamic, circular nature of group dynamics.

It should also be pointed out that the four categories illustrated in Figure 16.1 should not be viewed as independent or unrelated. For example, leadership behavior and individual satisfaction are both associated with the development of group cohesion. They also have an influence on each other. So, while situational, personal, leadership, and team factors are presented separately in the present chapter, in real groups they are interwoven.

A final point that must be made is that in some cases the decision to assign studies to categories is difficult. In the final analysis, we placed them where they seemed to fit best. Thus, for example, role involvement research is discussed in the section on "team factors." It must be kept in mind, however, that individuals, not teams, understand, accept, and/or carry out roles. Consequently, the relationship of cohesion to role involvement also could have been introduced in the "personal factors" section.

---

1. This conceptual framework is a modification of one proposed by Carron (1982). The 1982 Carron framework was presented in the form of a linear model that contained *inputs* (situational factors, leadership factors, individual factors, and team factors), *throughputs* (task and social cohesion), and *outputs* (individual and team outcomes). The fundamental purpose of that framework was to organize (and communicate to the reader) information about cohesion. It was never intended to be a definitive view of the elements that cause cohesion and/or result from cohesion—although it was interpreted that way by a number of authors because it satisfied a need to test a theoretical model. The principle function of Figure 1 is to provide a framework to communicate information on factors that have been found to correlate with group cohesion.

Situational Factors and Cohesion

Cultural and Organizational Considerations

In the previous chapter, a distinction was made between task and social cohesion, each of which is of two types: individual attractions to the group and group integration. Carron and his colleagues (1985) assumed that the resulting four manifestations illustrated in Figure 15.2 provide most of the differences in cohesiveness among sport teams. However, they did acknowledge that other conditions in the situation also help to keep a group together.

One of these situational conditions that leads to togetherness is *contractual responsibilities*. Eligibility and/or transfer rules, geographical restrictions, and the contractual obligations that exist in professional and amateur sport can constrain the movement of athletes from one team to another. Contractual responsibilities are one major difference between a social group and a sport team. Members generally can leave social groups if they wish; they cannot do so in most sport situations if they want to continue participating.

The discussion between Pat Riley and Patrick Ewing when Riley took over as coach of the New York Knicks illustrates a slightly different perspective of the relationship between cohesion and contractual commitments (see Box 16.1). A contract not only makes it impossible for an athlete to leave a team; it also makes it difficult for the team to get rid of an athlete.

There are also *normative pressures* associated with cohesiveness. These are a product of our society's low regard for "quitters." Quitters are considered irresponsible and undependable. Consequently, once an individual joins a group, there are pressures on him/her to continue to maintain involvement.

A third situational factor that could contribute to the development of cohesiveness is the organization's *orientation.* In our own research with exercise groups, for example, we have found that perceptions of greater social cohesion are a significant discriminator between individuals who regularly attend versus those who drop out of programs organized in private fitness clubs (Spink & Carron, Study 2, 1994). On the other hand, in university settings, regular attendees hold higher perceptions of task cohesion than dropouts (Spink & Carron, Study 1, 1994).

The *level of competition* also seems to play a role in the development of group cohesion (Granito & Rainey, 1988; Gruber & Gray, 1982). When Granito and Rainey (1988)

Box 16.1 *Situational factors and team cohesion*	
Focus	**Quotation**
Contractual obligations and cohesion	I pledged that . . . we were committed to bringing in players who wanted to win . . . "If there's a player on this team who thinks his big-money contract guarantees him a position, and if that player doesn't produce, he's making the biggest mistake of his life." Patrick [Ewing] was hearing news. Big-contract players rarely get traded. (Riley, 1993, p. 238)

assessed the cohesion of high school and college football teams, they found that task cohesion was greater in the high school teams. Also, Gruber and Gray found social cohesion was higher in elementary school and junior high school basketball teams than in senior high school teams. Why this might be the case, however, is the critical question. Possibly, consensus and task social unity are achieved more easily with less experienced athletes.

Geographical Considerations

Geographical factors such as *physical and functional proximity* also contribute to group cohesiveness. When team members are in close proximity to one another in playing position or locker location, for example, they become closer. Consequently, when groups of individuals are brought into closer proximity, cohesiveness increases. This is probably a result of the increased opportunities to interact and communicate about task and social issues (see Illustration 16.1).

The classic study often used to illustrate the relationship between cohesion and proximity was carried out by Festinger, Schachter, and Back (1950, 1963). In the late 1940s, they studied the social patterns of married students attending the Massachusetts Institute of Technology and living in the housing developments of Westgate and Westgate West. The measure of cohesiveness used was the question, "What three people in Westgate or Westgate West do you see most often socially?" (Festinger et al. 1950, 1963, p. 37). By considering the courts and buildings within the community as individual groups, Festinger and his colleagues were able to compare the proportion of in-group to out-group choices. Physical proximity was found to be the major contributor to the development of friendships within the communities.

A group's permeability—the degree to which it is open to non-group members or other groups—has an influence on cohesiveness. Groups that are less permeable, possibly because they are socially or physically isolated from other groups, draw upon their own membership

Illustration 16.1. "Coach . . . are you sure being in close proximity will make us more cohesive?"

to fulfill important psychological needs. Communication and interaction occur predominantly or exclusively within the group. Also, the group becomes more cohesive.

There is also an association between group *size* and cohesion. As a general rule, cohesion decreases as group size increases. Neil Widmeyer and his colleagues carried out two studies that generally demonstrated this (the Widmeyer et al., 1990 research was discussed in detail in Chapter 3). In the first study, in a 3-on-3 recreational basketball league teams were formed consisting of 3, 6, or 9 members. The results showed that task cohesion decreased as roster size increased (although social cohesion was highest in the 6-person groups).

For their second study, Widmeyer and his colleagues examined the relationship between the size of the group competing at any given time in a recreational volleyball game and group cohesion. Teams competed in 3 versus 3, 6 versus 6, and 12 versus 12 competitions. The level of group cohesion was greatest in the 3-person teams; with increasing team size, there was a progressive decrease in cohesiveness.

Personal Factors and Cohesion

Demographic Attributes

As Figure 16.1 illustrates, a second category of factors associated with the development of group cohesion is the characteristics of the group members. When there is *similarity in demographic attributes* of individual members—attributes such as social background, race, and sex of the group members—cohesion is enhanced. In a discussion relating to this point, Stanley Eitzen (1975) noted,

> *the more alike the members of a group, the more positive the bond . . . This is usually explained by the assumption that internal differentiation on some salient characteristic such as religion, race, and socioeconomic status leads to greater likelihood of clique formation. (p. 41)*

Box 16.2 contains an example of the difficulties faced by Jackie Robinson when he broke the color barrier in major league baseball. Robinson's experiences notwithstanding, it is difficult to determine from available research whether similarity in personal attributes is important for team cohesiveness. Widmeyer, Silva, and Hardy (1992) identified 32 potential antecedents of cohesion and then had American and Canadian athletes rate how important each of those antecedents is for both task and social cohesion. Among the lowest ranking (i.e., rated as least important) was similarity in social background and racial similarity. What isn't known from the research of Widmeyer and his colleagues, of course, is whether the behaviors of athletes are consistent with their cognitions.

Thus, for example, evaluating race as irrelevant for group cohesiveness is not equivalent to behaving as if race was irrelevant.

The *sex* of group members is another personal attribute considered to be associated with cohesiveness. Reis and Jelsma, 1978 suggested that the basic orientation of males and females toward competitive sport is different. Males most strongly endorse competition, winning, and beating one's opponent whereas females most strongly endorse participating in the game, interacting with teammates and opponents, and socializing. Thus, males are expected to be higher in task cohesiveness, females in social cohesiveness.

However, research has not borne this perspective out. Widmeyer and Martens (1978) failed to find any sex differences in cohesiveness, Widmeyer and his colleagues (1985) found that female team-sport athletes were higher in task cohesiveness than male team-sport athletes, and Thompson and Albinson (1991) found that male members of rowing crews were higher in task cohesiveness than female members of rowing crews. The pattern of findings is sufficiently equivocal to conclude that there are no systematic differences in cohesion associated with the gender of the athletes.

Cognitions

Shared perceptions. Another general factor traditionally considered to be associated with greater cohesiveness is *shared perceptions,* including similarity in attitudes, beliefs, and motives. The relationship of similarity in perceptions to cohesion was emphasized by Alvin Zander (1982), who observed that "birds of feather flock together, and create a more distinct entity when they do . . . Persons whose beliefs do not fit together well have a hard time forming a strong group" (p. 3).

In social and work groups at least, attitude similarity also seems to operate in a reciprocal fashion with group cohesiveness. That is, an initial similarity in attitude increases the likelihood that individuals will come together and develop group cohesiveness. And, over time, the group's work, experiences together, and cohesiveness increase the degree to which individual members adopt similar attitudes (Terborg, Castore, & DeNinno, 1976).

Self-deception. The perception of the group also becomes distorted when cohesiveness is high; there is a tendency toward *self-deception.* Other group members, and the group's accomplishments, behaviors, and performances are overvalued while those of opponents are undervalued or underestimated.

Attributions for responsibility. When individuals are members of a group they perceive to be highly cohesive, there is a greater likelihood that they will assume more *responsibility for negative outcomes* (Bird, Foster, & Maruyama, 1980; Brawley, Carron, & Widmeyer,

Box 16.2 *Personal factors and team cohesion*	
Focus	**Quotation**
Similarity and cohesion	Those early days were awfully tough on Jackie. I remember times on the train when nobody would sit with him or talk with him. Pee Wee [Reese] always seemed to be the first to break the tension. He kidded Jackie before anyone else did and made him a part of the team. He was probably the first Dodger to have a meal with him off the field. Pee Wee was a real leader on our club, and when he started being friendly with Jackie, everybody started being friendly. In the beginning Jackie was alone at the dining table. By the middle of the year you couldn't get a seat at the dining table with him; there were so many guys. (Bobby Bragan, quoted in Allen, 1987, pp. 102-103)

1987; Schlenker & Miller, 1977b). For example, Brawley and his colleagues (1987, Study 3) had athletes from a wide cross-section of sports use their teammates as a benchmark to estimate degree of personal responsibility for the team's win or loss. Athletes rating their team high in task cohesiveness assumed a level of personal responsibility that was equal to that of the average team member, regardless of outcome (i.e., winning or losing). However, those athletes rating their team low in task cohesion showed a self-protective and self-serving pattern of attribution by accepting less responsibility for the loss than the average team member. Brawley et al. suggested that while "failure may be as damaging to personal self-esteem for players perceiving high task cohesion as it is for those perceiving low task cohesion, it may be easier for the former athletes to bear when they see their teammates sharing equally in the responsibility" (p. 291).

Self-handicapping. Perceptions of the team's cohesiveness are also related to *self-handicapping* (Carron, Prapavessis, & Grove, 1994; Hausenblas & Carron, 1996). The term self-handicapping was introduced by Jones and Berglas (1978, Berglas & Jones, 1978) to represent the strategies that individuals use prior to an important achievement situation in order to protect their self-esteem. As Berglas and Jones pointed out, self-handicapping "enhances the opportunity to externalize (or excuse) failure and to internalize (reasonably accept credit for) success" (p. 406). Thus, for example, an athlete who doesn't practice prior to a championship because of a real or imagined injury can use that injury and lack of practice as reasons for a loss. Also, the athlete's self-esteem is protected because the loss occurred as a result of events outside of personal control. Conversely, if the athlete is successful, his/her self-esteem is enhanced because the victory was obtained despite the presence of an injury and lack of practice.

When we undertook our research on self-handicapping with male (Carron, Prapavessis, & Grove, 1994) and female athletes (Hausenblas & Carron, 1996), we were uncertain about how cohesion would be related to self-handicapping. Two diametrically opposite scenarios seemed possible. On the one hand, it seemed reasonable to expect that the need to use self-handicapping strategies would be reduced in cohesive groups. In cohesive groups, responsibility for failures is shared equally, and the individual has a better relationship with and greater support from teammates. Thus, the cohesive group represents an environment in which the individual is buffered from threats to self-esteem and, consequently, the need to use self-handicapping strategies should be reduced.

On the other hand, it also seemed reasonable to predict that the need to use self-handicapping strategies would be increased in cohesive groups. In cohesive groups, members have less tendency to take advantage of others, feel greater responsibility for the group and its members, have a tendency to make more sacrifices for the group, and feel a greater responsibility to conform to group expectations. Thus, the cohesive group also represents an environment in which the individual experiences greater pressure to carry out group responsibilities and satisfy the expectations of highly valued teammates. Failure to do so would be threatening to self-esteem. As a result, the need to establish reasons for potential failure could be increased.

In both the Carron et al. (1994) study with male athletes and Hausenblas and Carron (1996) study with female and male athletes, support was obtained for the latter possibility. That is, those athletes who had a high tendency to use self-handicaps rated the severity of the self-handicaps they had experienced in the week prior to an important competition as high when then they perceived that the task cohesion of their team was high. Conversely, when the team was perceived to be low in task cohesion, self-handicapping also was low.

Affect

As Roy Baumeister and Mark Leary (1995) noted, feelings of belongingness influence our affect and emotions. If the bonds in our relationships are strong, we feel more content, more satisfied, and less anxious. Conversely, if the bonds are weak or severed, the result is "potent negative feelings" (Baumeister & Leary, 1995, p. 508). What about relationships in sport teams? Is higher cohesion associated with improved mood states? A number of studies have been directed toward this issue.

State anxiety. One affective measure examined has been *anxiety.* As Bauemister and Leary suggested, it is "the extreme or prototype of negative affect . . . clearly linked to damaged, lost, or threatened social bonds" (p. 506). Cogan and Petrie (1995) found that an intervention program led to enhanced social cohesion and reduced somatic and cognitive anxiety in intercollegiate gymnasts. Also, Prapavessis and Carron (1996) reported that athletes from a variety of team sports possessing higher perceptions of the team's task cohesion also reported lower levels of cognitive anxiety.

A slightly different approach was taken by Mark Eys and his colleagues (Eys, Hardy, Carron, & Beauchamp, 2003). Athletes from a variety of sports not only rated their state anxiety prior to competition, they also indicated the degree to which that anxiety was either facilitative or debilitative. It is possible, for example, for an athlete to be quite nervous prior to competition but to consider that as positive (i.e., facilitative: "I'm ready") or negative (debilitative: "I'm too nervous to play well"). Eys and his colleagues found that athletes higher in task cohesion perceived their cognitive and somatic state anxiety symptoms as more facilitative.

Individual satisfaction. Another affective measure that has received some attention is satisfaction (Martens & Peterson, 1971; Widmeyer & Williams, 1991). Rainer Martens and James Peterson (1971) proposed that cohesion, satisfaction, and performance are related to each other in a circular fashion. That is, the presence of cohesiveness contributes to team performance and, ultimately, to team success. In turn, success produces higher satisfaction in the individual athlete and this leads to the development of a greater sense of cohesiveness. When Jean Williams and Colleen Hacker (1982) tested the cause-effect relationships among performance, cohesion, and satisfaction in women's intercollegiate field hockey teams, they found support for the Martens and Peterson proposal.

In coacting sports such as golf, satisfaction may be one of the most important positive correlates of team cohesion. The relative importance to cohesion of team size, athlete satisfaction from team membership, athlete similarity, the coach's efforts to foster cohesion, prior team success, the presence and importance of team goals, participation in team goal setting, communication, and prior liking were assessed by Widmeyer & Williams (1991). They found that the best single predictor of both task and social cohesion in female golfers from Division I intercollegiate teams was satisfaction.

Depression. Baumeister and Leary pointed out that, "Depression may be precipitated by a variety of events, but failing to feel accepted or included is certainly one of them . . . both general depression and social depression . . . are inversely related to the degree to which one feels included and accepted by others (1995, p. 506). However, a study by Henderson, Bourgeois, LeUnes, and Meyers (1998) found that athletes perceiving higher and lower task cohesion had lower depression scores than athletes in the intermediate range in perceptions of team cohesion.

Conversely, Peter Terry and his colleagues (Terry, Carron, Pink, Lane, Jones, & Hall, 2000), in a comprehensive study of cohesion and mood in 415 athletes from the sports of rowing, netball and rugby, did obtain results consistent with the proposition advanced by Baumeister and Leary. On the basis of their results, Terry et al. concluded that different manifestations of cohesiveness are associated with different manifestations of mood, and a remarkable consistency was present across the three samples. In the rowers, and netball and rugby players, the group integration-task measure of cohesion was inversely related to feelings of depression.

Behavior

Sacrifice behavior. The perception that individual group members have of the group changes when they make investments in that group. Alvin Zander (1982) emphasized this point, writing, "A participant who is asked to give up something of value for her group becomes, because of this sacrifice, more attracted to that body" (p. 7). Just as importantly, perhaps, an individual's sacrifice also changes the way other group members perceive the group. Elder and Clipp (1988) studied World War II veteran's groups 40 years after the war. Although a sense of unity was still present in all units, that sense of unity was greatest in units that had experienced deaths in combat, moderate in units that had been in combat but had not suffered any fatalities, and least in units that had not been in combat.

The role that sacrifice plays in promoting both cohesion and conformity to group norms in sport teams was examined by Prapavessis and Carron (1997) with state-level cricket teams. The many ways that sacrifices in a team sport can be manifested were assessed—sacrifices by the self or by teammates, in either the immediate situation (e.g., practices and competitions) or in a situation removed from other team members (e.g., sacrifices in personal life or at work). Prapavessis and Carron found that sacrifice contributes to task and social cohesion and, in turn, task and social cohesion contribute to increased conformity to important group norms. The sacrifices found to have the most powerful impact on cohesion were those made by the self and teammates at practices or competitions. Further, it was found that sacrifices by the self and teammates had their largest impact on task cohesion.

Adherence behavior. Cohesion is the construct representing a tendency for members to stick together. So, not surprisingly, cohesion is associated with adherence in sport teams (Brawley, et al. 1988, Study 1; Widmeyer et al. 1988, Study 2; Prapavessis & Carron, 1997). Robinson and Carron (1982) tested high school males from what they called a continuum of participation: starters (had regular opportunity to compete in games), survivors (practiced with the team but never had the opportunity to compete in a game), and dropouts (had quit the team of their own volition). Systematic differences were found between the starters, survivors, and dropouts. Athletes who left the team reported having the lowest sense of belonging, yet rated the team as most cohesive. Conversely, the starters possessed the highest sense of belonging, but held the lowest perceptions of the team's cohesiveness.

There are a number of aspects of adherence besides dropout behavior—including absenteeism, lateness, early departure, and reduced work output. Research has shown that athletes who hold the perception that their team is more cohesive are more likely to be on time for practice, to be present at practices and games (Carron et al., 1988, Study 1), and to feel that their team is able to withstand the negative impact of disruptive events (Brawley, et al., 1988, Study 1).

There is also evidence that athletes who perceive their team to be less cohesive are more likely not to work hard at practice. This was demonstrated by Prapavessis and Carron (1997) in a study where the cohesion of 261 athletes from a variety of sports was assessed. Their coaches, who had agreed to cooperate in the project, were provided with a standard warmup program to use prior to practices. Also, the athletes were led to believe that they might be randomly selected to participate in a project designed to assess their fitness level. The 20 athletes who had scored at the extremes in task cohesion were targeted. The researchers arrived at practice just after the standard warmup and, using a field protocol, assessed the heart rate, blood lactate, and oxygen consumption of a targeted athlete. That athlete was subsequently brought to the lab and a maximal oxygen uptake test was administered to provide a standard for comparison against the work output measures obtained at practice. A difference in maximal work output at practice was present between the athletes who viewed their teams as high versus low in task cohesion. The athletes who held higher perceptions of their team's task cohesiveness worked at a level that was significantly closer to their maximum.

Social loafing. In Chapter 3, social loafing—the reduction in individual effort shown when people work in groups versus when they work alone—was discussed (Latané, 1981; Latané, Williams, & Harkins, 1979; Williams, Harkins, & Latané, 1981). Although a meta-analysis by Karau and Williams (1993) showed that social loafing is pervasive across tasks, gender, and culture, they found that it can be reduced under some circumstances. Two of the conditions that can reduce social loafing are a) the potential to identify individual outputs and b) the presence of a relationship among the group members (Karau & Williams, 1993; Williams, Nida, Baca, & Latané, 1989).

McKnight, Williams, and Widmeyer (1991) had swimmers compete, either in relay teams of four swimmers or alone, to assess the impact of cohesion and identifiability on social loafing. A high-identifiability situation was obtained by informing the swimmers of their individual and relay split times in the presence of teammates and spectators. For the low-identifiability situation, the swimmers were informed privately of their time for the individual event and only the total time for the team was given for the relay event. McKnight et al. found that when task cohesion was low, only high identifiability was effective in reducing social loafing. That is, when the times of the swimmers were private, individuals socially loafed. On the other hand, in relay teams characterized by high task cohesion, social loafing did not occur regardless of whether personal output could be identified or not.

Naylor and Brawley (1992) took a somewhat difference approach than McKnight et al. Rather than examine social loafing behavior itself, they assessed whether members who perceived that their team was high in cohesion would be less likely to think that their teammates were engaging in social loafing. They found that this was the case. In interactive sports (i.e., basketball and volleyball), lower task cohesion was associated with stronger beliefs that teammates socially loafed. In coactive sports (i.e., swimming), lower social cohesion was associated with stronger beliefs that teammates socially loafed.

Naylor and Brawley did interject a note of caution, however. Team members who perceive their team to be highly cohesive might feel pressure to report (or refuse to entertain the possibility) that loafing is occurring less frequently than it actually is. Ignoring social loafing would help to preserve feelings of unanimity.

Leadership Factors and Cohesion

The third major correlate of group cohesion is leadership. As Williams and Widmeyer (1991) observed, when coaches place a great deal of importance on group cohesion and then take steps to enhance it, the cohesiveness in their teams increase. The interrelationship among leaders, subordinates, cohesiveness, and group performance is complex, however. For example, a group in mutiny against its leadership could be highly cohesive but would also be strongly oriented to perform poorly or contrary to the organization's goals (Schachter, Ellertson, McBride, & Gregory, 1951). This can occur in sport—at least in professional sport as the quote in Box 16.3 illustrates. Hockey coach Punch Imlach recognized that it is possible for the athletes to unite and undermine team management.

Leader Behavior

One general aspect of leadership that is related to the development of group cohesion is the leader's behavior. In work groups, which are by nature task-oriented, leader behaviors directed toward the completion of the task are most important. Clarifying group goals and developing strategies to achieve these helps to produce a cohesive unit.

In a study which examined the relationship between coaching behaviors and team cohesion with high school football players, Kirk Westre and Maureen Weiss (1991) found that higher levels of training and instruction behavior, social support behavior, positive feedback, and a democratic style of decision making (see Chelladurai's multidimensional model of leadership in Chapter 14) were associated with higher levels of task cohesion in athletes.

Steve Kozub (1993) reported similar findings in a study carried out with high school basketball teams. He found that athletes who perceived that their coaches demonstrated higher levels of training and instruction behavior, social support behavior, and a democratic decision style, perceived their team as more task cohesive.

Lee, Kim, and Lim (1993) obtained slightly different results using a stratified random sample of Korean high school athletes from a variety of sports. The only two leader behaviors associated with athlete perceptions of task cohesion were social support behavior and a democratic style.

The level of group cohesion present also influences the specific type of leader behavior that is most effective (Schriesheim, 1980). In groups that are low in cohesiveness, task-oriented behaviors produce better performance, greater role clarity, and higher individual satisfaction. In groups that are high in cohesiveness, person-oriented behaviors are better.

Box 16.3
Leadership factors and team cohesion

Focus	Quotation
A cohesive team united against team management	Any group of players on any pro team—hockey, basketball, whatever—can get together and undermine the coach or manager to the point that he's fired. But it is mainly teams that are going nowhere anyway who have the time and inclination to do that. The winners work at their game, their profession, instead of shafting management. (Imlach & Young, 1982, p. 164)

Decision Style

Another element in leadership that contributes to group cohesion is decision style (Bovard, 1951; Carron & Chelladurai, 1981). Stronger perceptions of cohesiveness are present when a more democratic (participative) approach is used to arrive at a decision. For example, Brawley, Carron, and Widmeyer (1993) found that those athletes who had had more participation in team goal setting possessed a stronger sense of task and social cohesion. Also, in the Westre and Weiss (1991), Kozub (1993) and Lee et al. (1993) studies which were discussed above, it was observed that athletes who perceived that their coach used a democratic style also perceived the group to be more task cohesive.

Also, in his study, Kozub (1993) found that a delegative decision style on the part of coaches also was associated with greater cohesion. It may be that any decision style that provides for greater athlete input leads to feelings of greater 'ownership' of the decision and the group. A feeling develops that it 'was our decision for our group.'

Team Factors and Cohesion

It was pointed out in Chapter 9 that there are four aspects commonly associated with the structure of a group: position, status, roles, and norms. Given that cohesion is the glue that binds the group together, it might be expected that the four aspects of group structure would be related to cohesion. Generally results have supported this expectation (the relationship of position to cohesion has not been explored).

Status

In their research with Indian and Canadian high school and intercollegiate athletes, Jacob and Carron (1997) failed to find a relationship between task cohesion and *status congruency* (i.e., the discrepancy between an athlete's perception and teammates' perceptions of the athlete's status in the group). However, Jacob and Carron did find that the higher the athletes' perceptions of task cohesion, the smaller the degree to which they attached *importance to status*.

The *starting status* of athletes seems to influence the way they perceive the cohesiveness of their team (Granito & Rainey, 1988; Gruber & Gray, 1982; Spink, 1992). For example, Granito and Rainey (1988) found that the starters on high school and college football teams held stronger perceptions of task cohesion than the nonstarters. However, on the basis of his findings, Spink (1992) suggested that team success is an important moderating variable. When he compared the starters and nonstarters of less successful volleyball teams, Spink found the same pattern of results as Granito and Rainey; the starters perceived their teams to be higher in task cohesion. When the starters and nonstarters of more successful teams were compared, however, no differences in cohesion were present. Team success seems to override the negative impact of not starting and contributes to maintaining task cohesion.

Role Involvement

Role involvement is inextricably linked to team unity. John Wooden recognized this; commenting on the development of his great teams at UCLA, he noted,

> *[I built teams] by defining roles for each individual and making each individual feel that their role is as important as any other role. Now there's a lead role and then there's the supporting cast, but if you don't have the good supporting cast, the thing as a whole is going to fail. (John Wooden, quoted in Fisher and Thomas, 1996, p. 90)*

In both team and individual sports, various aspects of role involvement and cohesion are strongly related (Brawley, Carron, & Widmeyer, 1987; Dawe & Carron, 1990; Grand & Carron, 1982). For example, Brawley, Carron, and Widmeyer (1987) reported correlations of .56, .63, and .57 between task cohesion (i.e., Group Integration-Task) and role clarity, role acceptance, and role performance respectively for individual sport athletes. For team sport athletes, the comparable correlational values were .38, .49, and .43.

When role clarity, role acceptance, and task cohesion are examined over the course of a season, the results contribute to the suggestion that role involvement and cohesion are related in a circular fashion. For example, Dawe and Carron (1990) evaluated the task cohesion, role clarity, and role acceptance of high school hockey players three times over the course of a season. Task cohesion measured early in the season was related to role clarity (r = .54) and role acceptance (r = .60) measured later in the season. At the same time, role clarity and role acceptance measured early in the season were related to task cohesion measured later in the season (r = .42 and .53 respectively). The strength of the relationship was slightly stronger when cohesion was assessed early in the season and the two aspects of role involvement were assessed later in the season.

In the research cited above, role clarity was measured as a unidimensional construct. As was pointed out in Chapter 12, Mark Beauchamp and his colleagues (Beauchamp, Bray, Eys, & Carron, 2002) recently proposed a conceptual model that contains four types of role ambiguity (which is the reverse of role clarity): ambiguity associated with scope of responsibilities, ambiguity associated with the behaviors required to carry out role responsibilities, ambiguity associated with how role performance will be evaluated, and, finally, ambiguity associated with the consequences of a failure to carry our role responsibilities.

Eys and Carron (2001) found that two measures of task cohesion (individual attractions to the group task and group integration-task) were negatively related to the four manifestations of role ambiguity. That is, as role ambiguity increased, task cohesion decreased.

Group Norms

There is little doubt that groups exert influence on their members, and that more cohesive groups have greater potential influence than less cohesive groups. An example of the former (i.e., that groups exert influence on their members) is the classic study by Kurt Lewin (1943, reported in Forsythe, 1983). Because of the shortage of beef during World War II, Lewin was asked by the National Research Council to develop a strategy for changing food preferences in the general population. A brief period of time was provided in which to convince volunteer homemakers to serve readily available but less desirable products to their families. Lewin set up an experimental situation in which two different approaches were tried. In the first, an attempt was made to change *individual* attitudes and behaviors. Groups of homemakers listened to a lecture that incorporated appeals to patriotism, information on the nutritional benefits of the alternate foods, and possible recipes. *There was no interaction among the homemakers*. In the second approach, an attempt was made to change the attitudes and behaviors of a *group*. Situations for group interaction were introduced in which the same information used in the lecture was discussed by groups of homemakers. The groups were then urged to reach consensus on an issue.

Subsequently, in a follow-up, Lewin found that only 3% of the homemakers who had heard the lecture in the individual approach had served the less desirable food products to their families. On the other hand, 32% of homemakers who had been involved in the group approach had served at least one dish. Later, Lewin and his colleagues followed up on this work with a number of other similar studies and found the same pattern of results. In summary, he concluded that, "it's easier to change individuals formed into a group than to change them separately" (Lewin, 1951, p. 228, quoted in Forsythe, 1983).

Examples of the latter point raised above (i.e., that more cohesive groups have greater potential influence than less cohesive groups) are present in research in laboratory contexts (Berkowitz, 1954; Schachter, Ellertson, McBride, & Gregory, 1951), with industrial groups (Mikalachki, 1969), with military crews (Berkowitz, 1956), and in academic settings (Miesing & Preble, 1985). A positive relationship is present between group cohesion and individual conformity—when cohesion is higher, conformity to group norms is greater.

In the context of sport, Shields, Bredemeier, Gardner, and Boston (1995) found that team cohesion was positively related to normative expectations that peers would cheat and aggress, and that the coach would condone cheating. Also, Prapavessis and Carron (1997) found that perceptions of task cohesion were positively related to conformity to the group norms identified as important by athletes.

Collective Efficacy

According to Zaccaro et al. (1995), collective efficacy represents "a sense of collective competence shared among individuals when allocating, coordinating, and integrating their resources in a successful concerted response to specific situational demands" (p. 309). It does seem reasonable to assume that when cohesion is higher, the sense of collective confidence in a team also would be higher. Subsequent studies have supported this assumption. For example, Spink (1990) found that perceptions of cohesion were higher for elite athletes and recreational volleyball players who perceived high collective efficacy in their respective teams. Subsequent research (e.g., Kozub & McDonnell, 2001; Paskevich, 1995; Paskevich, Brawley, Dorsch, & Widmeyer, 1995) has produced similar findings and also contributed to the suggestion that task cohesion is more strongly related to collective efficacy than social cohesion.

How are cohesion and collective efficacy related to team performance? The quote by Michael Jordan in Box 16.4 serves to highlight the fact that all three are interrelated (although the specific term *collective efficacy* is not used by Jordan). Paskevich (1995, Study 3) examined the interrelationships among cohesion, collective efficacy, and performance in 25 intercollegiate volleyball teams. He found that collective efficacy is a mediator between team task cohesion and team performance (i.e., win-loss record). That is, greater task cohesion contributes to greater collective efficacy, which, in turn, contributes to better team performance.

A final, very important team factor associated with cohesion that must be discussed is team performance. However, because of its importance, it is dealt with independently in the section that follows.

Team Success and Cohesion

Historical Perspectives

The popular perspective on the importance of team cohesion is well illustrated in the following quote by Phil Jackson, then coach of the Los Angeles Lakers:

With this current group there is one thing that worries me. I still sense a lack of cohesiveness, the oneness every team requires to win a title. There are always signs—anticipating when a teammate will be beat on defense, trusting someone will be in a designated spot, displaying the unwillingness

Box 16.4 *Team factors and cohesion*	
Focus	**Quotation**
Cohesion, collective efficacy, and team performance	Naturally, there are going to be ups and downs, particularly if you have individuals trying to achieve at a high level. But when we stepped in between the lines, we knew what we were capable of doing. When a pressure situation presented itself, we were plugged into one another as a cohesive unit. That's why we were able to come back so often and win so many close games. And that's why we were able to beat more talented teams. (Michael Jordan, 1994, p. 23).

to lose. So far, I haven't seen these, and time is running out. Achieving one-ness does not guarantee success, but it greatly enhances a team's chances. Except in a rare blowout, no matter how poorly you may perform, there comes a point late in every NBA game when the margin is not substantial, maybe six or eight points. The team closest to that oneness is usually tri-umphant. (Jackson & Arkush, 2004, pp. 169-170)

But, what does science say about cohesion and team success? Traditionally, one of the most heavily debated issues associated with the study of group cohesion has been its rela-tionship to team success. That debate arises largely because over an extended period of time research findings spanned the continuum of possibilities. First, there have been stud-ies where low cohesion has been found to be associated with high success. The 1960 German gold medal rowing eight and the 1962 German world champion rowing eight studied by Lenk (1969) is an often-cited example. Despite being in constant open conflict, the crew achieved at the highest level possible. As another example, Landers and Luschen (1974) observed that the most successful bowling teams they studied had the lowest lev-els of group cohesion.

There have also been studies in which cohesion also has been found to be unrelated to performance. A study by Melnick and Chemers (1974) with intramural basketball teams provides a good example.

Finally, there have been studies in which cohesion has been found to be positively associated with team success. In contrast to the results of Melnick and Chemers, many of those have been from the sport of basketball. For example, cohesion has been associated with greater team success in high school (Carron & Chelladurai, 1981; Shangi & Carron, 1987), intramural (Landers, Wilkinson, Hatfield, & Barber, 1982), and college basketball teams (Arnold & Straub, 1972).

An effective way to resolve the inconsistencies in research is a statistical tool called meta-analysis—the empirical combination of the results from all the studies in a domain of interest. In 2002, Carron, Colman, Wheeler, and Stevens carried out a meta analysis of 46 studies that had examined the association between team cohesiveness and team suc-cess. An overall moderate to large positive relationship was found. Moreover, the type of cohesiveness present—task versus social—is irrelevant insofar as team success is con-cerned. That is, when Carron and his colleagues subdivided the measures according to whether they represented task or social cohesiveness, moderate to large positive relation-ships between team success, and both task and social cohesion were observed.

Moderators of the Cohesion-Performance Relationship

In their meta-analysis, Carron and his colleagues examined whether either gender or type of sport had an influence on the magnitude of the cohesion-performance relationship.

Females and males. The group dynamics literature has many examples of where the responses of males and females have been shown to differ. Carron et al. found that the cohesion-performance relationship is no exception; the association between cohesion and performance is significantly stronger in female teams than it is in male teams.

Type of sport. A longstanding view, often advanced, has been that in some types of sports—wrestling, gymnastics, and golf would be a few examples—cohesion is irrelevant.

The athletes compete alone (although a team score might be calculated), so the presence of cohesion (or conflict for that matter) is irrelevant to the team's success. Interestingly, analyses of the outcome of the Ryder Cup (the golf competition between European and American professionals) have not endorsed this perspective. For example, Alan Shipnuck (2004), commenting on the most recent triumph of the Europeans, suggested,

> *This was not an upset. The Europeans' overwhelming victory . . . was their fourth in the last five, and their seventh in the last 10. They were the better team, and they are the better team. Accept it. Believe it. Sure, none of the dozen men responsible for Euro-trashing the U.S. have won a major championship, and only [one] . . . is in the Top 10 in the World Ranking. The American team, by contrast, boasted five players who have one at least one major, and five of the top 11 in the world. None of that matters in the Ryder Cup match-play format. It is a different game altogether . . . with their passionate, cohesive play . . . Europe not only beat the lifeless Yanks but also embarrassed them" (p. 86)*

Shipnuck's view on the importance of team cohesion in a sport such as golf is supported by research evidence. Carron and his colleagues found that a moderate to large cohesion-team success relationship is present in both coactive sports such as golf and interactive sports such as basketball.

Cohesion to Performance versus Performance to Cohesion

Another important issue that has sparked some interest concerns the magnitude of the cohesion-performance relationship versus the performance-cohesion relationship. Box 16.5 contains the view advanced by television commentator and former coach John Madden, who argued that the relationship is largely one way: success breeds cohesion but the opposite isn't necessarily the case.

The issue is particularly important because strong causal inferences can be drawn from research designs where the two measures are separated by a period of time. Thus, for example, in the context of a sport, if early season cohesion is correlated with midseason performance, it can be concluded that greater cohesion led to superior performance. Similarly, if early season performance is correlated with midseason success, it can be concluded that the greater success led to the higher cohesion.

In their meta-analysis, Carron et al. reported that both task and social cohesion were positively related to team success and team success was positively related to both task and social cohesion. So, John Madden (see Box 16.5) was partly correct. Highly successful teams are more likely to develop a sense of togetherness or family. On the other hand, unsuccessful teams that can begin to develop greater cohesiveness should increase their chances of becoming more successful.

Adversity

Although it is easy to appreciate how positive events and good times in the life of a group can produce feelings of togetherness, it's less obvious how failure or some other shared negative experience can also do so. But this could be the case (e.g., Kennedy & Stephan, 1977). Certainly, not every negative experience leads to increased cohesiveness. But, there are many instances where adversity, failure, threats from outside, and frustration serve to draw groups closer together. England after the Battle of Dunkirk and during the Battle of Britain is one example. The war was not going well but the entire population drew together for a common purpose. They shared a common highly emotional experience and developed a stronger sense of "we/us" clearly distinct from "they/them."

Turner, Hogg, Turner, and Smith (1984) have offered an explanation for this phenomenon that evolves from the research on social categorization and forced compliance. Social categorization involves attaching labels to people or putting them into categories. Research has shown that simply being defined as a group member (prior to any contact or involvement) is sufficient for an individual to feel attracted to a group. Committed recruits who have never attended a practice or played a game with a team will begin to feel that they have the same interests, characteristics, and values as team members. When those recruits eventually join the team (and their claim to being a member of the social category becomes even stronger), their commitment to the group also increases. When commitment is extremely high, a negative experience can serve as a catalyst to enhance cohesiveness (e.g., England during the Battle of Britain).

In forced compliance situations, the individual must behave in accordance with some standard or rule. When this happens, there is a tendency to adopt private attitudes that are consistent with the public behavior. When there is a feeling of personal responsibility and the resulting behavior leads to negative consequences, there is an even greater tendency to shift personal attitudes in line with the behavior. What all of this means is that when individuals hold a strong perception (attitude) that they are members of a group—they perceive themselves in the "group member" category and willingly acting on its behalf—their sense of commitment to that group is enhanced if the costs of group membership are high.

To draw on the Battle of Britain example again, the population was forced to use food stamps and ration what they used. Hardships resulted. This didn't lead to riots and protests but, rather, to an attitude that the deprivation was appropriate given the nature of the times.

Box 16.5
The dynamic relationship of team success and team cohesion

Focus	Quotation
The cohesion-performance and performance-cohesion relationships	The more the Raiders won, the closer the team got. In any sport, success breeds togetherness. But don't be fooled, togetherness doesn't breed success. If a bad team tries to develop togetherness, that's nice; but it's still a bad team. Take the Pittsburgh Pirates. When they won the 1979 World Series, they were "family," they were a good team. But when the Pirates dropped out of contention after that, they weren't family anymore. They were a bad team—that's why they weren't a family. (Madden and Anderson, 1986, p. 212)

Turner et al. have offered a good example that helps to illustrate this mechanisms underlying self-categorization:

> *If one is a Christian in the Roman empire, knows that a likely outcome is being thrown to the lions, chooses to continue being a Christian, and that outcome eventuates, then at least before being eaten one should tend to justify and explain one's actions in terms of one's definition of oneself as a Christian (which should be enhanced as a result). (p. 98)*

A similar process can occur in sport teams when an unexpected, devastating defeat occurs. The media and fans are critical and often look for scapegoats. Psychologically, the team then "circles the wagons" to withstand the threats, criticisms, and pressures directed against it. An example of this occurred in the 1988 Stanley Cup playoffs (see Box 16.6). After leading the league in the regular season, the Calgary Flames were defeated in four straight games in a quarterfinal series.

Turner et al., in two laboratory studies, tested their proposition that perceptions of commitment and perceived responsibility help to account for increased cohesiveness after a defeat. In one study, they manipulated the degree of choice individuals had about doing a group task as well as about the success and failure experienced. A second study was similar except that individual commitment to the group was manipulated. It was found that the failures produced greater cohesion than the successes when group members had a high degree of choice about their behavior or a high commitment to their membership in the group. On the other hand, lower cohesiveness was produced when choice and commitment were low.

Box 16.6	
Negative consequences and team cohesion	
Focus	**Quotation**
Cohesion and adversity	Some disgruntled fans may already be calling them the Shames, but the Calgary Flames aren't ashamed of anything . . . "We have nothing to be ashamed of," Coach Terry Crisp reminded his players. "It was a four-game sweep, but we were in every game . . ." There will be a lot of analyzing why the league's top regular-season team came to such a sour end just nine games into the playoffs. Fingers will be pointed at [the] forwards . . . who failed to score the way they had all season. More fingers will point at a power play that went from the league's best to pitifully anemic and at [the] goaltender . . . who never came up with a really big save when his team needed it most. But those fingers, said team leader Lanny McDonald, will be pointed only by people outside Calgary's dressing room. "It's a team effort out there. You all take credit when you win and you all take the blame when you lose." ("Flames not", 1988, C-1)

Some Potential Negatives Consequences of Cohesion

Although cohesion generally is assumed (and is) a positive group property, it does have the potential to be negative under some circumstances. At least that's what James Hardy and his colleagues found when they asked athletes to indicate whether they felt there were disadvantages to high task and social cohesion on a team and, if so, to identify those disadvantages. Fifty-six percent of athletes reported potential disadvantages to developing high social cohesion while 31% reported disadvantages to high task cohesion.

Some of the reported disadvantages to high social cohesion included wasting task-related time, difficulties focusing and committing to task related goals, problematic communication between friends, and the potential for social isolation of those outside the main group.

The high task cohesion-related disadvantages included, for example, decreased social relations, communication problems, reduced personal enjoyment, and increased perceived pressures. The Hardy et al. study does provide another perspective on cohesion. However, there seems to be little doubt that the benefits of a cohesive team far outweigh any disadvantages that may be present.

SECTION 6

TEAM PROCESSES

If we've gone to Glenn [Robinson] three or four times in a row on offense, he'll make sure to tell me to go down on the blocks because the ball is coming to me . . . we'll call his favorite inbounds play, but he'll say, "No, let's run yours." We try to make sure that everything stays in balance, because then it's harder to stop either one of us. One of the reasons we've been so successful this year is that we have an even better understanding than in the past that we're both at our best when we're sharing the load. (Milwaukee Bucks' Vin Baker quoted in Taylor, 1996b, p. 56)

Chapter Seventeen

TEAM GOALS

> Pat [Summit, coach of the national champion Tennessee Lady Vols] was fed up . . . she told us to quit acting like babies. She also set game go als. For instance, if we made more than 15 turnovers or gave up too many rebounds, we'd have to run extra sprints. I think that really helped to turn things around. (Lady Vols' team member Chamique Holdsclaw, quoted in Anderson, 1997b, p. 49)

Teams are composed of individuals who interact and communicate in a group context; Sections 2 and 3 of this book focused on aspects of group composition and the group environment that have an influence on individual and team outcomes (see Figure 1.4 again). Similarly, team member interactions and communications lead to the development of a team structure (discussed in Section 4) and the growth of social and task cohesion (discussed in Section 5). In the present section, the focus is on team processes.

At their core, team processes represent the dynamic interactions that are a fundamental, integral characteristic of group involvement. The quotation used to introduce this section is illustrative. Over time and with experience, Glenn Robinson and Vin Baker apparently came to an implicit understanding about what was necessary to maintain team cohesion and team effectiveness.

As was pointed out in Chapter 1, team processes don't literally follow from the development of group structure and group cohesion—the pattern illustrated in Figure 1.4. Team processes—interaction, communication, decision making, group goal setting, and so on—are an integral part of group life from the moment individuals come together to form into a group. In fact, some processes, such as interaction and communication, may even precede and contribute to group formation. For example, interactions and communications among strangers may lead them to recognize similarities in beliefs, common goals, and/or a mutual attraction. As a consequence, group formation may follow. In short, while team processes are influenced by group composition, environment, structure, and cohesion (the linear model represented in Figure 1.4), the relationship is more reciprocal and dynamic. The chapters in Section 6 focus on various facets of team dynamics.

Goals and Goal Setting

The Nature of Goals

As the term would suggest, a goal is a target, objective, standard, destination, aim, or end toward which effort is directed. As Alvin Zander (1971) has pointed out in his book *Motives and goals in groups*, the nature of goals and goal setting in groups is a complex interplay of personal and collective concerns (see Figure 17.1). Members set goals for themselves and for the group. Also, the group has its own set of goals. Finally, the group sets goals for individual members.

In an attempt to examine the relationships illustrated in Figure 17.1, Dawson, Bray, and Widmeyer (2002) questioned varsity athletes from 17 teams. Consistent with Zanders' proposal (outlined in Figure 17.1), they found that team sport athletes have personal goals while the team as a collective has group goals. Dawson and her colleagues also found that athletes have goals for their team; in over 40% of the cases, however, those goals exceeded the team's goals. The researchers suggested that a possible reason for this discrepancy was that the athletes were not involved in the goal-setting process for the team.

Dawson and her colleagues also noted that most athletes did not feel that their teams set specific goals for individual team members. Specifically, only 27% of the athletes felt that anyone on the team—coach, team captain, or the team generally—had set out goals for them to accomplish. Apparently, the goals that sport teams have for individual athletes are general and implicit—play well, do your best, carry out your assignments. Unfortunately, goal setting works better when goals are specific and explicit.

The Benefits of Goal Setting

Much of the earliest research—which was undertaken in industrial psychology—was founded on the belief that individual productivity can be increased if individuals have a target or goal (Ryan, 1970). Moreover, that belief was not ill founded. In 1981, after Locke, Shaw, Saari, and Latham carried out a comprehensive review of research evidence, they concluded,

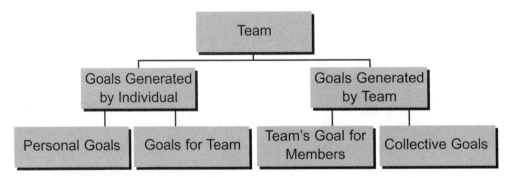

Figure 17.1. The relationship of group and individual goals
(Adapted from Zander, 1971)

the beneficial effect of goal setting on task performance is one of the most replicable findings in the psychological literature. Ninety percent of the studies showed positive or partially positive effects. Furthermore, these effects are found just as reliably in field settings as in the laboratory. (p. 145)

Subsequently, several meta-analyses empirically supported the conclusions of Locke and his colleagues (Mento, Steel, & Karren, 1987; Tubbs, 1986; Wood, Mento, & Locke, 1987). There is no doubt that goal setting works. In fact, Pinder (1984) has argued, "Goal setting theory has demonstrated more scientific validity to date than any other theory or approach to work motivation" (p. 169).

Goal setting doesn't just serve to improve productivity. As Edwin Locke and Gary Latham (1984) pointed out in their book, *Goal Setting: A Motivational Technique That Works*, it also improves work quality, reduces boredom, increases clarity of expectations, increases liking for the task, increases satisfaction with performance, increases recognition from peers and supervisors, enhances self-confidence, stimulates feelings of pride in achievement, and increases willingness to accept future challenges.

Goal Setting Mechanisms

What is it about goals and goal setting that leads to such reliable improvements in performance in work groups? Weldon and Weingart (1988) suggested that six processes play an important role in the relationship between group goals and the group's productivity. One of these is goals produce increased *effort*. When team goals are established, individuals are motivated to achieve them. In order to do so, they work with greater intensity and over longer durations than they would otherwise. The quote used to introduce this chapter speaks to how team goals can stimulate more effort. Coach Pat Summit felt that at least two factors contributing to a lack of team success were turnovers and the number of rebounds given up. By setting goals in these areas, she directed her athletes' attention and efforts toward performance elements considered important for team success.

A second process is *group planning and strategy development*. Goals serve to highlight what is important for collective success. Therefore, once they are established, members must determine how to achieve the group's goals. Third, the existence of group goals leads members to *monitor performance* and assess progress. As a consequence, motivation is improved. Having group goals also leads to *morale-building communications*, the fourth process suggested by Weldon and Weingart. When goals are present, they serve to arouse emotion, stimulate enthusiasm, and increase confidence among members. Fifth, with the introduction of group goals, members are likely to engage in what Weldon and Weingart called *extra-role behaviors*. These are behaviors that improve the performance of others or facilitate coordination among group members. Weldon and Weingart also suggested that a sixth, potentially negative process could be stimulated by the introduction of team goals. That is, there may be *reduced quality of performance* in those instances where the group's goal is to increase quantity of performance. Qualitative issues could become secondary to achieving more quantity or output.

Individual Goal Setting

Industrial and Work Settings

On the basis of a comprehensive review of the research evidence, Locke and his colleagues (1981) outlined a number of generalizations about the effectiveness of goal setting for individual productivity. These included the following:

1. Goals should be set out in specific and measurable terms. Vague, general, imprecise goals do not serve to direct the individual's attention to the important elements in the situation.
2. Goals should be as hard and as challenging as possible—with the qualifier that the individual must accept it and have the ability necessary to attain or closely approximate it.
3. Intermediate goals or subgoals should be used as links to long-term goals.
4. Feedback should be used in order for goals to have their maximum effectiveness as a source of motivation.
5. Support from the group leader is an important positive factor in the success of a goal-setting program.
6. Token rewards are useful for increasing commitment toward a specific goal.
7. Competition among individuals for goal achievement produces greater commitment and better performance.

The conclusions arrived at by Locke and his colleagues were subsequently supported by meta-analyses (Mento et al., 1987; Tubbs, 1986). In fact, in a commentary on Generalizations 1 and 2, Mento et al. proposed "if there is ever a viable candidate from the organizational sciences for elevation to the lofty status of a scientific law of nature, then the relationships between goal difficulty/specificity and task performance are most worthy of serious consideration" (p. 74). What about goal setting in sport?

Sport Setting

Box 17.1 provides an example of individual goal setting in a team sport. Steve Nash, then at Santa Clara University, outlined how playing in the NBA was his holy grail, a personal goal that was a daily source of motivation (and a goal that he subsequently achieved).

Considerable research interest in sport psychology has been directed toward understanding the dynamics of personal goal setting. This should not be surprising given that many athletes of different abilities and in different contexts engage in the practice. As an example at the elite sport level, Weinberg, Burton, Yukelson, and Weigand (2000) conducted a study on 328 Olympic athletes to explore their use of goal setting. Their results highlighted that all the athletes had utilized goal setting to some degree and that the majority of the goals were related to improving performance followed by winning and having fun. In addition, the athletes (a) demonstrated a preference for moderately difficult goals, (b) used goal setting somewhat frequently, and (c) believed their goals to be reasonably effective. These results concerning the use of goal setting were quite similar to those previously found by the same authors examining collegiate level athletes (i.e., NCAA Division 1; Burton, Weinberg, Yukelson, & Weigand, 1998).

	Box 17.1 *The nature of goals in sport*	
Type of Goal	Illustration	
Individual Goals	The NBA is the major dream in my life and the grail I chase every day . . . I am obsessed with it. (Steve Nash, quoted in Crothers, 1995, p. 68)	
Team Goals	We told each other, all the time we were there [training in Albuquerque in preparation for the 1996 Olympic Games in Atlanta], that someone must win a medal . . . It didn't matter who. (South African marathoner Lawrence Peu, quoted in Montville, 1996a, p. 82).	
Strategic (Organizational) Goals	One thing I learned . . . is that you may not always be able to get the best players, but you can get the best of everything else . . . the best ushers, the best secretaries, the best trainers—everything that gives your organization the feeling of being first class. (Utah Jazz President Frank Layden, quoted in Taylor, 1997b, p. 46)	

Setting goals for the purpose of successful performance is not the only use for sport-related goals. Athletes who are injured and are in rehabilitation can also benefit from goal setting. A study conducted by Lynne Evans and Lew Hardy (2002a) confirmed this with 77 athletes who were out of competition due to injury for at least five weeks. These individuals were placed in either a goal-setting group, a social support group, or a control group. The goal-setting group adhered better to the rehabilitation regimen than the other two groups based on self-report measures and demonstrated higher self-efficacy regarding the rehab program than the control group. Follow-up interviews with nine of the injured athletes (Evans & Hardy, 2002b) highlighted numerous issues and concerns expressed by athletes not able to compete due to injury and also indicated that individuals in the goal-setting group seemed to prefer long-range goals. Although these individuals also set short-term goals to a greater degree than the other groups, Evans and Hardy suggested that long-term outcome goals might be highly valued for those individuals who foresee a lengthy rehabilitation.

Effectiveness of individual goal setting in sport. One principle question has been whether specific, difficult individual goals are superior to vague "do your best" instructions or to no goals. Contrary to the case in organizational settings, research results in sport have not been consistent. Some studies reported support for Generalizations 1 and 2 listed above (e.g., Hall & Byrne, 1988; Hall, Weinberg, & Jackson, 1987) but others have not (e.g., Weinberg, Bruya, Jackson, 1985, 1990; Weinberg, Bruya, Jackson, & Garland, 1987).

Consequently, Kyllo and Landers (1995) attempted to resolve the inconsistencies empirically through a meta-analysis of 36 studies in sport and exercise settings (the total number of comparisons in these 36 studies was 136). They categorized various studies on the basis of whether the goal set was improbable, difficult, moderate, or easy. Consistent with the results from industrial settings, they found that easy goals do not have any effect in a sport setting on performance. There is nothing motivating about easy goals and, therefore, they do not lead to improvements in performance.

Contrary to the findings from industrial settings, however, Kyllo and Landers found that neither improbable nor difficult goals have an effect on performance. Only moderate goals—in which the possibility of attainment is in the range of 10 to 50 percent—are effective in a sport setting.

Kyllo and Landers suggested that one explanation for the sport-industry difference might be ability. If sport performers do not think they have the ability to achieve their goals—and improbable and difficult goals could be perceived this way—then they are unlikely to strive toward their attainment. A second explanation could be self-efficacy; individuals in sport who are not confident that they can obtain a desired outcome will not be motivated to work toward that outcome.

In many sport psychology textbooks, a distinction is made between outcome goals and performance goals (e.g., Weinberg & Gould, 2003; Orlick, 1986). An outcome goal, such as winning a gold medal, represents an absolute standard. A performance goal represents a relative standard based on a previous personal or team performance; reducing the number of rebounds or turnovers is an example. Popular wisdom (i.e., prescriptions in sport psychology textbooks) holds that performance goals are superior to outcome goals for producing performance improvements. For example, Orlick (1986) advised,

> *day-to-day goals for training and for competition should focus on the means by which you can draw out your own potential. Daily goals should be aimed at the improvement of personal control over your performance, yourself, and the obstacles you face. (p. 10)*

Kyllo and Landers found, however, that relative (performance) goals are no more effective than vague (do your best) goals; the greatest improvements in performance are achieved through absolute (outcome) goals.

However, it is not necessarily the case that an individual has to use one type of goal setting or another. Could the use of *multiple goal setting strategies* be the most advantageous? Filby, Maynard, and Graydon (1999) asked 40 individuals to participate in an experiment that measured their ability to perform a soccer task. This task required the participant (in a minute and a half) to continuously kick a soccer ball at a target on a wall about 8 meters away; points were received on the basis of accuracy. Each participant was assigned to one of five goal-setting groups: (a) outcome goal only, (b) process goal only, (c) outcome and process goals, (d) outcome, performance, and process goals, and (e) no goal control. Their results supported the contention that multiple goal strategies are the most effective strategy. However, Filby and colleagues also cautioned that it is not just the combination of goals, but the setting of effective and properly prioritized goals that is important.

The third generalization listed by Locke and his colleagues from industrial settings was that intermediate goals or sub goals should be used as links to long-term goals. Kyllo and Landers found that this generalization also has relevance in sport. Both short-term goals and combined short-term and long-term goals are clearly superior to long-term goals. An athlete who has a long-term goal of running a mile in 5 1/2 minutes will have more success if he or she establishes short-term (intermediate) goals for weekly improvement.

There are a number of other conditions associated with the effectiveness of goal setting (Kyllo & Landers, 1995). For example, competition among team members who are involved in a goal-setting program is good. Goal setting produces an improvement in performance and competition adds to the extent of the improvement.

Also, goal setting is more effective when athletes either establish or are involved in establishing personal goals. Cooperative or participant-set goals produce double the effect of assigned goals. Possibly the sense of "ownership" of the goals is greater and, therefore, athletes work harder to achieve them.

Finally, goals that are public are vastly superior to goals that the individual holds privately. In fact, in the research examined by Kyllo and Landers, private goals had no appreciable effect on performance. Possibly, it is easier to give up on or reduce goals that are not public knowledge.

Team Goal Setting

Nature and Prevalence of Team Goals in Sport

What types of goals do teams set for themselves for practices? For competitions? In sport psychology, there has been a tendency to focus on individuals rather than groups, on individual goal setting rather than group goal setting. Thus, Brawley, Carron, and Widmeyer (1992) undertook a study to identify the nature of group goals in team sports. Athletes from various sports were asked to list up to five goals held by their team for both practices and for competitions. Overall, 70% of the goals were vague, general in nature, and not well described. Coaches and athletes do not tend to establish team goals that are specific and measurable.

Brawley and his colleagues found that in practices, teams have collective goals that focus on processes (performance) needed to achieve outcomes rather than on outcomes themselves (see Table 17.1). Thus, for example, a process goal for practice in hockey might be to skate hard in every drill, whereas an outcome goal might be to get fit. In competitions (see Table 17.1 again), the collective goals held by teams were relatively balanced between outcome goals and process goals. An outcome goal for hockey could be to win, whereas process goals might be to reduce an opponent's shots on net.

In general, Brawley and his colleagues found that "team goals were not stated in specific, quantitative, behavioral terms. The overwhelming majorities . . . were stated in general terms" (p. 331). Thus, the effectiveness of team goals needs to be questioned. If a goal is

Table 17.1
The nature of team goal setting in sport (Adapted from Brawley et al.,1992)

Situation	Type of Goal	Percent
Practices	Outcome (e.g., work hard)	10.2%
	Process (e.g., work on each of the special units)	89.8%
Competitions	Outcome (e.g., win)	53.1%
	Process (e.g., reduce penalty minutes)	46.9%

essentially a road map to a target, objective, or destination, the more detailed and specific the map, the greater its utility.

Team Goals and Performance

As Box 17.1 illustrates, even in a marathon, a highly individual event, individuals can have a collective goal. After considerable debate, South Africa provided the finances to support four runners to train in Albuquerque for the 1996 Olympic Games in Atlanta. Apparently, "there were a lot of people who thought this was a waste of money" (coach-manager Jacques Malan, quoted in Montville, 1996a, p. 82). As a consequence, the four runners believed that one of them—anyone of them—would have to win a gold to justify the considerable expense. One of them, Josia Thugwane, did win the gold in the marathon in Atlanta.

Team goal setting can serve to improve performance in targeted indices. A goal-setting program designed to increase the number of body checks in a university hockey team was instituted by Anderson, Crowell, Doman, and Howard (1988) at the request of senior players on the team. In the first year, they found that the number of body checks increased by 82%, while in the second year, the improvement was 141%. Also, these improvements in body-checking rates were not accompanied by substantial increases in the number of penalties.

Individual Goals versus Team Goals

In some instances, individual goals can detract from team goals. Consider, for example, the personal struggle embedded in the following quotation:

> There was one time when [Bobby] Orr and Phil Esposito were running neck-and-neck for the scoring championship. Time and again Bobby would find himself in excellent scoring positions but instead of firing the puck he would look around for someone to pass to and often it was Phil. So, finally, I asked my defenseman Carol Vadnais what was going on with Bobby and why he was squandering potential points. "Don't you know?" he said. "He's trying not to get too far ahead of Phil for the scoring title." He risked the Art Ross Trophy [for the most scoring points] in order to make the team play better. (Cherry & Fischler, 1982, p. 163)

If Orr or Esposito had personal goals for individual scoring and were also competing with one another for the attainment of these goals, their competition might have caused the team to break up into two camps. Or, as another example, a team could have a goal-setting program comprised of personal goals for offensive performance (e.g., points scored, number of assists) and team goals for defensive performance (e.g., reducing the number of shots attempted or points scored). In pursuing the individual goals, it is possible for the team goals to suffer.

In their discussion of team versus individual goals, Edwin Locke and Gary Latham (1984) pointed out that,

> The late Rensis Likert, a psychologist at the University of Michigan, argued that group goal setting fosters a higher degree of cooperation and

> *communication than individual goal setting, and thus is preferable . . .*
> *When the tasks to be accomplished are highly interdependent, group goals*
> *are indeed appropriate. But this is unlikely to be the case where the jobs*
> *are not interdependent. (p. 37)*

In short, Locke and Latham essentially proposed that team goals are better than individual goals in sports such as basketball, soccer, ice hockey, field hockey—sports where a high degree of task cooperation and coordination are necessary.

There is some research evidence, however, that group goals are also better even in so-called independent sports such as golf or wrestling. This was the conclusion from a study in which Tamao Matsui, Takashi Kakuyama, and Mary Lou Uy Onglatco (1987) compared the effects of three goal-setting conditions on performance in an additive problem-solving task (i.e., individual scores were added to produce a group score). In one of the conditions, the subjects set a personal goal and were then tested alone. In another condition, the subjects set both a personal goal and a goal for their group. Again, the individuals were tested alone. This condition is comparable to the situation that exists when a team score is obtained in a wrestling meet. The athletes compete independently but their results are combined to obtain a team score (see Illustration 17.1).

As Figure 17.2 shows, there was no difference in the level of the personal goal set by an individual working independently or in a group. The participants set the same personal target for performance whether they were working independently or with a partner. However, the goal set for the group was significantly higher than the average of the two personal goals. Individual performance in the group situations was also significantly better. Matsui et al. suggested that group goal setting is superior to individual goal setting because (1) the collective goals that individuals set are higher than the goals they set individually and (2) goal acceptance is better in groups. It was proposed that when individuals set a personal goal, they just work to the minimum level necessary to achieve that goal. When they set a group goal, however, they work to achieve and then surpass that goal.

In a follow-up study, Matsui et al. also found that when group goals are used, it is important to evaluate the individual contributions to the

Illustration 17.1. Group goals serve to improve performance.

group effort. Otherwise, performance is not as effective. This is consistent with what has been discussed in Chapter 3 in relation to social loafing. Individuals working in a group reduce their output if their contributions cannot be readily identified and distinguished from the contributions of others.

Another study that compared group and individual goal setting looked at novice bowlers in an eight-week instructional period. Scott Johnson, Andrew Ostrow, Frank Perna and Edward Etzel (1997) first established a bowling performance base-

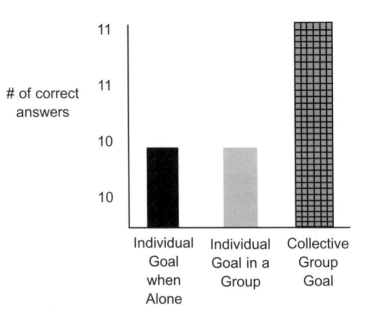

Figure 17.2. Goal setting and performance alone and in a group situation (Based on data from Matsui, Kakuyama, & Onglatco, 1987)

line for each individual during an initial two-week period. Then, in the intervention phase, participants in the individual goal-setting condition were given their personal performance baseline score and asked to write a personal goal for the day (which remained confidential). The participants in the group goal-setting condition were given the group's performance baseline score (which was obtained by averaging individual bowling scores) and asked to write a group goal for the day that was then discussed within the group. Johnson and his colleagues found that participants in the group goal-setting condition improved their personal bowling performance but participants in the personal goal-setting condition did not.

It is possible in most team sports to set up team goals and still have individual goals for offensive and defensive parameters. In a run-and-gun offense, for example, a team goal could be set for the number of shots taken each half in order to generate as much offense as possible. At the same time, it would also be possible to have individual goals for different team members that were compatible with this team goal. The best shooter could have personal goals for points scored, the playmaker for assists obtained, the rebounder for defensive and offensive rebounds, and so on.

Some Consequences of Team Goal Setting

Brawley, Carron, and Widmeyer (1993) undertook research to examine the psychological consequences for team members when team goal setting is undertaken for practices and competitions. They found that satisfaction with team goals for competition was higher when the clarity of the goals was greater and there was a greater belief by team members that the goal could be achieved. Also, the greater the task and social cohesion within the team, the greater was the satisfaction with the team's goals. Greater satisfaction with team goals for practice was present when task cohesion was higher and when the athletes perceived that the team goals produced behaviors (e.g., drills, skill development) directed toward goal achievement.

It was also observed that participation in team goal setting was associated with greater task and social cohesion. Brawley et al. (1993) suggested that when teams act together to participate in team goal setting, other psychological perceptions that reflect a sense of *groupness* are enhanced. That is, the interactions that occur within the group during participation in goal setting can lead to the development of common perceptions about the group—common beliefs about the team's goals, its unity, and the level of satisfaction present.

Finally, similar to setting individual goals, coaches and sport psychologist may use team goals to increase the collective motivation and effort as illustrated in the following quote by coach Phil Jackson of the NBA Los Angeles Lakers:

> *Giving goals was not a practice I followed with the Bulls, who were sufficiently self-motivated from Michael down to the twelfth man, watching countless games on television to scout their opponents. When I arrived in Los Angeles, I sensed that this team needed a measurable target to advance its cause. The players weren't nearly as driven. (Jackson & Arkush, 2004, p. 90)*

Strategic (Organizational) Goals

Locke and Latham (1984) introduced the concept of strategic goals to represent the standards, objectives, or goals of the whole organization or a significant portion of it. Box 17.1 provides a good illustration of how a sport organization can have organizational goals quite independent of team goals. Frank Layden, President of the Utah Jazz of the NBA, noted that his organization was striving for excellence in areas beyond just team success.

Strategic goals represent the general objectives of an organization and provide the basis for setting group (unit) goals, which in turn form the basis for setting individual goals. The quote in Box 17.1 notwithstanding, strategic goals generally include performance objectives, as the following quote from Jim Devellano, the vice president and general manager of the Detroit Red Wings hockey team, illustrates:

> *Devellano answered owner Mike Illitch's call to rebuild the once proud Detroit franchise. On the day he was introduced to the local media, Devallano promised fans a competitive team within five years and a Stanley Cup contender by the end of the 1980s. (p. 4)*

Detroit's strategic goal of first becoming competitive and then being a contender influenced the organization's decision to hire a coach and actively try to sign free agents. These decisions eventually also influenced the style of play of the team, the team's objectives, and ultimately the goals for individual players.

Strategic goals are different from both individual goals and group goals in multiplicity, breadth, complexity, duration, and specificity. Consequently, not all of the generalizations that apply to individual goal setting are equally applicable to strategic goals.

Goal *multiplicity* refers to the fact that it is possible for an individual athlete to have only one primary explicit goal but an organization usually has multiple strategic goals. For example, a coach may set one goal for her playmaking guard, such as "reduce the number of turnovers." Obviously, other aspects of the athlete's performance are also important. But turnovers could be the single element that the coach might want her athlete to emphasize. On the other hand, an organization develops different goals for its different departments or units. In the case of the Detroit Red Wings, for example, improving the team's standing might be the objective for the team; increasing attendance, profitability, and the number of support personnel in the organization might be objectives of the marketing division. The organization may also have goals for individual players that may run counter to the goals of the team and/or coach. Phil Jackson highlights this issue:

> [Owner Jerry] Buss wants to see Kobe and Shaq on the All-Star team every year, which is fine with me. But, as a coach, I want to see my team succeed, even if that in some way diminishes the contributions from the two superstars. (Jackson & Artush, 2004, p. 90)

Goal *breadth* is also different among individual, group, and strategic goals. Strategic goals are much broader in scope than group goals that, in turn, are broader than individual goals. When Devallano promised that the Red Wings would be competitive in five years, he set out a broad objective. At the team level, a number of specific goals would be set up to help translate that general objective into something specific and measurable. If the team had weak personnel, for example, one way to become competitive would be to emphasize sound defensive hockey. Thus, team goals could be generated to focus on the elements of good defense, such as goals against average, number of shots permitted in the prime scoring areas, number of 2-on-1 opportunities given up, and so on. In turn, at the individual level, goals would be set out to complement the achievement of the team goals. Thus, each athlete might have an individual goal established to reduce his plus-minus rating (i.e., the difference between being on the ice when a goal is scored for versus against the team).

Strategic goals, although they appear simple, are more *complex* than group or individual goals. This should be evident from the example above and in Box 17.1. Any organization that has the strategic goal of improvement in performance, in attendance, and in the number of personnel, must also identify the actions that are important to achieve each. At each level the focus of the actions becomes narrower. What must be done at the management level? At the team level? At the individual level? Unless the strategic goals are well thought out, appropriate group and individual goals cannot be established.

A fourth difference among individual, group, and strategic goals lies in their *duration*. The Detroit Red Wings example also serves to illustrate this facet. In terms of the duration of time involved, the strategic goal of being competitive within five years would take the longest to accomplish. Group and individual goals would be set out for each year, segments of the year, and/or each game.

A final difference is in the degree of *specificity versus generality* present. Group and individual goals are usually presented in very specific terms. Also, they're more effective because of it. There is some question whether strategic goals should be general or specific. Locke and Latham pointed out that there are advantages and disadvantages with each course of action. A strategic goal that is general in nature—"becoming competitive," for example—not only provides greater flexibility in terms of establishing (and changing) possible courses of action, it allows greater flexibility in interpreting goal achievement. A last-place team might become more competitive in its division by increasing its standing two or three places to become the sixth best team in the total league. It could be argued quite reasonably that the team had achieved its strategic goal and, therefore, was successful. On the other hand, if the strategic goal was phrased specifically—"end up first in the division and be among the top four teams in the total league," for example—it could be argued that it had not achieved its strategic goal and was unsuccessful.

Specific strategic goals are an advantage when an organization is suffering from a lack of direction and/or must change its focus. Then, all of the energies of the organization can be clearly focused on the attainment of that specific goal and there is no misunderstanding about the direction the organization must take.

Chapter Eighteen

COOPERATION AND COMPETITION IN GROUPS

The competition in [Bela] Karolyi's gym was intense by design. The day after each meet, Karolyi's wife, Martha, also a coach, would stretch the girls in the order in which they placed in the competition, carefully pulling and pushing on their muscles and joints like clay sculptor's hands. Kristie Phillips and Phoebe Mills, the two hotshots, almost always finished first and second, so Martha stretched them in that order—a subtle but clear privilege in a place were privileges were doled out by the teaspoon. The message: You're worth only as much as your latest ranking. Karolyi wanted the girls to battle each other every day in the gym. "These girls are like little scorpions," he once said. "You put them all in a bottle, and one will come out alive. That scorpion will be champion." If one girl didn't perform a routine to his liking, he often made one of her teammates do extra work, building a climate of resentment among them where only the strongest would survive. (Ryan, 1995, p. 22)

In this opening quote, from Joan Ryan's book, *Little girls in pretty boxes: The making and breaking of elite gymnasts and figure skaters,* the intense competition among teammates in an elite gymnastics club coached by Bela Karolyi is discussed. This constant and intense competition often left the gymnasts tired, frustrated, and resentful.

From the perspective of a scientist, the gymnasts' situation could be examined in three ways—from an individual perspective, from a within-group perspective, and from a between-group perspective. In other words, it is possible to look at the situation by trying to determine what Kristie and each of the other gymnasts were like in terms of their personal aspirations, motivations, and frustrations. It is also possible to look at the situation by trying to better understand the pattern of interactions between Kristie and her teammates. Finally, it also is possible to look at the impact of the situation in terms of the Olympic team's relationships with other teams. The kind of insight obtained from each approach is different. Social scientists Muzafer Sherif and Carolyn Sherif (1979) emphasized this point when they pointed out, *we cannot legitimately extrapolate from the individual's motivational urges and frustrations to . . . experiences and behaviors in group situations as if the interaction processes and reciprocities within a group were a play of shadows. It is equally erroneous to extrapolate from the properties of relations within a group to explain relations between groups, as though the area of interaction between groups consisted of a vacuum. (p. 9)*

The study of intragroup and intergroup processes has intrigued a wide spectrum of social scientists because the issues involved have such universal importance. For example, in order to understand team dynamics in sport, stereotyping and social discrimination in society, the functioning of action groups in politics, and the causes and consequences of aggression at a national and international level, it is necessary to understand intragroup and intergroup processes. It is not surprising then that numerous books have been devoted to research and theory on the topic; e.g., *Making groups effective* (Zander, 1982), *The social psychology of intergroup relations* (Austin & Worchel, 1979), *Group conflict and cooperation* (Sherif, 1966). The present book is concerned with intragroup and intergroup processes in sport teams. In the present chapter, the dynamics of cooperation and competition and their influence on intra- and intergroup relations are discussed.

Nature of Cooperation and Competition

Cooperation and competition have been viewed in a number of different but related ways. For example, Morton Deutsch (1949) emphasized the *distribution of rewards* when he defined a cooperative situation as one in which the gains by one individual contribute to a gain by all individuals. Rewards are shared equally, independent of the amount of contribution by various group members. An example of cooperation exists in professional sport when a team wins a championship and the league bonus is distributed equally among team members.

In a competitive situation, the gains by one individual reduce the potential for gains by other individuals. Rewards are provided on the basis of each individual's relative contribution or success. Consequently, rewards are shared unequally. The prize money awarded in professional golf provides a good example.

Competition has also been referred to as a *zero-sum condition* because the rewards to a winner (+) are balanced off against the absence of rewards to the loser (-). The quote in Box 18.1 provides a good example. The Olympic team was comprised of a limited number of competitors. Thus, when the top seven athletes were selected, the eighth competitor was eliminated—a zero-sum situation.

Cooperation represents a nonzero-sum condition because rewards are available for all participants.

From a slightly different perspective, Marvin Shaw (1981) has considered cooperation and competition in terms of the *heterogeneity versus homogeneity of the group goals*. A characteristic of cooperative situations is that group members hold the same (homogeneous) perception of the group goal and are committed to achieving it. Box 18.1 provides a good illustration of the existence of homogeneous goals in a gymnastics team. In spite of a serious injury, Nadia Comeneci competed in an attempt to achieve the gold in the

---

Box 18.1
The nature of competition and cooperation in teams

Factor	Example
Competition as a zero-sum activity	Kristie [Phillips] finished the Trials in eighth place, one spot short of being named an alternate. She would go to the Olympics only if someone got hurt . . . None of the girls would let Kristie set the boards for their vaults because they feared she might sabotage the equipment to cause an injury . . . "If I had a magic wand," Kristie was heard to say one day, "I'd wish one of the girls would get hurt." (Ryan, 1995, p. 115-116)
Cooperation as a homogeneous perception of a common goal	[Nadia Comeneci was hurt and couldn't compete] Everything was lost...I was so frustrated that I couldn't speak, . . . Nadia did not say a word . . . The green light went on and Nadia walked up to the beam . . . I couldn't look . . . I was 90 percent sure that she would fall...There was Nadia, one hand and three fingers from the other hand on the beam, moving slowly . . . It was so obvious, with her big bloodied bandage, that she was injured, and therefore so incredible that she had performed a near-perfect one-handed routine . . . The score came up, 9.95. We were back in first place. Nadia walked quietly back to the bleachers. She had made her contribution to the team's victory. (Karolyi & Richardson, 1994, p. 87-90)

---

team competition of the 1979 World Championships. In competitive situations, members either have different (heterogeneous) perceptions of the group goal or they have personal goals that interfere with the achievement of the group goal.

It is possible to have cooperation and competition both within groups and between groups. Figure 18.1 contains examples of four possible combinations of intra-and inter-group processes. In the top example, there is cooperation within each group and these groups are competing against each other—a situation which exists in most team sport situations. The second example contains intragroup and intergroup cooperation. This is rare in sport but it does exist; e.g., when the teams in a conference get together to establish rules and regulations that govern eligibility, the rules of play and so on.

The third example illustrated in Figure 18.1, competition within and between groups, is characteristic of the situation that exists in many gymnastics clubs. The following quote is illustrative:

> She [Susan—an elite gymnast] would support her teammates, as long as she clearly was better than them. As soon as their performances neared hers, Susan would begin to view them as an opponent. As she stated: "I [was] very supportive of my teammates, only if they never beat me." She also noted: "I had no problem coaching somebody up. I had no problem supporting somebody up as long as they stayed underneath that clear

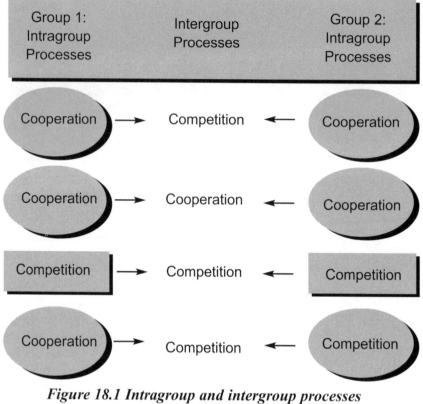

Figure 18.1 Intragroup and intergroup processes
(Adapted from Carron, 1980)

window. I mean window ceiling. Ya know, if they even came close to me, forget it. I'm not helping you." (Krane, Greenleaf, & Snow, 1997, p. 65)

In competitions with other clubs, a team score is important but each gymnast also strives to have the best personal score.

In the final example in Figure 18.1, there is competition within one group and cooperation within the other. Also, there is competition between the two groups. The following quote from NBA coach Pat Riley illustrates this scenario:

The day training camp opened, everyone was surprised to see one core player arrive in the best shape of his career . . . his physique looked hand-carved. But his motivation for secretly working out all summer wasn't simply driven by how much more he could give the team. It was for personal gain. He wanted to show he could challenge the greatest offensive weapon in the history of the NBA, Kareem Abdul-Jabbar. Sometimes a rising challenge within a team creates healthy change. It spurs everyone to do their best and to prove their worth. Was this the drive for excellence or a self-ishness of spirit? In this case it was the latter—a lightning rod for the resentment gathering between teammates. (Riley, 1993, p. 43)

As Riley noted, the same action might be spurred by two different motives. Similarly, in the same league, one team might have total cooperation whereas a second might be characterized by total competition.

The Robbers Cave Experiment

In 1954, a classic research project that became known as the *Robbers Cave Experiment* was initiated by a research team led by Muzafer and Carolyn Sherif (Sherif, Harvey, White, Hood, & Sherif, 1961). The main purpose of their study was to examine intragroup and intergroup relations in a natural environment. To achieve this objective, a boys' camp was set up in an isolated setting in Robbers Cave State Park in Oklahoma. In the original selection of the 11-year-old boys and their eventual assignment to one of two groups, care was taken to insure that there were no idiosyncratic characteristics that could have contributed to alternate explanations for the results. Thus, an attempt was made to insure that the boys selected were homogeneous in age, race, religion, and socioeconomic status and relatively similar in appearance. No previous friendships were present and the assignments to each of the two groups were organized so that each group was matched for ability and size.

The two groups were brought to the camp separately and, in the initial phase (which lasted for a week), kept segregated. This strategy provided the researchers with an opportunity to chart the development of group structure in the two settings. Thus, the researchers were able to chart the emergence of status hierarchies, leadership roles, group norms, and so on. The researchers were also able to observe the appearance of various intragroup processes, such as cohesiveness, goal setting, cooperation, and competition. Near the end of the initial phase, the groups became aware of each other. Gradually, the boys' interests became more and more centered on the presence of the other group. In their conversations, the distinction between "we" and "they" was prevalent, and interest was expressed in holding some competitions between the group.

When the competitions were arranged and initiated, it marked the beginning of the second stage of the study. During this period, the researchers were able to chart the development of intergroup cooperation and competition. Initially, there was some intergroup tension resulting from the competition but it was minimal (e.g., teasing, mild insults). Eventually, however, open hostilities resulted when one group (the Eagles) burned the other group's (the Rattlers) flag after losing a tug-of-war. This marked the beginning of a period of escalating intergroup tension and hostility. At various times, the boys had to be physically restrained from fighting each other. Eventually, the researchers took the two groups to different parts of the camp.

In an attempt to reduce the hostility, the researchers brought the boys together during the third phase in a variety of different noncompetitive situations. They ate together, watched films, and played games. When this failed to reduce the hostility, a series of crises were staged which required a cooperative effort from both groups. In this fourth phase, the boys worked together to locate the disruption to their water supply, pull a broken truck, rent movies, and prepare meals. The Sherifs and their colleagues referred to the challenges requiring joint effort as superordinate goals—goals that required the combined resources of the total group for success. During this fourth phase, intergroup hostility and group polarization were reduced and intergroup contact, friendships, and cooperation were increased.

Behavioral Consequences of Cooperation and Competition

Reactions to Teammates and the Opposition

A number of studies in addition to the work of the Sherifs and their colleagues have shown that the combination of intragroup cooperation and intergroup competition is associated with some relatively consistent behavioral patterns (e.g., Tyerman & Spencer, 1983). An overview of these is presented in Table 18.1. Some of these behavioral patterns are inter-related in the sense that they represent a growing tendency by the ingroup to differentiate itself from the outgroup.

Social categorization is one reflection of an attempt to differentiate the ingroup from outgroups and/or nongroup members. When a group forms, social categorization helps it establish a sense of identity and serves to differentiate it and its members from others. As Tajfel and Turner (1979) pointed out,

> *the mere perception of belonging to two distinct groups—that is, social cat-egorization per se—is sufficient to trigger intergroup discrimination favor-ing the in-group. In other words, the mere awareness of the presence of an out-group is sufficient to provoke intergroup competitive or discriminatory responses on the part of the in-group. (p. 38)*

Table 18.1
Behavioral consequences of cooperation and competition

Factor	Consequences	Reference
Social Categorization	Outgroup members are categorized into restrictive perceptual categories and stereotyping occurs.	Tajfel & Turner (1979)
Outgroup Rejection	Ratings of interpersonal attraction favor ingroup members. Friendship choices are predominantly ingroup. Ingroup similarities and outgroup differences are exaggerated.	Brewer (1979) Coser (1956)
Evaluation Bias	An evaluative bias develops which favors the group's members and its products.	Dustin & Davis (1970) Bettencourt, Brewer, Croak, & Miller (1992)
Group Cohesion	Group cohesion is increased but it is influenced by success. Winning teams show increases, losing teams show decreases.	Sherif, Harvey, White, Hood, & Sherif (1961)
Leadership Style	An autocratic decision style is increasingly used and favored over a democratic style.	Blake & Mouton (1961) Sherif, Harvey, White, Hood, & Sherif (1961)

Box 18.2
Behavioral consequences of competition

Factor	Example
Social Categorization	[My opponents] are my enemies, threats, challenges, but all of them had to be conquered. (Krane et al., 1997, p. 62)
Evaluation Bias	There was no question in my mind that Nadia would once again win the all-around title. She was in good shape, and her reputation would help her. There was no question in my mind that unless Nadia made a major mistake, no one could take that title away from her. (Coach Bela Karolyi quoted in Karolyi & Richardson, 1994, p. 92)
Outgroup Rejection	[Coach] would say, "You don't speak to competitors, they are enemies." (Krane et al., 1997, p. 59)
Group Cohesion	The joy in the locker room—champagne spraying into every corner, wives, friends, and broadcasters all sharing the moment—lasted for a good two hours, yet it felt like barely fifteen minutes. But the afterglow has never gone away. That's how you feel when something significant has been achieved. (Riley, 1993, pp. 180-181)
Use of an Autocratic Style	[Coach] was extremely, extremely competitive-minded.... whatever he says is gospel. I mean, he was just, he was a god-like figure to me. He had that power. (Krane et al., 1997, p. 59)

"We" versus "they" is a simple form of social categorization. With the introduction of competition, the categorizations used by ingroup members become more stereotypical. Box 18.2 illustrates social categorizations that were manifested by a gymnast.

Groups that are in competition also show a strong *evaluative bias* in favor of the ingroup. In relation to the perceptions held for other groups and their members, there is a tendency to overestimate ingroup successes and strengths—the group's product is considered more favorably (e.g., Dustin & Davis, 1970; Janssens & Nuttin, 1976). An example of evaluation bias is presented in Box 18.2.

There is also a tendency to misjudge the motives and intentions of other groups. For example, Doise (1978) found that ingroup members attributed more cooperative motives to themselves and fellow group members than to the outgroup and its members.

Another consequence of intergroup competition is that there is increased *outgroup rejection* (see Box 18.2 again). This is strongly related to the evaluative bias mentioned above. When cooperative groups are competing with other groups, ratings of interpersonal attraction favor the ingroup and there are a greater number of friendship choices within the group (Brewer, 1979; Coser, 1956). Also, groups in competition have a tendency to emphasize their differences rather than their similarities. Commonalities between the groups are downplayed or ignored and any minor differences that exist become exaggerated (Coser, 1956).

The *style of leadership* used by leaders and endorsed by subordinates is also influenced by cooperation and competition (see Box 18.2). Cooperative groups inherently are more prone to a participative decision style. With the introduction of competition, however, there is a tendency to shift to a more autocratic style and this is generally considered to be acceptable to the group as a whole.

Blake and Mouton (1979) have referred to the process of increased autocracy in competition as *leadership consolidation.* Those group members who are slightly more dominant, exercise greater initiative, and provide more and better input during the cooperative phase, assume a greater proportion of the leadership responsibility during competition. In their research with industrial work groups, Blake and Mouton also observed that leadership replacement occurs in groups that fail. Group members who take a leadership role lose status and influence when the group is unsuccessful. Consequently, they are replaced by other group members.

Intragroup cooperation with intergroup competition also influences the development of *group cohesion,* a consequence that was evident in the Robbers Cave Experiment. A clearly defined group structure emerged and cohesiveness was present within the two groups of boys during the initial phase of the study. Then, when competition was initiated, the two groups became even more close knit and cohesive. The Sherifs and their colleagues also found, however, that success and failure had an influence on the relative level of cohesion—a result which also has been observed in sport teams (see Chapter 16). With group success, cohesiveness was strengthened; with failure, it was weakened. An example of increased cohesiveness with group success is illustrated in Box 18.2.

Why Does Cohesion Increase in Competition?

Kenneth Dion (1979) has suggested that there are four possible interpretations for the increases that occur in ingroup cohesiveness during competition. One is based on Heider's (1958) *balance theory* that is founded on the premise that individuals seek out perceptual consistency. This consistency is achieved by balancing positive perceptions (+) with negative perceptions (-). When ingroup membership is perceived in a positive way, the outgroup will be perceived in a negative way so that balance and consistency are achieved.

A *reinforcement* explanation is based on the fact that the group can serve as a vehicle for the achievement of extrinsic rewards. Competition provides an opportunity to secure rewards, such as social approval, trophies, and so on. The ingroup is perceived more favorably because it is the vehicle through which the individual can receive rewards. This explanation also helps to account for the decrease in cohesiveness in groups that fail—as a result of failure, the group is not providing the reinforcement necessary to maintain committed group membership.

Competition also poses a *threat* to goal attainment, prestige, and self-evaluation. When groups are threatened from outside, they tend to draw closer together.

The final explanation offered by Dion is associated with a *self-enhancement* hypothesis. Would I be likely to feel good about my membership in an inferior group? The ingroup is perceived to be superior to the outgroup in order to protect and enhance self-esteem.

The Case of Minimal Groups

Henri Tajfel and John Turner (1979) have found that cohesiveness, social categorization, evaluative bias, and outgroup rejection occur even in what are referred to as *minimal groups*—ad hoc categories of individuals formed on the basis of some trivial criteria. For example, an instructor might tell a group of students that they all achieved the same grade in a psychology exam. With only this trivial characteristic in common, the individuals would begin the process of self-categorization (i.e., consider themselves as "we" and other individuals in the class as "they").

In the Tajfel and Turner research, the individuals are unfamiliar with each other, there is no face-to-face social interaction, and there is no opportunity to gain from favoring ingroup individuals. Nonetheless, a bias becomes evident almost immediately; individuals show favoritism toward the ingroup and discriminate against the outgroup.

Tajfel and Turner have suggested that one of the reasons why people respond in this way is that they have a strong need to protect and enhance their self-esteem. When they enter into a group, a social bond forms with other group members. One significant contributor to individual self-esteem is our social identity resulting from our membership in groups. Other groups in which the individual is not a member provide a reference for comparison. When the comparison yields a positive evaluation, it also provides prestige. When the comparison yields a negative evaluation, however, prestige suffers.

Reducing the Tension Between Groups

If increased cohesiveness, social categorization, evaluative bias, and outgroup rejection can occur in competing social groups and even in minimal groups, it can be expected that they are also present in sport groups—teams that are engaged in intergroup competition. The negative behavioral consequences listed in Table 18.1 seem to be inevitable. In professional sport, these behaviors might be considered desirable and coaches might be interested in promoting their development. But in amateur and youth sport, an attempt should be made to reduce their influence as much as possible.

Steven Worchel (1979), in a review dealing with the reduction of intergroup conflict in society, has presented four strategies that have been used with varying success: increasing intergroup contact, utilizing group representatives, finding a common enemy and, promoting intergroup cooperation.

Intergroup *contact* can be used in youth sport. Encouraging interaction, and communication and insuring that the athletes are brought into close physical proximity will help to reduce stereotyping and discrimination and break down the barriers between groups. Worchel pointed out, however, that there are mixed opinions on the effectiveness of intergroup contact as a general strategy for reducing conflict between societies or racial groups. On the one hand, some research has shown that the increased familiarity that results from contact with members of the other group does draw individuals from different groups together. On the other hand, there is also evidence that increased contact has either had no impact or has increased intergroup hostility. We only have to consider the "hot spots" around the world to understand that having contact and/or being in close physical proximity to members of different groups (religious, ethnic, political) does not ipso facto lead to harmony.

Another strategy which has been used—particularly if the groups are very large—is to have leaders or *group representatives* meet and then report back to their groups. This approach also is not very successful for reducing intergroup conflict, however. Only the group representatives are strongly influenced; the attitudes and beliefs held by individual group members remain largely unaffected. It is doubtful that this approach would produce beneficial effects in amateur sport situations.

A third strategy that has been used is to establish a *common enemy*. The assumption underlying this approach is that a threat that is mutually perceived will draw the two groups closer together. Drawing on the work of the Sherifs (Sherif & Sherif, 1969), Worchel argued against this approach. Facing a common threat does not break down the barriers between groups; it simply serves to set up new barriers (against the common threat). Also, when the common threat has been removed, the hostilities between the two groups flare up again.

An effective approach to reducing conflict between groups is to promote intergroup *cooperation*. This was the strategy used by the Sherifs and their colleagues in the Robbers Cave experiment when they developed superordinate goals for the two groups. "When groups in a state of friction are brought into contact under conditions embodying superordinate goals whose attainment is compellingly desired by each group, but which cannot be achieved by the efforts of one group alone, they will tend to cooperate toward the common goal" (Sherif, 1979, p. 260). For example, two competing sport teams may come together to discuss the scheduling and location of their upcoming competitive season. When a goal is developed (scheduling and game locations) which becomes the focus for the two groups, there is an increase in interaction and communication, negotiation, and so on. As a consequence, the principals involved establish a sense of "we" and the distinctions between "we" and "they" become blurred.

Performance Consequences of Cooperation and Competition

It was pointed out above that in a cooperative situation, the gains by one individual contribute to a gain by all (see Illustration 18.1). This is the case in relay events where an exceptional time by one individual benefits the whole team. In a competitive situation, on the other hand, the gains by one individual reduce the potential for gains by other individuals. This is the situation that exists in individual sprint events. There is only one first-place finisher, one second-place finisher, one third, and so on. Although competition and cooperation are the two predominant possibilities in sport, a third is possible in educational settings—individualism. With an individualistic situation, each person is rewarded on the basis of personal merit. As a consequence, any number of people can reach the highest category and be appropriately rewarded. During elementary school track and field days, this is what often occurs. A first-place ribbon is awarded to every child who surpasses a baseline (threshold) time in the track events or achieves a set distance (or height) in the field events.

What are the merits of competition versus cooperation versus individualism for performance? Advocates of competition have cited the advantages of working independently, not having to share the credit or blame, accepting the challenges of social comparison. Advocates of individualism point out that it offers many of the same advantages plus one other—the individual's goal is to achieve success in the task and not to

beat another person. Advocates of cooperation, on the other hand, point to the
social benefits of working with others
(e.g., increased interaction, communication, trust, tolerance) as well as to the
greater opportunities provided for
learning from others. Which of these
three approaches produces the best performance?

A series of meta-analyses have been
undertaken to determine what process—
cooperation, competition, or individualism—produces the best performance
(Johnson, Maruyama, Johnson, Nelson,
& Skon , 1981; Quinn, Johnson, &
Johnson, 1995; Slavin, 1983). For
example, in 1981, Johnson, and his colleagues (1981) drew together 122 studies published since the 1920s. On the
basis of their meta-analysis, Johnson
and his colleagues concluded that

***Illustration 18.1. Cooperation results in
increased group performance.***

- Cooperation is superior to competition for achievement and productivity;
- Cooperation is superior to individualism for achievement and productivity;
- Cooperation without intergroup competition is superior to cooperation with
  intergroup competition for achievement and productivity; and
- There is no difference between competition and individualism for achieve-
  ment and productivity.

Furthermore, it was stated that these four relationships were present for virtually
every subject area, including language arts, reading, math, science, social studies, psychology, and physical education. The only situations in which Johnson and his colleagues
found cooperation was not superior to individualism and competition were rote learning
and correcting tasks.

Moderators of Cooperation and Competition

The Johnson et al. conclusions were subsequently criticized for being too simplistic and
for not taking into account some of the factors that have been shown to modify the effect
of cooperation and competition (e.g., Cotton & Cook, 1982; Maruyama, 1991; McGlynn,
1982). Some of these moderating variables, which were highlighted by John Cotton and
Michael Cook (1982), are task interdependence, task complexity, and group size.

Competition is considered to be better for performance in independent tasks such as
archery. No task interaction among members of the team is required. On the other hand,
cooperation is considered to be more effective for performance in interdependent

tasks—those tasks characteristic of team sports, such as basketball. As the following quote from NBA coach Pat Riley illustrates, cooperation increases the probability of team success:

> *There are protective defenses and there are destructive defenses. This one, which we called "FIST," was designed to destroy. It relied on our guys [the LA Lakers] covering their basic assignments and moving in at the right movement to trap the ball-handler, like the five fingers of a single hand closing into a powerful fist. When we executed it well, FIST totally changed the rhythm of a game. It forced our opponents to play quicker, and to make more mistakes, creating a lot of fast-break opportunities for us. It was a strategy that could only work through intense cooperation. (Riley, 1993, pp. 72-73)*

Another aspect of the task that has an impact on the effectiveness of cooperation and competition is its complexity. Tasks such as basketball, badminton, judo, and volleyball are very complex, and, therefore, are learned and performed better under cooperative situations. Tasks assessing reaction time in the laboratory are simple; consequently, competition is better for their successful achievement.

Group size is also a moderating variable. Cooperation is superior in large groups while competition is superior in smaller groups (fewer than six members). In large groups, coordinating the group's resources and ensuring that individual members have opportunities for interaction and communication are important considerations. These are more easily accomplished with a cooperative orientation.

Further, in sport and physical activity, the gender of the participants may also be a moderator of the effectiveness of cooperation versus competition. For example, Duda (1987) and Gill (1986) examined gender differences in goal orientations that are specific to sports and physical activities. Both authors found that males were more likely than females to have competitive orientations and to emphasize winning in a sport setting.

Marsh and Peart (1988) examined competitive and cooperative physical fitness training programs for high school girls. They found that both the competitive and cooperative programs increased physical fitness. However, the cooperative program also enhanced physical self-concept and appearance self-concept, whereas the competitive programs lowered physical and appearance self-concept. Since females have lower participation rates than males for sport and physical activity, these results may have implications for exercise and sport adherence in females. That is, if females prefer cooperative physical activity situations, programs that emphasize cooperation may result in increase adherence compared to competitive programs.

Reward Systems and Cooperation and Competition

Robert Slavin (1983) conducted another meta-analysis concerned with identifying what *group-oriented approach* in education is most effective for promoting student learning. Table 18.2 presents an overview of the six possible techniques. As this summary shows, Slavin distinguished between tasks in which a division of labor is either possible or not (and therefore, specialization by group members is also possible or not). He also made a distinction among three reward systems: (1) where the group is rewarded because of the summed contributions of individual members (e.g., golf teams, wrestling teams);

(2) where the group is rewarded for a single group product (e.g., rowing teams, volleyball teams); and, (3) where each person is rewarded on the basis of personal accomplishment (e.g., individuals train together and then compete independently at a competition).

Slavin found that group rewards are essential in order for group-oriented approaches to be successful. When individuals work together in a group and then are rewarded on the basis of their individual performance (the last column in Table 18.2), there are no advantages over working alone. In order for the group to be effective (i.e., for cooperation to occur), a group payoff is necessary.

Social loafing can also occur in education (as any person who has ever worked within a group to produce a term paper can testify). Thus, individual accountability is an important consideration when individuals work in groups. When individual contributions can be readily identified (the first column as well as the lower cell in the middle column of Table 18.2), group work is superior to working alone.

In Table 18.2, sport examples are used for illustrative purposes. Nonetheless, there is some question about how relevant Slavin's conclusions are for sport and physical activity. The transfer of generalizations across different situations is often suspect and this may be particularly so in this instance. Ultimately, in education, individual outcomes and performances are of primary importance. Group activities are simply used as a means toward

Table 18.2

Group-oriented approaches to the enhancement of individual learning in educational settings (Adapted from Slavin, 1983)

Task Structure	Group Rewards for Individual Learning	Group Rewards for a Group Product	Individual Rewards Following Group Involvement
No Division of Labor is Possible in the Group Task.	Each person carries out the same task in the group and individual scores are summed to produce a group score; e.g., team bowling.	Each person carries out the same task in the group. A single group product is produced; e.g., rowing teams.	Each person carries out the same task in the group and individual score are based on individual achievement; e.g., a group of wrestlers in the same weight class training for the Olympics.
A Division of Labor is Possible in the Group Task.	Each person becomes expert in one component of the task and individual scores are summed to produce a group score; e.g., college tennis	Each person becomes an expert in one component of the task. A single group product is produced; e.g., volleyball teams	Each person becomes an expert in one component of the task. Each person's score is based on personal achievement; e.g., members of a track team training for the Olympics

this end. In many sport situations, however, group outcomes are of primary importance. Individual activities are a means toward this end.

Traditionally, it has been believed that competition is a fundamental aspect of sport and physical activity. Also, traditionally it has also been held that competition is more effective for the learning and performance of sport skills. This isn't necessarily the case. A strong case can be made for cooperation from a performance perspective. As was pointed out above, high task interdependence, high task complexity, and large groups favor the use of a cooperative rather than a competitive approach. Task interdependence is a characteristic of many sports—basketball, soccer, ice and field hockey, volleyball, and so on. Similarly, every sport is complex for a young athlete who is trying to master a new skill. Finally, there are very few sport groups that consist of less than six members. There are situations where competition may be more effective but these should be identified before it is automatically assumed that competition is always superior.

Chapter Nineteen

GROUP INTERACTION AND COMMUNICATION

> The stories about big-time trades, in which a superstar joins another superstar, always raise the question of "chemistry." How will the superstars react to each other? Will one ball be enough? One stretch limo? One whatever. In this case, with three superstars involved, with the noisiest one joining the residents who already have won a championship together, the questions of chemistry are even more obvious.
>
> "What I think we have now are three great leaders," [coach Rudy] Tomjanovich says. "We have Hakeem [Olajuwon], who is not afraid to speak his mind. We have Clyde [Drexler], who is a little more vocal, and then we have Charles [Barkley], who is an outspoken person, who likes the attention. I think it all works positively."
> (Montville, 1996b, p. 46)

The scenario represented in the quote used to introduce this chapter is familiar to anyone who has ever been involved in a group activity. Individual group members have different needs, attitudes, personalities, and interests and this is reflected through group interaction and communication. In the quote, Rudy Tomjanovich, coach of the NBA Houston Rockets, described the different communication patterns of his three leaders. All were different but this did not disrupt the chemistry on the team.

Interaction and communication are essential in order for the group to come to an understanding about itself and where it is going. For this reason, these processes are fundamental to the development and maintenance of group structure. They also play a role in other group processes, including group goal setting, cooperation and competition, and the development of group task and social cohesion. Communication is also fundamental to effective team performance—as the quote in Box 19.1 illustrates. A lack of communication between two Los Angeles Lakers' basketball players led to a breakdown at a critical period in the game. In short, interaction, communication, and group decision-making are important, primary group processes (see Illustration 19.1). The focus of this chapter is on different aspects of group interaction and communication.

Box 19.1
Examples of the nature of group communication in sport

Focus	Illustration
The role of communication in team performance	A few seconds before the final buzzer, two [LA] Lakers failed to communicate on a simple switch. Mike Dunleavy, a Houston guard with a great shooting touch, got left wide open, and sank a jump shot that put the Rockets one point ahead. (Riley, 1993, p. 51)
Communication as a nonverbal process	I remember Olympic villages that were magical. I recall a spirit of mutual admiration and a unique level of communication, despite language barriers. Hands would fly, bodies would dance, and songs and jokes would make the village electric with music and laughter. (Karolyi & Richardson, 1994, p. 216)
Improved communication through team socialization	This is one of the best teams we have ever had in terms of camaraderie and team chemistry . . . At the beginning of the year, the make-up of the team was challenged with eleven freshman making the roster. As the season progressed, the chemistry of the team became real tight, we became more and more of a family, almost like a brotherhood. The team did everything together, they would eat together, socialize together, pick each other up in practice, genuinely ask how each other is doing, and, in general, interact like a close knit family. (Yukelson, 1997, p. 85)

Group Communication

There appears to be no true consensus among researchers on the definition of communication. For instance, Dance and Larson (1976) surveyed a variety of journals and publications from a diversity of fields and found 126 different definitions. Webster's dictionary refers to communication as "a giving or exchanging of information, messages, etc." (1971, p. 126). Although it is often assumed that communication is a verbal process, the giving or exchanging of information can be expressed in many different ways—verbal, nonverbal, written, and visual. In Box 19.1, the United States Olympic gymnastics coach, Bela Karolyi, recounts how Olympic athletes were able to communicate despite the presence of language barriers.

Heterogeneity versus Homogeneity and Communication

Communication in groups is influenced by variability in the personal characteristics of the group members. The nature and extent of that influence depends on the characteristics in which the group members are similar or different. Heterogeneity among individuals in a group may be present in either of two important dimensions (Burgoon, Heston, & McCroskey, 1974). One of these is represented by non-changeable or slowly changing

Illustration 19.1. Lack of communication can reduce team performance

("static") characteristics, such as age, sex, religion, language, culture, and educational attainment. The second dimension is represented by more changeable, ("dynamic") characteristics, such as attitudes, knowledge, and beliefs.

A group is heterogeneous to the degree that differences in these static and dynamic characteristics are present. Thus, for example, a sport team that contains individuals from different cultural backgrounds who speak different languages and practice different religions would be highly heterogeneous.

Principles of Communication

There are three principles of group communication that are related to the concepts of homogeneity and heterogeneity (Burgoon, Heston, & McCroskey, 1974). The first is that *communication patterns are normally homogeneous*; individuals tend to communicate with others who are similar to them in attitudes and characteristics. Members of a university basketball team tend to communicate most frequently and easily with other team members, gymnasts with other gymnasts, and so on.

The second principle is that *communication is more effective among people who are homogeneous*. The more that individuals are alike as team members, the greater is the likelihood that they will share common meanings in language, common motives, and common values. It is evident that individuals who share a common culture share idiosyncrasies in speech. The use of "eh" by Canadians, "mate" by Australians, and "you all" by Americans from the southern United States helps to illustrate this point. How difficult would it be for Sherlock Holmes to establish the country of origin for the three individuals in this conversation?

A: "It's sure nice to see you all again."
B: "It looks like the instructor is late, eh?"
C: "She'll be right mate!"

The third principle is that *effective communication leads to increased homogeneity* in dynamic characteristics—attitudes, knowledge, and beliefs. This reflects the cyclical relationship of communication and homogeneity. Homogeneity increases the likelihood that communication will occur and that communication will be effective. In turn, communication increases the likelihood that the individuals involved will adopt similar attitudes and beliefs and share common perceptions. (Burgoon, Heston, & McCroskey, 1974). Birds of a feather really do seem to flock together insofar as communication is concerned.

A note of caution is also necessary. As Donelson Forsyth (1983) noted, "The ability to communicate with others is a mixed blessing" (p.161). Communication can be used by the sender to exchange information or create misunderstandings, to reduce conflicts or accelerate the growth of problems, to test new ideas or produce conformity.

There are also a number of problems that can arise in the processing of information by the receiver (Campbell, 1958, in Forsyth, 1983). These include *leveling,* whereby a communication is reduced and simplified, *ordering,* in which the beginning and the end of a communication are better retained than the middle portion, *sharpening,* in which a communication is reinterpreted by emphasizing some components and deemphasizing others, and *assimilating,* in which the meaning of a communication is shifted so that it matches a previous important message.

Although the three principles of communication are undoubtedly in operation and have relevance in sport teams, it is not clear how they influence team effectiveness. There is no empirical evidence available and the anecdotal accounts are varied. The complexity of the homogeneity-group effectiveness relationship was highlighted in the quote by Ken Dryden presented in Chapter 4. Dryden, a former goaltender, pointed out that the Montreal Canadiens, like most sport teams, were heterogeneous in static and dynamic characteristics. That is, differences were present among team members in culture and language, age, religion, ability, educational attainment, and personality. According to Dryden, at first glance, these differences weren't evident; the Canadiens seemed perfectly compatible personally and professionally. He pointed out, however, that a second glance showed that heterogeneity was present along Anglophone versus Francophone lines and it influenced communication. And, finally, Dryden stated that a third glance showed that no divisions existed because the differences that were present were unconscious, unintended, unnoticed, and irrelevant to the team.

Other sport teams have not been as fortunate; the heterogeneity that was present in static and dynamic characteristics became significant. Dave Meggyesy (1971), in his book, *Out of Their League,* recalled how racial tensions on the 1967 St. Louis Cardinals eventually destroyed the fabric of the group:

> *In 1967, the racial tension that I'd seen simmering for years on the Cardinals finally reached the boiling point. What I saw around the locker room made me expect a race war at any moment. I was first introduced to racism on the team . . . in my rookie year, 1962; room assignments, wings of the dormitory, and the dining room were all segregated. In the half hour between the end of practice and dinner, all the white ball players would head up to the town's only bar, the Lantern. I never saw a black football player in the Lantern at any time during my first five years with the team . . . Racism was not a matter of individual quirks in the St. Louis organization; it was part of the institution . . . Near the end of the 1967 season,*

these tensions had become so intense that there was almost no communication between black and white ball players. It was a miracle we weren't forced to field two separate teams. (pp. 167-171)

The members of the Canadiens were able to overcome, ignore, or work around their differences; the members of the Cardinals were not. The Canadiens were remarkably successful, as the six Stanley Cup Championships won while Dryden was their goaltender clearly show. The Cardinals were highly unsuccessful. What isn't clear is what came first, the attitude that the heterogeneity that was present in the group wasn't important or the team's success. Did increased communication contribute to a reduction in the importance attached to the heterogeneity among members and, subsequently, to team success? Or, did team success contribute to a reduction in the importance attached to the heterogeneity among members, which led to increased communication? Probably both causal relationships were in operation but there has not been any direct test of this supposition.

Communication in Sport Teams

In an effort to better examine and understand team interaction and communication in sport groups, Philip Sullivan and Deborah Feltz (2003) developed the Scale for Effective Communication in Sports Teams (SECTS). This questionnaire assesses four distinct components of verbal and non-verbal communication among team members. One dimension, referred to as *acceptance,* reflects communication practices that promote inclusion and support of team members such as honesty and openness in discussions. A second dimension, *distinctiveness*, refers to verbal and non-verbal communications promoting the "we" mentality of the group. Sullivan and Feltz included the use of nicknames, slang, and gestures understood only by group members as indicative of this dimension.

Positive and negative conflict, the remaining two dimensions, obviously represent quite opposing types of communication. *Positive conflict* communications represent the non-emotional and constructive attempts to rectify problems within the group. Examples might include the ability to compromise and willingness to engage in open discussion. Communicating in a destructive fashion to deal with problems (e.g., shouting, losing temper, etc.) is reflective of the *negative conflict* dimension.

The Sullivan and Feltz approach represents the first attempt at a comprehensive conceptualization of communication for sport teams and, as such, has not yet been examined extensively in relation to other variables. It seems intuitive that developing team members' abilities to communicate in an accepting, positive fashion, while promoting distinctiveness and reducing negative interaction will result in greater integration of athletes and better team performance. Interestingly, however, in some competitive environments the use of negative conflict can be viewed in a positive manner, as the following quote illustrates:

Even as Duke was winning its second straight NCAA title, in 1992, Christian Laettner mocked Bobby Hurley, sneered at Grant Hill and hazed Cherokee Parks. They each responded on the court by doing something to repudiate Laettner's harsh judgment of them. "When Laettner yelled at somebody, people said, 'Oh, they have friction,'" says Blue Devil coach Mike Krzyzewski. "Baloney. We had communication. Friction is when no one says anything." (Wolff & Spear, 1995, p.35)

Understanding effective methods to improve communication that matches the various personalities and goals of the team is an important step.

Improving Communication

Alvin Zander (1982) and David Yukelson (1993) have offered a number of practical solutions on how to improve communication among team members. One is to insure that team members know each other's duties and responsibilities. Providing opportunities to socialize also helps team members become comfortable with each other (see Box 19.1). The physical environment also is important. Consequently, the practice and dressing room areas should be made conducive to easy interchange by insuring physical proximity. Each team member should be shown that his/her contributions are valuable to the team. If team members are friendly, any differences of opinion should be made evident in order to promote discussion and communication. Team members should be actively encouraged to modify their ideas and compromise if differences have caused conflict. Finally, cooperation should be promoted and rivalry reduced by emphasizing the group and deemphasizing personal goals and objectives.

Group Communication as a Source of Motivation

Interaction and communication among members of task-oriented groups also serves to facilitate group motivation. This was demonstrated through an analysis of the group dynamics in a mountain climbing team which was conducted by Richard Emerson (1966) during the 1963 American expedition to Mount Everest. The team consisted of Western mountaineers and a support group.

When the climb was initially planned, the objective was to ascend Everest by a route known as the South Col. However, subsequently, as the team began its initial approach, some members put pressure on the group to attempt the climb by way of a more difficult and uncertain route known as the West Ridge. This interest in the West Ridge route developed into what Emerson referred to as a "pathological motivation" (p. 219).

In order to resolve the increasing conflict over the group's route (goal), it was agreed to subdivide the expedition into two primary objectives: the South Col route and the West Ridge route. Three separate units then evolved: a South Col team with 5 participants, a West Ridge team with 5 participants (one was killed in an ice-avalanche early in the climb), and a Peripheral South Col team in various roles marginal to the actual climb.

Emerson collected data over a period of 92 days: the duration of time it took the West Ridge team to reach the summit. The South Col team completed their phase of the expedition and reached the summit after 70 days. Data collection had to be as unobtrusive as possible, so Emerson used four approaches. One approach consisted of providing each subject with a diary for personal and research use. Prepared questions were woven into the diary for the regular recording of cognitions and feelings. Some questions appeared daily (e.g., "Tomorrow I (should, will, would like to . . .")), others every second, fourth, or eighth day. Another approach involved the use of stimulus statements. Emerson, as a participant observer, introduced "stimulus-statements" into his natural discussion with participants and then recorded whether the feedback he received was optimistic or pessimistic in nature. Using a tape recorder, Emerson also recorded group discussions, including planning sessions, bull sessions, and reconnaissance meetings. Finally, all inter-camp radio communications were automatically recorded on tape.

Emerson felt that uncertainty about goal outcome is the crucial variable in maintaining goal-directed behavior (i.e., goal striving). Consequently, he proposed that the primary function of communication in task-oriented groups is to sustain uncertainty in order to maintain group motivation at a high level. There was considerable support for this proposal. In all task communications, there was an overwhelming tendency for the reply to both negative and positive stimulus statements to be pessimistic in nature. This is summarized in Table 19.1. Thus, for example, a positive suggestion such as "the weather is ideal for making good progress" would be reacted to with a negative reply such as "but we haven't capitalized on it very well." Conversely, a negative suggestion such as "the weather hasn't been very good for making progress" would be reacted to with a negative reply such as "and it will probably get worse." In both cases, the negative reply served a practical purpose—to sustain uncertainty in the group and help it maintain high motivation in reference to its goal.

As Table 19.1 shows, there was one exception to this pattern of generally negative feedback—when the South Col team communicated about the West Ridge team. The South Col team had very little motivation for the West Ridge objective and they perceived that this aspect of the expedition was likely to fail. When members of the South Col team were presented with pessimistic stimulus statements about the West Ridge goal, there was an overwhelming tendency to respond positively.

It was suggested by Emerson that the general tendency to respond negatively in order to sustain uncertainty and motivation occurs when individuals are involved in collaborative problem-solving requiring coordination and cooperation. The West Ridge goal was seen as a threat to the South Col goal—the original objective that remained the principal goal for the expedition-as-a-whole. Members of both the West Ridge team and the South Col team considered the South Col goal important and attempted to sustain high motivation for it by responding pessimistically. Similarly, the West Ridge team considered the

Table 19.1

Communication feedback to optimistic and pessimistic stimulus statements about goals under varying conditions of uncertainty and motivation (Adapted from Emerson, 1966)

Prevailing Condition					
Group	Goal	Outcome	Motivation	Stimulus	Negative Feedback (%)
West Ridge	West Ridge	Outcome Uncertain	Very High	Optimistic	84.2%
				Pessimistic	81.6%
West Ridge	South Col	Success Likely	High	Optimistic	75.0%
				Pessimistic	57.9%
South Col	South Col	Success Likely	Very High	Optimistic	83.3%
				Pessimistic	62.5%
South Col	West Ridge	Failure Likely	Low	Optimistic	84.6%
				Pessimistic	27.3%

West Ridge goal important and attempted to sustain high motivation for it by responding pessimistically. But, the South Col team was not supportive of the West Ridge goal and, therefore, responded in a manner not designed to sustain high motivation.

Group Decision Making

Group Polarization

Group polarization is the term used to represent the shift that occurs in the attitudes of individual members following group interactions and communication. This shift leads to a riskier position if the initial tendency was toward moderate risk, or to a more conservative position if the initial tendency was toward caution (see Figure 19.1). Thus, for example, two noon-hour joggers privately might be mildly tempted to enter a marathon. If they sat down together to discuss the pros and cons, group polarization would occur if they decided to enter the marathon.

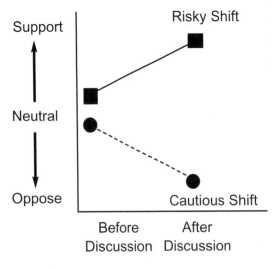

Figure 19.1. The group-polarization hypothesis

Much of the early research in the area of group polarization centered around an attempt to understand the risky shift phenomenon—the tendency for groups to adopt riskier positions than individuals. A major contribution to this research came from Nathan Kogan and Michael Wallach, who developed the *Choice Dilemma Inventory.* (Kogan & Wallach, 1964). This inventory consists of 12 real-life dilemmas in which a central character is confronted with a choice between two alternatives. One is risky; the other more conservative. The decision that a subject (or group) must come to is what advice to give this central character. One of the dilemmas that deal with a sport situation is as follows:

> *Mr. D. is the captain of College X's football team. College X is playing its traditional rival, College Y, in the final game of the season. The game is in its final seconds, and Mr. D's team, College X, is behind in the score. College X has time to run one more play. Mr. D., the captain, must decide whether it would be best to settle for a tie score with a play which would be almost certain to work or, on the other hand, should he try a more complicated and risky play which could bring victory if it succeeded, but defeat if not.*
>
> *Imagine that you are advising Mr. D. Listed below are several probabilities or odds that the risky play will work. Please check the lowest probability that you would consider acceptable for the risky play to be attempted. (Kogan & Wallach, 1964, p. 257)*

Participants in the role of an advisor are required to select the minimum probable level for success that would lead them to advise the central character to take the riskier but more attractive alternative. In the Choice Dilemma Inventory, the options are presented on a scale varying from 1 chance in 10 of being successful to 10 chances in 10 of being successful. In order to examine the effect of the group influence on decision-making, participants initially respond to the 12 problems independently. After this, the participants are put into a group situation where the issues are discussed and then a group decision is reached.

How realistic are the dilemmas and the decisions? Interestingly, on New Year's Day in 1988, life imitated science. In the Sugar Bowl, the Auburn Tigers, trailing 16-13, had the ball on the Syracuse Orangemen's 13 yard-line with four seconds left in the game. Auburn's coach, Pat Dye, was faced the same dilemma as Mr. D, the Kogan and Wallach character—kick a field goal for a tie or run a play from scrimmage in an attempt to win. Dye chose to kick. And, it was successful. Sportswriter Douglas Looney described the situation following the game:

> *Stoney-faced and sullen, Auburn coach Pat Dye tried to defend his non-sporting decision to play for a tie against undefeated Syracuse in the Sugar Bowl: "My decision was not to get beat." Not to get beat? No coach worth his whistle ought to think like this . . .*
>
> *"Our guys were not real happy," said [Kicker Win] Lyle. "They really didn't like it when I went out there. They were screaming that they wanted to go for the touchdown . . . Afterward, the more Syracuse coach Dick MacPherson thought about what had happened, the madder he got. "Why didn't Dye ask his players what they wanted to do?" he said, fuming. Obviously, coaches don't ask their players to make such decisions, but MacPherson was angry beyond logic. (Looney, 1988, p.22)*

From the accounts presented, it seems apparent that the Auburn players endorsed the riskier alternative. If they had been questioned as a group, they probably would have advocated trying for the touchdown and a win. However, what would their response have been if they had been questioned in private? How would each player have advised Dye if he had talked to his coach in a one-on-one situation?

When Wallach, Kogan, and Bem (1962) examined these questions in an experimental situation, they found that individuals are much more prepared to take chances when they are in a group than when they are alone. As Table 19.2 shows, the group score for risk for males and females is 9.4% greater than the average individual response. Thus, (a) if Pat Dye had discussed the issues with his coaching staff and/or his players, (b) if he and they had been slightly inclined to gamble, and (c) the ultimate decision had been voted on by the total group, then the chances of Auburn taking a gamble would have increased by 9.4%. Wallach and his colleagues also found that when individual judgments are collected after the group discussion, males show a 10.4% increase in endorsement for risk; females, an 8.2% increase. So there's an even greater chance that Dye would have taken the gamble following a discussion even if he had made the decision alone. Finally, as Table 19.2 shows, when individual judgments (in the case of males only) are delayed and collected from two to six weeks later, the tendency toward risk increases even more. It's probably of

Table 19.2
Shifts in the level of risk perceived to be
acceptable alone versus in a group situation
(Adapted from Wallach, Kogan, & Bem, 1962)

Comparisons	Shift Toward Greater Risk (%)	
	Males	Females
Individual Pretest vs. Group Decision	9.4%	9.4%
Individual Pretest vs. Individual Posttest	10.4%	8.2%
Individual Pretest vs. Individual Delayed Posttest	12.2%	—

little value to know that if the issues had been discussed and then Pat Dye had had six weeks to make a decision, there's a 12.3% greater chance that he would have chosen to run a play rather than kick a field goal.

It was pointed out earlier that group discussions increase the likelihood of a risky shift if the members in the group are initially predisposed toward some risk. During the 1960s, 1970s, and 1980s, literally hundreds of studies on attitudes, values, judgments, cognitions, and perceptions have shown that this is the case (e.g., Myers, 1982). At the same time, however, numerous studies have also shown that there were instances when the opposite process occurred. That is, if the members in a group are initially predisposed toward caution, a cautious shift occurs. Thus, if Dye and his coaching staff had privately believed that the conservative option of kicking was the best, then any discussion that followed would have simply strengthened that belief. In short, group discussions seem to produce group polarization—the tendency to adopt a more extreme position (either risky or cautious) than the one initially held by the individual members. The direction of movement toward either extreme depends upon what point-of-view was initially dominant.

Explanations for Group Polarization

A number of overlapping explanations have been advanced to account for group polarization effects (Pruitt, 1971). These can be summarized into four general explanations: diffusion of responsibility, leadership, persuasive arguments, and social comparison (see Table 19.3).

The basis for the *diffusion of responsibility* explanation is the fact that, in groups, responsibility for a decision can be shared. When individuals operate alone, it cannot. All people have some anxiety about the potential negative consequences of an unfavorable outcome emanating from an incorrect decision. When an individual arrives at a decision alone, he or she must assume full responsibility for the consequences. But, when a decision is made in concert with others, the responsibilities are diffused among all of the members of the group.

A number of *leadership* theories have also emerged in which the qualities of the dominant individuals in the group discussion are highlighted. In these explanations, it is

Table 19.3
Explanations advanced to account for
the group polarization effects in
decision making (Adapted from Pruitt, 1971)

Theory	Description
Diffusion of Responsibility	The responsibility for negative consequences can be diffused among all of the members of the group.
Leadership	Dominant individuals, because of their personal traits, more extreme views, confidence, or assertiveness, are more influential and persuasive in the group.
Persuasive Arguments	The group discussion produces relevant arguments about the utility or merits of a position.
Social Comparison	The group discussion brings out the dominant values in the group. Individuals compare themselves against that standard and adopt a position which is at least as risky or as cautious.

proposed that group leaders, either because of their personal traits (e.g., high need for risk), more extreme views, greater confidence, or greater assertiveness, are more influential and persuasive in the group.

In the *social comparisons* approach, it is assumed that the energy behind the shift is the presence of some commonly held human values (Pruitt, 1971). Thus, if the majority of group members privately endorse (value) a risky alternative, that perspective will be intensified within the group discussions. Conversely, if the majority privately values a cautious position, group discussions will serve to increase the attractiveness of the cautious perspective.

The basis for the *persuasive arguments* approach is the belief that individuals try to process information in a logical, rational fashion. They compare their views with the views of other group members; they weigh the evidence, and then go with the best option (Isenberg, 1986). In a group discussion, the majority of good arguments are generally advanced in favor of the dominant position—which might be for caution or for risk. Group members judge this information and shift toward greater endorsement of that position.

Although there has been some level of support for all of these explanations, historically the latter two approaches (social comparison and persuasive arguments) have been considered to offer the best explanation for group polarization effects. The social comparison approach begins with the assumption that all people have a desire to present themselves well and be perceived in a socially desirable way. As a consequence, when an individual is faced with a decision, he or she attempts to determine what view others might hold. After this comparison is made between the position held by others and by the self, the individual further endorses his/her initial decision. This endorsement is the same or slightly more extreme (for either risk or for caution depending upon the problem) than is considered to be typical of other individuals in the group. In the group discussion that follows, direct social comparison occurs. When it becomes apparent through the discussion that others also hold similar views, there is a shift in the direction represented by the greater social value.

According to the persuasive arguments approach, "the dominant value or values in a decision problem elicit persuasive arguments in group discussion that convince group members to move further in the direction of these values" (Pruitt, 1971, p. 354). Thus, a coach faced with a difficult decision will draw on past experiences and weigh the pros and cons of both options. The number and the persuasiveness of these experiences will contribute to an initial impression. Then, when the issue is discussed in a group setting with the team or other coaches, persuasive arguments in favor of the initial impression cause a further shift.

Researchers continue to test the relative merits of the persuasive arguments and social comparison approaches, but increasingly scholars are developing explanations that bridge them (Bettenhausen, 1991). A meta-analysis of 21 studies published between 1974 and 1982 (Isenberg, 1986) concluded that social comparison and persuasive arguments approaches occur in combination to produce group polarization, but the persuasive argument effects tend to be larger. Thus, social comparison and persuasive argument approaches provide complementary, rather than alternative, explanations of group polarization.

Groupthink

The Nature of Groupthink

A major weakness with decision-making in groups has been the tendency for group members to exert and respond to normative pressure rather than to make a decision based on factual information (Miranda, 1994). Social psychologist Irving Janis (1972, 1982) introduced the term *groupthink* to represent this weakness. He defined groupthink as "a mode of thinking that people engage in when they are deeply involved in a cohesive-ingroup, when members' strivings for unanimity override their motivation to realistically appraise alternative courses of action" (p. 8).

The catalyst for Janis' work was his interest in exploring the reasons behind some well-known, disastrous group decisions—the Bay of Pigs invasion, the inadequate defense of Pearl Harbor prior to World War II, and the escalation of the Vietnam War (see Box 19.2). There are some close parallels between the process of group polarization and the process of groupthink. In groupthink, as in group polarization, "members show interest in facts and opinions that support their initially preferred policy and take up time in their meetings to discuss them, but they ignore facts and opinions that do not support their initially preferred policy" (Janis, 1972, p. 10).

Symptoms of Groupthink

Janis identified eight symptoms of groupthink. These are presented in Table 19.4. This table also contains an example to show how this phenomenon might occur in sport situations. The sport example used is the 1972 hockey series between Canada and the U.S.S.R. This series represented the first meeting between North American professionals and European amateurs and the anticipation and excitement were high. The U.S.S.R. had

| | Box 19.2 |
| | *Examples of groupthink* |

Example	Anecdote
Pearl Harbor	In the weeks before the 1941 Pearl Harbor attack, military commanders in Hawaii were continually informed about Japan's preparations for attack. Then military intelligence lost radio contact with Japanese aircraft carriers, which had begun flying toward Hawaii. Air reconnaissance could have sited the carriers or provided a warning of the impending attack. But the complacent commanders decided against such precautions. Thus, no alert was sounded until the Japanese were directly attacking the defenseless ships and airfields.
The Bay of Pigs Invasion	On April 17, 1961, 1,400 Cuban exiles landed at the Bay of Pigs in Cuba. Their mission was to establish a beachhead and to join Cuban rebels in the Escambray Mountains. Together these forces were expected to unite the Cuban people in a rebellion to overthrow Castro. The exiles were armed by the United States. Their mission had been planned by one of the best intelligence organizations in the world, the Central Intelligence Agency (CIA), and approved by President John F. Kennedy. Despite all of these advantages, the whole plan was a disaster. Castro's army was well prepared for the invasion; there was little discontent among the Cuban people; and 80 miles of dense swamp separated the Bay of Pigs from the Escambray Mountains. Nearly all of the invaders were soon killed or captured. The United States was humiliated and Cuba allied itself even closer to the U.S.S.R.
The Vietnam War	President Lyndon Johnson and his "Tuesday lunch group" of policy advisers devised the Vietnam war based on the belief that U.S. aerial bombardment and search and destroy missions would bring North Vietnam to peace while maintaining the support of South Vietnam. This decision was made despite warnings from government intelligence experts. The Vietnam war caused 56,500 American deaths and more than 1 million Vietnamese deaths, cost Johnson his presidency, and created huge budget deficits.

assumed international dominance in Olympic and World Cup competitions in a sport that most Canadians viewed chauvinistically. Generally, the prevailing mood prior to the series was that now that Canada was able to use her best players she would be able to demonstrate quite clearly who was superior. Subsequent events proved otherwise. Jack Ludwig (1972), in his book *Hockey Night in Moscow*, clearly shows how the process of groupthink developed in the preparation of Team Canada.

An *illusion of invulnerability* was created when preliminary reports confirmed the generally held expectation that the NHL was decidedly superior. Although some evidence

Table 19.4
The symptoms of groupthink
(The list of symptoms are from Janis, 1972.
The illustrations are from Ludwig, 1972.)

Symptom	Description	Illustration
Illusion of invulnerability	A highly optimistic picture is presented to the group.	[Scouts] brought back only good news, nothing calculated to get Team Canada stampeding into midnight practice sessions. Only one player on the USSR could make the NHL. (p. 230)
Collective efforts to rationalize	Alternate opinions and warnings are ignored.	I myself, watching the practices, saw everything . . . [but] discounted what I saw . . . my blindness to what was before my eyes made me ignore what was, later, so painfully obvious. (p. 23)
Unquestioned belief in the group's inherent morality	The group is assumed to possess an inherent superiority over the opposition.	I wouldn't have bet on the Russians if somebody had offered odds of 100-1. I would have assumed, as I think most Canadians did, that people who don't speak the Queen's English can hardly be expected to keep up with those that do. (p. 24)
Stereotyped views of the opposition	The opposition is viewed in stereotypical terms.	Their defensemen were slow, their pass patterns were slower, their attack telegraphed and easily broken up by the NHL players who, unlike athletes in an unfree society like the USSR, are taught to think for themselves. (p. 23)

was available that the Russian team was talented, this was discounted or ignored—as Janis would say, there was a *collective effort to rationalize.* The Ludwig quotation used in Table 19.4, which illustrates an *unquestioned belief in the group's inherent morality,* was obviously written tongue-in-cheek but it does reflect the prevailing sentiment at that time. An important aspect of groupthink is the implicit belief that "goodness is on our side." Consistent with this perspective is the use of *stereotyped views to characterize the opposition.* The presence of these stereotypes contributes to an expectation that the opposition's responses can be readily predicted and countered.

These initial four symptoms are generally related to the development of a positive appraisal of the relative strengths and merits of the group with respect to its opposition. The group also works toward the achievement of consensus among its membership, a process associated with the next four symptoms.

Alternate perspectives are discouraged as the group applies *direct pressures to conform* on its members. At the same time, members engage in *self-censorship* in order to produce a unanimous group perspective. Ultimately, opposition to the group's decision is

Table 19.4 (continued)

Symptom	Description	Illustration
Direct pressures to conform	Pressure is brought to bear against members who present alternative views.	Isn't it time the media laid off the NHL, who, through the cooperation of the US clubs, made it possible to have the greatest hockey players ever assembled represent Canada. (Conn Smythe, in Ludwig, 1972, p. 16)
Self censorship of deviations	Members censor themselves in order to produce a unanimous group position.	Experts, like ex-hockey star . . . Aggie Kukulowicz, made sharp observations about how the Russians might handle Team Canada, and then, like a scientist refusing to believe the results of an experiment because the results don't fit in with his hypotheses, scrapped his observations and came out for Team Canada "in eight straight." (p. 24)
Shared illusions of unanimity	Members believe that the group position is universally shared.	We concluded what we *had* to conclude and remain faithful to . . . the icy nights under a street light in Hockeyland, Canada, that the *drill* was on the Russian side, the *talent* with Team Canada. (p. 26)
Emergence of self-appointed mindguards	Members protect the group from adverse information.	Any player good enough to make the NHL . . . was NHL stuff, and that, like beauty being truth and truth being beauty, was all there was to know, and all one needed to know. (pp. 26-27)

virtually eliminated and there is a *shared illusion of unanimity*. Although individual members may have private misgivings, public proclamations suggest otherwise. And, finally, there is *emergence of self-appointed mindguards:* group members who suppress any dissenting views in order to preserve group solidarity.

Antecedents of Groupthink

Groupthink, however, does not always occur in group decision making. Janis (1982) has suggested that there are several antecedent conditions which increase the probability that groupthink will occur (see Figure 19.2). First, *high levels of cohesion* would make the group more susceptible to pressures toward conformity and facilitate the occurrence of groupthink. However, research by Bernthal and Insko (1993) showed that groups with high social cohesion were more likely to experience groupthink than were groups high in task cohesion. Thus, promoting a task orientation during decision making, rather than a social orientation, might diffuse the danger of groupthink in highly cohesive groups.

Second, groups whose members have very weak ties with and awareness of external groups are more vulnerable to groupthink. Janis (1982) indicated that *insulated groups*

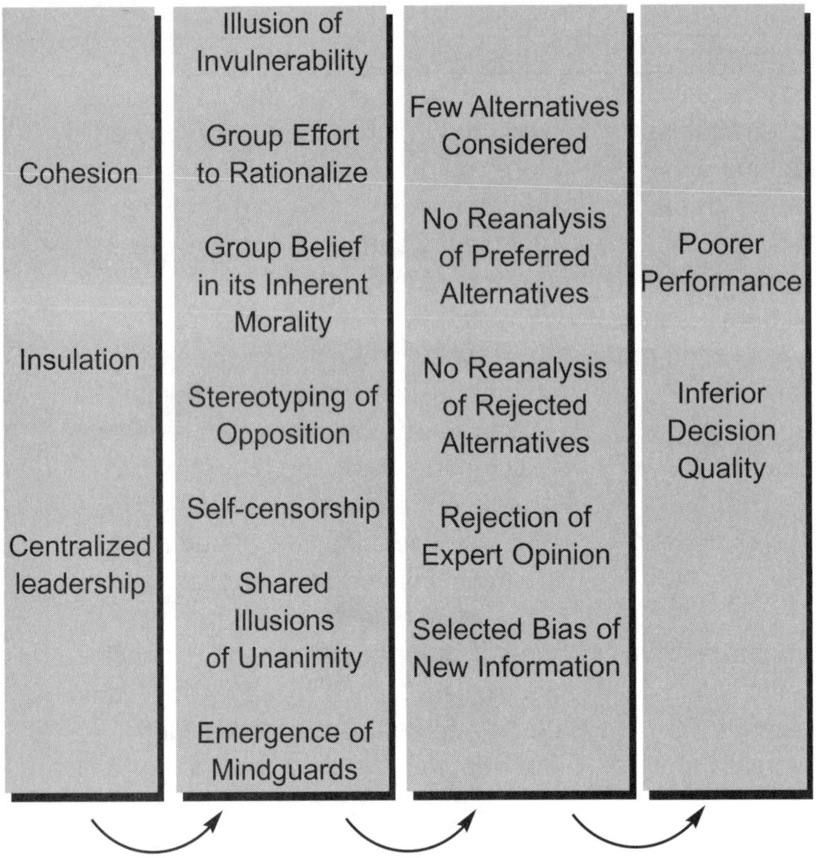

| Cohesion

Insulation

Centralized leadership | Illusion of Invulnerability

Group Effort to Rationalize

Group Belief in its Inherent Morality

Stereotyping of Opposition

Self-censorship

Shared Illusions of Unanimity

Emergence of Mindguards | Few Alternatives Considered

No Reanalysis of Preferred Alternatives

No Reanalysis of Rejected Alternatives

Rejection of Expert Opinion

Selected Bias of New Information | Poorer Performance

Inferior Decision Quality |

Figure 19.2. A model for groupthink
(Adapted from Janis, 1972)

experience a feeling of invulnerability and tend to consult less frequently with external experts.

Third, a *directive (i.e., autocratic) leadership style*, where the leaders actively advocate the adoption of their favored solution, is conducive to the development of groupthink. With an open (i.e., democratic) style, leaders withhold their personal opinions, solicit input on the pros and cons of alternate positions, encourage meetings when they are absent, and welcome healthy criticism. The following is an example of open style leadership used by Lou Whittaker, a world famous rock climber, who led the first mountaineering team to reach the summit of the world's tallest mountain, Mt. Everest:

> It is important to listen, even when you feel certain you are correct. One time, we wasted eight days waiting for the snows to settle, but I had been in a few avalanches so I had more experience than those who hadn't been in avalanches. I dug a lot of people out, so I could say, "This is a slope that we could lose our whole party on. I think we should turn around." But instead of saying, "We should turn around," I say, "I think we should turn around," and then we would talk it over. That's an example of trying to get the best out of everybody. We can get the best of everybody only when we keep valuing those around us, making sure that we don't have blind spots. (Fisher & Thomas, 1996, p. 144)

Fourth, groups composed of persons similar in backgrounds and ideologies are more prone to groupthink. The presence of *homogeneity* leads to the production of fewer solutions and a narrower group focus when examining issues of concern and evaluating solutions.

Finally, the *nature of the task* can influence the occurrence of groupthink. For example, groups involved in solving problems associated with a crisis situation are more likely to be victims of groupthink.

Preventing Groupthink

Some of the strategies that have been advanced to prevent groupthink are evident in Figure 19.2. Initially, a *large number of alternatives* should be solicited and then listed. The group has greater flexibility when more options are available. When the list of alternatives is completed, one or two will be obviously preferable to the group; others will be rejected almost immediately. The *preferred alternatives should be reconsidered*, examined for defects, and discussed in terms of the strategies necessary for implementation and possible problems associated with that implementation. At the same time, the *rejected alternatives should be reconsidered* and examined for any advantages that might have been overlooked previously.

Cohesive groups value consistency, conformity, and consensus. Consequently, another technique to prevent groupthink is to solicit the *input of experts* outside the group. These experts bring a different perspective and are not committed to the need for group solidarity. New information—facts, strategies, alternatives—may arise when the group is well along in its deliberations. Nonetheless, the desire for closure should be resisted and the new information scrutinized completely.

Finally, *contingency plans* should be developed for all of the possible outcomes of the decision. If a sport group decides after considerable discussion to introduce compulsory drug testing for everyone in the organization, it must also establish contingency plans (i.e., "if this . . . then this") for all the possibilities. What if some athletes, coaches, or administrative personnel refuse to be tested? What if an athlete, coach, or administrator tests positive? An attempt to develop contingencies also serves as a protection against groupthink.

Group Attributions

The Attributional Process

Individuals within groups also repeatedly come to decisions about events and people. They draw conclusions about motives and traits, causes and effects, and the assignment of credit and blame. The products of these decisions are referred to as attributions. The following quote from gymnastics coach Bela Karolyi illustrates the different attributes that could be given to account for success or failure across a variety of sports:

> *Some sports, like football and hockey, involve teammates. The responsibility for success or failure is shared. Then there are sports like cycling, skiing, or the bobsled. Once again success or failure is not solely the responsibility of the athlete. There is always something else that can be blamed. "It wasn't me that lacked preparation, it wasn't my mistake, my ski wasn't waxed correctly, my tire blew out, the snow wasn't fast enough." Then there is gymnastics. In gymnastics there is nothing but the athlete. If her body does not respond correctly then that is her fault. There is ultimate satisfaction because the one responsibility for the victory is the gymnast— no one else. (Karolyi & Richardson, 1994, p. 187)*

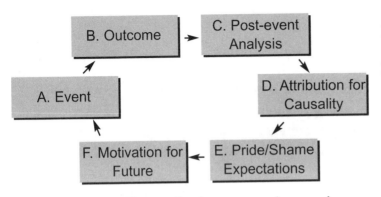

Figure 19.3. The attribution process in overview (Adapted from Carron, 1981b)

The general attributional process is illustrated in Figure 19.3. When an event—a competition between two teams—occurs (A), there is an outcome (B), such as a win or loss. Following this outcome, the athletes both publicly or privately analyze what happened (C) and then come to some conclusion (D) about the major causes or reasons. The attributions chosen contribute to feelings of pride or shame, as well as to expectations for subsequent performance (E). Thus, for example, if a team wins and its members primarily attribute that success to superior talent, feelings of pride develop, as well as an expectation that the team is likely to be successful in the future. In turn, these perspectives contribute to team motivation (F).

The attributional process has been described as *common sense* or *naive psychology* because all people have a natural need to understand the events and people around them. By understanding "why," the individual is better able to anticipate, plan, and even control future outcomes. Thus, in the example above, if the team had lost and its members had decided that this occurred because they were in poor physical condition, steps could be taken to rectify this problem. On the other hand, if they decided that the loss was due to poor coaching, absenteeism by key personnel, or poor motivation, different steps would be taken to rectify these problems.

General Nature of Attributions

Although an individual may select any of a number of different attributions (explanations) for why an event occurred, Bernard Weiner and his colleagues (1974, 1979; Weiner, Freeze, Kukla, Reed, Rest, & Rosenbaum, 1972) have proposed that attributions generally fall into three main dimensions that, in combination, produce eight different categories (see Table 19.5). One of these, the *locus of control* dimension, refers to whether the perceived cause is internal or external to the performer. Thus, a team that loses could feel that the primary reason was their own lack of ability (an internal attribute) or the superior ability of their

Table 19.5
Weiner's classifications scheme for causal attributions, with examples included in each cell

		Internal	External
	Stable	*Ability*	*Equipment*
Controllable	Unstable	*Effort*	*Practice Cancellation*
	Stable	*Size*	*Opponent's Ability*
Uncontrollable	Unstable	*Mood, Health*	*Luck, Weather, Officiating*

opponents (an external attribute). A second dimension in the Weiner model, *stability*, refers to whether the attribute is likely to change markedly over a relatively short period of time. Luck is an unstable cause for an outcome— there's no reason to believe that it will be a factor every time two teams compete. On the other hand, the skill of an opponent is a stable attribute because it could be expected to remain relatively constant. The third dimension is *controllability*. Some causes are under the direct control of the team or its opponents whereas others are not under anyone's control. Training, for example, can be controlled; the weather cannot.

It was pointed out above (see Figure 19.3 again) that when a particular cause for an outcome is established, it also leads to feelings of pride or shame and to the development of expectations for subsequent performance. The locus of control dimension, for example, has a major impact on feelings of pride/shame. If a team feels that personal factors, such as hustle, effort, and hard work, were the major reasons for a victory, it experiences pride and satisfaction. On the other hand, if it feels that a lack of hustle, effort, and hard work were the major reasons for a loss, it feels shame and dissatisfaction.

The stability dimension has its major influence on expectations for future performance. Similar outcomes are expected from causes that are stable (i.e., an opponent is highly competent), whereas a different outcome is expected from causes that are unstable (i.e., an opponent was extremely lucky).

Finally, the controllability dimension is associated with reactions to others. Praise, rewards, and/or approval are expected for controllable successes; punishment, criticism, and/or disapproval are expected for failures that are controllable.

Attributions in Achievement Situations

The research that has examined causal attributions in achievement situations has produced some reasonably consistent generalizations. One of these is that when individuals are working *independently on a laboratory task*, they have a tendency to take personal credit for success. And, when failure is experienced, they have a tendency to deemphasize the importance of personal factors and to shift the blame to external conditions (e.g., Gill & Gross, 1979; Roberts, 1978). In short, individuals working alone in laboratory situations adopt what are referred to as *self-serving* explanations for successes and failures (see Illustration 19.2).

A second generalization is that when individuals are working *collectively on a laboratory task*, there is a greater tendency for members of successful groups to assume greater responsibility for the group's performance than members of unsuccessful groups (e.g., Forsyth & Schlenker, 1977). Also, members of successful groups tend to view their contribution as greater than that of the average group member, while members of unsuccessful groups tend to view their contribution as less than that of the average group member (e.g., Wolosin, Sherman, & Till, 1973). In short, individuals working in groups in laboratory situations adopt self-serving explanations for group successes and failures.

Illustration 19.2. "It's not my fault."

The relevance of results from laboratory studies for real life situations was questioned, however, for maximizing the likelihood of finding a self-serving effect. Mullen and Riordan (1988) argued that laboratory achievement tasks "have tended to be novel or trivial, ambiguous, minimally involving from the subjects' point of view, to provide bogus and contrived, rather than actual and meaningful, performance outcomes, and to elicit unrealistically high performance expectancies from subjects" (p. 4).

Mullen and Riordan (1988) suggested that research from sport situations provides a better test of the attributional process. Sport competitions generally are not as novel and ambiguous as laboratory-based performance tasks. Second, sport competitions are usually perceived as more important and tend to generate more ego involvement. And third, the performance expectancies and outcomes in sport events are likely to be more meaningful and realistic.

In a meta-analytic review of 22 studies, Mullen and Riordan (1988) examined the self-serving attributional phenomenon in sport. In general, they found that self-serving attributions also occur in sport. That is, personal ability is used to a far greater extent as an explanation for successful performances than for unsuccessful performances. In this regard, success is generally considered to be a product of high ability but failure is not considered to be a product of low ability. Mullen and Riorden also found that after winning and losing, athletes assign a similar rating to the amount of effort they expended, the difficulty of their opponent, and the amount of luck (good versus bad) they experienced.

Team size also seems to have a moderating influence. Athletes who are members of larger teams are more self-serving in their perceptions of the reasons for success and failure. That is, as the size of a team increases, there is a greater tendency to assign more credit to personal ability following success and to assign lesser amounts of credit to personal ability following failure. This can be illustrated by the following two quotations:

"We won and my ability is a major reason why."

and

"We lost but it had very little to do with my ability."

Team-Enhancing Attributional Strategies

When athletes explain team outcomes, there is a tendency for members of successful teams to either share equally or give a disproportionate amount of credit to their teammates. Similarly, members of unsuccessful teams either share equally or take a disproportionate amount of the blame (e.g., Gill, 1980; Taylor & Doria, 1981). This pattern of causal attribution represents a *team-enhancing* rather than a self-enhancing perspective.

The differences between self-enhancing and team-enhancing strategies are summarized in Table 19.6. In the case of the latter, the team is emphasized and protected. With success, care is taken to insure that the credit is distributed equally among all of the team members and that the individual's personal role is deemphasized. With failure, scapegoating is avoided—responsibility is either distributed equally among all team members or each individual assumes a disproportionate amount of blame. This was the case in research conducted by Zaccaro, Peterson, and Walker (1987). They found that in sports with

Table 19.6

Team enhancing versus self-enhancing attributional strategies for team outcomes

Attributional Strategy	Team Success	Team Failure
Team-Enhancing	The role of the team is emphasized. Credit is distributed among other team members.	The role of the team or the self is emphasized. Responsibility is shared equally or the individual assumes a disproportionately greater amount of personal blame.
Self-Enhancing	The role of the self is emphasized. Greater personal credit is assumed for the outcome.	The role of others is emphasized. Greater responsibility is assigned to teammates.

increased interdependence of members' actions, self-attributions tended to decrease and team attributions tended to increase for successful performances.

Diane Gill (1980) has suggested that team-enhancing strategies are used in sport because a team norm is in operation—a norm which leads members to place the group's welfare first. Protecting teammates and the team after a failure and crediting them after a victory helps to insure the team unity is maintained.

Imamoglu (1991) has suggested that group studies on attributional tendencies indicate that individuals generally are concerned not only with maintaining a positive image but also with establishing satisfying relationships with other people. Individuals seem to compromise between their needs and tendencies to maintain a positive image and to also maintain smooth interpersonal relationships with other people.

Moderators of the Use of Team-Enhancing Strategies

Three factors have a moderating influence on the degree to which a team-enhancing versus a self-enhancing strategy is used in the assignment of the responsibility for team outcomes. One is team *cohesiveness*. When low-cohesive groups fail, a self-serving pattern of attributions is not unusual. Members feel minimal association with the group and, therefore, protect their own interests by attributing the majority of the blame to their teammates. When high-cohesive groups fail, however, members protect the solidarity of the group by adopting a team-enhancing pattern of attributions. They assume a level of responsibility for failure that is at least equal to the average group member. This pattern has been demonstrated both with ad hoc laboratory groups (e.g., Schlenker & Miller, 1977a) and with intact sport teams (Bird, Foster, & Maruyama, 1980; Brawley, Carron, & Widmeyer, 1987)

A second factor is the amount of *interaction and communication* present. Individuals who are not in groups but are working in highly cooperative situations involving considerable face-to-face interaction reduce the extent to which they use a self-serving strategy and increase the extent to which they use a team-enhancing strategy (Gill, 1980; Schlenker, Soraci, & McCarthy, 1976). Close associations and interactions lead to the development of a collective perspective. Consequently, an attributional pattern emerges that is also similar to that of a group rather than of an independent individual.

The *individual's role* in the group also has a moderating influence on the degree to which self-enhancing strategies are used. This was demonstrated in a study reported by Bruce Caine and Barry Schlenker (1979). Army cadets participated in 3-man groups on a problem-solving task. The written instructions provided prior to the experiment contributed to each participant's expectation that he was a group leader, a follower, or an equal. Bogus feedback was then provided after the problem-solving that led the individuals to perceive that their groups had either been successful or unsuccessful.

Individuals in the roles of followers and equals showed a self-serving pattern in their attributional analysis. They assumed a high level of personal responsibility if their group was successful but a much-reduced level if the group was unsuccessful. On the other hand, individuals in the role of group leaders assumed a high level of personal responsibility after both success and failure. The attributional analysis used after success was self-enhancing but the one after failure was team-enhancing.

Cognitive and Motivational Bases for Attributions

When it became obvious that different patterns were present in the types of attributions that were used following success and failure, attempts were made to understand why. One proposal advanced has been referred to as a *motivational or functional* model (Kelley, 1967). This approach is based on the assumption that individuals are motivated by a desire to maintain or enhance their self-esteem. Thus, success attributed to personal factors represents a self-enhancing strategy; failure attributed to external factors represents a self-protecting strategy.

A second explanation advanced has been referred to as a *cognitive* model because it focuses on the logical, rational basis for assigning responsibility (Miller & Ross, 1975). The cognitive model is based on the assumption that individuals logically search, analyze, and draw inferences from past experiences to arrive at the reason(s) why an outcome occurred. Thus, an athlete who has consistently been outstanding in sport all her life might be expected logically to attribute winning to personal factors (ability, effort) rather than to external factors (easy opponent, luck).

An experiment was conducted by Schlenker and Miller (1977b) in order to directly compare the motivational and cognitive models. They had individuals work in groups of four on a problem-solving task. Three of the people in the group were confederates; the fourth was the only true participant. The experimental situation was manipulated so that, the majority of the time, the group used the solution offered by the participant. Following the problem-solving phase, one half of the participants were informed that their group had been successful on the task; the other half, that their group had not done very well. The participants were then asked to evaluate their own absolute responsibility as well as their responsibility relative to other members of the group. The participants who were in groups that had been successful quite accurately assumed the majority of responsibility. They had had the greatest input into their group's decisions and they assigned the greatest amount of credit to themselves. Participants who were in groups that had been unsuccessful, however, displayed a self-serving bias. They rated their input into the group's decisions and their responsibility as equal to that of the other members of the group. The Schlenker and Miller results show that although individuals may process information and make attributions in a logical fashion in some instances, there is also a strong motivation to maintain self-esteem.

The Actor-Observer Bias

Actor-observer bias represents a type of attributional bias. It is defined as "a pervasive tendency for actors to attribute their actions to situational requirements, whereas observers tend to attribute the same actions to stable personal dispositions" (Jones & Nisbett, 1971, p. 80). For example, a basketball player (the actor) who fails to make free throws in practice may attribute her poor performance to extenuating circumstances (e.g., it's only practice). However, the coach (the observer) may attribute the athlete's poor performance to more stable characteristics (unfocused athlete, poor shooter).

Judy Van Raalte, Brit Brewer, and Al Petitpas (1995) tested the actor-observer bias with 22 intercollegiate sport coaches and 42 intercollegiate lacrosse players. They found that both coaches and teammates tended to attribute athletes' behaviors to dispositional characteristics of the athletes. In short, coaches and teammates were prone to the actor-observer attributional bias.

In another study examining the locus of control perceived by competitive swimmers, Wolfson (1997) demonstrated a slightly different perspective of the actor-observer bias. Swimmers did not draw on extenuating circumstances to explain own failures while drawing on stable explanations to explain the failures of teammates. Rather, they felt that all swimmers experienced the same external factors to some degree. However, individual swimmers did feel that they were slightly more susceptible or affected by external (i.e., water temperature, luck, spectators, time/day of event, coaching received) and internal factors (i.e., skill, effort, mood, training amount, personality).

> Overall, it is conceivable that teammates and coaches may see athletes as personally responsible for behaviors even when it is obvious environmental factors were the cause. Thus, Van Raalte, Brewer, and Petitpas noted that it is extremely important for coaches to be aware of the actor-observer bias since the attributions for specific behaviors can influence coaches' expectation for athletes' future performances. They also stated that "attributing all sport performances to dispositional characteristics of athletes may actually inhibit athletic performance. Coaches should exercise caution and consider situational factors when explaining athlete behavior" (p. 90).

Chapter Twenty

COLLECTIVE EFFICACY

> I think this team can be our best . . . A lot of time [in the past] it felt as if we'd wait for someone to hit a three-run homer. With the power we had the past couple of years I believed we could win our division every year. But when you get to the postseason, especially with the kind of pitching you see at that level, you have to ask guys to bunt and move people over, and we never had that ability . . . now we can do that to go along with the power. (John Smoltz, in Verducci, 1997, pp. 33-34)

Efficacy represents the strength of the belief that an objective can be achieved or the responsibilities necessary to produce a desired outcome can be carried out successfully. It is similar to confidence except that confidence is considered to be global in nature whereas efficacy is viewed as situational specific. For example, a team could have high perceptions of efficacy in terms of its offensive capabilities but not its defensive capabilities. Or, it could have confidence in its offensive and defensive capabilities but not in terms of the team leadership.

Most of the early research on efficacy was undertaken with individuals rather than groups. Albert Bandura (1982), a psychologist who was the primary catalyst for efficacy research, elaborated on why self-efficacy is important:

> *In their daily lives people continuously make decisions about what courses of action to pursue and how long to continue those they have undertaken. Because acting on misjudgments of personal efficacy can produce adverse consequences, accurate appraisal of one's own capabilities has considerable functional value. Self-efficacy judgments, whether accurate or faulty, influence choice of activities and environmental settings. People avoid activities that they believe exceed their coping capabilities, but they undertake and perform assuredly those that they judge themselves capable of managing (Bandura, 1977). Judgments of self-efficacy also determine how much effort people will expend and how long they will persist in the face of obstacles or aversive experiences. When beset with difficulties, people who entertain serious doubts about their capabilities slacken their efforts or give up altogether, whereas those who have a strong sense of efficacy exert greater effort to master the challenge. (p. 123)*

In short, self-efficacy has a direct influence on motivation—on the activities people select, on the intensity with which they carry them out, and on the degree to which they persist in the face of adversity.

Although Bandura's original discussions were centered on self (personal) efficacy, he also pointed out that "people do not live their lives as social isolates. Many of the challenges and difficulties they face reflect group problems requiring sustained collective effort to produce any significant change" (Bandura, 1982, p. 143). Groups vary in their perceptions of collective competency and expectations for success. Bandura referred to these perceptions and expectations as *collective efficacy*. Not surprisingly, collective efficacy influences the selection of group activities, the effort directed by the group toward those activities, and the persistence exhibited in the face of adversity.

The Nature of Collective Efficacy

The essence of collective efficacy was captured in a definition advanced by Steven Zaccaro and his colleagues (Zaccaro, Blair, Peterson, & Zazanis, 1995). They suggested it is "*a sense of collective competence shared among individuals when allocating, coordinating, and integrating their resources in a successful concerted response to specific situational demands*" (p. 309).

Zaccaro et al., expanding on their definition, emphasized that one key aspect of collective efficacy is the concept of *shared beliefs*. Thus, for example, the quote from John Smoltz used to introduce this chapter reflects his confidence in his team. But, does it represent collective efficacy? Smoltz, a pitcher with the Atlanta Braves—possibly the most successful National League baseball team of the 90s—expressed his belief in the Braves' ability to win the world championship. The addition of people with key offensive skills, such as bunting and being able to move the runner over, were assumed to complete the package for the Braves. Although Smoltz's views might represent collective efficacy, more information is needed. The degree to which the other members of the Braves shared Smoltz's belief would be a measure of the degree to which the Braves possessed collective efficacy. If Smoltz was alone in his belief, or if his belief was only shared by a small number of other team members, it could be concluded that the Braves did not possess collective efficacy.

A second key aspect of the Zaccaro et al. definition is its focus on members' perceptions of competence in the group's *coordinative capabilities*. When individuals work in any collective endeavor, they are required to carry out a number of interpersonal functions—exchange information, coordinate responses (e.g., advance a base runner by bunting), and so on. Coordination is required even in individual sports such as wrestling. For example, Zaccaro and his colleagues pointed out that in team competitions, individuals may have to alter their approach and adopt a riskier strategy if the team is not doing as well as was initially projected. Collective efficacy reflects a shared belief that members of a group can work well together in a coordinative fashion.

A third key aspect of the Zaccaro definition is related to the *collective resources* available. For collective efficacy to be present, group members must believe that the group has sufficient skills, knowledge, and abilities within its membership for task success. In addition, as important as it is to have the necessary resources, it is equally important for members to have the collective perception that members are willing to use those skills, knowledge, and abilities for the group. In the Smoltz quote, half of this requirement is explicit—Smoltz suggested the Braves now possessed the resources necessary. In the absence of any reservations on Smoltz's part, it probably can be assumed that he believed that members of the Braves would use those resources for the team—would bunt to move runners along.

The final key aspect of the Zaccaro et al. definition relates to the *situational specificity* of collective efficacy. Thus, for example, it is possible for team members to have considerable collective efficacy for the team's defensive capabilities but minimal collective efficacy for its offensive capabilities. Similarly, a team may have high collective efficacy for competitions within its conference. Faced with an unfamiliar opponent, however, collective efficacy may be lower.

Collective Efficacy and Performance

From an anecdotal standpoint, many coaches, players, business leaders, and so on have alluded to the influence of collective efficacy (although perhaps not in those terms) on a group's performance. In fact, as the following quote by Phil Jackson illustrates, sometimes strategies are specifically employed to lower an opponent's collective efficacy in an effort to win:

> *We must find a way to force the [National Basketball Association's San Antonio] Spurs who haven't lost since March 23, to doubt themselves. The best way is through our own high level of execution . . . encourage them to wonder how in the world they will get any decent scoring opportunities. Gradually the frustration will mount, creating confusion, creating—-doubt. Once those doubts creep in, they tend to fester, gaining power with every errant pass, every missed assignment, every call that should have gone the other way. (Jackson & Artush, 2004, p. 178)*

From an empirical standpoint, a meta-analysis conducted by Gully, Incalcaterra, Joshi, and Beaubien (2002) examined the relationship between collective efficacy and performance among teams from a variety of different research contexts, including business, industry, management, and social psychology, as well as one study from the sport environment (i.e., collective efficacy and performance relationship in hockey; Feltz & Lirgg, 1998). The end result was a collection of 67 studies and 114 effect sizes (i.e., comparisons). Based on the statistical analysis of these studies, Gully and colleagues concluded that collective efficacy (or *team efficacy*, the term they used) was positively related to performance. In other words, greater collective efficacy leads to better performance.

Two interesting points were made by Gully et al. (2002) in a discussion of their findings. First, they noted that the collective efficacy-performance relationship was stronger than a cohesion-performance relationship found in a previous meta-analysis (Gully et al., 1995). However, it should be remembered that a sport-specific meta-analysis showed a strong cohesion-performance relationship is present (Carron et al., 2002; see Chapter 16 again). The bottom line? Both cohesion and collective efficacy play an important role in a team's performance.

A second point raised by Gully et al. (2002) was that the degree of group interdependence serves as a moderator in collective efficacy-performance relationship. That is, for tasks requiring considerable interaction and coordination, and having goals shared among group members (i.e., in contrast to group tasks carried out relatively independently), the collective efficacy-performance relationship is stronger. This has particular relevance for the sport environment. For example, a higher degree of collective efficacy in team sports that are inherently interdependent (e.g., basketball, hockey, volleyball) would likely be more important than, perhaps, is the case in individual sports where athletes compete as a team (e.g., track and field, wrestling, swimming).

While the Gully et al. meta-analysis focused primarily on work groups, additional research has examined the collective efficacy-performance relationship in sport. In one of the most comprehensive sport studies of collective efficacy conducted to date (but not included in the Gully et al. meta-analysis), Paskevich (1995) examined the interrelationships among collective efficacy, cohesion, and performance in volleyball teams. The multidimensional instrument developed by Paskevich (1995) focused on collective efficacy for a variety of task-related skills and abilities that require integration and coordination. The skills and abilities assessed included collective efficacy for a) offense, b) defense, c) the transition between the two, d) communication, e) motivation, f) overcoming obstacles in association with teammates (i.e., fatigue, bad officiating, poor practice sessions), g) team confidence in the face of obstacles (i.e., injuries to key personnel), and h) general collective efficacy. Paskevich (1995, Study 3) found that total collective efficacy (i.e., a combination of the eight measures listed above) obtained at the beginning of the season was a reliable predictor of a team's winning percentage at midseason.

It seems reasonable to suggest, based on the above research, that a team's belief in its capabilities to successfully execute various functions will be related to its performance. Interestingly, two studies by Greenlees, Graydon, and Maynard (1999, 2000) examined *why* collective efficacy is influential (i.e., mechanisms of the collective efficacy-performance relationship). Overall, their results suggested that individuals who perceived a higher degree of collective efficacy expended more effort in a task following failure (Greenless et al., 1999) and persisted in pursuing their goals to greater degree (Greenlees et al., 2000) than those with lower perceptions of collective efficacy

Sources of Collective Efficacy

As Figure 20.1 shows, collective efficacy can develop from a number of sources, including prior performance, vicarious experiences, verbal persuasion, leadership behaviors, group size, and group cohesion (Bandura, 1977, 1982, 1986; Zaccaro et al., 1995).

Prior Performance

Prior performance is generally acknowledged to be the most powerful source of efficacy. When a group has been successful, a perception of efficacy develops which is accompanied by an expectation for future successes in similar situations (see Illustration 20.1). The quote in Box 20.1 serves to illustrate this. Sheilagh Croxon (2003), a former head coach of the Canadian synchronized swimming team, described the preparation of the national synchro team for the 2000 Olympics; a team that had not achieved its goals on the world stage prior to attending training camp in 1998. A big issue for the team was "Building Belief" (p. 8) and the importance of reflecting on positive past perform-ances was viewed as a criti-cal element in enhancing collective efficacy.

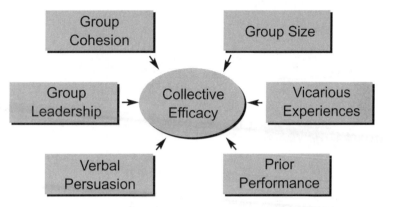

Figure 20.1. *The sources of collective efficacy (Adapted from Bandura, 1977, 1982, 1986; Zaccaro et al., 1995)*

A reliable relationship between performance and collective efficacy has been demonstrated in laboratory studies (Forward & Zander, in Zander, 1971; Hodges & Carron, 1992), ice hockey (Feltz, Bandura, Albrecht, & Corcoran, 1988; Feltz, Corcoran, & Lirgg, 1989), and volleyball (Paskevich, 1995; Spink, 1990). In the study by Hodges and Carron (1992) participants were brought into the laboratory in groups of three and tested on a hand dynamometer—ostensibly to obtain a measure of each individual's general strength. The collective efficacy of the triad was then manipulated through bogus feedback. The triads in the high collective efficacy condition were informed that their group had scored at the 75th percentile on the laboratory's norms. The triads in the low collective efficacy condition were informed that their group had scored at the 25th percentile on the laboratory's norms.

The triads then competed against a triad of confederates in a contest that involved holding a medicine ball aloft for as long as possible. The participants used a regular med-icine ball; the medicine ball used by the confederates was filled with foam rubber. In Trial 1, where the confederate group was victorious, the high collective efficacy triads were slightly superior in performance to the low collective efficacy triads. This is illustrated in Figure 20.2. In Trial 2, however, the differences became more accentuated. Triads that began with high collective efficacy and then failed on Trial 1 increased their effort con-siderably in Trial 2. Conversely, the triads that began with low collective efficacy and then failed in Trial 1 gave up quickly.

Vicarious Experiences

Perceptions of efficacy can also develop from vicarious experi-ences—seeing other groups have success. If those other groups are highly similar in competence, abil-ity, or some other important char-acteristic and are successful, it contributes to the development of feelings of efficacy (McCullagh,

Illustration 20.1. *Collective efficacy can make a difference!*

Box 20.1
Some examples of the sources of collective efficacy

Source of Efficacy	Quotation
Prior Performance	At the 1999 Pan American Games, we defeated the Americans and won gold medals in both the duet and the team event . . . The team was on an incredible high for about two weeks after the Games, and then I notice the doubts starting to creep back in. The athlete began to express sentiments like "Do you think it was a fluke that we beat the Americans? . . . This experience emphasized to me how important it is to reflect frequently on your successes, no matter how big or small—they are so easily forgotten (Croxon, 2003, p.9)
Vicarious Experiences	We had always ranked a player's performance against that of his teammates until someone pointed out that these comparisons were self-defeating . . . [so] we began comparing them to people on other teams with similar positions and similar role definitions . . . several of our players . . . were soon performing far above their levels of the previous season. (Pat Riley, 1993, pp. 162-168)
Verbal Persuasion	Olympic athletes and coaches from other sports . . . regularly came and spoke about their Olympic journeys, challenges, and experiences. Their stories provided inspiration and guidance. (Croxon, 2003, p.10)
Leadership	Knowing we were using new and different methods and working with excellent people helped to build the athletes' confidence in their abilities and improvements. (Croxon, 2003, p. 9)
Cohesion	Early in our Olympic year, we started work with the Outward Bound organization. Our first session was on a cold February day. The outdoor games and challenges were fun; however, it was obvious that this team was still in the infancy stages of problems solving. Everyone wanted to speak at once, and there were so many ideas that it took us a long time to solve simple problems. By the time we attended our second session in August, just prior to departure for Sydney, we were a highly functioning team . . . The difference between February and August was simply time together, time to learn and respect what each individual brought to the group. (Croxon, 2003, p. 9)

1987). Conversely, expectations for success are lowered when similar others are observed to fail despite high effort.

While the quote in Box 20.1 also illustrates the value of goal setting, it does provide a good example of the influence of vicarious experiences. Pat Riley, during his tenure as coach of the Los Angeles Lakers, motivated his players by having them compare themselves to similar others—rather than to superstar teammates such as Magic Johnson and

Kareem Abdul-Jabbar. It was pointed out earlier that efficacy influences the selection of activities, and the effort and persistence directed toward those activities. The comparison with similar others worked directly on the self-efficacy of the Lakers—behavior was focused and effort and persistence were increased.

Vicarious experiences have been referred to by Bandura (1982, 1986) as *modeling influences*. Two approaches used to model behavior are to use a live model or a symbolic model. The former might include watching a team considered to be comparable in competition against an upcoming opponent. Symbolic modeling could involve watching a

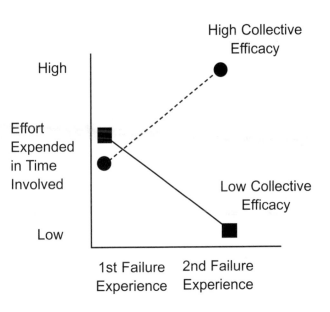

Figure 20.2. The effect of failure on groups high versus low in collective efficacy (Adapted from Hodges & Carron, 1992)

training film—an approach that is used with some success in the military. Whatever the approach used for both individuals and groups, models (i.e., vicarious experiences) are a less powerful source of efficacy than actual performance.

Verbal Persuasion

Verbal persuasion—the encouragement and support of others—also can be effective for developing self-efficacy (Bandura, 1986; Chambliss & Murray, 1979). It is generally considered to be the weakest source of efficacy, however.

Insofar as collective efficacy is concerned, Zaccaro and his colleagues (1995) argued that verbal persuasion in the form of "leadership actions that persuade and develop subordinate competency beliefs may be as critical a determinant . . . as the group's prior performance experiences, if not more so" (p. 317). To date, there is no evidence to support the Zaccaro et al. suggestion. It does seem unlikely that groups that lack the efficacy to successfully carry out a task can be convinced otherwise. A "win it for the Gipper" pep talk may always produce results in movies but its success rate is probably much lower in real life. However, it is still common for coaches or organizations to utilize inspirational speeches or speakers (as described by Sheilagh Croxon in Box 20.1) as a protocol to develop team confidence.

Group Cohesion

Zaccaro et al. also suggested that the degree to which *cohesion* is present also would influence the level of collective efficacy in the group. Spink (1990) found that this was the case; individual volleyball players who perceived their team to be more task cohesive also perceived their team to be more collectively efficacious. Box 20.1 highlights that the development of team cohesion was another critical factor in building belief for the Canadian synchronized swimming team heading into the 2000 Olympics.

The efficacy-cohesion relationship is likely reciprocal; teams that have greater collective efficacy could be expected to be more cohesive and teams that are more cohesive could be expected to have greater collective efficacy (Zaccaro et al., 1995). In his research, Paskevich (1995, Study 3) examined and supported this supposition. Teams higher in task cohesion in early season had greater collective efficacy later in the season. Similarly, the teams that were higher in collective efficacy in early season had greater task cohesion later in the season. These results were subsequently supported by Kozub and McDonnell (2000), in an examination of the cohesion-collective efficacy relationship in rugby.

Group Leadership

Another source of collective efficacy for the group is its leadership. According to Zaccaro et al. (1995), leaders contribute "directly to collective efficacy by specifically enhancing group functioning" (p. 318). Thus, for example, in Chelladurai's (1990) model of leadership (which was discussed in Chapter 14), athletes have preferences for specific leader behaviors. In turn, leadership has consequences for athlete performance and satisfaction—and, although it is not in Chelladurai's model, efficacy. It is reasonable to assume, for example, that athletes who have a preference for a large amount of training and instruction from their coach will be more confident if the coach demonstrates this behavior. Similarly, if the team collectively prefers an autocratic decision style, a democratic approach is likely to induce non-confidence. Finally, the group members' confidence in the expertise and knowledge levels of those in leadership positions can also influence perceptions of collective efficacy (see Box 20.1).

Group Size

Zaccaro and his colleagues also suggested that group size could be associated with collective efficacy. They also noted, however, that nature of the relationship is uncertain. On the one hand, larger groups possess more resources. Consequently, increasing the size of a group might be expected to increase the belief of group members that their group has sufficient skills, knowledge, and abilities within its membership for task success.

On the other hand, however, it is more difficult to coordinate the actions of members when groups are larger. Also, there is more likelihood that social loafing will increase with increases in group size. Consequently, increasing the size of the group might lead members to question the group's ability to work effectively. Recent research has been equivocal regarding the influence of group size. Watson, Chemers, and Preiser (2001) found that increasing group size in basketball teams was predictive of lower collective efficacy while Magyar, Feltz, and Simpson (2004) found no relationship was present between these two variables in rowing crews.

Motivational Climate

Additional results found in the study by Magyar and colleagues (2004) highlighted another potential source of collective efficacy: motivational climate. Whether the team's environment is focused on mastery (e.g., learning and improvement in group processes) or performance (e.g., competition among team members, punishment for errors) can influence how confident the team is as a whole. More specifically, Magyar et al. found that collective efficacy was enhanced to a greater degree in a mastery-oriented motivational climate.

As another example, Heuzé, Sarrazin, Masiero, Raimbault, and Thomas (2005), examining 146 basketball and handball athletes, found that those who perceived a more task-oriented environment (i.e., promotion of learning by the coach and fellow athletes) also indicated higher perceptions of collective efficacy compared with an ego-oriented environment (e.g., promotion of athlete comparison and the development of a fear of mistakes).

As a final note to this section on the potential sources of collective efficacy in a sport environment, a comprehensive study examining the contributions of some of the above predictors as well as additional sources of collective efficacy was undertaken by Watson, Chemers, and Preiser (2001). They utilized a hierarchical approach to examine which individual and group level variables would be related to collective efficacy with 28 collegiate basketball teams. The variables examined included self-efficacy, optimism, leader confidence, leader evaluation, team performance, individual performance, and perceptions of team performance over two time periods. Watson et al. reported that collective efficacy at the beginning of the season was predicted by personal beliefs such as self-efficacy and optimism, while collective efficacy at the end of the season was predicted by self-efficacy, past performance, and perceptions of leader quality.

SECTION 7

FORMING THE GROUP

Running a football franchise is not unlike running any other business: You start with a structural format and basic philosophy and then find the people who can implement it . . . There were certain qualities I was seeking in those we brought into the organization:

- *I needed to feel comfortable with them . . .*
- *I wanted functional intelligence, because I knew that one person who is not very bright but very aggressive in pushing his ideas can destroy an organization . . .*
- *We needed knowledge and experience in the business dynamics of the National Football League . . .*
- *I wanted people who could be enthusiastic and inquisitive, and who would thrive on work. (Walsh, 1990, pp. 123-132)*

Chapter Twenty-One

TEAM BUILDING IN SPORT

> I call them Lavisms . . . the things you know he's going to say everyday, like 'step by step' and 'brick by brick to the Brickyard' (a reference to the Bruins' progress to Indianapolis, the site of the Final Four). (UCLA Bruins' Kris Johnson, in Anderson, 1997a, p. 52)

The quote from Bill Walsh to introduce this section and the quote by Kris Johnson to introduce this chapter serve to highlight the essence of team building. Bill Walsh, then coach of the San Francisco 49ers, outlined how he rebuilt 'the laughingstock of the NFL' from losers into champions—into what has been referred to as the *team of the eighties*. The 49ers' management selected personnel with specific qualities in order to build an organization that continued to thrive after Walsh left the team.

The Kris Johnson quote provides insight into UCLA coach Steve Lavin's attempts to rebuild the Bruins' into a cohesive unit in the months after he replaced coach Jim Harrick (who was fired two weeks prior to the start of the season). Harrick had recruited all of the players, many of whom were on UCLA's National Championship team two years previously. As UCLA player Cameron Dollar noted about the team Lavin inherited, "We all had different ways we wanted to go" (Anderson, 1997a, p. 52). Lavin had to build the team step-by-step, brick-by-brick into a unified collective.

The Nature of Team Building

Team Building Defined

Team building, one of the most enduring themes in the organizational development literature, has been defined in a variety of ways (cf. Hardy & Crace, 1997). In summarizing the definitions offered in the organizational development literature, Brawley and Paskevich (1997) concluded that team building is "a method of helping the group to (a) increase effectiveness, (b) satisfy the needs of its members, or (c) improve work conditions" (p. 13). In short, team building can be characterized as team enhancement or team improvement for both task and social purposes (see Illustration 21.1).

Neuman, Edwards, and Raju (1989) highlighted the importance of team building in business and industry in a meta-analysis of 126 studies that employed various organizational interventions to modify satisfaction and/or other attitudes (e.g., attitudes about self, attitudes about others, attitudes about the job, attitudes about the organization). Results of the meta-analysis revealed that team building was the most effective intervention for improving individual satisfaction and changing attitudes.

General Strategies in Team Building

Members of groups in every context often feel that their particular group could be more efficient, or more pleasant, or more productive. Thus, not surprisingly, team-building interventions have been undertaken has been in a variety of settings, including religious groups, airline cockpit teams, medical teams, multicultural staffed corporate headquarters, sport groups, rehabilitation programs, and fitness classes (Bettenhausen, 1991; Prapavessis, Carron, & Spink, 1997; Rejeski, Brawley, & Etinger, 1997; Spink & Carron, 1993).

When the objective has been to develop a more effective productive group, one of four general types of team-building interventions has been used either alone or in combination (Beer, 1976; Blake & Mouton, 1964). In the first, the focus is on *group goal-setting*. Through the team-building intervention, collective goals are either established or clarified and actions to achieve those goals are identified.

In the second approach, the focus is on *interpersonal relationships* among group members. As might be expected, the interpersonal approach is used when conflicts are present or task and social communications among members are poor. Consequently, the team-building intervention is designed to improve relationships among members.

In a third approach to team building, the focus is on *individual role involvement.* It was pointed out in Chapter 12 that when group members do not understand, accept their role, and/or are unhappy with their role, cohesion is low and group effectiveness suffers. In the role approach to team building, the focus is on clarifying team members' roles, increasing their role acceptance and satisfaction, and insuring role performance

These first three approaches are largely directed toward group members (i.e., subordinates). In the fourth, the *managerial grid approach,* the focus is on managers or group leaders. Here, standardized instruments and exercises are used to try to provide leaders with insights and strategies that will help them move an organization toward both enhanced productivity and increased concern for people.

Illustration 21.1. Team building can improve group performance

Benefits of Team Building

According to Woodcock and Francis (1994), when team building is successful, a close, effective work group is established that possesses six characteristics. In Box 21.1, these six characteristics are illustrated by using Pat Riley's (1993) experiences when he was hired by the New York Knicks to produce a contender for the NBA championship. It should be kept in mind that Woodcock and Francis viewed the six characteristics as *resulting* from team building; in Box 21.1, some of the quotes by Pat Riley represent dynamics that *preceded* or *paralleled* the introduction of team building.

The first benefit is to produce *a team leadership that is coherent, visionary and acceptable* (Woodcock & Francis, 1994). As a result of Riley's efforts with individuals and the team as a collective, the Knicks were focused as a group and knew who they were and where they were going when they went into the season.

A second benefit to be derived from a team-building program is that team *members understand and accept their roles and responsibilities* (Woodcock & Francis, 1994). In his first step in building a better team, Pat Riley directed his attention toward the core of the team, Patrick Ewing. Although the quote does not explicitly highlight it, Riley was anxious to insure that Ewing understood and accepted not only the projections for the team but his own role.

Following a successful team-building intervention, *members of the team emotionally "sign up" and dedicate their efforts to collective achievement* (Woodcock & Francis, 1994). When team unity on the Knicks broke down, Riley had the members of various cliques on the team (e.g., the core players, the rebels, a social isolate, the complainers, etc.) take their chairs into various places in the room "to define reality . . . [to hold] up a mirror so they could see what they were making of themselves: human isolates in a hostile sea, linked only by their gripes" (Riley, 1993, p. 240). As the quote in Box 21.1 illustrates, following this session, the cliques rededicated their efforts to the team's collective interests.

According to Woodcock and Francis, a fourth consequence of team building is that the group develops a positive, energetic, and empowering climate. The attitude symbolized by the quote in Box 21.1 is intended to highlight this characteristic. A collective attitude developed around defense that helped produce a sense of team identity.

When team building has been successful, group meetings, both informal and formal, are *efficient and make good use of time and available resources.* If the team building has helped to clearly define or clarify the group's goals, produce role clarity and acceptance, improve interpersonal relationships, and so on, then team meetings can be more focused and efficient. In Box 21.1, Riley outlined how he introduced an adjunct program. Through the implementation of programs designed to improve flexibility and strength, cardiovascular fitness, diet and nutrition, it was expected that the base for team success would be developed.

Finally, if a team-building program is successful, *weaknesses in the team will have been diagnosed and their negative effects reduced or eliminated.* In Box 21.1, Riley has given credit to team president Dave Checketts for freeing up money under the NBA salary cap so players critical to team success could be hired.

As the quotes in Box 21.1 illustrate, Riley's team building also focused on member roles, team goals, interpersonal relationships, and team leadership. As a consequence, he felt that "the 1991-1992 season brought the Knicks a fantastic turnaround in team fortunes

---

Box 21.1
The desired benefits of team-building interventions

Area	Illustration
Leadership is coherent, visionary, and acceptable. Roles and functions are understood.	The Knicks had started the season with a single goal: to become the hardest-working, best-conditioned, toughest, most professional, unselfish, and disliked team in the NBA. (Riley, 1993, p. 235)
	I also told [Patrick Ewing] that . . . the pressure on him would be unmatched because he'd be expected to stand as the core of a championship team. (Riley, 1993, p. 238)
Members emotionally sign up and dedicate their efforts to collective achievements.	We had an hours-long discussion about tolerance, openness, and the spirit of understanding. About how losing brings out insecurities, blaming. About sharing the weight. Things got better after that. The core became stronger, the rebels became more cooperative, the stand-aparts began to take a stake in the team's morale. (Riley, 1993, p. 240-242)
A positive, energetic empowering climate is present in the group.	Whenever a Chicago Bull went to the basket, intending to throw down a dunk that would rock the stadium, we [the Knicks] would come to stop him—just as hard as he had come to score. Whenever he showed us how much he wanted to win, we had to show him that we wanted the same thing, just as much. We simply didn't want to defer. Without that attitude we'd be handing the Bulls a license to tear our hearts out for the next several years. (Riley, 1993, p. 248)
Meetings are efficient in terms of time and resources.	We brought on . . . probably the best weight and strength coach in the league. We spent a lot of time before and after each practice warding off potential [injuries] through weight and flexibility training, cardiovascular fitness, diet and nutrition counseling . . . All year long, no big-time injuries hit us. We were the healthiest team in the league. (Riley, 1993, p. 235)
Weaknesses in team capability are diagnosed and reduced or eliminated.	A tremendous share of credit for the Knicks' reemergence goes to team president Dave Checketts, who renegotiated contracts to get the team under the salary cap and made our team building trades possible. (Riley, 2993, p. 237)

. . . We achieved the team's best season in nineteen years and built the base to do even better the year that followed" (Riley, 1993, p. 235).

Team-Building Programs in Sport

Although team building has received considerable attention in business and industry, attention in sport beyond anecdotal reports is sparse (e.g., Brennan, 1990; Riley, 1993). In general, two types of team-building protocols have been used in sport and exercise settings: *indirect* and *direct*. These two approaches are discussed in the sections that follow.

Direct Team-Building Interventions

Coaches as team builders. With the direct approach, the individual responsible for introducing and implementing the team-building intervention works directly with the athletes. That individual could be the *coach*—as was the case with both Pat Riley's team building with the New York Knicks (see Box 21.1 again) and Pat Summit's team building with the Tennessee Lady Vols basketball team:

> *"They have to understand that this is a team sport," Summit says. "Tennessee is not a star system. I tell them if they're prepared to be unselfish, the rewards are tremendous." Her philosophy got tested this season when freshman Chamique Holdsclaw won the Kodak All-American award. "She became a media darling, but there were seniors who had waited their turn to shine," Summit says. The coach sat everyone down and talked about their goal, the national championships. "I asked them to name last year's All Americans. They couldn't. But we all know which team won last year's championship!" (Huntington, 1996, p. 79)*

Team building by coaches is not an unusual event; they either implicitly or explicitly work constantly on developing a more cohesive, effective team. Occasionally, however, a team-building *consultant* is brought in by the coach to work directly with the team to increase its cohesiveness and effectiveness or eliminate problems that have arisen.

A consultant's approach. David Yukelson (1997) has used team-building strategies with various Penn State teams. As he noted,

> *since communication is directly related to group cohesion and team effectiveness, and success is highly dependent upon teamwork and having consensus on group goals and objectives, I spend a great deal of time with teams discussing strategies for developing and maintaining group cohesion as well as methods for improving harmonious team relations. (Yukelson, 1997, p. 75)*

Generally, Yukelson's team-building intervention proceeds through four stages: assessment of the situation, education, brainstorming, and establishing team-building goals.

According to Yukelson, the team-building consultant initially must gain an awareness of the team dynamics. He suggested that, "this is perhaps the most important part of any good team-building intervention" (Yukelson, 1997, p. 86). In order to increase the accuracy of his *assessment* and, ultimately, the effectiveness of the intervention, Yukelson pointed out that the team-building consultant must be accessible and be perceived to be an integral part of the team. During the assessment phase, Yukelson observes, listens, and talks with the coaches, athletes, trainers, and support staff. He also meets with the team to determine its goals, expectations, perceptions, and concerns.

During the *education* phase, Yukelson provides the athletes with an overview of the nature of groups and how they develop. According to Yukelson, the education phase helps to lay a solid foundation for the implementation of sport psychology interventions.

The purpose of the *brainstorming* phase is to identify the areas to be targeted for team-building intervention. The team generates a list of needs that must be addressed. The needs identified by the athletes serve as goals for the team-building intervention. Yukelson noted he then develops a team-building program tailored to the specific needs of the team. This involves the development of action plans targeted at each need identified.

During the season, goals, roles, and team structure can change and communication can break down. Thus, according to Yukelson, in order for team-building consultants to be effective, they must become a member of the coaching staff and be available to the team members when consultation is required.

Another team-building approach. Another example of a direct team-building approach was used by sport psychology consultant Neil Widmeyer with the approval of Coach E.J. McGuire of the Guelph Storm Junior-A hockey (Widmeyer & McGuire, 1996). Team goal setting was the specific team-building intervention used. In order to identify and implement their team goal-setting program, Widmeyer and McGuire used an educational phase, a goal-development phase, an implementation phase, and a renewal phase.

In the *educational phase* (which occurred at the beginning of the season), the athletes were provided a brief overview of the benefits of goal setting generally and team goal setting specifically. The purpose of the educational phase was to teach team members the principles of goal setting, outline the techniques for setting goals, and convince them of the benefits of having specific team goals.

During the *goal-development phase,* lists of the specific offensive and defensive statistics that the team routinely collected during the course of each game were presented to each athlete. For example, two offensive parameters charted were shots on net and offensive face-offs, while two defensive parameters included were penalty-killing percentage, and defensive face-offs. Each athlete independently selected the five parameters he considered most critical for team success. Following this, athletes formed into subgroups of four to present their list and arrive at a consensus for the subgroup. Then, the athletes met in a total group to establish consensus on the five parameters considered critical to team success.

As Widmeyer and McGuire pointed out, the approach they used was based on sound goal-setting theory. By insuring that all team members (not just older, higher status, and/or more experienced athletes) had input into the establishment of team goals, Widmeyer and McGuire also insured that cohesion would be positively affected and goal clarity and influence would be greater.

Following the identification of the five parameters to be adopted as team goals, the process was repeated to arrive at an appropriate level for the goal for an upcoming six-game segment. Using the previous year's statistics as a guide and taking into account the nature of their opponents, the athletes initially arrived at a goal level independently. Then, as was the case above, consensus was achieved in a subgroup and then in the total group.

During the *implementation phase,* a statistician charted the team's performance on the five parameters. Thus, differences between the level for the team goal and the team's performance could be monitored.

As was indicated above, initially the level for a team goal was set for an upcoming six-game segment. The *renewal phase,* therefore, was used to update the level for each team goal at the start of each successive six-game segment. Using their previous performance and next six opponents as a reference, the athletes established a revised level for each offensive and defensive team goal. Widmeyer and McGuire noted that while the consultant coordinated the team goal setting process for the first six-game segment, the team captain acted as the coordinator for the remainder of the segments.

Indirect Team-Building Interventions

In indirect team-building interventions, the consultant works with the coach (not the team). The coach or leader then introduces the team-building interventions to the team. Thus, the intervention is indirect since it must filter through the coach.

Carron and his colleagues took an indirect approach in a series of team-building projects (Carron, Spink, & Prapavessis, 1997; Carron & Spink, 1993; Prapavessis, Carron, & Spink, 1997; Spink & Carron, 1993). Typically, the team-building intervention involved four components: introduction, conceptual, practical, and intervention stage. The first three stages (i.e., introduction, conceptual, and practical) occurred in a seminar/workshop conducted by a sport psychologist with the present. The final stage (i.e., intervention) involved the introduction of the team-building strategies by the coach with the team.

In the *introductory stage*, the coach was provided with a brief overview of the general benefits of group cohesion (see Chapter 16) and the reasons for introducing team building. For example, in their study, Prapavessis, Carron, and Spink (1997) outlined research findings pertaining to the relationship of cohesion to team success soccer coaches participating in a team-building session.

The *conceptual stage* was used to provide a model to better understand group dynamics (see Figure 21.1). A conceptual model has three advantages. First, it facilitates communication with the coaches because complex concepts can be simplified and more readily described and comprehended. Second, the interrelationship among the various components of the team-building protocol can be highlighted. And third, the focus of the possible interventions can be more easily distinguished.

As Figure 21.1 shows, the conceptual framework is linear in nature, consisting of inputs, throughputs, and outputs. Cohesion (task and social), the output, was presented as the product of three categories of factors:

- The team's environment (e.g., proximity and distinctiveness),
- The team's structure (e.g., group norms, leadership, and role clarity), and
- The team's processes (e.g., cooperation, sacrifices, cooperation, goals and objectives).

As Figure 21.1 shows, the team's structure and its environment represent the inputs in the conceptual model. These two inputs are assumed to affect the throughput (i.e., team processes), which in turn is assumed to affect the output (i.e., group cohesion).

In the *practical stage*, the coaches engaged in brainstorming in an attempt to generate specific team-building strategies for their specific situation. Representative examples of strategies listed from sport brainstorming sessions are presented in Table 21.1. Also, the

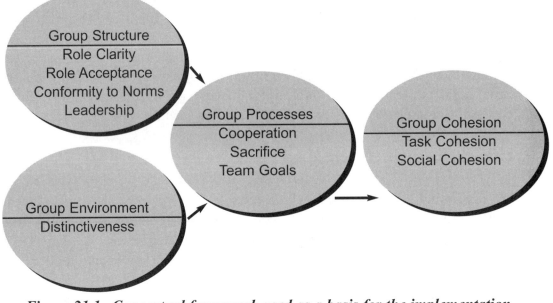

***Figure 21.1. Conceptual framework used as a basis for the implementation
of a team-building program in sport and fitness groups
(Prapavessis, Carron, & Spink, 1996)***

rationale provided to the coaches for including each of the factors in a team-building program is included.

In the *intervention stage*, the team-building protocols were introduced to the team by
the coaches. To ensure that the team-building strategies were used, trained assistants monitored the sessions on a weekly basis.

Team-Building Research

Despite the intuitive appeal of team building as an intervention strategy to increase team
cohesiveness and team effectiveness, research evidence has not shown consistently positive effects. For example, Prapavessis, Carron, and Spink (1997) conducted a study with a
soccer league in which the teams were subdivided into three categories: a team-building
intervention condition, an attention-placebo condition, or a control condition. The team-
building strategies established in the workshops were implemented throughout the six-
week regular season. When the teams in the three conditions were retested at the end of
the season, no differences in cohesion were found.

Similarly Cogan and Petrie (1995) established a team-building program for intercollegiate gymnasts. Questionnaires administered six time (three in preseason and three in season) showed that cohesion levels remained unchanged from the first to the final test session.

Finally, Bloom and Mack (1999) conducted six team-building sessions with a group
of equestrians that included improving athlete leadership, establishing appropriate
norms for interpersonal interactions, and improving communication patterns. Although
the athletes perceived that team functioning did improve, no changes were found in the
level of cohesiveness present.

Table 21.1

Examples of specific strategies coaches used to enhance group cohesiveness
(Adapted from Prapavessis, Carron, & Spink, 1996)

Category	Rationale	Strategies
Team Environment		
Distinctiveness	The presence of team distinctiveness contributes to cohesiveness.	Insure that all team members have and use the identical sweat suit.
Togetherness	When group members are repetitively placed in close physical proximity, cohesiveness is enhanced.	Reserve a section of lockers in the same section in the locker room.
Team Structure		
Role clarity & acceptance	When team members clearly understand, accept their role and are satisfied with their role, cohesiveness is enhanced.	Schedule weekly meetings with athletes to outline and reinforce their role responsibilities.
Conformity to team norms	Conformity to team social and task norms contributes to enhanced cohesiveness.	Have captains establish a behavioral code and have weekly sessions to discuss issues of noncompliance.
Team leadership	A participative style of decision-making contributes to enhanced cohesiveness.	Establish an elected player's council to bring forward issues to discuss with the coach.
Group Processes		
Individual sacrifices	When high-status team members make sacrifices for the group, cohesiveness is enhanced	Request that team captains assume the responsibility for integrating rookies into the social network of the team.
Goals and objectives	Member participation in team goal setting contributes to enhanced cohesiveness.	Meet weekly with the total team to establish process, performance, and outcome goals for the upcoming week.
Cooperation	Cooperative behavior contributes to enhanced cohesiveness.	Have veterans provide individual instruction and assistance to athletes unfamiliar with the system.

Conversely, McClure and Foster (1991) did observe improved group cohesion following a 15-week team-building program that also focused on college gymnastics. The team-building program would be difficult to replicate, however, because it did not target specific components of group functioning.

References

Aamodt, M. G. (1981). Criteria used by fans in All-Star Game selections. *Journal of Sport Psychology, 3*, 355-357.

Aamodt, M. G., Kimbrough, W. W., & Alexander, C. J. (1983). A preliminary investigation of the relationship between team racial heterogeneity and team performance in college basketball. *Journal of Sport Sciences, 1,* 131-133.

Abdul-Jabbar, K., & Knobler, P. (1983). *Giant steps: The autobiography of Kareem Abdul-Jabbar.* Toronto, ON: Bantam House.

Adams, R. S., & Biddle, B. J. (1970). *Realities of teaching: Explorations with video tape.* New York: Holt, Rinehart, & Winston.

Agnew, G., & Carron, A. V. (1994). Crowd effects and the home advantage. *International Journal of Sport Psychology, 25,* 53-62.

Allen, M. (1987). *Jackie Robinson: A life remembered.* New York: Franklin Watts.

Allen, M. P., Panian, S. K., & Lotz, R. E. (1979). Managerial succession and organizational performance: A recalcitrant problem revisited. *Administrative Science Quarterly, 24,* 167-180.

Allport, F. H. (1924). *Social Psychology.* Cambridge, MA: Riverside.

Alsop, J. (1982). *FDR: A centenary remembrance.* New York: Viking Press.

Altman, I. (1975). *The environment and social behavior.* Monterey, CA: Brooks/Cole.

Anderson, D. C., Crowell, C. R., Doman, M., & Howard, G. S. (1988). Performance posting, goal setting, and activity-contingent praise as applied to a university hockey team. *Journal of Applied Psychology, 73,* 87-95.

Anderson, K. (1997a, March 3). Winner takes all? UCLA knocked off Duke in a matchup that has never failed to foretell the national champion. *Sports Illustrated, 86,* 50-53.

Anderson, K. (1997b, April, 7). Surprise, surprise. Few people expected Tennessee to repeat as the women's champion, but guess what? *Sports Illustrated, 86,* 42-49.

Anderson, L. R. (1978). Groups would do better without humans. *Personality and Social Psychology Bulletin, 4,* 557-558.

Anshel, M. H. (1995). Examining social loafing among elite female rowers as a function of task duration and mood. *Journal of Sport Behavior, 18,* 39-49.

Anshel, M. H., & Sailes, G. (1990). Discrepant attitudes of intercollegiate athletes as a function of race. *Journal of Sport Behavior, 13,* 87-101.

Argyle, M. (1969). *Social interactions.* London: Methuen & Co.

Arnold, G. E., & Straub, W.F. (1972). Personality and group cohesiveness as determinants of success among interscholastic basketball teams. In I. D. Williams & L. M. Wankel (Eds.), *Proceedings of the Fourth Canadian Symposium on Psycho-Motor Learning and Sport Psychology*, (pp. 346-352). Ottawa, ON: Fitness and Amateur Sport Directorate, Department of National Health and Welfare.

Arrow, H., Poole, M. S., Henry, K. B., Wheelan, S., & Moreland, R. (2004). Time, change, and development: The temporal perspective on groups. *Small Group Research, 35,* 73-105.

Austin, W. G., & Worchel, S. (1979). *The social psychology of intergroup relations.* Belmont, CA: Wadsworth.

Bacharach, S. B., Bamberger, P., & Mundell, B. (1993). Status inconsistency in organizations: From social hierarchy to stress. *Journal of Organizational Behavior, 14,* 21-36.

Baker, P. (1981). The division of labor: Interdependence, isolation, and cohesion in small groups. *Small Group Behavior, 12,* 93-106.

Bales, R. F. (1966). Task roles and social roles in problem solving groups. In B. J. Biddle & E. J. Thomas (Eds.), *Role theory: Concepts and research* (pp. 254-262). New York: John Wiley.

Bales, R. F., & Slater, P. E. (1955). Role differentiation in small decision-making groups. In T. Parsons & R. F. Bales (Eds.), *The family socialization and interaction process* (pp. 259-306). Glencoe, IL: The Free Press.

Ball, D. W. (1973). Ascription and position: A comparative analysis of 'stacking' in professional football. *Canadian Review of Sociology and Anthropology, 10,* 97-113.

Balmer, N. J., Nevill, A. M. and Williams, M. (2001). Home advantage in the Winter Olympics (1908-1998). *Journal of Sports Sciences, 19,* 129-139.

Bandura, A. (1977). Self-efficacy: Toward a unifying theory of behavioral change. *Psychological Review, 84,* 191-215.

Bandura, A. (1982). Self-efficacy mechanism in human agency. *American Psychologist, 37,* 122-147.

Bandura, A. (1986). *Social foundations of thought and action: A social cognitive theory.* Englewood Cliffs, NJ: Prentice-Hill.

Bandura, A. (1997). *Self-efficacy: The exercise of control.* New York: W. H. Freeman & Co.

Bar-Eli, M., Levy-Kolker, N., Pie, J. S. and Tenenbaum, G. (1995). A crisis-related analysis of perceived referee's behavior in competition. *Journal of Applied Sport Psychology, 7,* 63-80.

Barnett, V. and Hilditch, S. (1993). The effect of an artificial pitch surface on home team performance in football (soccer). *Journal of the Royal Statistical Society, 156,* 39-50.

Bass, B. M. (1960). *Leadership, psychology, and organizational behavior.* New York: Harper.

Bass, B. M. (1962). *The orientation inventory.* Palo Alto, CA: Consulting Psychologists Press.

Bass. B. M. (1980). Team productivity and individual member competence. *Small Group Behavior, 11,* 431-504.

Bass, B. M. (1985). *Leadership and performance beyond expectations.* New York: The Free Press.

Bass, B. M., Dunteman, G., Frye, R., Vidulich, R., & Wambach, H. (1963). Self, interaction, and task orientation inventory scores associated with overt behavior and personal factors. *Educational and Psychological Measurement, 23,* 101-116

Baum, A., & Valins, S. (1977). *Architecture and social behavior: Psychological studies of social density.* Hillsdale, NJ: Erlbaum.

Baumeister, R. F. (1985, April). The championship choke. When a title is on the line, jubilant home crowds can root athletes on to win. *Psychology Today, 19,* 48-52.

Baumeister, R. F. (1995). Disputing the effects of championship pressures and home audiences. *Journal of Personality and Social Psychology, 68,* 644-648.

Baumeister, R. F., Hamilton, J. C., & Tice, D. M. (1985). Public versus private expectancy of success: Confidence booster or performance pressure? *Journal of Personality and Social Psychology, 48,* 1447-1457.

Baumeister, R. F., Hutton, D. G., & Cairns, K. J. (1990). Negative effects of praise on skilled performance. *Basic and Applied social Psychology, 11,* 131-148.

Baumeister, R. F., & Leary, M. R. (1995). The need to belong: Desire for interpersonal attachment as a fundamental human motivation. *Psychological Bulletin, 117,* 497-529.

Baumeister, R. F., & Steinhilber, A. (1984). Paradoxical effects of supportive audiences on performance under pressure: The home field disadvantage in sports championships. *Journal of Personality and Social Psychology, 47,* 85-93.

Beam, J. W., Serwatka, T. S., & Wilson, W. J. (2004). Preferred leadership of NCAA Division I and II intercollegiate student-athletes. *Journal of Sport Behavior, 27,* 3-17.

Beauchamp, M. R., & Bray, S. R. (2001). Role ambiguity and role conflict within inter-dependent teams. *Small Group Research, 32,* 133-157.

Beauchamp, M. R., Bray, S. R., Eys, M. A., & Carron, A. V. (2002). Role ambiguity, role efficacy, and role performance: Multidimensional and mediational rela-tionships within interdependent sport teams. *Group Dynamics: Theory, Research, and Practice, 6(3),* 229-242.

Beauchamp, M. R., Bray, S. R., Eys, M. A., & Carron, A. V. (2003). The effect of role ambiguity on competitive state anxiety. *Journal of Sport and Exercise Psychology, 25(1),* 77-92.

Beauchamp, M. R., Bray, S. R., Eys, M. A., & Carron, A. V. (in press). Leadership behaviors and multidimensional role ambiguity perceptions in team sports. *Small Group Research.*

Bechtel, M., Kim, A., & Mravic, M. (2000). He still gives a shirt. *Sports Illustrated, 93(19),* 44-50.

Beer, M. (1976). The technology of organiza-tion development. In M. D. Dunnette (Ed.), *Handbook of industrial and organi-zational psychology* (pp. 937-933). Chicago, IL: Rand McNally.

Behling, O., & Schriesheim, C. (1976). *Organizational behavior: Theory, research and application.* Boston, MA: Allyn & Bacon.

Benjafield, J., Liddell, W. W., & Benjafield, I. (1989). Is there a home disadvantage in professional sports championships? *Social Behavior and Personality, 17,* 45-50.

Berger, J., Fisek, H., Norman, R. Z., & Zelditch, M. (1977). *Status characteris-tics and social interaction: An expectation states approach.* New York: Elsevier.

Berghorn, F. J., Yetman, N. R., & Hanna, W. E. (1988). Racial participation and integra-tion in men's and women's intercollegiate basketball: Continuity and change. *Sociology of Sport Journal, 5,* 107-124.

Berglas, S., & Jones, E. E. (1978). Drug choice as a self-handicapping strategy in

response to non-contingent success. *Journal of Personality and Social Psychology 36,* 405-417.

Bergman, B. R. (1986). *The economic emer-gence of women.* New York: Basic Books.

Berkowitz, L. (1954). Group standards, cohe-siveness, and productivity. *Human Relations, 7,* 509-514.

Berkowitz, L. (1956). Group norms among bomber crews: Patterns of perceived crew attitudes, "active" crew attitudes, and crew liking related to air crew effective-ness in Far Eastern combat. *Sociometry, 19,* 141-153.

Bernthal, P. R., & Insko, C. A. (1993). Cohesiveness without groupthink: The interactive effects of social and task cohe-sion. *Group and Organizational Management, 18,* 66-87.

Bettencourt, B. A., Brewer, M. B., Croak, M. B., & Miller, N. (1992). Cooperation and the reduction of intergroup bias: The role of reward structure and social orientation. *Journal of Experimental Social Psychology, 28,* 301-319.

Bettenhausen, K. L. (1991). Five years of groups research: What we have learned and what needs to be addressed. *Journal of Management, 17,* 345-381.

Bird, A. M. (1977). Team structure and success as related to cohesiveness and leadership. *Journal of Social Psychology, 103,* 217-223.

Bird, A. M., Foster, C. D., & Maruyama, G. (1980). Convergent and incremental effects of cohesion on attributions for self and team. *Journal of Sport Psychology, 2,* 181-194.

Birrell, S., & Richter, D. M. (1994). Is a dia-mond forever? Feminist transformations of sport. In S. Birrell & C. L. Cole (Eds.), *Women, sport, and culture* (pp. 221-244). Champaign, IL: Human Kinetics.

Blais, M. (1995). *In these girls, hope is mus-cle.* New York: Atlantic Monthly Press.

Blake, R., & Mouton, J. (1964). *The manage-rial grid.* Houston: Gulf Publishing.

Blake, R. R., & Mouton, J. S. (1979). Intergroup problem solving in organizations: From theory to practice. In W. G. Austin & S. Worshel (Eds.), *The social psychology of intergroup relations* (pp. 19-32). Monterey, CA: Brooks/Cole.

Bloom, G. A., & Mack, D. E. (1999). Improving team effectiveness: A direct approach to team-building. Cited in Stevens, D. E. (2002). Building the effective team. In J. M. Silva III and D. E. Stevens (Eds.), *Psychological foundations of sport*, (pp. 306-327). Boaton, MA: Allyn & Bacon.

Bouton, J., Albert, K., & Kennedy, K. (2002). Locker room confidential. *Sports Illustrated, 96(13),* 25.

Bovard, E. W. (1951). Group structure and perception. *Journal of Abmormal and Social Psychology, 46,* 389-405.

Bradley, B. (1976). *Life on the run.* New York: Bantam Books.

Bradley, J. E. (1996, October 28). Six shooters. A half-dozen players to a side is the rule in the rural West. *Sports Illustrated, 85,* 66-80.

Brawley, L. R., Carron, A. V., & Widmeyer, W. N. (1987). Assessing the cohesion of teams: Validity of the Group Environment Questionnaire. *Journal of Sport Psychology, 9,* 275-294.

Brawley, L. R., Carron, A. V., & Widmeyer, W. N. (1988). Exploring the relationship between cohesion and group resistance to disruption. *Journal of Sport and Exercise Psychology, 10,* 199-213.

Brawley, L. R., Carron, A. V., & Widmeyer, W. N. (1992). The nature of group goals in sport teams: A phenomenological analysis. *The Sport Psychologist, 6,* 323-333.

Brawley, L. R., Carron, A. V., & Widmeyer, W. N. (1993). The influence of the group and its cohesiveness on perceptions of group-related variables. *Journal of Sport and Exercise Psychology, 15,* 245-260.

Brawley, L. R., & Paskevich, D. M. (1997). Conducting team building research in the context of sport and exercise. *Journal of Applied Psychology, 9,* 11-40.

Bray, R. M., Kerr, N. L., & Atken, R. S. (1978). Effects of group size, problem difficulty, and sex on group performance and member reactions. *Journal of*

Personality and Social Psychology, 36, 1224-1240.

Bray, S. R. (1999). The home advantage from an individual team perspective. *Journal of Applied Sport Psychology,* 11, 116-125.

Bray, S. R., Balaguer, I, & Duda, J. L. (2004). The relationship of task self-efficacy and role efficacy beliefs to role performance in Spanish youth soccer. *Journal of Sports Sciences, 22,* 429-437.

Bray, S. R., Beauchamp, M.R., Eys, M. A., & Carron, A. V. (2004). *Need for clarity as a moderator of the role ambiguity – satisfaction relationship.* Manuscript submitted for publication.

Bray, S. R., & Brawley, L. R. (2002). Role efficacy, role clarity, and role performance effectiveness. *Small Group Research, 33,* 233-253.

Bray, S. R., Brawley, L. R. & Carron, A. V. (2002). Efficacy for interdependent role functions: Evidence from the sport domain. *Small Group Research, 33,* 644-666.

Bray, S., & Carron, A.V. (1993). The home advantage in alpine skiing. *The Australian Journal of Science and Medicine in Sport, 25,* 76-81.

Bray, S. R., Culos, S. N., Gyurcsik, N. C., Widmeyer, W. N., & Brawley, L. R. (1998). Athletes' causal perspectives on game location and performance: The home advantage? *Journal of Sport and Exercise Psychology, 20,* S-100.

Bray, S. R., Jones, M. V. and Owen, S. (2002). The influence of competition location on athletes' psychological states. *Journal of Sport Behavior, 25,* 231-242.

Bray, S. R. and Martin, K. A. (2003). The influence of competition location on individual sport athletes' performance and psychological states. *Psychology of Sport and Exercise,* 4, 117-123.

Bray, S. R., & Widmeyer, W. N. (1995). Athletes' perceptions of a home advantage in women's basketball. *Journal of Applied Sport Psychology, 7* (Suppl.), S43.

Bray, S. R. and Widmeyer, W. N. (2000). Athletes' perceptions of the home advantage: An investigation of perceived causal factors. *Journal of Sport Behavior, 23,* 1-10.

Breglio, J. (1976). *Formal structure and the recruitment of umpires in baseball organizations.* Paper presented at the American Sociological Association Annual Meeting, New York, NY.

Brennan, S. J. (1990). *Competitive excellence. The psychology and strategy of successful team building.* Omaha, NE: Peak Performance.

Brewer, M. B. (1979). The role of ethnocentricism in intergroup conflict. In W.G. Austin & S. Worchel (Eds.), *The social psychology of intergroup relations* (pp.71-84). Belmont, CA: Wadsworth.

Brown, R. (1988). *Group processes: Dynamics within and between groups.* Oxford, UK: Blackwell.

Brown, R. W. (1965). *Social psychology.* New York: Free Press.

Brown Jr., T. D., Van Raalte, J. L., Brewer, B. W., Winter, C. R. and Cornelius, A. E. (2002). World Cup soccer home advantage. *Journal of Sport Behavior, 25,* 134-144.

Buchanan, H. T., Blankenbaker, J., & Cotton, D. (1976). Academic and athletic ability as popularity factors in elementary school children. *Research Quarterly, 47,* 320-325.

Burgoon, M., Heston, J. K., & McCroskey, J. (1974). *Small group communication: A functional approach.* New York: Holt, Rinehart & Winston.

Burns, J. M. (1978). *Leadership.* New York: Harper.

Burton, D., Weinberg, R., Yukelson, D., & Weigand, D. (1998). The goal effectiveness paradox in sport: Examining the goal practices of collegiate athletes. *The Sport Psychologist, 12,* 404-418.

Buys, C. J. (1978a). Humans would do better without groups. *Personality and Social Psychology Bulletin, 4,* 123-125.

Buys, C. J. (1978b). On groups would do better without groups: A final note. *Personality and Social Psychology Bulletin, 4,* 568.

Caine, B. T., & Schlenker, B. R. (1979). Role position and group performance as determinants of egotistical perceptions in cooperative groups. *Journal of Psychology, 101,* 149-156.

Cantona, E., & Fynn, A. (1996). *Cantona on Cantona.* London: Deutsch.

Capel, S. A., Sisley, B. L., & Desertrain, G. S. (1987). The relationship between role conflict and role ambiguity to burnout in high school coaches. *Journal of Sport Psychology, 9,* 106-117.

Caplow, T. (1964). *Principles of organization.* New York: Harcourt, Brace & World.

Carli, L. L. (2001). Gender and social influence. *Journal of Social Issues, 57,* 725-741.

Carron, A. V. (1978). Role behavior and coach-athlete interaction. *International Review of Sport Sociology, 13,* 51-65.

Carron, A. V. (1980). *Social psychology of sport.* Ithaca, NY: Mouvement.

Carron, A. V. (1981a). Processes of group interaction in sport teams. *Quest, 33,* 245-270.

Carron, A.V. (1981b). *Social psychology of sport: An experiential approach.* Ithaca, NY: Mouvement.

Carron, A. V. (1982). Cohesiveness in sport groups: Interpretations and considerations. *Journal of Sport Psychology, 4,* 123-138.

Carron, A. V. (1984a). Cohesion in sport teams. In J. M. Silva III & R. S. Weinberg (Eds.), *Psychological foundations of sport* (pp. 340-351). Champaign, IL: Human Kinetics.

Carron, A. V. (1984b). *Motivation: Implications for coaching and teaching.* London, ON: Sports Dynamics.

Carron, A. V. (1986). The sport team as an effective group. In J. M. Williams (Ed.), *Applied sport psychology: Personal growth to peak performance* (pp. 75-88). Palo Alto, CA: Mayfield.

Carron, A. V., Ball, J. R., & Chelladurai, P. (1977). Motivation for participation, success in performance and their relationship to individual and group satisfaction. *Perceptual and Motor Skills, 45,* 835-841.

Carron, A. V., & Bennett, B. B. (1977). Compatibility in the coach-athlete dyad. *Research Quarterly, 48,* 671-679.

Carron, A.V., & Brawley, L.R. (2000). Cohesion: Conceptual and measurement issues. *Small Group Research, 31,* 89-106.

Carron, A. V., Brawley, L. R., & Widmeyer, W. N. (1998). The measurement of cohesiveness in sport groups. In J. L. Duda (Ed.), *Advancements in sport and exercise psychology measurement* (pp. 213-226. Morgantown, WV: Fitness Information Technology.

Carron, A. V., & Chelladurai, P. (1978). Psychological factors and athletic success: An analysis of coach-athlete interpersonal behavior. *Canadian Journal of Applied Sport Sciences, 3,* 43-50.

Carron, A. V., & Chelladurai, P. (1981). The dynamics of group cohesion in sport. *Journal of Sport Psychology, 3,* 123-139.

Carron, A. V., Colman, M. M., Wheeler, J., & Stevens, D. (2002). Cohesion and performance in sport: A meta-analysis. *Journal of Sport and Exercise Psychology, 24,* 168-188.

Carron, A. V., & Garvie, G. T. (1978). Compatability and successful performance. *Perceptual and Motor Performance, 46,* 1121-1122.

Carron, A. V., Prapavessis, H., & Grove, J. R. (1994). Group effects and self-handicapping. *Journal of Sport and Exercise Psychology, 16,* 246-258.

Carron, A. V., & Spink, K. S. (1993). Team building in an exercise setting. *The Sport Psychologist, 7,* 8-18.

Carron, A. V., Spink, K. S., & Prapavessis, H. (1997). Team building and cohesiveness in the sport and exercise setting: Use of indirect interventions. *Journal of Applied Sport Psychology, 9,* 61-72.

Carron, A. V., Widmeyer, W. N., & Brawley, L. R. (1985). The development of an instrument to assess cohesion in sport teams: The group environment questionnaire. *Journal of Sport Psychology, 7,* 244-266.

Carron, A. V., Widmeyer, W. N., & Brawley, L. R. (1988). Group cohesion and individual adherence to physical activity. *Journal of Sport and Exercise Psychology, 10,* 119-126.

Carron, A. V., Widmeyer, W. N., & Brawley, L. R. (1989). Perceptions of ideal group size in sport team. *Perceptual and Motor Skills, 69,* 1368-1379.

Carron, A. V., Widmeyer, N. W., & Brawley, L. R. (1996). *Achievement and group size: Two toucans can but one toucan can too—and better.* Unpublished manuscript, University of Western Ontario, London, ON.

Cartwright, D., & Zander, A. (1968). *Group dynamics: Research and theory.* New York: Harper & Row.

Cattell, R. B. (1948). Concepts and methods in the measurement of group syntality. *Psychological Review, 55,* 48-63.

Cattell, R. B. (1953). New concepts for measuring leadership in terms of group syntality. In D. C. Cartwright & A. Zander, (Eds.), *Group dynamics: Research and theory.* New York: Row & Peterson.

Centra, J. A., & Creech, F. R. (1976). *The relationship between student, teacher, and course characteristics and student ratings of teacher effectiveness.* SIR Report No. 4. Princeton, NJ: Educational Testing Services.

Chambliss, C. A., & Murray, E. J. (1979). Cognitive procedures for smoking reduction: Symptom attribution versus efficacy attribution. *Cognitive Therapy and Research, 3,* 91-96.

Chase, M. A., & Dummer, G. M. (1992). The role of sports as a social status determinant for children. *Research Quarterly for Exercise and Sport, 63,* 418-424.

Chelladurai, P. (1978). *A contingency model of leadership in athletics.* Unpublished doctoral dissertation, University of Waterloo, Waterloo, ON, Canada.

Chelladurai, P. (1984). Discrepancy between preferences and perceptions of leadership behavior and satisfaction of athletes in varying sports. *Journal of Sport Psychology, 6,* 27-41.

Chelladurai, P. (1984). Leadership in sports. In J. M. Silva III & R. S. Weinberg (Eds.), *Psychological foundations of sport* (pp.

329-339). Champaign, IL: Human Kinetics.

Chelladurai, P. (1990). Leadership in sports: A review of relevant research. *International Journal of Sport Psychology, 21,* 328-354.

Chelladurai, P. (1993). Styles of decision making in coaching. In J. M. Williams (Ed.), *Applied sport psychology: Personal growth to peak performance* (pp. 99-109). Mountain View, CA: Mayfield.

Chelladurai, P., & Arnott, M. (1985). Decision styles in coaching: Preferences of basketball players. *Research Quarterly for Exercise and Sport, 56,* 15-24.

Chelladurai, P., & Carron, A. V. (1977). A reanalysis of formal structure in sport. *Canadian Journal of Applied Sport Sciences, 2,* 9-14.

Chelladurai, P., & Carron, A. V. (1978). *Leadership.* Ottawa, ON: Sociology of Sport Monograph Series, Canadian Association for Health, Physical Education, and Recreation.

Chelladurai, P., & Carron, A. V. (1981). Applicability to youth sports of the Leadership Scale for Sport. *Perceptual and Motor Skills, 53,* 361-362.

Chelladurai, P., & Carron, A. V. (1982). Task characteristics and individual differences and their relationship to preferred leadership in sports. *Proceedings of the North American Society for the Psychology of Sport and Physical Activity.*

Chelladurai, P., & Carron, A. V. (1983). Athletic maturity and preferred leadership. *Journal of Sport Psychology, 5,* 371-380.

Chelladurai, P., & Haggerty, T. R. (1978). A normative model of decision styles in coaching. *Athletic Administrator, 13,* 6-9.

Chelladurai, P., Malloy, D., Imamura, H., & Yamaguchi, Y. (1987). A cross-cultural study of preferred leadership in sports. *Canadian Journal of Sport Sciences, 12,* 106-110.

Chelladurai, P., & Saleh, S. D. (1978). Preferred leadership in sports. *Canadian Journal of Applied Sport Sciences, 3,* 85-92.

Cherry, D., & Fischler, S. (1982). *Grapes: A vintage view of hockey.* Englewood Cliffs, NJ: Prentice-Hall.

Chesler, D. J., Van Steenberg, N. J., & Brueckel, J. E. (1955). Effect of morale on infantry team replacement and individual replacement systems. *Sociometry, 18,* 587-597.

Christie, R., & Geis, F. L. (1970). *Studies in Machiavellianism.* New York: Academic Press.

Cikler, J. (1967). The rise, the development and the extinction of a soccer team of boys. *International Review of Sport Sociology, 2,* 33-46.

Cissna, K. N. (1984). Phases in group development. The negative evidence. *Small Group Behavior, 15,* 3-32.

Clarke, S. R. and Norman, J. M. (1995). Home advantage of individual clubs in English soccer. *The Statistician, 44,* 509-521.

Cogan, K. D., & Petrie, T. A. (1995). Sport consultation: An evaluation of a season-long intervention with female college gymnasts. *The Sports Psychologist, 9,* 282-286.

Coleman, J. S. (1961). *The adolescent society.* New York: Free Press.

Collins, B. (1970). *Social psychology.* Don Mills, ON: Addison-Wesley.

Colman, M. M. (2001). *Group norms: Theory to practice.* Paper presented at the meeting of the Association for the Advancement of Applied Sport Psychology, Orlando, Fl.

Colman, M. M., & Carron, A. V. (2001). The nature of norms individual sport teams. *Small Group Research, 32,* 206-222.

Comrey, A. L. (1953). Group performance in a manual dexterity task. *Journal of Applied Psychology, 37,* 207-210.

Comrey, A. L., & Deskin, G. (1954a). Further results on group manual dexterity in men. *Journal of Applied Psychology, 38,* 116-118.

Comrey, A. L., & Deskin, G. (1954b). Group manual dexterity in women. *Journal of Applied Psychology, 38,* 178-180.

Cooper, R., & Payne, R. (1967, January). Personality orientations and performance in football teams: Leaders and subordinates' orientations related to team success. *Organizational Psychology Group Report No. 1.*

Cooper, R., & Payne, R. (1972). Personality orientations and performance in soccer teams. *British Journal of Social and Clinical Psychology, 11,* 2-9.

Coser, L. A. (1956). *The functions of social conflict.* Gelcoe, IL: Free Press.

Cota, A. A., Evans, C. R., Dion, K. L., Kilik, L., & Longman, R. S. (1995). The structure of group cohesion. *Personality and Social Psychological Bulletin, 21,* 572-580.

Cotton, J. L., & Cook, M. S. (1982). Meta-analysis and the effects of various reward systems: Some different conclusions from Johnson et al. *Psychological Bulletin, 92,* 176-183.

Courneya, K. S., & Carron, A.V. (1990). Batting first versus last: Implications for the home advantage. *Journal of Sport and Exercise Psychology, 12,* 312-316.

Courneya, K. S., & Carron, A. V. (1991). Effects of travel and length of the home stand/road trip on the home advantage. *Journal of Sport and Exercise Psychology, 13,* 42-49.

Courneya, K. S., & Carron, A. V. (1992). The home advantage in sport competitions: A literature review. *Journal of Sport and Exercise Psychology, 14,* 13-27.

Craighead, D. J., Privette, G., Vallianos, F., & Byrkit, D. (1986). Personality characteristics of basketball players, starters, and nonstarters. *International Journal of Sport Psychology, 17,* 110-119.

Crandall, C. S. (1988). Social contagion of binge eating. *Journal of Personality and Social Psychology, 55,* 588-598.

Cratty, B. J. (1983). *Psychology in contemporary sport: Guidelines for coaches and athletes* (2nd ed.). Englewood Cliffs, NJ: Prentice-Hall.

Crosbie, P. V. (1975). Social exchange and power compliance: A test of humans' propositions. In P. V. Crosbie (Ed.), *Interaction in small groups* (pp. 356-373). New York: Macmillan.

Crothers, T. (1995, December 11). Little magic: Canadian export Steve Nash doesn't get much TV time at Santa Clara, but he might be the best point guard in the country. *Sports Illustrated, 83,* 62-68.

Croxon, S. (2003). Preparing for Olympic glory. *Coaches Report, 9(4),* 7-11.

Curtis, B., Smith, R. E., & Smoll, F. L. (1979). Scrutinizing the skipper: A study of leadership behaviors in the dugout. *Journal of Applied Psychology, 64,* 391-400.

Curtis, J. E., & Loy, J. W. (1978). Race/ethnicity and relative centrality of playing positions in team sports. In R. S. Hutton (Ed.), *Exercise and Sport Sciences Reviews* (Vol. 6, pp. 285-313). Philadelphia, PA: Franklin Institute Press.

Daiss, S., LeUnes, A., & Nation, J. (1986). Mood and locus of control of a sample of college and professional basketball players. *Perceptual and Motor Skills, 63,* 733-734.

Dance, F. E., & Larson, C. E. (1976). *The functions of human communication: A theoretical approach.* New York: Holt, Rinehalt, & Winston.

Danielson, R. R. (1976). *Contingency model of leadership effectiveness: An empirical investigation of its application in sport.* Proceedings of the International Congress on Physical Activity Sciences (pp. 131-155). Quebec City, Quebec.

Dark, A., & Underwood, J. (1980). *When in doubt, fire the manager.* New York: Dutton.

Davies, M. F. (1994). Personality and social characteristics. In A. P. Hare, H. H. Blemberg, M. F. Davies, & M. V. Kent (Eds.). *Small Group Research: A Handbook* (pp. 41-80). Norwood, NJ: Ablex.

Dawe, S. & Carron, A. V. (1990, October). *Interrelationships among role acceptance, role clarity, task cohesion, and social cohesion.* Paper presented at the Canadian Psychomotor Learning and Sport Psychology Annual Meeting, Windsor, Ontario.

Dawson, K. A., Bray, S. R., & Widmeyer, W. N. (2002). Goal setting by intercollegiate sport teams and athletes. *Avante, 8,* 14-23.

Deep, S. D., Bass, B. M., & Vaughn, J. A. (1967). Some effects on business gaming of previous quasi-t group situations. *Journal of Applied Psychology, 51,* 426-431.

Dennis, P.W. and Carron, A. V. (1999). Strategic decisions of ice hockey coaches as a function of game location. *Journal of Sports Sciences*, 17, 263-268.

Dennis, P. W., Carron, A. V. and Loughead, T. M. (2002). The relationship between game location and decisions by National Hockey League officials. *Avante, 8(2),* 67-73.

Deutsch, M. (1949). A theory of cooperation and competition. *Human Relations, 2,* 129-152.

Dimock, H. (1941). *Rediscovering the adolescent.* New York: Association Press.

Dion, K. L. (1979). Intergroup conflict and intergroup cohesiveness. In W.G. Austin & S. Worchel (Eds.), *The social psychology of intergroup relations* (pp. 211-224). Belmont, CA: Wadsworth.

Dion, K. L. (2000). Group cohesion: From "field of forces" to multidimensional construct. *Group Dynamics: Theory, Research and Practice, 4,* 7-26.

Doise, W. (1978). Intergroup relations and polarization of individual and collective judgments. *Journal of Personality and Social Psychology, 12*, 136-143.

Donnelly, P. (1975). *An analysis of the relationship between organizational half-life and organizational effectiveness.* Paper presented at the advanced topics course, Department of Sport Studies, University of Massachusetts, Amherst.

Donnelly, P., Carron, A. V., & Chelladurai, P. (1978). *Group cohesion and sport.* Ottawa, ON: CAHPER Sociology of Sport Monograph Series.

Dowie, J. (1982). Why Spain should win the World Cup. *New Scientist, 94,* 693-695.

Driskell, J. E., & Mullen, B. (1990). Status, expectations, and behavior: A meta-analytic review and test of the theory. *Personality and Social Psychology Bulletin, 16,* 541-553.

Dryden, K. (1983). *The game: A thoughtful and provocative look at a life in hockey.* Toronto, ON: Macmillan.

Dryden, K., & Mulvoy, M. (1973). *Face-off at the summit.* Toronto, ON: Little, Brown & Co.

Duda, J. L. (1987). Toward a developmental theory of children's motivation in sport. *Journal of Sport Psychology, 9*, 130-145.

Duffy, L. J. and Hinwood, D. P. (1997). Home field advantage: Does anxiety contribute? *Perceptual and Motor Skills, 84, 283-286.*

Dunnette, M. D., Campbell, J., & Jaastad, K. (1963). The effect of group participation on brainstorming effectiveness for two industrial samples. *Journal of Applied Psychology, 47,* 30-37.

Dunteman, G., & Bass, B. M. (1963). Supervisory and engineering success associated with self, interaction and task orientation scores. *Personnel Psychology, 16,* 16-22

Durand, D. E. (1977). Power as a function of office space and physiognomy: Two studies of influence. *Psychological Reports, 40,* 755-760.

Dustin, D. W., & Davis, H. P. (1970). Evaluative bias in group and individual competition. *Journal of Social Psychology 80,* 103-108.

Eagly, A. H., & Johnson, B.T. (1990). Gender and leadership style: A meta-analysis. *Psychological Bulletin, 108,* 233-256.

Eagly, A. H., & Karau, S. J. (1991). Gender and the emergence of leaders: A meta-analysis. *Journal of Personality and Social Psychology, 60,* 685-710.

Eagly, A. H., Makhijani, M. G., & Klonsky, B. G. (1992). Gender and the evaluation of leaders: A meta-analysis. *Psychological Bulletin, 111,* 3-22.

Edney, J. J., & Grundmann, M. J. (1979). Friendship, group size, and boundary size: Small group spaces. *Small Group Behavior, 10,* 124-135.

Edney, J. J., & Jordan-Edney, N. L. (1974). Territorial spacing on a beach. *Sociometry, 37,* 92-104.

Edney, J. J., & Uhlig, S. R. (1977). Individual and small group territories. *Small Group Behavior, 8,* 457-468.

Edwards, J., & Archambault, DE. (1989). The homefield advantage. In J. H. Goldstein (Ed.), *Sports, games and play: Social and psychological viewpoints* (2nd. Ed., pp. 333-370). Hillsdale, NJ: Erlbaum.

Eitzen, D. S. (1975). Group structure and group performance. In D. M. Landers, D. V. Harris, & R. W. Christina (Eds.), *Psychology of sport and motor behavior (pp. 41-45).* University Park, PA: College of HPER, Pennsylvania State University.

Eitzen, D. S. (1976). Sport and social status in American public secondary education. *Review of Sport and Leisure, 1,* 139-155.

Eitzen, D. S., & Furst, D. (1989). Racial bias in women's collegiate volleyball. *Journal of Sport and Social Issues, 13,* 46-51.

Eitzen, D. S., & Sanford, D. C. (1975). The segregation of blacks by playing position in football: Accident or design? *Social Science Quarterly, 55,* 948-959.

Eitzen, D. S., & Yetman, N. R. (1972). Managerial change, longevity, and organizational effectiveness. *Administrative Science Quarterly, 17,* 110-116.

Elder, G. H., & Clipp, E. C. (1988). Wartime losses and social bonding and influences across 40 years in men's lives. *Psychiatry, 51,* 177-198.

Elliott, J. (2004, October 4). Turned around by a tackle. *Sports Illustrated, 101*, 57-58.

Emerson, R. (1966). Mount Everest: A case study of communication feedback and sustained group goal-striving. *Sociometry, 29,* 213-227.

Enoch, J. R., & McLemore, S. D. (1967). On the meaning of group cohesion. *Southwestern Social Science Quarterly, 48,* 174-182.

Erle, F. J. (1981). *Leadership in competitive and recreational sport.* Unpublished master's thesis, University of Western Ontario, London, ON, Canada.

Escovar, L. A., & Sim, F. M. (1974). *The cohesion of groups: Alternative conceptions.* Paper presented the meeting of the Canadian Sociology and Anthropology Association, Toronto, ON, Canada.

Evan, W. M. (1963). Peer-group interaction and organizational socialization: A study of employee turnover. *American Sociological Review, 28,* 436-440.

Evans, L., & Hardy, L. (2002a). Injury rehabilitation: A goal setting intervention study. *Research Quarterly for Exercise and Sport, 73,* 310-319.

Evans, L., & Hardy, L. (2002b). Injury rehabilitation: A qualitative follow-up study. *Research Quarterly for Exercise and Sport, 73,* 320-329.

Evans, N. J., & Jarvis, P. A. (1980). Group cohesion: A review and reevaluation. *Small Group Behavior, 11,* 359-370.

Eys, M. A., Beauchamp, M. R., & Bray, S. R. (in press). A review of team roles in sport. In S. Hanton & S. D. Mellalieu (Eds.), *Literature reviews in sport psychology.* Hauppauge, NY: Nova Science Publishers, Inc.

Eys, M. A., & Carron, A. V. (2001). Role ambiguity, task cohesion, and task self-efficacy. *Small Group Research, 32,* 356-373.

Eys, M.A., Carron, A.V., Beauchamp, M.R., & Bray, S.R. (2003). Role ambiguity in sport teams. *Journal of Sport and Exercise Psychology, 25(4),* 534-550.

Eys, M.A., Carron, A.V., Beauchamp, M.R., & Bray, S.R. (in press). Athletes' perceptions of the sources of role ambiguity. *Small Group Research.*

Eys, M. A., Carron, A. V., Bray, S. R., & Beauchamp, M. R. (2003). Role ambiguity and athlete satisfaction. *Journal of Sports Sciences, 21,* 391-401.

Eys, M. A., Hardy, J., Carron, A. V., & Beauchamp, M. R. (2003). The relationship between task cohesion and competitive state anxiety. *Journal of Sport & Exercise Psychology, 25,* 66-76.

Fabianic, D. (1984). Organizational effectiveness and managerial succession: An update of an old problem. *Journal of Sport Behavior, 7,* 139-152.

Fabianic, D. (1994). Managerial changed and organizational effectiveness in major league baseball: Findings for the eighties. *Journal of Sport Behavior, 17,* 135-147.

Farber, M. (1995, November 13). Sweeping change: After a horrendous start, the Montreal Canadiens are rolling, thanks to a new coach from the old days. *Sports Illustrated, 83,* 36-39.

Farber, M. (1996, October 7). Scouting reports. *Sports Illustrated, 85,* 68-77.

Farber, M. (1997a, January 13). Soaring. *Sports Illustrated, 86,* 52-54.

Farber, M. (1997b, March 24). The worst job in sports. *Sports Illustrated, 86,* 66-72.

Farber, M. (1997c, April 7). The big picture. Striving for long-term success, the Indians' John Hart has made tough player moves *Sports Illustrated, 86,* 82-89.

Farber, M. (2000). Chain of command. *Sports Illustrated, 93(15),* 76-87.

Feinstein, J. (1987). *A season on the brink: A year with Bobby Knight and the Indiana Hoosiers.* New York, NY: Simon & Schuster.

Feld, N. D. (1959). Information and authority: The structure of military organization. *American Sociological Review, 24,* 15-22.

Feltz, D. L. (1978). Athletics in the status system of female adolescents. *Review of Sport and Leisure, 3,* 98-108.

Feltz, D. L., Bandura, A., Albretcht, R. R., & Corcoran, J. P. (1988). *Perceived team efficacy in collegiate hockey.* Proceedings for the North American Society for the Psychology of Sport and Physical Activity.

Feltz, D. L., Corcoran, J. P., & Lirgg, C. D. (1989). *Relationships among team confidence, sport confidence and hockey performance.* Proceedings for the North American Society for the Psychology of Sport and Physical Activity.

Feltz, D. L., & Lirgg, C. D. (1998). Perceived team and player efficacy in hockey. *Journal of Applied Psychology, 83,* 557-564.

Festinger, L., Pepitone, A., & Newcomb, T. (1952). Some consequences of deindividuation in a group. *Journal of Abnormal and Social Psychology, 47,* 382-389.

Festinger, L., Schachter, S., & Back, K. (1963). *Social pressures in informal groups.* Stanford, CA: Stanford University Press. (Originally published in 1950).

Fiedler, F. E. (1954). Assumed similarity measures as predictors of team effectiveness. *Journal of Abnormal and Social Psychology, 49,* 381-388.

Fiedler, F. E. (1967). *A theory of leadership effectiveness.* New York: McGraw-Hill.

Fiedler, F. E., & Chemers, M. M. (1974). *Leadership and effective management.* Glenview, IL: Scott, Foresman & Co.

Filby, W. C., Maynard, I. W., & Graydon, J. K. (1999). The effect of multiple-goal strategies on performance outcomes in training and competition. *Journal of Applied Sport Psychology, 11,* 230-246.

Fisher, B., & Thomas, B. (1996). *Real dream teams: Seven practices used by world-class leaders to achieve extraordinary results.* Delray Beach, FL: St. Lucie.

Flames not hiding heads. (1988, April 27). *London Free Press,* p. C1.

Fletcher, D., & Hanton, S. (2003). Sources of organizational stress in elite sports performers. *The Sport Psychologist, 17,* 175-195.

Forsyth, D. R. (1983). *An introduction to group dynamics.* Belmont, CA: Wadsworth.

Forsyth, D. R., & Schlenker, B. R. (1977). Attributing the causes of group performance: Effects of performance quality, task importance, and future testing. *Journal of Personality, 45,* 220-236.

Frazier, S. E. (1988). Mood state profiles of chronic exercisers with differing abilities. *International Journal of Sport Psychology, 19,* 65-71.

French, J. R. P., & Raven, B. (1959). The bases of social power. In D. Cartwright (Ed.), *Studies in social power* (pp. 150-167). Ann Arbor, MI: Institute for Social Research.

Gaertner, K. N., & Nollen, S. D. (1992). *Turnover intentions and desire among executives.* Human Relations, 45, 447-465.

Gammage, K. L., Carron, A. V., & Estabrooks, P. A. (2001). Team cohesion and individual productivity: The influence of the norm for productivity and the identifiability of individual effort. *Small Group Research, 32,* 3-18.

Gamson, W. A., & Scotch, N. A. (1964). Scapegoating in baseball. *American Journal of Sociology, 70,* 69-72.

Garland, J., Kolodny, R., & Jones, H. (1965). A model for stages of development in social work groups. In S. Bernstein (Ed.), *Exploration in group work.* Boston, MA: Milford House.

Gastil, J. (1994). A meta-analytic review of the productivity and satisfaction of democratic and autocratic leadership. *Small Group Research, 25,* 384-410.

Gayton, W. F., Brioda, J. and Elgee, L. (2001). An investigation of coaches' perceptions of the cause of home advantage. *Perceptual and Motor Skills, 92,* 933-936.

Gayton, W. F., & Langevin, G. (1992). Home advantage: Does it exist in individual sports? *Perceptual and Motor Skills, 74,* 706.

Gayton, W. F., Matthews, G. R., & Nickless, C. J. (1987). The home field disadvantage in sports championships: Does it exist in hockey? *Journal of Sports Psychology, 9,* 183-185.

Gayton, W. F. and Coombs, R. (1995). The home advantage in high school basketball. *Perceptual and Motor Skills, 81,* 1344-1346.

George, J. J. (1989). Finding solutions to the problem of fewer female coaches. *The Physical Educator, 46,* 2-8.

Gersick, C. J. G. (1988). Time and transition in work teams: Toward a new model of group development. *Academy of Management Journal, 31,* 9-41.

Gill, D. L. (1977). Cohesiveness and performance in sport groups. *Exercise and Sport Sciences Reviews, 5,* 131-155.

Gill, D. L. (1979). The prediction of group motor performance from individual member ability. *Journal of Motor Behavior, 11,* 113-122.

Gill, D. L. (1980). Success-failure attributions in competitive groups: an exception to egocentricism. *Journal of Sport Psychology, 2,* 106-114.

Gill, D. L. (1984). Individual and group performance in sport. In J. M. Silva & R. S. Weinberg (Eds.). *Psychological foundations of sport* (pp. 315-328). Champaign, IL: Human Kinetics.

Gill, D. L. (1986). Competitiveness among females and males in physical activity classes. *Sex Roles, 15,* 233-247.

Gill, D. L., & Gross, J. B. (1979). The influence of group success-failure on selected interpersonal variables. In G. C. Roberts & K. M. Newell (Eds.), *Psychology of motor behavior and sport – 1980* (pp. 61-71). Champaign, IL: Human Kinetics.

Gillick talks to Bell, agent about DH role. (1988, March 4). *London Free Press,* p. C2.

Goldman, M., (1965). A comparison of individual and group performance for varying combinations of initial ability. *Journal of Personality and Social Psychology, 1,* 210-216.

Goldman, F. W., & Goldman, M. (1981). The effects of dyadic group experience in subsequent individual performance. *Journal of Social Psychology, 115,* 83-88.

Golembiewski, R. (1962). *The small group.* Chicago, IL: University of Chicago.

Gordon, S. (1988). Decision-making styles and coaching effectiveness in university soccer. *Canadian Journal of Sport Sciences, 13,* 56-65.

Goyens, C., & Turowetz, A. (1986) *Lions in winter.* Scarborough, ON: Prentice-Hall.

Grand, R.H. & Carron, A.V. (1982, October). *Development of the Team Climate Questionnaire.* Canadian Psychomotor Learning and Sport Psychology Symposium, Edmonton, Alberta.

Granito, V. J., & Rainey, D. W. (1988). Differences in cohesion between high school and college football teams and starters and nonstarters. *Perceptual and Motor Skills, 66,* 471-477.

Green, R. B., & Mack, J. (1978). Would groups do better without social psychologists? A response to Buys. *Personality and Social Psychology Bulletin, 4,* 561-563.

Greenfield, J. (1976). *The world's greatest team: A portrait of the Boston Celtics 1957-1969*. New York: Random House.

Greenlees, I. A., Graydon, J. K., & Maynard, I. W. (1999). The impact of collective efficacy beliefs on effort and persistence in a group task. *Journal of Sports Sciences, 17,* 151-158.

Greenlees, I. A., Graydon, J. K., & Maynard, I. W. (2000). The impact of individual efficacy beliefs on group goal selection and group goal commitment. *Journal of Sports Sciences, 18,* 451-459.

Greer, D. L. (1983). Spectator booing and the home advantage: A study of social influence in the basketball arena. *Social Psychology Quarterly, 46,* 252-261.

Greer, H. (2002). Five ways to motivate a team. *Coach and Athletic Director, 72,* 40-41.

Griffen, R. (2004, October 17). Beware Rocket's red glare from mound. Toronto Star, p. E 4.

Gross, N., & Martin, W. (1952). On group cohesiveness. *American Journal of Sociology, 57,* 533-546.

Gruber, J. J., & Gray, G. R. (1981). Factor patterns of variables influencing cohesiveness at various levels of basketball competition. *Research Quarterly for Exercise and Sport, 52,* 19-30.

Gruber, J. J., & Gray, G. R. (1982). Response to forces influencing cohesion as a function of player status and level of male varsity basketball competition. *Research Quarterly for Sport and Exercise, 53,* 27-36.

Grusky, O. (1963). Managerial succession and organizational effectiveness. *American Journal of Sociology, 69,* 21-31.

Grusky, O. (1964). Commentary and debates: Scapegoating in baseball. Reply. *American Journal of Sociology, 70,* 72-76.

Gully, S. M., Devine, D. J., & Whitney, D. J. (1995). A meta-analysis of cohesion and performance: Effects of level of analysis and task interdependence. *Small Group Research, 25,* 497-520.

Gully, S. M., Incalcaterra, K. A., Joshi, A., & Beaubien, J. M. (2002). A meta-analysis of team-efficacy, potency, and performance: Interdependence and level of analysis as moderators of observed relationships. *Journal of Applied Psychology, 87,* 819-832.

Gzowski, P. (1981). *The game of our lives.* Toronto, ON: McClelland & Stewart.

Hackman, J. R., & Oldham, G. R. (1980). *Work redesign.* Reading, MA: Addison-Wesley.

Habib, D. G. (2002). Dissension in the dressing room. *Sports Illustrated, 96(19),* 80.

Hall, E. T. (1966). *The hidden dimension.* Garden City, NY: Doubleday.

Hall, H. K., & Byrne, A. T. J. (1988). Goal setting in sport: Clarifying recent anomalies. *Journal of Sport and Exercise Psychology, 10,* 184-198.

Hall, H. K., Weinberg, R. S., & Jackson, A. (1987). Effects of goal specificity, goal difficulty, and information feedback on endurance performance. *Journal of Sport Psychology, 9,* 43-54.

Hallinan, C. J. (1991). Aborigines and positional segregation in Australian rugby league. *International Review of Sociology of Sport, 26,* 69-79.

Hardy, C. J., & Crace, R. K. (1997). Foundations of team building: Introduction to the Team Builder Primer. *Journal of Applied Sport Psychology, 9,* 1-10.

Hardy, C. J., & Latané, B. (1988). Social loafing in cheerleaders: Effects of team membership and competition. *Journal of Sport & Exercise Psychology, 10,* 109-114.

Hardy, J., Eys, M. A., & Carron, A. V. (in press). Disadvantages from high task cohesion? A qualitative approach. *Small Group Research.*

Hare, A. P. (1976). *Handbook of small group research (2nd ed.).* New York: Free Press.

Hare, A. P. (1981). Group size. *American Behavioral Scientist, 24,* 695-708.

Hare, A. P., & Bales, R. F. (1963) Seating position and small group interaction. *Sociometry, 26,* 480-486.

Harkins, S. G., Latané, B., & Williams, K. (1980). Social loafing: Allocating effort or taking it easy. *Journal of Experimental Social Psychology, 16,* 457-465.

Hassmen, P., & Blomstrand, E. (1995). Mood state relationships and soccer team performance. *The Sport Psychologist, 9,* 297-308.

Hausenblas, H. A., & Carron, A. V. (1996). Group cohesion and self-handicapping in female and male athletes. *Journal of Sport and Exercise Psychology, 18,* 132-143.

Hayman, H. (1981). Minority group sports involvement in New Zealand: The New Zealand Maori. *Research Papers in Physical Education, 3,* 1-22.

Haythorn, W. W. (1968). The composition of groups: A review of the literature. *Acta Psychologica, 28,* 97-128.

Heaton, A. W., & Sigall, H. (1989). The "championship choke" revisited: The role of fear of acquiring a negative identity. *Journal of Applied Social Psychology, 19,* 1019-1033.

Heider, F. (1958). *The psychology of interpersonal relations.* New York: Wiley.

Henderson, J., Bougeois, A. E., LeUnes, A., & Meyers, M. C. (1998). Group cohesion, mood disturbance, and stress in female basketball players. *Small Group Research, 29,* 212-225.

Hendry, L. B. (1968) Assessment of personality traits in the coach-athlete relationship. *Research Quarterly, 39, 543*-551.

Henschen, K. P. (1986). Athletic staleness and burnout: Diagnosis, prevention, and treatment. In J. M. Williams (Ed.), *Applied sport psychology: Personal growth to peak performance* (pp. 327-342). Palo Alto, CA: Mayfield

Hersey, P., & Blanchard, K. H. (1969). Life style theory of leadership. *Training and Development Journal, 23,* 26-34.

Hersey, P., & Blanchard, K. H. (1977). *Management and organizational behavior* (3rd Ed.). Englewood Cliffs, NJ: Prentice-Hall.

Hersey, P., & Blanchard, K. H. (1982). Leadership style: Attitudes and behaviors. *Training and Development Journal, 36,* 50-52.

Herzog, W., & Horrigan, K. (1987). *White rat: A life in baseball.* New York: Harper & Row.

Heslin, R. (1964). Predicting group task effectiveness from member characteristics. *Psychological Bulletin, 62,* 248-256.

Heuzé, J, Sarrazin, P., Masiero, M., Raimbault, N., & Thomas, J. (2005). *The relationships of perceived motivational climate to cohesion and collective efficacy in elite female teams.* Manuscript submitted for publication.

Highlen, P. S., & Bennett, B. B. (1979). Psychological characteristics of successful and nonsuccessful elite wrestlers: An exploratory study. *Journal of Sport Psychology, 1,* 123-137.

Highlen, P. S., & Bennett, B. B. (1983). Elite divers and wrestlers: A comparison between open- and closed-skill athletes. *Journal of Sport Psychology, 5,* 390-409.

Hill, W. F., & Gruner, L. (1973). A study of development in open and closed groups. *Small Group Behavior, 4,* 365-381.

Hodges, L., & Carron, A. V. (1992). Collective efficacy and group performance. *International Journal of Sport Psychology, 23,* 48-59.

Hoffer, R. (1996, March 11). King no more: By forcing Los Angeles to trade him, Wayne Gresky escaped a losing team—but he also tarnished his image. *Sports Illustrated, 84,* 22-28; 33.

Hoffman, L. R. (1965). Group problem solving. *Advances in Experimental Social Psychology, 2,* 99-132.

Holland, A., & Andre, T. (1999). Student characteristics and choice of high school remembrance role. *Adolescence, 34,* 315-338.

Hollander, E. P. (1961). Some effects of perceived status on responses to innovative behavior. *Journal of Abnormal and Social Psychology, 63,* 247-250.

Hollander, E. P. (1967). *Principles and methods of social psychology.* New York, NY: Oxford University.

Homans, G. C. (1950). *The human group.* New York: Harcourt, Brace & World.

Hopkins, T. K. (1964). *The silent language.* New York: Doubleday.

Horne, T., & Carron, A. V. (1985). Compatibility in coach-athlete relationships. *Journal of Sport Psychology, 7,* 137-149.

Huddleston, S., Doody, S. G., & Ruder, M. K. (1985). The effect of prior knowledge of the social loafing phenomenon on performance in a group. *International Journal of Sport Psychology, 16,* 176-182.

Huntington, A. S. (1996, July). She makes women winners. *Glamour,* p .79.

Imamoglu, E. O. (1991). Interpersonal consequences of expressing personal or team affect for team success of failure among Turkish students. *The Journal of Psychology, 125,* 509-523.

Imlach, P., & Young, S. (1982). *Heaven and hell in the NHL.* Toronto, ON: McClelland & Stewart.

Inciong, P. (1974). *Leadership style and team success.* Unpublished doctoral dissertation, University of Utah.

Indik, B. (1965). Organization size and member participation: Some experimental tests of alternative explanations. *Human Relations, 18,* 339-350.

Ingham, A. G., Levinger, G., Graves, J., & Peckham, V. (1974). The Ringlemann Effect: Studies of group size and group performance. *Journal of Experimental Social Psychology, 10,* 371-384.

Irvine, D. M., & Evans, M. G. (1995). Job satisfaction and turnover among nurses: Integrating research findings across studies. *Nursing Research, 44,* 246-253.

Irving, P. G., & Goldstein, S. R. (1990). Effect of home-field advantage on peak performance of baseball pitchers. *Journal of Sport Behavior, 13,* 23-27.

Isenberg, D. J. (1986). Group polarization: A critical review and meta-analysis. *Journal of Personality and Social Psychology, 50,* 1141-1151.

Iso-Ahola, S. (1977a). Immediate attributional effects of success and failure in the field: Testing some laboratory hypotheses. *European Journal of Social Psychology, 7,* 275-296.

Iso-Ahola, S. (1977b). Effects of team outcome on children's self-perceptions: Little League baseball. *Scandinavian Journal of Psychology, 18,* 38-42.

Jackson, P. & Arkush, M. (2004). *The last season.* New York: Penquin Press.

Jackson, S. E., Brett, J. F., & Sessa, V. I., Cooper, D. M., Julian, J. A., & Peyronnin, K. (1991). Some differences make a difference: Individual dissimilarity and group heterogeneity as correlates of recruitment, promotions, and turnover. *Journal of Applied Psychology, 76,* 675-689.

Jackson, S. E., & Schuler, R. S. (1985). A meta-analysis and conceptual critique of research on role ambiguity and role conflict in work settings. *Organizational Behavior and Human Decision Process, 36,* 16-78.

Jacob, C. S. (1995). *The nature of status in sport teams.* Unpublished doctoral dissertation, University of Western Ontario, London, ON, Canada.

Jacob, C. S., & Carron, A. V. (1994). Sources of status in intercollegiate sport teams. *Journal of Sport and Exercise Psychology, 16* (Suppl.), S67.

Jacob, C. S., & Carron, A.V. (1996). Sources of status in sport teams. *International Journal of Sport Psychology, 27,* 369-382.

Jacob, C. S., & Carron, A. V. (1998). The association between status and cohesion in sport teams. *Journal of Sports Sciences, 16,* 187-198.

Jacob Johnson, C. S. (2004, Summer). Status in sport teams: Myth or reality? *International Sports Journal,* 55-64.

Jambor, E. A., & Weekes, E. M. (1996). The nontraditional female athlete: A case study. *Journal of Applied Sport Psychology, 8,* 146-159.

Janis, I. L. (1972). *Victims of groupthink.* Boston, MA: Houghton-Mifflin.

Janis, I. L. (1982). *Groupthink: Psychological studies of policy decision and fiascoes* (2nd ed.). Boston, MA: Houghton Mifflin.

Janssens, L., & Nuttin, J. R. (1976). Frequency perception of individual and group successes as a function of competition, coaction, and isolation. *Journal of Personality and Social Psychology, 80,* 103-108.

Jehue, R., Street, D., & Huizenga, R. (1993). Effect of time zone and game time changes on team performance: National Football League. *Medicine and Science in Sports and Exercise, 25,* 127-131.

Johnson, D.W. & Johnson, F.P. (2000). *Joining together: Group theory and group skills* (7th ed.). Needham Heights, MA: Allyn & Bacon.

Johnson, D. W., Maruyama, G., Johnson, R., Nelson, D., & Skon, L. (1981). The effects of cooperative, competitive, and individualistic goal structures on achievement: A meta analysis. *Psychological Bulletin, 89,* 47-62.

Jones, G.R. (2001). *Organizational theory: Text and cases* (3rd ed). Upper Saddle River, NJ: Prentice Hall.

Jones, E. E., & Berglas, S. (1978). Control of attributions about the self through self-handicapping strategies: The appeal of alcohol and the role of underachievement. *Personality and Social Psychology Bulletin, 4,* 200-206.

Jones, E. E., & Nisbett, R. E. (1971). The actor and the observer: Divergent perceptions of the causes of behavior. In E. E. Jones, D. E. Kanouse, H. H. Kelley, R. E., Nisbett, S. Valins, & B. Weinder (Eds.), *Attributions: Perceiving the causes of behavior* (pp. 79-94). Morristown, NJ: General Learning Press.

Jones, G., Leonard, W. M. II, Schmitt, R. L., Smith, D. R., & Tolone, W. L. (1987). A loglinear analysis of stacking in college football. *Social Science Quarterly, 68,* 70-83.

Jones, M. B. (1974). Regressing group on individual effectiveness. *Organizational Behavior and Human Performance, 11,* 426-451.

Jones, M. V., Bray, S. R. and Bolton, L. (2001). Do cricket umpires favour the home team? Officiating bias in English club cricket. Perceptual and Motor Skills, *93, 359-362.*

Johnson, S. R., Ostrow, A. C., Perna, F. M., & Etzel, E. F. (1997). The effects of group versus individual goal setting on bowling performance. *The Sport Psychologist, 11,* 190-200.

Jordon, M. (1994). *I can't accept not trying.* New York: Harper Collins.

Jurkovac, T. (1985). *Collegiate basketball players' perceptions of the home advantage.* Unpublished master's thesis, Bowling Green State University, Bowling Green, OH, USA.

Kahn, R. (1972). *The boys of summer.* New York: Harper & Row.

Kahn, R. L., Wolfe, D. M., Quinn, R. P., Snoek, J. D., & Rosenthal, R. A. (1964). *Occupational stress: Studies in role conflict and role ambiguity.* New York: Wily.

Kane, M. J. (1988). The female athletic role as a status determinant within the social systems of high school adolescents. *Adolescents, 23,* 253-264.

Karau, S. J., & Williams, K. D. (1993). Social loafing: A meta-analytic review and theoretical integration. *Journal of Personality and Social Psychology, 65,* 681-706.

Karolyi, B., & Richardson, N. (1994). *Feel no fear: The power, passion and politics of a life in gymnastics.* New York: Hyperion.

Kelley, H. H. (1967). Attribution theory in social psychology. In D. Levine (Ed.), *Nebraska Symposium on Motivation: Vol. 15. Perspectives on Motivation* (pp. 192-240). Lincoln, NE: University of Nebraska Press.

Kennedy, J., & Stephan, W. (1977). The effects of cooperation and competition on in-group-outgroup bias. *Journal of Applied Social Psychology, 7,* 115-130.

Kenny, D. A., & Lavoie, L. (1985). Separating individual and group effects. *Journal of Personality and Social Psychology, 48,* 339-348.

Kenow, L. J., & Williams, J. M. (1992). Relationship between anxiety, self-confidence, and the evaluation of coaching behaviors. *The Sport Psychologist, 6,* 344-357.

Kernaghan, J. (1987, September 15). The best brings out the best. *The London Free Press,* p. C1.

Kerr, J. H. and Vanschaik, P. (1995). Effects of game venue and outcome on psychological mood states in rugby. *Personality and Individual Differences,* 19, 407-410.

Khrushchev, N. (1970). *Khrushchev remembers.* Toronto, ON: Little, Brown & Co.

Kim, M.S. (2001). Satisfaction and perception of performance norms of sport teams. *Perceptual and Motor Skills, 92,* 1201-1204.

Kim, M.S., & Cho, I. C. (1996). Self-monitoring and perception of performance norms of sport teams. *Perceptual and Motor Skills, 83,* 129-130.

King, K. (2004). The coach's door is open. *Sports Illustrated, 100(17),* 164-165.

King, L. A., & King, D. W. (1990). Role conflict and role ambiguity: A critical assessment of construct validity. *Psychological Bulletin, 107,* 48-64.

King, P. (2003). Are you kidding me? *Sports Illustrated, 98(1),* 52-53.

King, P. (2004, October 4). Selling point. *Sports Illustrated, 101,* 80-81.

Kirschenbaum, D. S., & Smith, R. J. (1983). A preliminary study of sequence effects in simulated coach feedback. *Journal of Sport Psychology, 5,* 332-342.

Klein, M., & Christiansen, G. (1969). Group composition, group structure and group effectiveness of basketball teams. In J. W. Loy & G. S. Kenyon (Eds.), *Sport, culture and society* (pp. 397-408). New York: Macmillan.

Klonke, C. (1988). Jacques Demers: Head coach. *Goal: Detroit Red Wings,* 25. New York: Professional Sports Publications.

Klonsky, B. (1975*). The effects of formal structure and role skills on coaching recruitment and longevity: A study of professional baseball teams.* Unpublished paper, Department of Psychology, Fordham University.

Kluckhohn, C., & Murray, H. A. (1949). *Personality in nature, society and culture.* New York: Knopf.

Knowles, E. S. (1983). Social physics and the effects of others: Tests of the effect of audience size and distance on social judgements and behavior. *Journal of Personality and Social Psychology, 45,* 1263-1279.

Kogan, N., & Wallach, M. A. (1964). *Risk taking: A study of cognition and personality.* New York: Holt, Rinehart, & Winston.

Kornspan, A. S., Lerner, B. S., Ronayne, J., Etzel, E. F., & Johnson, S. (1995). The home disadvantage in the National Football League's conference championship games. *Perceptual and Motor Skills, 80,* 800-802.

Kozub, S. A. (1993). *Exploring the relationships among coaching behavior, team cohesion, and player leadership.* Unpublished doctoral dissertation, University of Houston, TX.

Kozub, S. A., & McDonnell, J. F. (2000). Exploring the relationship between cohesion and collective efficacy in rugby teams. *Journal of Sport Behavior, 23,* 120-129.

Krane, V., Greenleaf, C. A., & Snow, J. (1997). Reaching for gold and the price of glory: A motivational case study of an elite gymnast. *The Sport Psychologist, 11,* 53-71.

Kravitz, D. A., Cohen, J. L., Martin, B., Sweeney, J., McCarty, J., Elliott, E., & Goldstein, P. (1978). Humans would do better without other humans. *Personality and Social Psychology Bulletin, 4,* 559-560.

Kravitz, D. A., & Martin, B. (1986). Ringelmann rediscovered: The original article. *Journal of Personality and Social Psychology, 50,* 936-941.

Kroll, W. (1967). Sixteen personality factor profiles of collegiate wrestlers. *Research Quarterly, 38,* 49-57.

Kyllo, L. B., & Landers, D. M. (1995). Goal setting in sport and exercise: A research synthesis to resolve the controversy. *Journal of Sport and Exercise Psychology, 17,* 117-137.

Laios, A., Theodorakis, N., & Gargalianos, D. (2003). Leadership and power: Two important factors for effective coaching. *International Sports Journal, 7,* 150-154.

Landers, D. M., & Lueschen, G. (1974). Team performance outcome and cohesiveness of competitive co-acting groups. *International Review of Sport Sociology, 9,* 57-69.

Landers, D. M., Wilkinson, M. O., Hatfield, B. D., & Barber, H. (1982). Causality and the cohesion-performance relationship. *Journal of Sport Psychology, 4,* 170-183.

Lapchick, R. E. (2003). *2003 racial and gender report card.* Orlando, FL: University of Central Florida, The Institute for Diversity and Ethics in Sport.

Latané, B. (1981). The psychology of social impact. *American Psychologist, 36,* 343-356.

Latané, B., Williams, K., & Harkins, S. (1979). Many hands make light the work: The causes and consequences of social loafing. *Journal of Personality and Social Psychology, 37,* 822-832.

Laughlin, P., Branch, L., & Johnson, H. (1969). Individual versus triadic performance on unidimensional complementary tasks as a function of initial ability level. *Journal of Personality and Social Psychology, 12,* 144-150.

Lavoie, M. (1989). Stacking, performance differentials, and salary discrimination in professional ice hockey: A survey of the evidence. *Sociology of Sport Journal, 6,* 17-35.

Lee, H. K., Kim, B. H., & Lim, B. J. (1993). The influence of structural characteristics on team success in sport groups. *Korean Journal of Sport Science, 5,* 138-154.

Lehman, D. R., & Reifman, A. (1987). Spectator influence on basketball officiating. *Journal of Social Psychology, 127,* 673-675.

Lenk, H. (1969). Top performance despite internal conflict: An antithesis to a functional proposition. In J. Loy & G. Kenyon (Eds.), *Sport, culture and society: A reader on the sociology of sport.* Toronto, ON: MacMillan.

Leonard, W. M. (1977). Stacking and performance differentials of whites, blacks and latins in professional baseball. *Review of Sport and Leisure, 2,* 77-106.

Leonard, W. M. (1987). "Stacking" in college basketball: A neglected analysis. *Sociology of Sport Journal, 4,* 403-409.

Leonard, W. M. (1989). The "home advantage": The case of the modern Olympiads. *Journal of Sport Behavior, 12,* 227-241.

Levine, J. M., & Moreland, R. L. (1991). Culture and socialization in work groups. In L. B. Resnick, J. M. Levine, & S. D. Teasley (Eds.), *Perspectives on socially shared cognition* (pp. 257-282). Washington, DC, American. Psychological Association.

Lewin, K. (1935). *A dynamic theory of personality.* New York: McGraw-Hill.

Lewin, K. (1943). Forces behind food habits and methods of change. *Bulletin of the National Research Council, 108,* 35-65.

Lewin, K., & Lippitt, R. (1938). An experimental approach to the study of autocracy and democracy: A preliminary note. *Sociometry, 1,* 292-300.

Lewis, G. H. (1972). Role differentiation. *American Sociological Review, 37,* 424-434.

Liddell W. W., & Slocum, J. W. (1976). The effects of individual-role compatibility upon group performance: An extension of Schutz's FIRO theory. *Academy of Management Journal, 19,* 413-426.

Lieber, J. (1987, October 5). A test of unity and loyalty. *Sports Illustrated, 67,* 41-43.

Locke, E. A. (1976). The nature and causes of job satisfaction. In M. D. Dunnette (Ed.), *Handbook of industrial and organizational psychology.* Chicago: Rand McNally.

Locke, E. A., & Latham, G. P. (1984). *Goal setting: A motivational technique that works.* Englewood Cliffs, NJ: Prentice-Hall.

Locke, E. A., Shaw, K. N., Saari, L. M., & Latham, G. P. (1981). Goal setting and task performance: 1969-1980. *Psychological Bulletin, 90,* 125-152.

Loden, M. (1985). *Feminine leadership or how to succeed in business without being one of the boys.* New York: Time Books.

Looney, D.S. (1988, January 11). Why, oh why did Pat stand pat? *Sports Illustrated, 68,* 22-23.

Lott, A. J., & Lott, B. E. (1965). Group cohesiveness as interpersonal attraction: A review of relationships with antecedent and consequent variables. *Psychological Bulletin, 64,* 259-309.

Loughead, T. M., Carron, A. V., Bray, S. R. and Kim, A. (2003). Facility familiarity and the home advantage in professional sports. *International Journal of Sport Psychology and Exercise Psychology, 1,* 264-274.

Loy, J. W. (1970). *Where the action is: A consideration of centrality in sport situations.* Paper presented at the Canadian Psychomotor Learning and Sport Psychology Symposium, Windsor, ON, Canada.

Loy, J. W., & McElvogue, J. F. (1970). Racial integration in American sport. *International Review of Sport Sociology, 5,* 5-24.

Loy, J. W., McPherson, B. D., & Kenyon, G. (1978). *Sport and social systems: A guide to the analysis, problems, and literature.* Reading, MA: Addison-Wesley.

Loy, J. W., & Sage, J. N. (1968). *The effects of formal structure on organizational leadership: An investigation of interscholastic baseball teams.* Paper presented at the 2nd International Congress of Sport Psychology, Washington, D.C.

Loy, J. W., Theberge, N., Kjeldsen, E., & Donnelly, P. (1975). *An examination of hypothesized correlates of replacement processes in sport organizations.* Paper prepared for presentation at the International Seminar for the Sociology of Sport, University of Heidelberg.

Ludwig, J. (1972). *Hockey night in Moscow.* Toronto, ON: McClelland & Stewart.

Mabry, E. A., & Barnes, R. E. (1980). *The dynamics of small group communication.* Englewood Cliffs, NJ: Prentice-Hall.

MacMullan, J. (1997, January 20). Inside the NBA. *Sports Illustrated, 86,* 86-88.

Madden, J., & Anderson, D. (1986). *One knee equals two feet: (And everything else you need to know about football).* New York: Jove Books.

Maguire, J. (1988). Race and position assignment in English soccer: A preliminary analysis of ethnicity and sport in Britain. *Sociology of Sport Journal, 5,* 257-269.

Magyar, T. M., Feltz, D. L., & Simpson, I. P. (2004). Individual and crew level determinants of collective efficacy in rowing. *Journal of Sport and Exercise Psychology, 26,* 136-153.

Mahoney, M. J., & Avener, M. (1977). Psychology of the elite athlete: An exploratory study. *Cognitive Therapy and Research, 1,* 135-142.

Mann, R. D. (1959). A review of the relationship between personality and performance in small groups. *Psychological Bulletin, 56,* 241-270.

Mariotti, J. (2004, August 18). Dream team, fans deserve each other. Chicago Sun-Times. Retrieved August, 18, 2004, from http://www.suntimes.com/output/mariotti/cst-spt-jay18.html

Marsh, H. W., & Peart, N. D. (1988). Competitive and cooperative physical fitness training programs for girls: Effects on physical fitness and multidimensional self-concepts. *Journal of Sport and Exercise Psychology, 10,* 390-407.

Marsh, R. L., & Heitman, R. J. (1981). The centrality phenomenon in football: Senior Bowl, 1975-1981. *Journal of Sport Behavior, 4,* 111-118.

Marshall, J., & Heslin, R. (1975). Boys and girls together: Sexual composition and the effect of density and group size on cohesiveness. *Journal of Personality and Social Psychology, 31,* 952-961.

Marshall, T. H. (1963). *Sociology at the crossroads.* London: Heinemann.

Martens, R. (1970). Influence of participation motivation on success and satisfaction in team performance. *Research Quarterly, 41,* 510-518.

Martens, R., Landers, D. M., & Loy, J. W. (1972). *Sport cohesiveness questionnaire.* Washington, DC: AAHPERD Publications.

Martens, R., & Peterson, J. (1971). Group cohesiveness as a determinant of success and member satisfaction in team performance. *International Review of Sport Sociology, 6,* 49-71.

Martin, B., & Pepe, P. (1987). *Billyball.* Garden City, NY: Doubleday & Co.

Maruyama, G. (1991). Meta-analyses relating goal structures to achievement: Findings, controversies, and impacts. *Personality and Social Psychology Bulletin, 17,* 300-305.

Massengale, J., & Farrington, S. (1977.) The influence of playing position centrality on the careers of college football coaches. *Review of Sport and Leisure, 2,* 107-115.

Matsui, T., Kakuyama, T., & Onglatco, M. L. (1987). Effects of goals and feedback on performance in groups. *Journal of Applied Psychology, 72,* 407-415.

McCallum, J. (1988, March 21). King for a year. *Sports Illustrated, 68,* 15.

McCallum, J. (1996, November 25). The man. By speaking his mind, Grant Hill had demonstrated that he's the guy who now drives the Pistons. *Sports Illustrated, 85,* 40-48.

McCallum, J. (2005, January 17). Super side-kick. *Sports Illustrated, 102,* 58.

McCullagh, P. (1987). Modeling similarity effects on motor performance. *Journal of Sport Psychology, 9,* 249-260.

McClure, B. A., & Foster, C. D. (1991). Group work as a method of promoting cohesiveness within a women's gymnastics team. *Perceptual and Motor Skills, 73,* 307-313.

McDaniel, E. D., & Feldhusen, J. F. (1971). College teaching effectiveness. *Today's Education, 60,* 27.

McGehee, R. V., & Paul, M. J. (1986). Racial makeup of central, stacking, and other playing positions in southeastern conference football teams, 1967-1983. In L. V. Vander & J. H. Humphrey (Eds.), *Psychology and Sociology of Sport. Current Selected Reseach,* Volume 1 (pp 177-190). Clemson, SC: Clemson University.

McGlynn, R. P. (1982). A comment on the meta-analysis of goal structures. *Psychological Bulletin, 92,* 184-185.

McGrath, J. E. (1962). The influence of positive interpersonal relations on adjustment and effectiveness in rifle teams. *Journal of Abnormal and Social Psychology, 65,* 365-375.

McGrath, J. E. (1964). *Social psychology: A brief introduction. New* York: Holt, Rinehart & Winston.

McGrath, J. E. (1984). *Groups: Interaction and performance.* Englewood Cliffs, NJ: Prentice-Hall.

McGrath, J. E., & Altman, I. (1966). *Small group research.* New York: Holt, Rinehart & Winston.

McGuire, A. (1987). Introduction. In J. Feinstein, *A season on the brink: A year with Bobby Knight and the Indiana Hoosiers.* New York: Simon & Schuster.

McGuire, F. A. (1985). Leisure co-participant preferences of the elderly: Age-homogeneity versus age-heterogeneity. *Leisure Sciences, 7,* 115-124.

McKnight, P., Williams, J. M., & Widmeyer, W. N. (1991, October). *The effects of cohesion and identifiability on reducing the likelihood of social loafing.* Presented at the Association for the Advancement of Applied Sport Psychology Annual Conference, Savannah, GA.

McPherson, B. D. (1976a). Involuntary turnover: A characteristic process of sport organizations. *International Review of Sport Sociology, 4,* 5-16.

McPherson, B. D. (1976b). Involuntary turnover and organizational effectiveness in the National Hockey League. In R. S. Gruneau & J. G. Albinson (Eds.), *Canadian sport: Sociological perspectives* (pp. 259-264). Don Mills, ON: Addison-Wesley.

McTeer, W., White, P. G., & Persad, S. (1995). Manager/coach midseason replacement and team performance in professional team sport. *Journal of Sport Behavior, 18,* 58-68.

Meggyesy, D. (1971). *Out of their league.* New York: Paperback Library.

Melnick, M. J. (1982). Six obstacles to effective team performance: Small group considerations. *Journal of Sport Behavior, 5,* 114-123.

Melnick, M. J. (1988). Racial segregation by playing position in English football league: Some preliminary observations. *Journal of Sport and Social Issues, 12,* 122-130.

Melnick, M. J. (1996). Maori women and positional segregation in New Zealand netball: Another test of the Anglocentric hypothesis. *Sociology of Sport Journal, 13,* 259-273.

Melnick, M. J., & Chemers, M. (1974). Effects of group social structure on the success of basketball teams. *Research Quarterly, 45,* 1-8.

Melnick, M. J., & Loy, J. W. (1996). The effects of formal structure on leadership recruitment: An analysis of team captaincy among New Zealand provincial rugby teams. *International Review for Sociology of Sport, 31,* 91-107.

Mennecke, B. E., Hoffer, J. A., & Wynne, B. E. (1992). The implications of group development and history for group support system theory and practice. *Small Group Research, 23,* 524-572.

Mento, A. J., Steel, R. P., & Karren, R. J. (1987). A meta-analytic study of the effects of goal setting on task performance: 1966-1984. *Organizational Behavior and Human Decision Processes, 39,* 52-83.

Meyers, A. W., Cooke, C. J., Cullen, J., & Liles, L. (1979). Psychological aspects of athletic competitors: A replication across sports. *Cognitive Therapy and Research, 3,* 361-366.

Michaelson, L. K., Watson, W. E., & Black, R. H. (1989). A realistic test of individual versus group consensus decision making. *Journal of Applied Psychology, 74,* 834-839.

Miesing, P., & Preble, J. F. (1985). Group processes and performance in a complex business simulation. *Small Group Behavior, 16,* 325-338.

Mikalachki, A. (1969). *Group cohesion reconsidered.* London, ON: School of Business Administration, University of Western Ontario.

Miller, D. T., & Ross, M. (1975). Self-serving biases in the attribution of causality: Fact or fiction? *Psychological Bulletin, 82,* 213-225.

Mills, T. M. (1984). *The sociology of small groups* (2nd ed.). Englewood Cliffs, NJ: Prentice-Hall.

Miranda, A. M. (1994). Avoidance of groupthink. Meeting management using group support systems. *Small Group Research, 25,* 105-136.

Mitchener, J. A. (1976). *Sports in America.* New York: Random House.

Mohr, P. B. and Larsen, K. (1998). Ingroup favoritism in umpiring decisions in Australian football. *Journal of Social Psychology, 138,* 495-504.

Montville, L. (1996a, October 21). Run for your life. Gold medalist Josia Thugwane hasn't found fame and fortune at home in South Africa. *Sports Illustrated, 85,* 72-87.

Montville, L. (1996b, November 4). Listen up! Newcomer Charles Barkley has already given—and gotten—an earful in Houston. *Sports Illustrated, 85,* 44-47.

Moore, J. C. and Brylinsky, J. A. (1993). Spectator effect on team performance in college basketball. *Journal of Sport Behavior, 16,* 77-84.

Moore, J. C. and Brylinsky, J. A. (1995). Facility familiarity and the home advantage. *Journal of Sport Behavior, 18,* 302-311.

Morgan, W. P. (1979). Prediction of performance in athletics. In P. Klavora & J. V. Daniel (Eds.), *Coach, athlete, and the sport psychologist* (pp. 173-186). Champaign, IL: Human Kinetics.

Morgan, W. P. (1980, July). Test of champions. *Psychology Today,* pp. 92-99.

Morgan, W. P., & Johnson, R. (1978). Personality characteristics of successful and unsuccessful oarsmen. *International Journal of Sport Psychology, 9,* 119-133.

Morgan, W. P., & Pollack, M. L. (1977). Psychologic characterization of the elite runner. *Annals of the New York Academy of Sciences, 301,* 382-403.

Mravic, M., & O'Brien, R. (1999, April). An age-old problem. *Sports Illustrated, 90(15),* 31-32.

Mudrack, P. E. (1989). Defining group cohesiveness. A legacy of confusion?_*Small Group Behavior, 20,* 37-49.

Mullen, B., & Riordan, C. A. (1988). Self-serving attributions for performance in naturalistic settings: A meta-analytic review. *Journal of Applied Social Psychology, 18,* 3-22.

Munroe, K., Estabrooks, P., Dennis, P., & Carron, A. (1999). A phenomenological analysis of group norms in sport teams. *The Sport Psychologist, 13,* 171-182.

Murray, M. C., & Mann, B. L. (1993). Leadership effectiveness. In J. M. Williams (Ed.), *Applied sport psychology: Personal growth to peak performance* (pp. 82-98). Mountain View, CA: Mayfield.

Myers, A. (1962). Team competition, success, and adjustment of team members. *Journal of Abnormal and Social Psychology, 65,* 325-332.

Myers, D. G. (1982). Polarizing effects of social interaction. In H. Brandstatter, J. H. Davis, & G. Stocker-Kreichgauer (Eds.), *Group decision making* (pp. 125-162). New York: Academic Press.

Nagle, F., Morgan, W.P., Hellickson, R., Serfass, R., & Alexander, J. (1975). Spotting success traits in Olympic contenders. *The Physician and Sports Medicine, 3,* 31-34.

Naylor, K., & Brawley, L. R. (1992, October). *Social loafing: Perceptions and implications.* Paper presented at the Joint Meeting of the Canadian Association of Sport Sciences and the Canadian Psychomotor learning and Sport Psychology Association Conference, Saskatoon, Saskatchewan.

Neave, N. and Wolfson, S. (2003). Testosterone, territoriality, and the 'home advantage'. *Physiology & Behavior, 78,* 269-275.

Neuman, G. A., Edwards, J. E., & Raju, N. S. (1989). Organizational development interventions: A meta-analysis of their effects on satisfaction and other attitudes. *Personnel Psychology, 42,* 461-483.

Nevill, A. M., Balmer, N. J. and Williams, A. M. (2002). The influence of crowd noise and experience upon refereeing decisions in football. *Psychology of Sport and Exercise, 3,* 261-272.

Nevill, A. M. and Holder, R. L. (1999). Home advantage in sport: An overview of studies on the advantage of playing at home. *Sports Medicine, 28,* 221-236.

Nevill, A. M., Newell, S. M. and Gale, S. (1996). Factors associated with home advantage in English and Scottish soccer matches. *Journal of Sports Sciences, 14,* 181-186.

Newcomb, T. M. (1951). Social psychological theory. In J. H. Rohrer & M. Sherif (Eds.), *Social Psychology at the crossroads.* New York, Harper.

Nieva, V. J., & Gutek, B. A. (1981). *Women and work: A psychological perspective.* New York: Praeger.

Nixon, H. L. (1977). Cohesiveness and team success: A theoretical reformulation. *Review of Sport and Leisure, 2,* 36-57.

Norris, J., & Jones, R. L. (1998). Towards a clearer definition and application of the centrality hypothesis in English professional association football. *Journal of Sport Behavior, 21,* 181-195.

O'Brien, R., & Hersch, H. (1997, April 14). Scorecard: Franchise players. *Sports Illustrated, 86,* 19-26.

Orlick, T. (1986). *Psyching for sport: Mental training for athletes.* Champaign, IL: Human Kinetics.

Orwell, G. (1949). *Nineteen eighty-four.* New York: Harcourt, Brace, & World.

Pace, A., & Carron, A.V. (1992). Travel and the home advantage. *Canadian Journal of Sport Sciences, 17,* 60-64.

Parkhouse, B. L., & Williams, J. M. (1986). Differential effects of sex and status on evaluation of coaching ability. *Research Quarterly for Exercise and Sport, 57,* 53-59.

Partridge, J., & Stevens, D. E. (2002). Group dynamics: The influence of the team in sport. In J. M. Silva & D. E. Stevens (Eds.), *Psychological foundations of sport.* (pp.272-290). Boston, MA: Allyn & Bacon.

Paskevich, D. M. (1995). *Conceptual and measurement factors of collective efficacy in its relationship to cohesion and performance outcome.* Unpublished doctoral dissertation, University of Waterloo, Waterloo, Canada.

Paskevich, D. M., Brawley, L. R., Dorsch, L. R., & Widmeyer, W. N. (1995). Implications of individual and group level analyses applied to the study of collective efficacy and cohesion. *Journal of Applied Sport Psychology, 7, (Suppl.),* S95.

Paulus, P. B., Annis, A. B., Seta, J. J., Schkade, J. K., & Matthews, R. W. (1976). Density does affect task performance. *Journal of Personality and Social Psychology, 34,* 248-253.

Pease, D. A., Locke, L. F., & Burlingame, M. (1971). Athletic exclusion: A complex phenomenon. *Quest, 16,* 42-46.

Perry, R. R., & Baumann, R. R. (1973). Criteria for the evaluation of college teaching: Their reliability and validity at the University of Toledo. In A. L. Sockloff (Ed.), *Proceedings: Faculty effectiveness as evaluated by students.* Philadelphia, PA: Temple University Measurement and Research Center.

Pfeffer, J., & Davis-Blake, A. (1986). Administrative succession and organizational performance: How administrator experience mediates the succession effect. *Academy of Management Journal, 29,* 72-83.

Pinder, C. (1984). *Work motivation.* Glenview, IL: Scott, Foreman.

Plimpton, G. (1978, March 5). 'Lord, No more than five'. *Sports Illustrated, 48,* 32-38.

Plunkett, J., & Newhouse, D. (1981). *The Jim Plunkett story: The saga of a man who cameback.* New York: Arbor House.

Pohlman, J. T. (1975). A multivariate analysis of selected class characteristics and student ratings of instruction. *Multivariate Behavioral Research, 10,* 81-91.

Pollard, R. (1986). Home advantage in soccer: A retrospective analysis. *Journal of Sport Sciences, 4,* 237-248.

Pollard, R. (2002). Evidence of a reduced home advantage when a team moves to a new stadium. *Journal of Sports Sciences, 20,* 969-973.

Powell, G. N. (1988). *Women and men in management.* Newbury Park, CA: Sage.

Powell, G. N. (1990). One more time: Do female and male managers differ? *Academy of Management Executive, 4,* 68-75.

Prapavessis, H., & Carron, A. V. (1996). The effect of group cohesion on competitive state anxiety. *Journal of Sport and Exercise Psychology, 18,* 64-74.

Prapavessis, H., & Carron, A. V. (1997). Cohesion and work output. *Small Group Research, 28,* 294-301.

Prapavessis, H., & Carron, A. V. (1997). The role of sacrifice in the dynamics of sport teams. *Group Dynamics, 1,* 231-240

Prapavessis, H., Carron, A. V., & Spink, K. S. (1997). Team building in sport. *International Journal of Sport Psychology, 27,* 269-285.

Prapavessis, H., & Gordon, S. (1991). Coach/player relationships in tennis. *Canadian Journal of Sport Sciences, 16,* 229-233.

Prelutsky, J. (1983). *Zoo doings.* New York: Greenwillow Books.

Price, S. L. (2001). Lords of discipline. *Sports Illustrated, 95(16),* 78-82.

Pruitt, D. G. (1971). Choice shifts in group discussion: An introductory review. *Journal of Personality and Social Psychology, 20,* 339-360.

Quinn, Z., Johnson, D. W., & Johnson, R. T. (1995). Cooperative versus competitive efforts and problem solving. *Review of Educational Research, 65,* 129-143.

Rail, G. (1987). Perceived role characteristics and executive satisfaction in voluntary sport associations. *Journal of Sport Psychology, 9,* 376-384.

Rainey, D. W., & Larsen, J. D. (1988). Balls, strikes, and norms: Rule violation and normative rules among baseball umpires. *Journal of Sport & Exercise Psychology, 10,* 75-80.

Rains, P. (1984). The production of fairness: Officiating in the National Hockey League. *Sociology of Sport Journal, 1,* 150-162.

Recht, L. D., Lew, R. A., & Schwartz, W. J. (1995). Baseball teams beaten by jet lag. *Nature, 377,* 583.

Reddy, W. B., & Byrnes, A. (1972). The effects of interpersonal group composition on the problem solving behavior of middle managers. *Journal of Applied Psychology, 56,* 516-517.

Rees, C. R., & Segal, M. W. (1984). Role differentiation in groups: The relationship between instrumental and expressive leadership. *Small Group Behavior, 15,* 109-123.

Reilly, R. (1987, November 9). Staying away in flocks. *Sports Illustrated, 67,* 38-43.

Reis, H. T., & Jelsma, B. (1978). A social psychology of sex differences in sport. In W. F. Straub (Ed.), *Sport psychology: An analysis of athlete behavior* (2nd ed.) (pp. 178-188). Ithaca, NY: Mouvement.

Rejeski, R. J., Brawley, L. R., & Ettinger, W. (1997, June*). Shaping active lifestyle in the elderly*. Paper presented at the American College of Sports Medicine Conference, Denver, CO.

Renger, R. (1993). A review of the Profile of Mood States (POMS) in the prediction of athlete success. *Journal of Applied Sport Psychology, 5,* 78-84.

Ridgeway, C. L. (2001). Gender, status, and leadership. *Journal of Social Issues, 57,* 637-655.

Riley, P. (1993). *The winner within: A life plan for team players.* New York: Berkeley Books.

Roberts, G. C. (1978). Children's assignment of responsibility for winning and losing. In F. Smoll & R. Smith (Eds.), *Psychological perspectives of youth sports* (pp. 145-171). Washington, DC: Hemisphere.

Robinson, T. T. & Carron, A.V. (1982). Personal and situational factors associated with dropping out versus maintaining participation in competitive sport. *Journal of Sport Psychology, 4,* 364-378.

Roy, G. (1974). The relationship between centrality and mobility: *The case of the National Hockey League.* Unpublished master's thesis, University of Waterloo, Waterloo, Canada.

Rumuz-Nienhuis, W., & Van Bergen, A. (1960). Relations between some components of attraction-to-group. *Human Relations, 13,* 271-277.

Rushall, B. S., & Smith, K. C. (1979). The modification of the quality and quantity of behavior categories in a swimming coach. *Journal of Sport Psychology, 1,* 138-150.

Rushin, S. (2003). Can this marriage be saved? *Sports Illustrated, 99(18),* 21.

Ryan, J. (1995). *Little girls in pretty boxes: The making and breaking of elite gymnasts and figure skaters.* Doubleday: New York.

Ryan, T. A. (1970). *Intentional behavior: An approach to human motivation.* New York: Ronald.

Ryckman, R. M., & Hamel, J. (1992). Female adolescents' motives related to involvement in organized team sports. *International Journal of Sport Psychology, 23,* 147-160.

Sage, G. H. (1972). *Machiavellianism among high school and college coaches.* In C. E. Mueller (Ed.), Proceedings of the Annual Meeting of the National College of Physical Education for Men. Minneapolis, MN: University of Minnesota.

Sage, G. H. (1974). *The effects of formal structure on organizational leadership: An investigation of collegiate football teams.* Paper presented at the Annual Meeting of the American Association for Health, Physical Education, & Recreation, Anaheim, CA.

Sage, G. H. (1975). An occupational analysis of the college coach. In D. W. Ball & J. W. Loy (Eds.), *Sport and social order: Contributions to the sociology of sport* (pp. 395-455). Reading, MA: Addison-Wesley.

Sage, G. H. (1998). *Power and ideology in American sport: A critical perspective* (2nd ed.). Champaign, IL: Human Kinetics.

Sage, G. H., Loy, J. W., & Ingham, A. G. (1970). *The effects of formal structure on organizational leadership: An investigation of collegiate baseball teams.* Paper presented at the Annual Meetings of the American Association for Health, Physical Education, and Recreation, Seattle, WA.

Salminen, S. (1993). The effect of the audience on the home advantage. *Perceptual and Motor Skills, 76,* 1123-1128.

Schachter, S. (1951). Deviation, rejection, and communication. *Journal of Abnormal and Social Psychology, 46,* 190-207.

Schachter, S., Ellertson, N., McBride, D., & Gregory, D. (1951). An experimental study of cohesiveness and productivity. *Human Relations, 4,* 229-238.

Schlenker, B. R. (1975). Group members attributions of responsibility for prior performance. *Representative Research in Social Psychology, 6,* 96-108.

Schlenker, B. R., & Miller, R. S. (1977a). Egocentricism in groups: Self-serving bias or logical infromation processing. *Journal of Personality and Social Psychology, 35,* 755-764.

Schlenker, B. R., & Miller, R. S. (1977b). Group cohesiveness as a determinant of egocentric perceptions in cooperative groups. *Human Relations, 30,* 1039-1055.

Schlenker, B. R., Phillips, S. T., Boniecki, K. A., & Schlenker, D. R. (1995). Where is the home choke? *Journal of Personality and Social Psychology, 68,* 649-652.

Schlenker, B. R., Soraci, S., & McCarthy, B. (1976). Self-esteem and group performance as determinants of egocentric perceptions in cooperative groups. *Human Relations, 35,* 755-764.

Schriesheim, C. A., Tepper, B. J., & Tetrault, L. A. (1994). Least preferred co-worker score, situational control, and leadership effectiveness: A meta-analysis of contingency model performance predictions. *Journal of Applied Psychology, 79,* 561-573.

Schriesheim, J. F. (1980). The social context of leader-subordinate relations: An investigation of the effects of group cohesiveness. *Journal of Applied Psychology, 65,* 183-194.

Schurr, K. T., Ashley, M. A., & Joy, K. L. (1977). A multivariate analysis of male athlete characteristics: Sport type and success. *Multivariate Experimental Clinical Research, 3,* 53-68.

Schutz, W. C. (1958). *FIRO: A three-dimensional theory of interpersonal behavior.* New York: Holt, Rinehart, & Winston.

Schutz, W. C. (1966). *The interpersonal underworld* (5th ed.). Palo Alto, CA: Science & Behavior Books.

Schwartz, B., & Barsky, S. F. (1977). The home advantage. *Social forces, 55,* 641-661.

Scott, J. (1969). *Athletics for athletes.* Hayward, CA: Quality Printing Services.

Seashore, S. E. (1954). *Group cohesiveness in the industrial work group.* Ann Arbor, MI: Survey Research Group, University of Michigan.

Shaffer, L. S. (1978). On the current confusion of group-related behavior and collective behavior: A reaction to Buys. *Personality and Social Psychology Bulletin, 4,* 564-567.

Shakespeare, W. (1896). *As you like it.* Boston, MA: Houghton.

Shakula, S. (2001, April 19). Sports arenas: For the love of the game or money? Retrieved November 5, 2004 from http://iml.jou.ufl.edu/projects/Spring01/Shakula/

Shangi, G., & Carron, A.V. (1987). Group cohesion and its relationship with performance and satisfaction among high school basketball players. *Canadian Journal of Sport Sciences, 12,* 20P.

Shaw, M. E. (1981). *Group dynamics: The psychology of small group behavior* (3rd ed.). New York: McGraw-Hill.

Shaw, M. E., & Harkey, B. (1976). Some effects of congruency of member characteristics and group structure upon group behavior. *Journal of Personality and Social Psychology, 34,* 412-418.

Shaw, M. E., & Webb, J. N. (1982). When compatibility interferes with group effectiveness. Facilitation of learning in small groups. *Small Group Behavior, 13,* 555-564.

Shields, D. L., Bredemeier, B. J., Gardner, D. E., & Boston, A. (1995). Leadership, cohesion, and team norms regarding cheating and aggression. *Sociology of Sport Journal, 12,* 324-336.

Shelley, M. W. (1964). The mathematical representation of the individual in models of organizational problems. In W. W. Cooper, H. J. Leavitt, & M. W. Shelley II

(Eds.), *New perspectives in organizational research* (pp.351-390). New York: Wiley.

Sherif, M. (1966). *Group conflict and cooperation: Their social psychology*. London: Routledge & Kegan Paul.

Sherif, M. (1979). Superordinate goals in the reduction of intergroup conflict: An experimental evaluation. In W.G. Austin & S. Worchel (Eds.), *The social psychology of intergroup relations* (pp. 257-261). Belmont, CA: Wadsworth.

Sherif, M., Harvey, O. J., White, B. J., Hood, W. R., & Sherif, C. W. (1961). *Intergroup cooperation and conflict: The Robbers Cave Experiment*. Norman, OK: Institute of Group Relations.

Sherif, M., & Sherif, C. W. (1956). *An outline of social psychology* (Rev. ed.). New York: Harper & Row.

Sherif, M., & Sherif, C. (1979). Research on intergroup relations. In W.G. Austin & S. Worchel (Eds.), *The social psychology of intergroup relations* (pp. 7-18). Belmont, CA: Wadsworth.

Shields, D. L., Bredemeier, B. J., Gardner, D. E., & Bostrom, A. (1995). Leadership, cohesion, and team norms regarding cheating and aggression. *Sociology of Sport Journal, 12*, 324-336.

Silva, J. M. III (1983). The perceived legitimacy of rule violating behavior in sport. *Journal of Sport Psychology, 5*, 438-448.

Silva, J. M., Schultz, B. B., Haslam, R. W., Martin, M. P., & Murray, D. F. (1985). Discriminating characteristics of contestants at the United States Olympic wrestling trials. *International Journal of Sport Psychology, 16*, 79-102.

Silver, M. (1995, September 4). The key link: At its best, the relationship between a coach and his quarterback can elevate a team. At its worst, it can destroy an entire season. *Sports Illustrated, 83*, 84-90.

Silver, M. (2001). No forward progress. *Sports Illustrated, 95(13)*, 38-

Silverman, I. W., & Stone, J. M. (1972). Modifying cognitive functioning through participation in a problem solving group.

Journal of Educational Psychology, 63, 603-608.

Slavin, R. E. (1983). When does cooperative learning increase student achievement? *Psychological Bulletin, 94*, 429-445.

Slusher, A., Van Dyke, J., & Rose, G. (1972). Technical competence of group leaders, managerial role, and productivity in engineering design groups. *Academy of Management Journal, 15*, 197-204.

Smith, D. R., Ciacciarelli, A., Serzan, J. and Lambert, D. (2000). Travel and the home advantage in professional sports. *Sociology of Sport Journal, 17*, 364-385.

Smith, S., & Haythorn, W. W. (1972). Effects of compatibility, crowding, groups size, and leadership seniority on stress, anxiety, hostility, and annoyance in isolated groups. *Journal of Personality and Social Psychology, 22*, 67-79.

Smith. R. E., Smoll, F. L., & Curtis, B. (1979). Coach effectiveness training: A cognitive-behavioral approach to enhancing relationship skills in youth sport coaches. *Journal of Sport Psychology, 1*, 59-75.

Smith. R. E., Smoll, F. L., & Hunt, E. (1977). A system for the behavioral assessment of athletic coaches. *Research Quarterly, 48*, 401-407.

Smith, S. (1990, February 12). Bulls' woes on road: It's official. *Chicago Tribune*, pp. 1, 5.

Smoll, F. L., & Smith, R. E. (1979). *Improving relationship skills in youth sport coaches*. East Lansing, MI: Institute for the Study of Youth Sports.

Smoll, F. L., Smith, R. E., Curtis, B., & Hunt, E. (1978). Toward a mediational model of coach-player relationships. *Research Quarterly, 49*, 528-541.

Snyder, E. E., & Purdy, D. A. (1987). Social control in sport: An analysis of basketball officiating. *Sociology of Sport Journal, 4*, 394-402.

Sommer, R. (1969). *Personal space*. Englewood Cliffs, NJ: Prentice-Hall.

Sorrentino, R. M., & Sheppard, B. H. (1978). Effects of affiliation-related motives on swimmers in individual versus group competition: A field experiment. *Journal of Personality and Social Psychology, 7,* 704-714.

Spense, E. (1980). *The relative contributions of ability cohesion, and participation motivation to team performance outcome in women's intramural basketball.* Unpublished undergraduate thesis, University of Waterloo, Waterloo, ON, Canada.

Spink, K. S. (1990). Group cohesion and collective efficacy of volleyball teams. *Journal of Sport and Exercise Psychology, 12,* 301-311.

Spink, K.S. (1992). Group cohesion and starting status in successful and less successful elite volleyball teams. *Journal of Sport Sciences, 10,* 379-388.

Spink, K. S., & Carron, A. V. (1993). The effects of team building on the adherence patterns of female exercise participants. *Journal of Sport and Exercise Psychology, 15,* 39-49.

Spink, K. S., & Carron, A. V. (1994). Group cohesion effects in exercise groups. *Small Group Research, 25,* 26-42.

Stabler, K., & Stainback, B. (1986). *Snake.* Garden City, NY: Doubleday.

Stasson, M. F., & Bradshaw, S. D. (1995). Explanations of individual-group performance differences. What sort of "bonus" can be gained through group interaction? *Small Group Research, 26,* 296-308.

Steiner, I. D. (1972). *Group processes and group productivity.* New York: Academic.

Steinzor, B. (1955). The spatial factor in face-to-face discussion groups. In A. P. Hare, E. F. Borgatta, & R. F. Bales (Eds.), *Small groups: Studies in social interaction* (pp. 348-352). New York: Alfred A. Knopf.

Stogdill, R. M. (1948). Personal factors associated with leadership: Survey of literature. *Journal of Psychology, 25,* 35-71.

Stogdill, R. M. (1964). *Team achievement under high motivation.* Columbus, Ohio: The Bureau of Business Research, College of Commerce and Administration, Ohio State University.

Stogdill, R. M. (1974). *Handbook and leadership: A survey of theory and research.* New York: Free Press.

Strachan, A. (1988, December 8). Reaching a dead end in Alberta. *The Globe and Mail,* p. 11.

Straub, W. F. (1978). How to be an effective leader. In W. F. Straub (Ed.), *Sport psychology; An analysis of athlete behavior* (pp. 257-266). Ithaca, NY: Mouvement.

Strauss, B. (2002). The impact of supportive spectator behavior on performance in team sports. *International Journal of Sport Psychology, 33,* 372-390.

Strodtbeck, F. L., & Hook, L. H. (1961). The social dimension of a twelve-man jury table. *Sociometry, 24,* 397-415.

Sullivan, P., & Feltz, D. L. (2003). The preliminary development of the Scale for Effective Communication in Team Sports (SECTS). *Journal of Applied Social Psychology, 33,* 1693-1715.

Sumner, J., & Mobley, M. (1981). Are cricket umpires biased? *New Scientist, 91,* 29-31.

Swift, E. M. (1988, April 11). Yanked about by the boss. Bringing their feud to ahead, George Steinbrenner sought to discredit, humiliate and unload Dave Winfield. *Sports Illustrated, 68,* 36-38.

Szreter, A. (2004, July4). Greeks upset the odds again. Retrieved August 13, 2004 from http://www.euro2004.com/tournament/matches/round=1623/match=1059194/Report=rw.html.

Tajfel, H., & Turner, J. (1979). An integrative theory of intergroup conflict. In W. G. Austin & S. Worchel (Eds.), *The social psychology of intergroup relations* (pp. 33-48). Belmont, CA: Wadsworth.

Taylor, D. M., & Doria, J. R. (1981). Self-serving and group-serving bias in attribution. *Journal of Social Psychology, 113,* 201-211.

Taylor, P. (1996b, December 30). Two Bucks worth. Vin Baker and Glenn Robinson are the NBA's most potent pair of forwards. *Sports Illustrated, 85,* 54-57.

Taylor, P. (1997b, April 28). Nice guys. Even with high play off hopes the Jazz would rather forgo a title than abandon its principles. *Sports Illustrated, 86,* 44-49.

Terborg, J., Castore, C., & DeNinno, J. (1976). A longitudinal field investigation of the impact of group composition on group performance and cohesion. *Journal of Personality and Social Psychology, 6,* 782-790.

Terry, P. C. (1984). The coaching preferences of elite athletes competing at Universiade '83. *Canadian Journal of Applied Sport Sciences, 9,* 201-208.

Terry, P. (1995). The efficacy of mood state profiling with elite performers: A review and synthesis. *The Sport Psychologist, 9,* 309-324.

Terry, P.C., Carron, A. V., Pink, M. J., Lane, A. M., Jones, G. J. W. & Hall, M. P. (2000). Perceptions of group cohesion and mood in sport teams. *Group Dynamics, 4,* 244-253.

Terry, P. C., Walrond, N. and Carron, A. V. (1998). The influence of game location on athletes' psychological states. *Journal of Science and Medicine in Sport, 1,* 29-37.

Tharp, R. G., & Gallimore, R. (1976, April). What a coach can teach a teacher. *Coaching Association of Canada Bulletin, 13,* 8-10; 21.

Theberge, N., & Loy, J. W. (1976). Replacement processes in sport organizations: the case of professional baseball. *International Review of Sport Sociology, 11,* 73-93.

Thelen, H. A. (1949). Group dynamics in instruction: The principle of least group size. *School Review, 57, 139-*148.

Thirer, J., & Rampey, M. S. (1979). Effects of abusive spectators' behavior on performance of home and visiting intercollegiate basketball teams. *Perceptual and Motor Skills, 48,* 1047-1053.

Thirer, J., & Wright, S. D. (1985). Sport and social status for adolescent males and females. *Sociology of Sport Journal, 2,* 164-171.

Thompson, S. A., & Albinson, J. (1991, October). *An investigation of factors affecting the development of cohesion among intercollegiate rowers.* Paper presented at the Canadian Psychomotor Learning and Sport Psychology conference, London, Ontario.

Thomsen, I. (2002, December). Lousy at a luxury price. *Sports Illustrated, 97(24),* 152.

Thuot, S. M., Kavouras, S. A. and Kenefick, R. W. (1998). Effect of perceived ability, game location, and state anxiety on basketball performance. *Journal of Sport Behavior,* 21, 311-321.

Tretiak, V. (1987). *Tretiak: The legend.* Edmonton, AB: Plains Publishing.

Triplett, N. (1897). The dynamogenic factors in pacemaking and competition. *American Journal of Psychology, 9,* 507-533.

Trist, E. L., & Bamforth, K. W. (1951). Some social and psychological consequences of the longwall method of coal-getting. *Human Relations, 4,* 3-38.

Tropp, K. J., & Landers, D. M. (1979). Team interaction and the emergence of leadership and inerpersonal attraction in field hockey. *Journal of Sport Psychology, 3,* 228-240.

Tubbs, M. E. (1986). Goal-setting: A meta-analytic examination of empirical evidence. *Journal of Applied Psychology, 71,* 474-483.

Tucker, L. W., & Parks, J. B. (2001). Effects of gender and sport type on intercollegiate athletes' perceptions of the legitimacy of aggressive behaviors in sport. *Sociology of Sport Journal, 18,* 403-413.

Tuckman, B. W. (1965). Developmental sequences in small groups. *Psychological Bulletin, 63,* 384-399.

Tuckman, B. W. & Jensen, M. A. C. (1977). Stages of small group development revisited. *Group and Organizational Studies, 2,* 419-427.

Turman, P. D. (2003). Coaches and cohesion: The impact of coaching techniques on team cohesion in the small group setting. *Journal of Sport Behavior, 26,* 86-104.

Turner, J. C. (1982). Towards a cognitive redefinition of the social group. In H. Tajfel (Ed.), *Social identity and intergroup relations.* Cambridge, UK: Cambridge University Press.

Turner, J. C., Hogg, M., Turner, P., & Smith, P. (1984). Failure and defeat as determinants of group cohesiveness. *British Journal of Social Psychology, 23,* 97-111.

Tutko, T. A., & Richards, J. W. (1977). *Psychology of coaching.* Boston, MA: Allyn and Bacon.

Tyerman, A., & Spencer, C. (1983). A critical test of the Sherif's robber's cave experiment: Intergroup competition and cooperation between groups of well-acquainted individuals. *Small Group Behavior, 14,* 515-531.

Valacich, J. S., Dennis, A. R., & Nunamaker, J. F. (1992). Group size and anonymity effects of computer-mediated idea generation. *Small Group Research, 23,* 49-73.

Van Bergen, A., & Koekebakker, J. (1959). "Group cohesiveness" in laboratory experiments. *Acta Psychologica, 16,* 81-98.

Van Raalte, J. L., Brewer, B. W., & Petitpas, A. J. (1995, March). The actor-observer bias in sport. *Applied Research in Coaching and Athletics Annual,* 80-92.

Varca, P. E. (1980). An analysis of home and away game performance of male college basketball teams. *Journal of Sport Psychology, 2,* 245-257.

Verducci, T. (1996, February 26). A new fresh: The rebuilding is nearly complete (once again) in San Diego, where the Padres look like contender. *Sports Illustrated, 84,* 68-71.

Verducci, T. (1997, May 5). Better than ever. As if power and superb pitching were not enough, the Braves now have speed to burn. *Sports Illustrated, 86,* 32-37.

Vincent, D. (2005, January 9). Old Fish helping young Warriors. *Toronto Star,* p. B2

Volp, A., & Keil, U. (1987). The relationship between performance, intention to drop out, and interpersonal conflict in swimmers. *Journal of Sport Psychology, 9,* 358-375.

Wahl, G., & Wertheim, L. J. (2003). A rite gone terribly wrong. *Sports Illustrated, 99(24),* 68-76.

Wallach, M. A., Kogan, N., & Bem, D. J. (1962). Group influence on individual risk taking. *Journal of Abnormal and Social Psychology, 65,* 75-86.

Walsh, J. M., & Carron, A. V. (1977). *Attributes of volunteer coaches.* Paper presented at the Annual Meeting of the Canadian Association of Sport Sciences, Winnipeg, Manitoba.

Walsh. B. (1990). *Building a champion. On football and the making of the 49ers.* New York, NY: St. Martin's.

Ward Jr., R. E. (1998). Rituals, first impressions, and the opening day home advantage. *Sociology of Sport Journal, 15,* 279-293.

Watson, C. B., Chemers, M. M., & Preiser, N. (2001). Collective efficacy: A multilevel analysis. *Personality and Social Psychology, 27,* 1057-1068.

Webster's new world dictionary (2nd ed.). (1971). New York, NY: Warner Books.

Weinberg, R. S., Bruya, L., & Jackson, A. (1985). The effects of goal proximity and goal specificity on endurance performance. *Journal of Sport Psychology, 7,* 296-305.

Weinberg, R. S., Bruya, L., & Jackson, A. (1990). Goal setting and competition: A reaction to Hall and Byrne. *Journal of Sport and Exercise Psychology, 12,* 92-97.

Weinberg, R. S., Bruya, L., Jackson, A., & Garland, H. (1987). Goal difficulty and endurance performance: A challenge to the goal attainability assumption. *Journal of Sport Behavior, 10,* 82-92.

Weinberg, R., Burton, D., Yukelson, D., & Weigand, D. (2000). Perceived goal setting practices of Olympic athletes: An exploratory investigation. *The Sport Psychologist, 14,* 279-295.

Weinberg, R., & Gould, D. (2003). *Foundations of sport and exercise psychology.* Champaign, IL: Human Kinetics.

Weinberg, R., Reveles, M., & Jackson, A. (1984).Attitudes of male and female athletes toward male and female coaches. *Journal of Sport Psychology, 6,* 448-453.

Weiner, B. (1974). *Achievement motivation and attribution theory.* Morristown, NJ: General Learning Press.

Weiner, B. (1979). A theory of motivation for some classroom experiences. *Journal of Educational Psychology, 71,* 3-25.

Weiner, B., Freeze, I., Kukla, A., Reed, L., Rest, S., & Rosenbaum, R. M. (1972). Perceiving the causes of success and failure. In E. E. Jones, D. E. Kanhouse, H. H. Kelley, R. E. Nisbett, S. Valins, & B. Weiner (Eds.), *Attribution: Perceiving the causes of behavior* (pp. 95-120). Morristown, NJ: General Learning.

Weiss, M. R., & Friedrichs, W. D. (1986). The influence of leader behaviors, coach attributes, and institutional variables on performance and satisfaction of collegiate basketball teams. *Journal of Sport Psychology, 8,* 332-346.

Weldon, E., & Weingart, L. R. (1988, August). *A theory of group goals and group performance.* Paper presented at the Annual Meeting of the Academy of Management, Anaheim, CA.

Wertheim, J. (2004, March). Good job. You're fired. *Sports Illustrated, 100(18),* 54-63.

Westre, K. R., & Weiss, M. R. (1991). The relationship between perceived coaching behaviors and group cohesion in high school football teams. *Sport Psychologist, 5,* 41-54.

Wharnsby, T. (2002, September 30). What's with all the goons? *Sporting News, 226(39),* 61.

Wheelan, S.A. (1999). *Creating effective teams: A guide for members and leaders.* Thousand Oaks, CA: SAGE Publications, Inc.

White, P., & Willits, K. (1991). Race as a predictor of playing position in Ontario youth soccer. *CAHPER Journal,* 5-10.

Whyte, W. F. (1943). *Street corner society.* Chicago, IL: University of Chicago.

Widmeyer, W. N. (1971). *The size of sport groups with special implications for the triad.* Unpublished paper. University of Illinois, Champaign, IL.

Widmeyer, W. N. (1977). *When cohesiveness predicts performance outcome in sport.* Unpublished doctoral dissertation, University of Illinois, Champaign, Il.

Widmeyer, W. N. (1990). Group composition in sport. *International Journal of Sport Psychology, 21,* 264-285.

Widmeyer, W. N., Brawley, L. R., & Carron, A. V. (1985). *The measurement of cohesion in sport teams: The Group Environment Questionnaire.* London, ON: Sports Dynamics.

Widmeyer, W. N., Brawley, L. R., & Carron, A. V. (1988). How many should I carry on my team? Consequences of group size. *Psychology of Motor Behavior and Sport: Abnstracts 1988.* Knoxville, TN: North American Society for the Psychology of Sport and Physical Activity.

Widmeyer, W. N., Brawley, L. R., & Carron, A. V. (1990). The effects of group size in sport. *Journal of Sport and Exercise Psychology, 12,* 177-190.

Widmeyer, W. N., & Gossett, D. M. (1978). *The relative contributions of ability and cohesion to team performance outcome in intramural basketball.* Paper presented at the Annual Meeting of the North American Society for the Psychology of Sport and Physical Activity, Tallahassee, FL.

Widmeyer, W. N. & Loy, J. W. (1981). *Dynamic duos: An analysis of the relationship between group composition and group performance in women's doubles tennis.* Paper presented at The Conference on the Content of Culture: Constants and Variants, Claremont, CA.

Widmeyer, W. N., & Loy, J. W. (1989). Dynamic duos: An analysis of the relationships between group composition and group performance in women's doubles tennis. In R. Bolton (Ed.), *Studies in Honor of J. M. Roberts.* New Haven: Human Relations Area Files.

Widmeyer, W. N., & Loy, J. W., & Roberts, J. (1980). The relative contribution of action styles and ability to the performance outcomes of doubles tennis teams. In C. Nadeau, W. Halliwell, K. Newell, & G. Roberts (Eds.), *Psychology of Motor Behavior and Sport-1979* (pp. 209-218). Champaign, IL: Human Kinetics.

Widmeyer, W. N., & Martens, R. (1978). When cohesion predicts performance outcome in sport. *Research Quarterly, 49,* 372-380.

Widmeyer, W. N. & McGuire, E .J. (1996, May). *Sport psychology for ice hockey.* Presentation to Ontario Intermediate Coaching Clinic, Waterloo, ON.

Widmeyer, W. N., Silva, J. M., & Hardy, C. J. (1992, October). *The nature of group cohesion in sport teams: A phenomenological approach.* Paper presented at Association for the Advancement of Applied Sport Psychology Conference, Colorado Springs, CO.

Widmeyer, W. N., & Williams, J. M. (1991). Predicting cohesion in a coacting sport. *Small Group Research, 22,* 548-570.

Wiley, R. (1988, January, 11). The puck stops here. *Sports Illustrated, 68,* 58-68.

Williams, J. M., & Hacker, C. M. (1982). Causal relationships among cohesion, satisfaction and performance in women's intercollegiate field hockey teams. *Journal of Sport Psychology, 4,* 324-337.

Williams, J. M., Jerome, G. J., Kenow, L. J., Rogers, T., Sartain, T. A., & Darland, G. (2003). Factor structure of the coaching behavior questionnaire and its relationship to athlete variables. *The Sport Psychologist, 17,* 16-34.

Williams, J. M., & White, K. A. (1983). Adolescent status systems for males and females at three age levels. *Adolescence, 18,* 381-389.

Williams, K., Harkins, S., & Latané, B. (1981). Identifiability as a deterrent to social loafing: Two cheering experiments. *Journal of Personality and Social Psychology 40,* 303-311.

Williams, K., Nida, S. A., Baca, L. D., & Latané, B. (1989). Social loafing and swimming: Effects of identifiability on individual and relay performance of intercollegiate swimmers. *Basic and Applied Social Psychology, 10,* 73-81.

Williams, R. L., & Youssef, Z. I. (1975). Division of labor in college football along racial lines. *International Journal of Sport Psychology, 6,* 3-13.

Wolff, A., & Spear, G. (1995, November 27). Chemistry 101. Here's the reason that the most talented teams don't always win

NCAA's. *Sports Illustrated Canada, 2,* 34-43.

Wolff, A. (1997, March 31). On to Indy. *Sports Illustrated, 86,* 34-41.

Wolfson, S. (1997). Actor-observer bias and perceived sensitivity to internal and external factors in competitive swimmers. *Journal of Sport Behavior, 20,* 477-484.

Wolosin, R.J., Sherman, S.J., & Till, A. (1973). Effects of cooperation and competition on responsibility attributions after success and failure. *Journal of Experimental and Social Psychology, 9,* 220-235.

Wood, R. E., Mento, A. J., & Locke, E. A. (1987). Task complexity as a moderator or goal effects: A meta-analysis. *Journal of Applied Psychology, 72,* 416-425.

Wood, W. (1987). Meta-analytic review of sex differences in group performance. *Psychological Bulletin, 102,* 53-71.

Woodcock, M., & Francis, D. (1994). *Teambuilding strategy.* Cambridge: University Press.

Worchel, S. (1979). Cooperation and the reduction of intergroup conflict: Some determining factors. In W.G. Austin & S. Worchel (Eds.), *The social psychology of intergroup relations* (pp. 174-187). Belmont, CA: Wadsworth.

Worchel, S. (1994). You can go home again: Returning group research to the group context with an eye on developmental issues. *Small Group Research, 25,* 205-223.

Wright, C. R., & House, T. (1989). *The diamond appraised.* New York: Simon & Schuster.

Wright, E. F., Voyer, D., Wright, R. D., & Roney, C. (1995). Supporting audiences and performance under pressure: The home disadvantage in hockey championships. *Journal of Sport Behavior, 18,* 21-29.

Wrong, D. H. (1979). *Power.* New York: Harper.

Yalom, I. D., & Rand, K. (1966). Compatibility and cohesiveness in therapy groups. *Archives of General Psychiatry, 15,* 267-275.

Yetman, N. R., & Berghorn, F. J. (1993). Racial participation and integration in intercollegiate basketball: A longitudinal perspective. *Sociology of Sport Journal, 10*, 301-314.

Yukelson, D. (1993). Communicating effectively. In J. M. Williams (Ed.). *Applied sport psychology. Personal growth to peak performance* (2nd ed.) (pp. 122-136). Mountain View, CA: Mayfield.

Yukelson, D. (1997). Principles of effective team building interventions in sport: A direct services approach at Penn State University. *Journal of Applied Sport Psychology, 9*, 73-96.

Yukelson, D., Weinberg, R., & Jackson, A. (1984). A multidimensional group cohesion instrument for intercollegiate basketball. *Journal of Sport Psychology, 6*, 103-117.

Zaccaro, S. J., Blair, V., Peterson, C., & Zazanis, M. (1995). Collective efficacy. In J. Maddux (1995), *Self-efficacy, adaptation, and adjustment* (pp. 305-328). New York: Plenum.

Zaccaro, S. J., Peterson, C., & Walker, S. (1987). Self-serving attributions for individual and group performance. *Social Psychology Quarterly, 50*, 257-263.

Zajonc, R. B. (1965). Social Facilitation. *Science, 149*, 269-274.

Zander, A. (1971). *Motives and goals in groups.* New York: Academic Press.

Zander, A. (1982). *Making groups effective.* San Francisco: Jossey-Bass.

Zander, A. (1985). *The purposes of groups and organizations.* San Francisco, CA: Jossey-Bass.

Zimmerman, E. (1985). Almost all you wanted to know about status inconsistency but never dared to measure: Theoretical deficits on status inconsistency. *Social Behavior and Personality, 13*, 195-214.

Index

About the Authors

Dr. Bert Carron is a professor in the School of Kinesiology at the University of Western Ontario in London, Ontario. He is a fellow in the American Academy of Kinesiology and Physical Education, the Association for the Advancement of Applied Sport Psychology, and the Canadian Psychomotor Learning and Sport Psychology Association. He is a past president of the Canadian Association for Sport Sciences and a former member of the board of directors of the Sports Medicine Council of Canada. In 1998, Bert was a co-recipient of the International Council of Sport Science and Physical Education's "Sport Science Award of the International Olympic Committee President." Currently, he is a member of the editorial board of *Journal of Sport and Exercise Psychology, the International Journal of Sport Psychology,* and *Small Group Research.* Bert's research focuses on group dynamics in sport teams and exercise groups.

Dr. Heather Hausenblas is the director of the Exercise Psychology Laboratory at the University of Florida. Her research focuses on the primary prevention of sedentary behavior and weight-related disorders. Heather has received grant support for her research from external funding agencies such as the National Institute of Mental Health and the National Institute of Child Health and Development. Heather currently serves on the editorial board for the Journal of Applied Sport Psychology. She recently was the recipient of the Early Career Distinguished Scholar Award for outstanding research contributions in the early stage of her scientific career from the North American Society for the Psychology of Sport and Physical Activity, as well as the Dorothy V. Harris Memorial Award for outstanding early career development in sport and exercise psychology from the Association for the Advancement of Applied Sport Psychology. Heather's writing includes three books and over 60 refereed publications in scientific journals. Heather, her husband Todd, and their two sons, Tommy and Scotty, live in Jacksonville, Florida.

Dr. Mark Eys is an assistant professor of sport and exercise psychology in the School of Human Kinetics at Laurentian University in Sudbury, Ontario. Mark's current research interests include role ambiguity and acceptance in sport and exercise groups, the measurement and correlates of cohesion, and social influences in exercise. He has published his research in the *Journal of Sports Sciences, International Journal of Sport and Exercise Psychology, Journal of Applied Sport Psychology,* and *Journal of Sport and Exercise Psychology.* In 2001, he was awarded the Canadian Interuniversity Sport (CIS) Coach of the Year for his work with the University of Western Ontario women's soccer program.